Umesh Santoshkumar Yashoda Rathod

STARTUP THEORIES, EXAMPLES, & ACTIVITIES

For Entrepreneurship Researchers, Educators, Startup Founders & Enthusiasts with lucid activities & images to develop an Entrepreneurial Mindset.

www.umeshrathod.in

Made with ♥ on the Notion Press Platform
www.notionpress.com

Jai Shri Mahakaal

कर्मण्येवाधिकारस्ते मा फलेषु कदाचन ।

मा कर्मफलहेतुर्भुर्मा ते संगोऽस्त्वकर्मणि ॥

Dedication

To all the educators & researchers making a difference to world we live & thrive-in

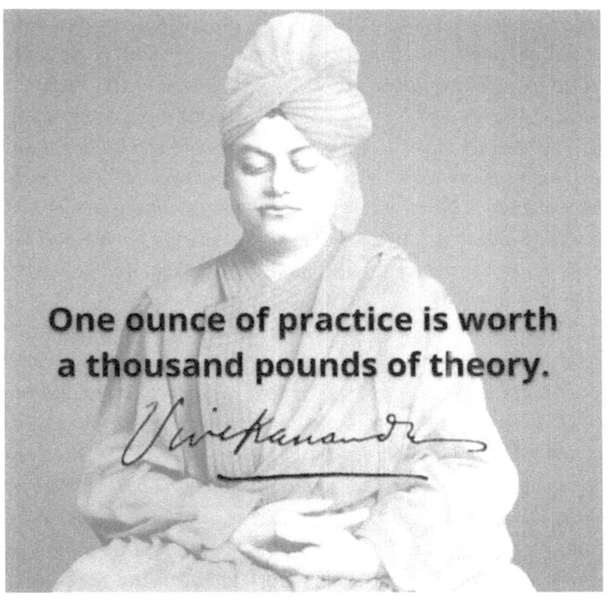
One ounce of practice is worth
a thousand pounds of theory.
Vivekananda

How is this book organized for the reader?

First, I have tried to keep this book as digestible & as short as possible. As a reader going through this book, you will come across several theories of startups/entrepreneurship which fall under a larger umbrella of categories based on their usability & inter-relations.

Second, I have tried to bring evident available literature together through this book. Other thing I wanted to do with the book was to provide a good mix of theory & practice strategies with activities to enhance the learning experience, I feel I 've only succeeded to an extent with this goal. The 2.0 version would be based on the feedback I received for this book. This book helps the readers to identify how the theories are interlinked & how the researchers have developed their framework. I have used pictures of the early researchers who have developed the theory along-with the conceptual theory design to make you aware who were the geniuses behind all the pain & it's overview which today makes the life of the everyday practitioner a little easy.

Theory is useful because merely knowing how things work often facilitates the change. As far as practical strategies go, I have kept it short & relatable. Let us be practical while we understand the theories which can help us make sound decisions in our journey ahead. One last thing I want to address is that after going through these theories one might rethink whether to pursue entrepreneurship or not. I should say, kill the self-doubt & give it a try. Most people gauge the depth of the sea just by standing at the shore. Finally, it is a humble attempt to make the startup enthusiasts, researchers & startup founders understand what startup theories all are about. I wish you a happy reading.

Note: Do not get puzzled to find the same theories in another categories. If any question comes up as you are reading, feel free to connect www.umeshrathod.in.. Thank you, let us get started.

Contents

Sr. No.	Categorized Startup Theories	Page No.
1	***Economics Related***	1
	1.1 Radical Subjectivism	1
	1.2 Jack of All Trades	4
	1.3 Creative Destruction	8
	1.4 Uncertainty-Bearing	12
	1.5 Agglomeration	15
	1.6 Knowledge Spillover	18
	1.7 Transaction Cost	22
	1.8 X-Efficiency	25
	1.9 Resource Scarcity	28
	1.10 Prospect	31
	1.11 Cantillon	34
2	***Sociological Related***	38
	2.1 Necessity Versus Opportunity	38
	2.2 Institutional	41
	2.3 Emancipation	45
	2.4 Withdrawal of Status Respect	49
	2.5 Social Capital	53
	2.6 Population Ecology	56
	2.7 Weak Ties	60
	2.8 Social Identity	63
	2.9 Information Processing	66
	2.10 Hoselitz	70
	2.11 Diffusion of Innovations	73
3	***Psychological & Trait Related***	78
	3.1 Ambiguity Tolerance	78
	3.2 Disagreeableness	81
	3.3 Impulsivity	83
	3.4 Passion	87
	3.5 Locus of Control	90
	3.6 Alertness	93
	3.7 Achievement Motivation	97
	3.8 Expectancy	101
	3.9 Self-Efficacy	104
	3.10 Regulatory Focus	107
	3.11 Cognitive Evaluation	111
	3.12 Planned Behavior	114

3.13 Resilience 117

4 *Managerial Related* 121

4.1 Stakeholder 121
4.2 Contingency 124
4.3 Disruptive Innovation 128
4.4 Strategic Disagreements 132
4.5 First Mover 135
4.6 Upper Echelons 138
4.7 Stewardship 141
4.8 Resource Based 144
4.9 Resource Dependency 147
4.10 Machiavellian 150
4.11 Born Global Startups 153
4.12 X-Efficiency (Ref 1.8) (25)
4.13 Resource Scarcity (Ref 1.9) (28)

5 *Process Related* 157

5.1 Harvard School 157
5.2 Effectuation 160
5.3 Bricolage 164
5.4 Experiential Learning 166
5.5 Emancipation (Ref 2.3) (45)

6 *Discovery* 170

6.1 Individual-Opportunity Nexus 170
6.2 Actualization 173
6.3 X-Efficiency (Ref 1.8) (25)
6.4 Alertness (Ref 3.6) (93)

7 *Financial* 177

7.1 Liquidity 177
7.2 Pecking Order 180
7.3 Signaling 184
7.4 Agency 187
7.5 Stewardship (Ref 4.7) (141)

8 *Biological Related* 191

8.1 Birth Order 191
8.2 Brain Parasite 194
8.3 Genetic 197
8.4 Great Man 200

	8.5 Lifecycle and Stages	203
	8.6 Niche	207
9	***Cultural Related***	210
	9.1 Misfit	210
	9.2 Cultural	213
	9.3 Religious	216
	9.4 Institutional (Ref 2.2)	(41)
	9.5 Withdrawal of Status Respect (Ref 2.4)	(49)
	9.6 Achievement Motivation (Ref 3.7)	(97)
10	***Technological***	219
	10.1 Marshall McLuhan	219
	10.2 Disruptive Innovation (Ref 4.3)	(128)
11	***Ethical***	224
	11.1 Utility	224
	11.2 Procedural Justice	227
12	***Other Startup Theories***	231
	12.1 Actor-Network	231
	12.2 Architectural	234
	12.3 Attribution	238
	12.4 Baumol's	242
	12.5 Bicultural	245
	12.6 Competence Destruction	249
	12.7 Critical	252
	12.8 Dynamic Capabilities	256
	12.9 Embeddedness	260
	12.10 Feminist	263
	12.11 Hubris	267
	12.12 Human Capital	269
	12.13 Hybrid Entrepreneurship	273
	12.14 Individual Ambidexterity	277
	12.15 Informal Entrepreneurship	281

12.16 Information Asymmetry 285
12.17 Lean Launchpad 288
12.18 Mental Disorders 292
12.19 Physiological 295
12.20 Real Options 299
12.21 Risk 302
12.22 Self-Competition 306
12.23 Serial Entrepreneurship 309
12.24 Slacker 312
12.25 Social Entrepreneurship 315
12.26 Social Exchange 320
12.27 Social Judgement 323
12.28 Spinout 328

References 332
Acknowledgement 348

Economic Theories

1.1 Radical Subjectivism

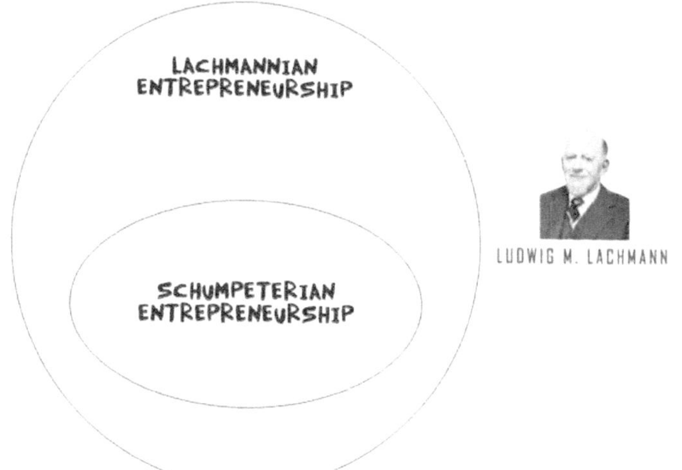

A German economist Ludwig M. Lachmann had proposed a radical subjectivist theory as an alternative to the existing Austrian School theories in entrepreneurship. According to Lachmann, entrepreneurs develop plans according to their subjective knowledge and expectations. Assumptions work because of the innovative creative mind of business visionaries, who might imagine many contending fates. Businesspeople persistently reconsider their arrangements as they experience new pieces of market data during trade encounters. Capital is viewed as ceaselessly recombining because of the course of capital refocusing. Mistakes lead to new transitory supplies of capital that should be redeployed towards new purposes. Lachmann accepts that people experience time contrastingly and that the best way to decipher occasions is to remake them from pieces of data after they have happened. As indicated by Lachmann, information incorporates understandings of the past & assumptions regarding what's to come However, expectations & interpretations are continuously changing as past events are reinterpreted by the new expectations form about the future. Hence, entrepreneurs should embrace the continuous revision of their plans.

Understanding the "Radical Subjectivism" theory:
It is unlikely that a business would use radical subjectivism as a guiding principle, as it does not provide a stable or reliable basis for decision-making. Business decisions are typically based on objective data, market research, and financial analysis, which require a degree of objectivity and rationality. However, there may be instances where businesses may incorporate certain elements of subjectivism, such as in branding and marketing. For example, a company may use subjective branding to appeal to the emotions and perceptions of its target market, rather than solely relying on objective product specifications. This may involve creating a brand image that conveys a particular lifestyle or values, such as using eco-friendly materials or promoting social responsibility. Such branding may be considered subjective in the sense that it relies on subjective perceptions and associations to appeal to customers, rather than objective facts or data. However, it is important to note that while businesses may use subjective branding or marketing strategies, they still rely on objective criteria such as market research, customer preferences, and financial analysis to make informed business decisions. Radical subjectivism is a philosophical position that is generally not applied in real-life situations as it denies the existence of objective reality and universal truths. However, there may be individuals or groups who subscribe to this philosophy and apply it in their personal lives or beliefs. One example of radical subjectivism in practice could be an individual who believes that their own perceptions and beliefs are the only reality and that everything else is subjective. This could lead to a rejection of objective reality and an insistence on their own subjective beliefs and experiences, even when presented with evidence to the contrary. Another example could be a group that rejects the existence of objective moral values and instead relies on individual or cultural perspectives to determine what is right or wrong. This could lead to a rejection of universally accepted ethical standards and a justification for actions that may be considered unethical or immoral by others. It is important to note, however, that radical subjectivism is a relatively

uncommon and controversial philosophical position, and it is not widely adopted or applied in mainstream society or business practices.

Classroom Activity: "The Radical Subjectivism Challenge"

Objective: To engage readers and encourage them to apply the concepts learned in a practical and creative manner. Participants will explore the principles of radical subjectivism and apply them to entrepreneurial scenarios, fostering critical thinking and innovative problem-solving skills.

Duration: 60-90 mins

Materials: Flipchart or whiteboard with markers, Sticky notes, Pens or pencils.

Instructions:

Activity	Instructions
Intro (10 mins)	Provide overview of the theory and its relevance to entrepreneurship. Highlight the key principles and concepts covered in the book. Emphasize the importance of critical thinking, subjective perception, and innovative approaches in entrepreneurship.
Group Discussion (15 mins)	Divide the participants into small groups of 3-5 individuals. Assign each group a specific scenario or problem related to entrepreneurship. Instruct the groups to discuss how the principles of radical subjectivism can be applied to their assigned scenario. Encourage participants to share their thoughts and perspectives, focusing on subjective perception, individual decision-making, and market dynamics.
Ideation Session (20 mins)	Provide each group with sticky notes or index cards & pens. Instruct the groups to brainstorm innovative solutions to the assigned scenario using the principles of radical subjectivism. Encourage participants to think outside the box, challenge conventional wisdom, and consider subjective preferences and perceptions. Set a time limit for this ideation session.
Presentation and Feedback (15 mins)	Ask each group to select a representative who will present their innovative solution to the rest of the participants. Each group should explain their thought process, the application of radical subjectivism principles, and the potential impact of their solution. After each presentation, open the floor for questions, comments, and feedback from the other participants. Encourage constructive dialogue and alternative viewpoints to further enrich the learning.

Wrap-up and Reflection (10 mins)	Summarize the main takeaways from the activity, emphasizing the practical applications of the theory of radical subjectivism in entrepreneurship. Facilitate a brief group discussion to reflect on the challenges faced, creative solutions proposed, and lessons learned during the activity. Provide recommendations for further exploration of the topic, additional readings, or resources to deepen their understanding of radical subjectivism.

Conclusion: The activity offers an interactive and engaging way for readers to apply the concepts of the theory of radical subjectivism to real-world entrepreneurial scenarios. By fostering critical thinking, subjective perception, and innovative problem-solving skills, participants can enhance their entrepreneurial mindset and develop a deeper understanding of how subjective factors shape decision-making and market dynamics.

1.2 Jack of all trades

Edward P. Lazear an economist from Stanford University, in a working paper had presented the theory of jack of all trades which got published in the American Economic Review in 2004. It tries to explain and predict who becomes an entrepreneur, and which entrepreneurs will be successful. According to him, individuals becoming entrepreneurs may have more balance in their investment strategy (on avg) as compared with individuals that specialize in employee roles. His thought is that business visionaries should be comfortable at various things, i.e., they are generalists instead of subject matter experts. For example, when initially beginning a restaurant one needs to identify sellers for sources like food, furniture, gear, and development. The individual should be comfortable with advertising (evaluating, advancement, placement, and product configuration) to get clients. The businessperson may likewise should have the option to plan a menu. Human resource management is additionally a significant ability of business visionaries to get their organizations going. The ability to influence or persuade financial backers to give money to get the business rolling might be significant. While it is far-fetched that any one individual will have these abilities, those that have more than others may be relied upon to be bound to begin a business and to prevail in business. Most examinations inspecting the theory show the quantity of utilitarian regions that businesspeople have had insight in. Overall, the evidence for this theory is mixed. Although some of the studies find support for the theory, even when constructed based on sex, nationality, age & other empirical examinations controlling unobservable characteristics that simultaneously determine skill accumulation and occupational choice seem to disprove the theory. Olmo Silva in his research concludes from his Italian sample that: "All in all, this analysis suggests that if an attitude matters for entrepreneurship, it does so as an innate ability.

Previous claims, on the 'causal' effect of acquiring a balanced skill-mix on the probability of becoming entrepreneur, should be more cautiously interpreted." Similarly, Åstebro & Thompson ('09) found that "that inventor-entrepreneurs typically have a more varied labor market experience, and that varied work experience is associated with lower household income". The debate centers around whether individuals can balance skills by varying their curricula studies, work functions & employers. If so, then individuals seeking to become entrepreneurs might intentionally pursue such variety. If not, that is, if individuals who become entrepreneur simply have a taste for variety that is innate, then no amount of purposeful variety seeking behavior can help. The fact that some studies show that individuals with varied experience and who are not entrepreneurs have lower earnings should give us pause. One is reminded of the individual who starts many things but never finishes, switches majors over & over, changes jobs with abandon, is shifty within their organization perhaps not exemplar to imitate?

Understanding the "Jack of all trades" theory:

A "jack of all trades" is a colloquial expression that refers to a person who is skilled in many different areas. In the context of businesses, a jack of all trades may refer to a company that offers a wide variety of products or services, rather than specializing in a specific area. Here are some examples of businesses that could be considered "jacks of all trades":

Amazon: It started as an online bookstore but has expanded to offer a wide variety of products, including electronics, home goods, groceries, and more. It also offers various services such as Amazon Prime, Amazon Web Services, and Amazon Music.

Walmart: It is a retail giant that offers a wide range of products, including groceries, clothing, electronics, home goods, and more. It also offers various services, such as pharmacy, automotive, and financial services.

Target: It is another retail chain that offers a wide variety of products, including clothing, home goods, electronics, groceries, and more. It also offers various services, such as pharmacy, optical, and photo printing.

Apple: It is primarily known for its technology products, such as the iPhone, iPad, and Mac computers. However, it also offers a wide range of services, such as Apple Music, Apple Pay, and the App Store.

Google: It is primarily known for its search engine, but it also offers a wide range of products and services, including Google Maps, Google Drive, Google Photos, and Google Play.

Microsoft: It is primarily known for its software products, such as Windows and Office. However, it also offers a wide range of hardware products, such as the Xbox gaming console, Surface tablets, and more.

These companies offer a broad range of products and services, allowing them to appeal to a wide variety of customers. However, this approach also comes with challenges, such as maintaining quality across different product lines and avoiding dilution of their brand identity.

Classroom activity: "The Jack of All Trades Challenge"

Objective: To engage readers and encourage them to explore the concept of multidisciplinary skills in entrepreneurship. Participants will reflect on the benefits and challenges of being a jack of all trades and develop strategies to leverage their diverse skill set effectively.

Duration: 60-90 mins

Materials: Flipchart or whiteboard with markers, Sticky notes or index cards & Pens or pencils.

Instructions:

Activity	Instructions
Introduction (10 mins)	Start by providing a brief overview of the theory and its relevance to entrepreneurship. Explain the concept of being a jack of all trades in the business world and highlight its benefits and challenges. Emphasize the importance of leveraging multidisciplinary skills for entrepreneurial success.
Individual Reflection (10 mins)	Ask participants to take a few mins to reflect on their own skill set and identify at least three different areas in which they possess knowledge or expertise. Encourage participants to consider both technical and non-technical skills and jot them down on sticky notes.
Group Discussion (20 mins)	Divide participants into small groups of 3-5 individuals. Instruct the groups to share their identified skills with one another and discuss how these skills can be valuable in an entrepreneurial context. Encourage participants to consider the potential intersections and combinations of their diverse skills, exploring unique value propositions and competitive advantages.
Skill Mapping (15 mins)	Provide each group with a flipchart or whiteboard and markers. Instruct the groups to create a visual representation of their combined skill sets, mapping out the various skills possessed by each group member. Encourage them to identify overlapping skills, complementary skill sets, & potential gaps within groups.
Case Study Analysis (20 mins)	Present a case study or scenario related to entrepreneurship that requires a diverse set of skills. Ask each group to analyze the case study, considering how their collective skill sets could be applied to tackle the challenges presented. Instruct them to discuss and propose innovative solutions, leveraging their multidisciplinary skills.
Presentation and Discussion (15 mins)	Ask each group to present their analysis of the case study and their proposed solutions. Encourage other participants to provide feedback, ask questions, and engage in a constructive discussion. Facilitate a dialogue about the advantages and limitations of being a jack of all trades and how to effectively leverage diverse skill sets.

Wrap-up and Reflection (10 mins)	Summarize the key takeaways from the activity, highlighting the value of multidisciplinary skills in entrepreneurship. Facilitate a brief group discussion to reflect on the challenges faced, innovative solutions proposed, and lessons learned during the activity. Encourage participants to consider how they can further develop and leverage their diverse skill sets in their entrepreneurial journeys.

Conclusion: The activity offers an opportunity to explore and leverage their multidisciplinary skills in an entrepreneurial context. By reflecting on their skill sets, engaging in group discussions, analyzing case studies, and proposing innovative solutions, participants can deepen their understanding of the theory of being a jack of all trades and its practical applications in entrepreneurship. This activity encourages participants to embrace their diverse skill sets and leverage them effectively to create unique value propositions in the business world.

1.3 Creative Destruction

Joseph Schumpeter criticized the classical approach to economics, which kept some variables fixed to deduce conclusions through logic, as too abstract and not grounded-in-reality. He was an Austrian economist writing in the 1930s about the nature of capitalism. He believed that capitalism could only be understood as a disequilibrium caused by continual change from innovation. Schumpeter viewed the entrepreneur as the key innovator & often argued that entrepreneurship is the key driver of economies, creating economic growth through the process of creative destruction. He distinguished between inventors & entrepreneurs, arguing that entrepreneurs are more important economic players than inventors because entrepreneurs are responsible for the actual implementation and dissemination of inventions. Inventors create new technologies and techniques, whereas entrepreneurs transform them into economic forces. Schumpeter is perhaps best known for his Theory of creative destruction which celebrates the destruction of old ways, companies, and legacies to make way for the new. Schumpeter's dynamic Theory contrasts with the older static theories of the circular flow of the economy. He argued that entrepreneurs produce innovations by creating new combinations with factors of production such as technologies and techniques. The entrepreneur innovates by introducing new products, opening new markets, new sources of inputs, or new forms of organization. Schumpeter is credited with placing human actors at the center of economic development processes. He argued that entrepreneurs seek to gain power through a capacity to resist social pressure and to overcome the limitations of existing skill sets. Perhaps one of the closest modern approximations to the notion of creative destruction is found in Clayton Christensen's disruptive innovation Theory. Stam in 2018 represented Schumpeter's theory of creative destruction as a great modern representation of innovative start-ups in entrepreneurship. Start-ups aim to solve existing problems experienced by the market and current incumbent offerings and aim to create a new solution that will eventually overtake the existing product or service in the market, thus destroying it. This can be seen in the rise of streaming services such as Netflix, which effectively dominated the home entertainment industry and rendered businesses such as Blockbuster obsolete.

Understanding the "Creative Destruction" theory:

Creative destruction is a term used in economics to describe the process by which new innovations and technologies displace older and less efficient ones, leading to the creation of new markets and industries. For example, the rise of digital photography and decline of traditional film photography is an example of creative destruction. For decades, film photography was the dominant technology for capturing and printing photographs. However, the introduction of digital cameras and the rise of digital photography disrupted the industry and led to the decline of film photography. Digital cameras were initially low quality and expensive, but over time they improved in quality and became more affordable. As a result, they became more popular among consumers, who were attracted to the convenience and cost savings of digital photography. This led to a decline in demand for traditional film photography, which was eventually phased out by many manufacturers. While the decline of film photography was painful for some, it also led to the creation of new markets and industries.

Digital photography allowed for new forms of image manipulation and sharing, leading to the rise of social media platforms like Instagram and Snapchat. It also led to the creation of new industries, such as online photo printing services and digital photography equipment manufacturers. Overall, the process of creative destruction in the photography industry led to the displacement of older technology and the creation of new markets and opportunities. This is a common pattern in many industries, where new innovations and technologies lead to the destruction of older, less efficient ones, and the creation of new markets and industries.

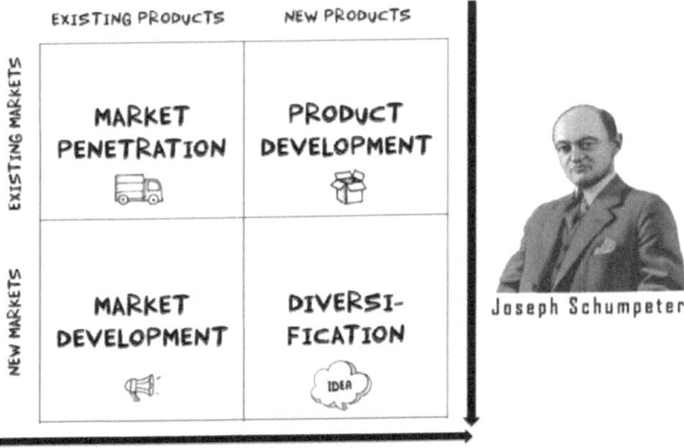

Classroom Activity: "The Creative Destruction Simulation"

Objective: To engage readers and provide them with a hands-on experience of how disruptive innovation and creative destruction impact industries and entrepreneurship. Participants will simulate the process of creative destruction & analyze its implications for entrepreneurial ventures.

Duration: 90-120 mins

Materials: Whiteboard with markers, Sticky notes, Pens & Laptop.

Instructions:

Activity	Instructions
Introduction (10 mins)	Provide an overview of the theory & its significance in entrepreneurship. Explain the concept of disruptive innovation and how it leads to the destruction & creation of industries. Emphasize adaptability, innovation, & entrepreneurial mindset in navigating the process of creative destruction.
Industry Analysis (20 mins)	Divide participants into small groups of 3-5 individuals. Assign each group a specific industry (e.g., music, transportation, retail) and instruct them to research and analyze the current state of that industry. Encourage exploration of recent innovations, emerging trends & potential disruptions within their assigned industry.

Group Discussion (15 mins)	Instruct each group to present their findings to the class. Encourage other participants to ask questions, share additional insights, and engage in a constructive discussion about the potential disruptions and challenges faced by the industries.
Creative Destruction Simulation (40 mins)	Explain the simulation activity to participants: they will imagine themselves as entrepreneurs operating within their assigned industries. Instruct each group to identify a traditional business or industry within their assigned sector that is ripe for disruption. Ask participants to brainstorm innovative ideas and business models that could potentially disrupt the identified traditional business or industry. Participants should consider how their proposed ideas leverage new technologies, customer preferences, and emerging trends to create a new market or significantly change the existing one. Instruct participants to create a brief pitch for their disruptive idea, highlighting its potential impact & competitive advantages.
Pitch (15 mins)	Ask each group to present their idea pitch to class. Encourage groups to be creative, persuasive, and concise in their presentations. After each pitch, allow time for questions, feedback, and discussions from the other participants.
Reflection & Analysis (20 mins)	Facilitate a group discussion to reflect on the simulation activity and the concepts of creative destruction. Ask participants to share their thoughts on the challenges faced during the simulation and the potential implications for existing industries and entrepreneurs. Discuss the importance of adaptability, continuous innovation, and embracing change in the entrepreneurial journey.
Wrap-up and Conclusion (10 mins)	Summarize the key takeaways from the activity, highlighting the impact of disruptive innovation and creative destruction in entrepreneurship. Encourage participants to further explore the theory of creative destruction through additional readings and case studies. Emphasize the importance of fostering an entrepreneurial mindset and embracing change as entrepreneurs navigate the dynamic business landscape.

Conclusion: The activity provides readers with a hands-on experience of how disruptive innovation and creative destruction shape industries and entrepreneurship. By analyzing industries, brainstorming disruptive ideas, and presenting their pitches, participants gain insights into creative destruction and its implications for entrepreneurial ventures. It encourages participants to think critically, embrace innovation, & adapt as they navigate the ever-evolving business landscape.

1.4 Uncertainty-Bearing

Frank Hyneman Knight, an American economist at the University of Chicago, developed the uncertainty-bearing Theory in the 1920s to explain the phenomenon of entrepreneurship.

The Roaring 20s: They brought with them renewed attention to the people and processes that served to bring innovations to market with increasing intensity, and the media of the day was in the habit of idealizing business tycoons. Much of the government had adopted a laissez-faire attitude toward business. Knight distinguished between risk that can be modeled probabilistically, from uncertainty, for which the probabilities are unknowable. For instance, uncertainty surrounds the implementation of new strategies, the development of new products or entry into new markets. Similarly, the positive consequences of acquiring a competitor may have unknowable probabilities. According to his Theory, bearing business uncertainty creates profit and the more uncertainty taken on, the more profit can be gained. The relationship between uncertainty and gain may be linear, or even exponential, where there are bigger payoffs when the uncertainty born is greater. The uncertainty-bearing Theory views entrepreneurs as bearers of uncertainty. It places great emphasis on the entrepreneur's ability to make decisions under uncertainty. The uncertainty perspective also suggests a normative dimension: that entrepreneurs who are willing to take on great uncertainty may deserve windfall profits the rare times they do succeed. Entrepreneurs take on uncertainty according to their inclinations and abilities. Knight argued that the greater their self-confidence, the more they can take on. Thus, uncertainty bearing is a capability that is a normal cost of doing business, where the payoffs are indefinite, future, and based on hopes and conjectures. The Theory also suggests that uncertainty can be reduced through pooling it among several entrepreneurs. Broadly pooling uncertainty may be especially important when pursuing windfall profits because the reward will be large enough to compensate several participants. Pooling may be less important for smaller payoff opportunities because they may not supply enough reward to make sharing worthwhile. Frank Knight (1921) saw the world as an environment that constantly brings new opportunities for businesses to form and make money.

However, with these new opportunities also come new risks. Knight observed that one reason humans developed institutions, such as financial firms, is to help eliminate the uncertainty that comes with entrepreneurship (Emmett, 2011). Stable institutions and regulations help reduce uncertainty by creating more predictable future outcomes.

Understanding the "Uncertainty-Bearing" theory:

Uncertainty bearing refers to the willingness of individuals or organizations to take risks and accept the potential consequences of uncertain outcomes. For example.

Entrepreneurs: They often take on significant financial risks, investing their own money and seeking funding from others to start a new venture. They do so in the face of uncertain outcomes, knowing that there is a chance the business may not succeed.

Investors: Investors often make decisions based on incomplete or imperfect information, taking risks in the hopes of earning a return on their investment.

Innovators: They invest time, money, & other resources into developing new ideas & technologies, knowing that there is a risk that their efforts may not result in a successful product or service.

Researchers: They often invest significant time and resources into research projects, with the hope that their efforts will result in new discoveries or insights.

Politicians: They make decisions based on imperfect information and must accept the potential consequences of those decisions, even if they are uncertain.

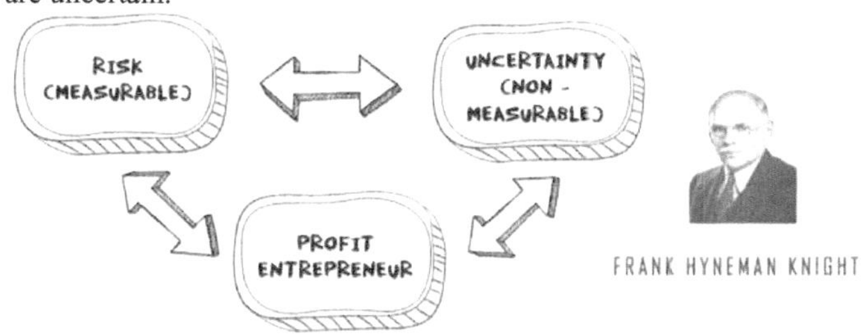

Classroom Activity: "Navigating the Sea of Uncertainty"

Objective: To engage readers and help them develop skills to effectively navigate and manage uncertainty in entrepreneurship.

Participants will explore different strategies, tools, and mindsets to embrace and mitigate uncertainty in their entrepreneurial ventures.

Duration: 90-120 mins

Materials: Flipchart or whiteboard with markers, Sticky notes or index cards & Pens or pencils.

Instructions:

Activity	Instructions
Intro (10 mins)	Provide an overview of the theory & its significance in entrepreneurship. Explain the concept of uncertainty & its impact on decision-making, risk-taking, & innovation. Emphasize developing skills & mindsets to effectively navigate & embrace uncertainty.
Brain-storming (20 mins)	Divide participants into small groups of 3-5 individuals. Instruct each group to brainstorm and list various uncertainties typically faced by entrepreneurs. Encourage participants to think broadly & consider both internal & external sources of uncertainty.
Theory Mapping (15 mins)	Provide each group with a flipchart or whiteboard and markers. Instruct the groups to create an uncertainty map by categorizing and organizing the uncertainties identified. Participants should group uncertainties based on their nature & its impact on the business.
Case Study Analysis (30 mins)	Present a case study or scenario involving significant uncertainty in the entrepreneurial context. Instruct each group to analyze the case study, identify the uncertainties present, and discuss potential risks and opportunities. Also ask participants to discuss and propose strategies to mitigate them.
Presen-tation and Discussion (25 mins)	Ask each group to present their analysis of the case study and their proposed strategies to manage uncertainty. Encourage other participants to provide feedback, ask questions, and engage in a constructive discussion. Facilitate a discussion.
Mindset & Skill Development (20 mins)	Lead a discussion on the mindset and skills required to effectively navigate uncertainty in entrepreneurship. Discuss concepts such as embracing ambiguity, building resilience, adaptive decision-making, continuous learning, & networking. Encourage participants to reflect on their own mindset & skills to self- improvement.

Action Planning (15 mins)	Instruct each participant to identify specific uncertainties they are currently facing or expect to face in their entrepreneurial journey. Ask them to write down actionable steps or strategies to embrace or mitigate them effectively.
Sharing and Reflection	Provide an opportunity for participants to share their action plans with the group, if they feel comfortable doing so. Facilitate a brief reflection session, encouraging participants to discuss how the activity has influenced their understanding of the theory.

Conclusion: The activity allows readers to explore and develop strategies to effectively manage uncertainty in entrepreneurship. By brainstorming uncertainties, analyzing a case study, and proposing strategies, participants gain insights into the theory of uncertainty-bearing and its practical applications. This activity encourages participants to embrace uncertainty as an opportunity for growth, develop the necessary mindsets and skills to navigate uncertainty, and take proactive steps to manage uncertainties in their entrepreneurial ventures.

1.5 Agglomeration

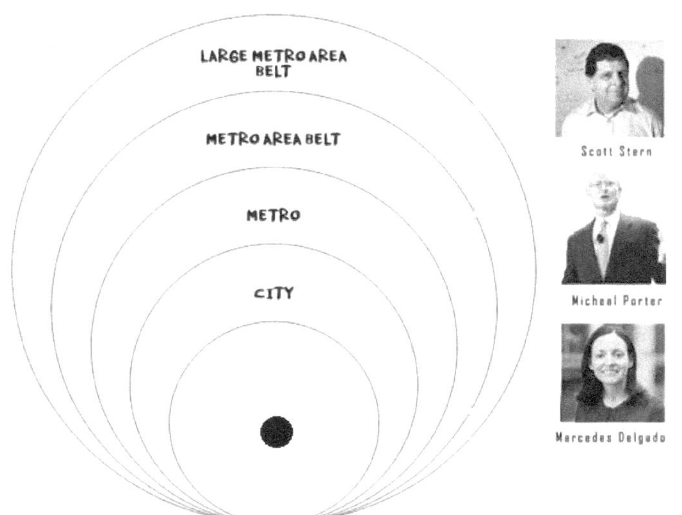

For quite a while there has been interest in whether or not a group's structure is due to business, or regardless of whether bunches advantage businesspeople (Delgado, Porter, and Stern, 2010). Bunches allude to geographic convergences of comparative firms, such the innovation firms in Silicon Valley. Specialists are intrigued to know whether groups breed and lift business visionaries to check whether favorable to bunch arrangements, like keen parks, bode well. Additionally, additionally need to know whether business visionaries are lucky to be in groups or not to advise mechanical strategy around business schooling and preparing (Cusmano, Morrison and Pandolfo, 2015). Spinouts: where workers from firms in a group pass on to begin integral or contending free endeavors, are viewed as critical to the variety and intensity of bunches. They are particularly significant because spinouts will in general remain nearby their parent firms and their own organizations. In this way, where there are numerous spinouts, there will in general be a bunching impact. In places where there exist less obstructions holding representatives back from turning out new pursuits, there are more spinouts (Cordes, Richerson and Schwesinger, 2014). For example, California doesn't uphold non-contend arrangements, so there is more potential for agglomeration. Since half of spinouts stay in the bunch (Berchicci, King and Tucci, 2011), the group develops through thickness and specialty advancement. An intriguing thought is the chance of a bunch impact whereby there is more worth made when numerous organizations of a similar kind contend close to one another. For example, groups incorporate a gathering of car vendors along the stretch of interstate, or downtown road of shoe stores.

Understanding "Agglomeration" the theory:

It is a phenomenon in which businesses and industries tend to cluster together in a specific geographic area, often leading to increased productivity and competitiveness. For example.

The tech industry in Silicon Valley is a prime example of agglomeration. The area around San Francisco and San Jose, California, is home to many of the world's leading technology companies, such as Apple, Google, and Facebook, as well as many start-ups and smaller tech firms. The concentration of tech companies in Silicon Valley has several benefits. First, it creates a pool of highly skilled workers, many of whom are trained at nearby universities such as Stanford and UC Berkeley. This concentration of talent and expertise can lead to greater innovation and productivity. Secondly, the proximity of tech companies to one another allows for greater collaboration and knowledge sharing. Employees can easily attend conferences and events, network with other professionals, and exchange ideas and best practices. This can lead to faster innovation, greater efficiency, and better solutions to common problems. Finally, the presence of many tech companies in Silicon Valley has also led to the creation of supporting industries, such as venture capital firms, law firms, and consulting firms. These industries help to fuel the growth of the tech industry and support its continued success.

Classroom Activity: "Agglomeration Innovations"

Objective: To engage readers and help them explore the concept of agglomeration in entrepreneurship. Participants will analyze the benefits and challenges of agglomeration and develop strategies to leverage the power of clustering & collaboration for entrepreneurial success.

Duration: 90-120 mins

Materials: Flipchart or whiteboard with markers, Sticky notes, Pens, or pencils.

Instructions:

Activity	Instructions
Introduction (10 mins)	Start by providing a brief overview of the "Theory of Agglomeration" and its relevance in entrepreneurship. Explain the concept of agglomeration, emphasizing the benefits of geographic clustering, knowledge spillovers, and collaboration among entrepreneurs. Highlight examples of successful agglomerations (e.g., Silicon Valley, Wall Street) to illustrate the impact of clustering on entrepreneurial ecosystems.
Group Discussion (20 mins)	Divide participants into small groups of 3-5 individuals. Instruct each group to discuss and share their understanding of agglomeration in entrepreneurship. Encourage participants to consider the advantages, challenges, & potential opportunities associated with agglomerations.
Agglomeration Mapping (15 mins)	Provide each group with a flipchart or whiteboard and markers. Instruct the groups to create an agglomeration map by identifying and visualizing existing entrepreneurial clusters or potential agglomerations in their local context. Participants should consider factors such as industry specialization, infrastructure, talent pool, and support organizations.

Case Study Analysis (30 mins)	Present a case study or scenario that highlights the benefits and challenges of agglomeration. Instruct each group to analyze the case study, considering how agglomeration influenced the success or failure of entrepreneurial ventures. Ask participants to discuss and propose strategies for leveraging the power of agglomeration and overcoming potential challenges.
Presentation and Discussion (25 mins)	Ask each group to present their analysis of the case study and their proposed strategies for agglomeration success. Encourage other participants to provide feedback, ask questions, and engage in a constructive discussion. Facilitate a dialogue about the importance of collaboration, networking, and knowledge-sharing within agglomerations.
Agglomeration Action Plan (20 mins)	Instruct each participant to identify one or two specific actions they can take to leverage or contribute to an existing agglomeration or build a new entrepreneurial cluster & write down their action plan on sticky notes. Participants should consider networking activities, collaboration opportunities, resource sharing, and knowledge exchange initiatives.
Sharing and Reflection (10 mins)	Provide an opportunity for participants to share their agglomeration action plans with the group, if they feel comfortable doing so. Facilitate a brief reflection session, encouraging participants to discuss how the activity has influenced their understanding and their plans.

Conclusion: It allows readers to delve into the theory of agglomeration and explore strategies to leverage clustering and collaboration for entrepreneurial success. By analyzing case studies, mapping agglomerations, and developing action plans, participants gain insights into the benefits, challenges, and opportunities associated with agglomerations. This activity encourages participants to actively participate in agglomerations, foster collaboration, and contribute to the growth of entrepreneurial ecosystems.

1.6 Knowledge spillover

The knowledge spillover Theory suggests that productive innovation comes from both incumbents (established firms) and new entrants (entrepreneurs and their organizations) (Acs et al., 2009; Audretsch and Lehmann, 2005). Knowledge is inherently leaky and moves through networks and via stakeholder mobility. This is probably a good assumption given that many organizations find it very difficult to keep secrets. Whistleblowers, for example, demonstrate limited secrecy when they leak information that is damning to their employers. Knowledge spillovers are the main sources of economic growth and development because they are sources of entrepreneurial opportunities. Entrepreneurship is about making new combinations, but the source of raw material for the combinations have to come from somewhere. Knowledge can leak from organizations in the form of spinouts (employees turned entrepreneurs), or when employees leave to work for other organizations (including direct competitors). They can also flow through explicit knowledge transfers (e.g., publications and patents). When incumbents are efficient at exploiting the knowledge they create, then there are fewer opportunities for new entrants (Agarwal et al., 2010). However, inefficient use of knowledge by incumbents causes it to leak out of those organizations making it possible for new entrants to utilize it. For instance, incumbents often invest in innovations that they do not subsequently utilize because they may deem the innovations to be counter to their firms' interests. Innovations can cannibalize sales or reduce the value of a firms' assets and resources or can threaten margins. As a result, employees who want to pursue innovations that are not supported by the parent firm may decide to leave to join other firms or to start new ventures. Many organizational actions and policies can be viewed as attempts suppress knowledge spillovers. For example, compensation schemes, non-compete contracts and intellectual property rights often make it difficult for entrepreneurs to utilize knowledge spillovers in their new ventures.

Understanding the "Knowledge Spill-over" theory:

Knowledge spillover refers to the situation where knowledge and ideas generated by one individual or organization spill over and benefit others. Here is an example of knowledge spillover: The development of the World Wide Web is an example of knowledge spillover. The World Wide Web was created by Tim Berners-Lee at CERN in Switzerland in the early 1990s. Berners-Lee developed the idea of hypertext, which allows users to navigate from one document to another via hyperlinks. The development of the World Wide Web was initially intended to solve a specific problem at CERN, but the knowledge and ideas generated by Berners-Lee spilled over and benefited many other individuals and organizations. The World Wide Web has had a profound impact on how we communicate, access information, and conduct business, and has spawned countless new industries and businesses. For example, the development of the World Wide Web has led to the creation of search engines like Google, social media platforms like Facebook, and online marketplaces like Amazon.

These businesses and industries have benefited from the knowledge and ideas generated by Berners-Lee and have built upon his initial work to create new products and services. The knowledge spillover from the development of the World Wide Web is an example of how knowledge and ideas generated by one individual or organization can have far-reaching effects and benefit many others.

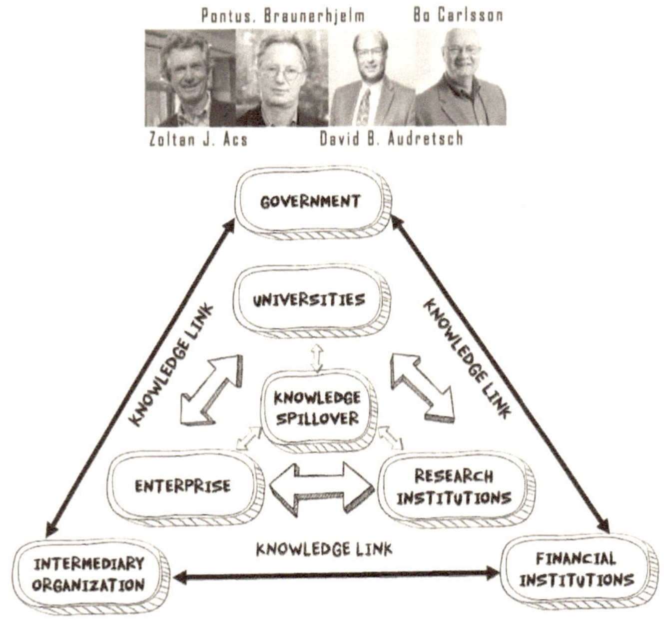

Classroom Activity: "Knowledge Spillover Lab"

Objective: To engage readers & provide them with an interactive experience to understand the concept and explore its implications in entrepreneurship. Participants will analyze knowledge spillover scenarios, identify potential spillovers, and develop strategies to leverage knowledge spillovers for entrepreneurial growth.

Duration: 90-120 mins

Materials: Flipchart or whiteboard, markers, Sticky notes & Pens, or pencils.

Instructions:

Activity	Instructions
Introduction (10 mins)	Provide a brief overview of the theory and its significance in entrepreneurship. Explain the concept of knowledge spillover, emphasizing the flow of knowledge across individuals, organizations, and industries. Highlight the potential benefits & challenges of knowledge spillovers for their ventures.
Brain-storming (15 mins)	Create small groups of 3-5 individuals. Instruct each group to brainstorm & identify potential knowledge spillover scenarios in entrepreneurship. Encourage participants to think broadly & consider various sources of knowledge & potential recipients.
Mapping (20 mins)	Provide each group with a flipchart or whiteboard. Instruct the groups to create a visual map of their identified knowledge spillover scenarios. Participants should categorize the spillovers, identify the sources of knowledge, & explore impacts on new ventures.
Case Study Analysis (30 mins)	Present a case study or scenario demonstrating knowledge spillover in action. Instruct each group to analyze the case study, identify the sources of knowledge spillover, and discuss the benefits or challenges faced by the ventures involved. Ask participants to propose strategies for leveraging knowledge spillovers.
Presentation and Discussion (25 mins)	Ask each group to present their analysis of the case study and their proposed strategies for leveraging knowledge spillovers. Encourage feedback, questions, and a constructive discussion among participants. Facilitate a dialogue on the importance of collaboration, networking, and open innovation in fostering knowledge spillovers.
Strategy Development (20 mins)	Instruct participants to reflect on their own entrepreneurial ventures or business ideas. Ask them to identify potential sources of knowledge spillover that could benefit their ventures. Participants should develop strategies to actively seek and leverage knowledge spillovers, such as networking, collaboration, or engagement.

Sharing and Reflection (10 mins)	Provide an opportunity for participants to share their knowledge of spillover strategies with the group. Facilitate a brief reflection session, encouraging discussion on the impact of the activity and plans for leveraging knowledge spillovers in their entrepreneurial journeys.

Conclusion: By brainstorming scenarios, analyzing case studies, and developing strategies, participants gain insights into the benefits and challenges of knowledge spillovers and how to leverage them effectively. This activity encourages participants to actively seek and embrace knowledge spillovers, foster collaborations, and build networks to drive entrepreneurial growth through the exchange of knowledge.

1.7 Transaction cost

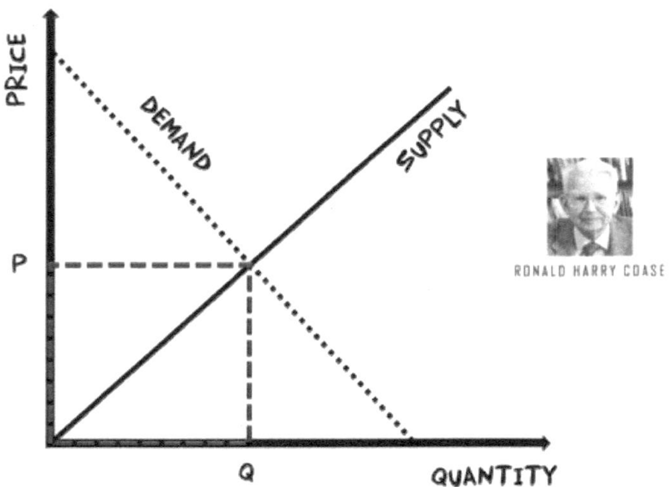

Transaction cost economics is often attributed to the work of Ronald H. Coase in the 1930s, who used it to explain the existence of organizations. Transaction costs occur whenever an economic exchange happens. Search and information costs describe the work of determining the availability of inputs and identifying the most affordable source of inputs in a market or finding the best partner for an exchange (Williamson, 1975). Oliver Williamson was awarded the 2009 Nobel Prize in part for his work on transaction cost Theory.

Bargaining costs describe the work of negotiating prices and agreements, such as contracts. Solid contracts may require considerable negotiation and the employment of lawyers with skill and experience with contract development. Policing costs describe the efforts needed to enforce agreements or to ensure that exchange terms are being met (Dahlman, 1979). For instance, such costs may be incurred when the legal system is needed to get a partner to do what they promised. Transaction costs add on to normal production costs related to buying inputs to produce outputs. Transaction costs are seen as information processing costs and are often reduced by resorting to hierarchies. For instance, if a firm vertically integrates its supply, then it can save some transaction costs relating to search, bargaining, and policing. Similarly, hybrid governance structures such as joint ventures and strategic alliances can be used to reduce transaction costs. Upon forming new ventures, entrepreneurs need to decide what to acquire in the spot market, what to acquire via contracts and relationships, and what to integrate into the venture. Typically, firms choose to integrate (buy or build) resources when specific investments are needed (e.g., a specialized machinery or highly custom software), whereas they tend to contract for more general resources like HR services, accounting services, & IT infrastructure (Williamson, 1975).

Understanding the "Transaction Cost" theory:

Transaction costs refer to the costs associated with making an economic transaction or exchange. These costs can include both direct costs (such as fees, commissions, and taxes) as well as indirect costs (such as time and effort spent searching for information or negotiating terms). For example.

Buying a house is an example of a transaction that incurs significant transaction costs. The costs of buying a house can include:

Real estate agent fees: In many cases, buyers work with a real estate agent who helps them find properties and negotiate with sellers. Real estate agents typically charge a commission, which can range from 2% to 6% of the sale price of the property.

Legal fees: Buyers may need to hire a lawyer to review contracts and ensure that the transaction is legally binding. Legal fees can range from a few hundred to several thousand dollars.

Inspection fees: Buyers often hire a home inspector to assess the condition of the property & identify any potential problems. Inspection fees can range from a few hundred to several thousand dollars.

Closing costs: When the transaction is complete, buyers are typically responsible for paying closing costs, which can include fees for title

searches, appraisals, and other services. Closing costs can range from 2% to 5% of the sale price of the property.
These transaction costs can add up quickly and can make buying a house a costly and time-consuming process. The existence of transaction costs can also discourage some buyers from entering the market, leading to lower levels of economic activity.

Classroom Activity: "Transaction Cost Analysis Game"

Objective: To engage readers of the book on the topic of the "Theory of Transaction Cost" and help them understand the concept through a hands-on and interactive game. Participants will analyze transaction costs in different scenarios, identify factors that contribute to transaction costs, and develop strategies to minimize transaction costs in entrepreneurial ventures.
Duration: 90-120 mins
Materials: Flipchart or whiteboard with markers, Sticky notes or index cards & Pens or pencils.
Instructions:

Activity	Instructions
Introduction (10 mins)	Provide a brief overview of the "Theory of Transaction Cost" and its relevance in entrepreneurship. Explain the concept of transaction cost and its impact on economic transactions in entrepreneurship. Highlight the importance of understanding transaction costs for effective decision-making and resource allocation.
Scenario Analysis (25 mins)	Divide participants into small groups of 3-5 individuals. Ensure each group has a mix of different backgrounds and experiences. Provide each group with a different entrepreneurial scenario involving various transactions. Instruct groups to analyze the scenario and identify potential transaction costs involved. Encourage consideration of both explicit and implicit costs.
Transaction Cost-Mapping (!5 mins)	Provide each group with a flipchart or whiteboard. Instruct groups to create a visual map of the transaction costs identified in their scenario analysis. Participants should categorize the costs, identify underlying factors, & explore strategies to mitigate them.

Case Study Discussion (30 mins)	Present a case study illustrating the impact of transaction costs on entrepreneurial ventures. Instruct groups to analyze the case study, considering the transaction costs involved and their consequences. Ask participants to discuss and propose strategies to reduce or manage transaction costs in the given case study.
Presen-tation and Discussion (25 mins)	Ask each group to present their case study analysis and proposed strategies for minimizing transaction costs. Encourage participants to provide feedback, engage in discussion, and explore the significance of transaction cost analysis.
Strategy Development (20 mins)	Instruct participants to reflect on their own entrepreneurial ventures or business ideas. Ask them to identify potential transaction costs and develop strategies to minimize or mitigate those costs. Participants should consider factors such as vertical integration, long-term partnerships, contract design, and optimization.
Sharing & Reflection (!0 mins)	Provide an opportunity for participants to share their transaction cost strategies with the group, if desired. Facilitate a reflection session, encouraging discussion on the impact of the activity & plans for reducing costs.

Conclusion: It allows readers to actively explore and understand the concept of transaction costs in entrepreneurship. Through scenario analysis, case study discussions, and strategy development, participants gain insights into the factors that contribute to transaction costs and strategies to mitigate them. This activity encourages participants to think critically, make informed decisions regarding resource allocation, and develop strategies to minimize transaction costs in their entrepreneurial ventures.

1.8 X-efficiency

Harvey Leibenstein, American economist, developed X-efficiency Theory in the 1960s. He views entrepreneurs as gap-fillers and input complementors. Gaps (X-inefficiency) emerge when there are inefficiencies in markets, such as when incumbents do not utilize their resources efficiently (Leibenstein, 1966;1978) because of political, normative, cognitive, and structural factors. A classic example is the startup without a union that enters a market where all the incumbents have strong unions. The cost advantage of disorganized labor may help firms with low-cost business models to thrive at the bottom of the market at margins that are uneconomical for incumbent firms to pursue within the target ranges given to them by their shareholders. If the maximum possible productive use of a resources is greater than the actual use by incumbents, an arbitrage opportunity emerges that an entrepreneur can exploit for profit. Entrepreneurs can also improve inputs by putting to use new resources, thus making existing production more efficient. Incumbents can ignore, waste, or misuse resources due to inertia, incompetence, or ignorance. Thus, the entrepreneur is seen as correcting market inefficiencies by improving the information flow in a market. X-efficiency Theory seems to align well with Kirzner's view of entrepreneurship as alertness to opportunities caused by the lack of insight of incumbents.

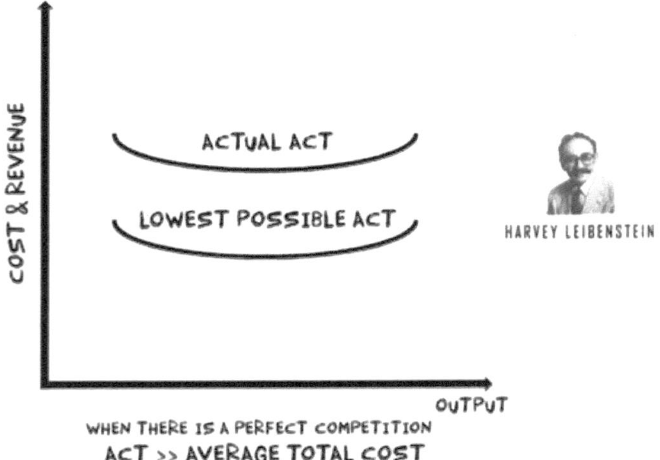

Understanding the "X-Efficiency" theory:

X-efficiency refers to the extent to which a firm can produce output using the least number of resources possible, given its level of technology and market conditions. For examples, A car manufacturing plant that has efficient processes and uses advanced technology to produce cars with fewer defects and higher quality than its competitors, while using fewer resources, such as labor and materials. A retail store that has streamlined its operations and supply chain to reduce costs and improve efficiency, allowing it to offer lower prices than its competitors while maintaining a similar level of quality. A hospital that has implemented efficient processes to reduce patient wait times, minimize errors, and increase the overall quality of care, while using fewer resources, such as staff time and medical supplies. A software development company that uses agile methodologies and efficient software development practices to quickly develop and launch high-quality software products, while using fewer resources, such as development time and hardware.

In each of these examples, the firm can produce output using the least number of resources possible, given its level of technology and market conditions. This allows the firm to be more competitive and profitable, and benefits consumers by offering higher quality products or services at a lower cost.

Classroom Activity for Educators: "The X-Efficiency Challenge"

Objective: To engage readers and help them understand the concept through an interactive and competitive game. Participants will analyze efficiency in different business scenarios, identify factors that contribute to X-inefficiency, and develop strategies to improve X-efficiency in entrepreneurial ventures.

Duration: 90-120 mins

Materials: Flipchart or whiteboard, Sticky notes, Pens or pencils & Timer or stopwatch.

Instructions:

Activity	Instructions
Intro (10 mins)	Provide an overview of the "Theory of X-efficiency" and its relevance in entrepreneurship. Explain the concept of X-efficiency, emphasizing firms' ability to achieve maximum output from inputs. Highlight the importance of identifying and addressing X-inefficiencies for improving productivity.
Analysis (25 mins)	Divide participants into small groups of 3-5 individuals. Ensure each group has a mix of different backgrounds and experiences. Provide each group with a business scenario involving processes or operations. Instruct groups to identify potential X-inefficiencies in the given scenario. Encourage participants to consider factors such as redundancies, resource allocation, and skill gaps.
Mapping (15 mins)	Provide groups with a flipchart or whiteboard. Instruct them to visually map the identified X-inefficiencies. Participants can categorize, analyze factors, & propose strategies to improve.

Challenge Game (40 mins)	Explain the game where groups compete to optimize a given business process within a time frame. Provide a sample process (e.g., order fulfillment) and set a time limit (e.g., 20 mins). Each group aims to achieve max. output using the provided resources and time.
Pitch & Evaluation (25 mins)	Ask each group to present their optimized process and explain their strategies for improving X-efficiency. Encourage participants to evaluate presentations based on criteria like resource utilization and process improvement. Facilitate a feedback session to encourage sharing of learnings.
Strategy Formation (15 mins)	Instruct participants to reflect on their own ventures. Ask them to identify potential X-inefficiencies and develop strategies to improve X-efficiency. Factors to consider: process optimization, employee training, technology utilization, resource allocation.
Share (5 mins)	Provide an opportunity for participants to share their X-efficiency strategies with the group.

Conclusion: It allows readers to actively explore and understand the concept of X-efficiency in entrepreneurship. Through scenario analysis, a competitive game, and strategy development, participants gain insights into the factors that contribute to X-inefficiency and strategies to improve X-efficiency. This activity encourages participants to think critically, identify and address inefficiencies, and develop strategies to optimize processes and resources in their ventures.

1.9 Resource Scarcity

New ventures need to grow at a fast pace to keep up with incumbent firms. Oxenfeld and Kelly (1969) propose resource scarcity Theory to explain which some new ventures choose franchising instead of chaining as a means of growth. A core assumption of the Theory is that new ventures are founded below minimum efficient scale, such that there is a negative relationship between growth rate and failure of new ventures (Audretsch, 1995). Franchising is a quick way to expand a new venture with little upfront capital because the franchisees provide their own capital for their franchises. Since new ventures are often not able to access mainstream financial markets (e.g., for loans, bonds, and equity), franchising is an important alternative. Startups may also be less able to retain earnings to expand, given their commitments to initial investors who may want a quick return (Combs and Ketchen, 1999). Shane (1996) argues that new ventures may also lack the local knowledge needed for expansion or may find it difficult to acquire the managerial talent (human resources) needed for chaining. With franchising, much of the risk of expansion is pushed to the franchisees. Once a franchiser grows to a certain size though, then it may gain access to new levels of financial capital and may seek to re-buy existing franchises (especially more profitable ones) or continue expansion via chaining. Alternatively, they may seek to increase their returns from each franchise. One problem with early franchising is that the franchising entrepreneurs may not be able to train franchisees adequately and may not able to monitor them effectively, creating the potential for lower quality growth (Stanworth and Curran, 1999).

Understanding the "Resource Scarcity" theory:

Resource scarcity in business refers to a situation where a company lacks access to certain resources that are necessary for its operations. For example.

Water scarcity: A drought may limit the availability of water for irrigation, which could affect crop yields and reduce the profits of agricultural companies.

Energy scarcity: An increase in the price of oil could increase the cost of production for a manufacturing company that relies on oil-based products.

Talent scarcity: A technology company may struggle to find qualified software engineers in a competitive job market, which could slow down its product development & growth.

Raw material scarcity: A technology company that produces electronic devices may face challenges when the supply of rare earth metals needed for its products is limited.

Classroom Activity: Resource Scarcity Simulation Game

Objective: To help participants understand and experience the challenges and decision-making involved in managing limited resources within a business or entrepreneurial context.

Duration: 80 – 90 mins.

Materials: Resource cards representing different types of resources (e.g., money, time, materials, skilled labor). Scarcity scenario cards describing various resource scarcity situations & pen & paper

Instructions:

Activity	Instructions
Intro (10 mins)	Introduce the concept and its importance in entrepreneurship. Explain that participants will be engaged in a simulation game to experience the challenges of managing limited resources.
Resource Allocation Game (30 mins)	Create groups of 3-5 individuals. Distribute resource cards to each group, ensuring a mix of different types of resources, they must allocate their available resources to address the situations effectively. Start with the first scarcity scenario card & provide the groups with a limited time (e.g., 5 mins) to discuss & allocate their resources accordingly. Ask each group to present their resource allocation decisions and explain their reasoning. Facilitate a brief discussion among the participants, highlighting the challenges & learnings.
Reflection and Discussion (15 mins)	After completing the initial round of scenarios, ask participants to reflect on their experience & discuss following questions as a group: • What challenges did you encounter while managing scarce resources? • What strategies did you employ to allocate resources effectively? • Did you have to make any trade-offs or sacrifices? List them • How did resource scarcity impact your decision-making process? • What lessons can you apply to real-life entrepreneurial situations?

Advanced Scarcity Scenario (15 mins)	Introduce a more complex & challenging scarcity scenario: • Give them a shorter time frame (e.g., 3 mins) to make resource allocation decisions. • After the allocated time, ask each group to share their decisions & discuss the reasoning behind them. • Facilitate a discussion about the additional challenges posed by the advanced scenario and the strategies employed by the groups to overcome them.
Key Takeaways and Application (10 mins)	Summarize key takeaways from the activity, emphasizing the importance of resource allocation and decision-making in entrepreneurship. Encourage participants to reflect on how they can apply the lessons learned in their real-life entrepreneurial endeavors. Provide additional resources or readings on resource scarcity theory for interested participants to explore further.

Conclusion: The activity focuses on resource allocation and decision-making in entrepreneurship. It could also encourage participants to reflect on how they can apply the lessons learned in their real-life entrepreneurial endeavors. Additionally, providing additional resources or readings on resource scarcity theory for interested participants to explore further can be mentioned. It will leave participants with a deeper understanding of the challenges posed by resource scarcity and equip them with valuable insights to navigate similar situations in their entrepreneurial pursuits.

1.10 Prospect

Prospect Theory was developed by behavioral economists Daniel Kahneman and Amos Tversky in the 1970s. Their aim was to better understand decision making processes by looking at how individuals assess the potential gains and losses from a decision separately. The most famous theory tied to the Theory is that most individuals fear losses more than they value gains. The Theory posits that when individuals think they are winning (gain domain frame), they become more risk-averse, whereas when they think they are losing (loss domain frame), they become inclined to take bigger risks to get back to a break-even position. According to Hsu et al. (2017): "So essentially, whether a person frames a situation as associated with gains or losses influences his or her attitude toward engaging in risky behaviors such as reentering entrepreneurship." Entrepreneurs judge whether they are in a gain or loss position based on a reference point. For instance, Hsu et al. use the entrepreneurs' wins and losses from prior entrepreneurial ventures as the reference point in their study. A key insight from the Theory is that entrepreneurs that have failed previously might interpret themselves as being in a loss position, which might encourage them to take even bigger risks in order to gain back what they lost. Looking at the chart below, the entrepreneur in the loss-frame would view him or herself as riding up a much steeper curve (i.e., the convex curve on the bottom left). This also suggests that an entrepreneur with already high income or previous success my subsequently take fewer risks because they would view themselves as riding up the concave curve on the top right. Busenitz et al. suggests that entrepreneurs might use other reference points than industry standards, for instance, psychic (or psychological) benefit from entrepreneurship (e.g., autonomy). Prospect Theory may thus help to explain why entrepreneurs take bold actions in the face of uncertainty. Prospect Theory seems highly related to the Regulatory focus Theory of entrepreneurship.

Understanding the "Prospect" theory:
Prospect theory is a behavioral economics theory that suggests that people make decisions based on their perception of potential losses and gains, rather than on objective probabilities. Here's an example of prospect theory in a business setting: A company is deciding whether to launch a new product line. The company's management team presents two scenarios to the board of directors:
Scenario A: There is a 50% chance of making a profit of Rs. 10 million and a 50% chance of making a loss of Rs. 5 million.
Scenario B: There is a 50% chance of making a profit of Rs. 5 million and a 50% chance of making a loss of Rs. 10 million.
According to prospect theory, people tend to be risk-averse when it comes to gains and risk-seeking when it comes to losses. In this case, the potential gains and losses are the same in both scenarios, but the way they are presented can have a significant impact on the decision. If the board of directors is risk-averse, they may choose Scenario A because the potential gain of Rs. 10 million is more attractive than the potential loss of Rs. 5 million. However, if they are risk-seeking, they may choose Scenario B because of the potential loss of Rs. 10 million is more attractive than the potential loss of Rs. 5 million.

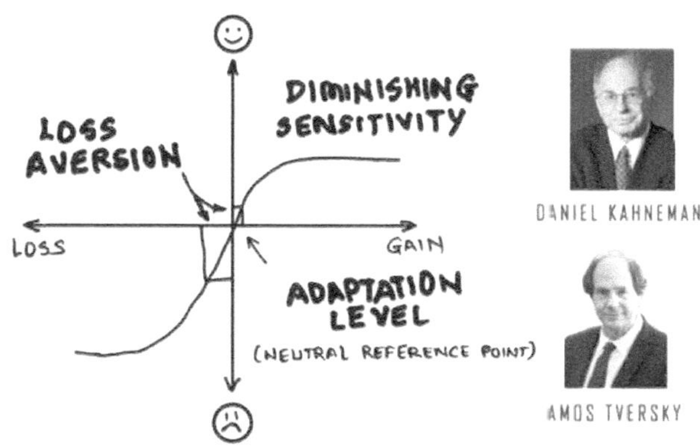

Classroom Activity: "Prospect Theory in Decision Making"

Objective: To help participants understand the theory and how it applies to decision making in an entrepreneurial context. Through this activity, readers will gain a practical understanding of how individuals perceive and evaluate risk and make decisions based on potential gains and losses.

Duration: 90 – 100 mins

Materials: Paper or digital notepads with Pens or pencils

Instructions:

Activity	Instructions
Intro (5 mins)	Introduce the theory as a behavioral economics theory. Explain that decisions are based on potential gains & losses instead of final outcomes.
Self Views (15 mins)	Participants reflect on their own entrepreneurial decision-making processes. Identify a specific entrepreneurial decision and consider perceived gains and losses.
Group Discussion (20 mins)	Divide participants into small groups (3-4 people). Groups discuss individual decisions and share potential gains and losses considered. Explore how perception of gains and losses influenced decision-making process, biases, and risk preferences.

Group Pitch (15 mins)	Groups present summaries of their discussions. Facilitate discussion on common themes or differences in decision-making processes. Participants share insights on how Prospect Theory applies to entrepreneurial decision making.
Case Study Analysis (30 mins)	Provide participants with a realistic entrepreneurial decision-making case study. Participants read case study individually and identify potential gains and losses faced by the entrepreneur. Small groups discuss the case study, considering the influence of Prospect Theory on decision-making process. Participants identify biases, reference points, or framing effects present in the case.
Wrap-up Discussion (!5 mins)	Bring groups back together for a discussion on the case study. Participants share observations and insights on how Prospect Theory affected the decision-making process. Discuss alternative decisions or strategies with class.

Conclusion: Participants would have gained a practical understanding of Prospect Theory and its implications for entrepreneurial decision making. They will develop awareness of biases and cognitive influences that can impact their decision-making processes. Armed with this knowledge, participants are better equipped to make informed decisions, consider potential gains and losses, and navigate the complexities of entrepreneurship.

1.11 Cantillon

The word "entrepreneur" has been traced back to Richard Cantillon, an Irish banker with French roots writing in the early 1700s, before Adam Smith. Cantillon distinguished between entrepreneurs with nonfixed incomes and employees with fixed incomes. Cantillon considered entrepreneurs as those who undertake to bear and overcome uncertainty by investing, paying expenses and hoping for a return. Cantillon viewed a wide slice of society as entrepreneurial because they bear uncertainty, including: *"All the other entrepreneurs, like those who take charge of mines, theaters, buildings, the traders by sea and land, restaurateurs, pastry cooks, innkeepers, etc., as well as the entrepreneurs of their own labor who need no capital to establish themselves, like journeymen artisans, coppersmiths, seamstresses, chimney sweeps, water transporters, live with uncertainty and proportion themselves to their customers. Master craftsmen like shoemakers, tailors, carpenters, wigmakers, etc., who employ journeymen according to the work they have, live with the same uncertainty since their customers may leave them any day."* He uses the example of the merchant that buys farm goods at the day's price thus incurring the risk of higher or lower prices upon arrival and sale in the city. The risk is created by uncertainty about supply and demand which always exists in a free city. Entrepreneurial uncertainty is a fact of the decentralized world where prices are not set in advance by a monopoly. The Theory recognizes the business cycle & turbulence created by unforeseen circumstances or natural forces in an economy. Entrepreneurs are seen to have an important role in the economy because they forecast the need for resources and invest in the future to help to balance supply and demand. Without entrepreneurs that take such risks in the face of uncertainty, the business cycle might be even more pronounced or acute.

Richard Cantillon

Understanding the "Cantillon" theory:

Cantillon refers to the idea that some individuals and firms in the economy are better positioned than others to benefit from changes in economic conditions. Here is an example of Cantillon effects in a business setting:

A company operates in an industry that is heavily regulated by the government. The company has been in business for many years and has established strong relationships with key government officials who are responsible for overseeing the industry. When a new regulation is proposed, the company can use its connections to influence the regulatory process in its favor. As a result, the company can adapt to the new regulation more easily than its competitors. The company can quickly adjust its operations and products to meet the new requirements, while its competitors struggle to keep up. This gives the company a significant advantage in the market and allows it to capture a larger share of the profits from the industry. This example illustrates how Cantillon effects can give certain firms a competitive advantage in the market. By having access to information, relationships, and resources that are not available to others, these firms are better positioned to benefit from changes in the economy or regulatory environment. As a result, they can capture a larger share of the profits and gain a stronger foothold in the market.

Classroom Activity: Unraveling the Theory of Cantillon

Objective: This activity aims to deepen understanding of the Theory of Cantillon, a fundamental concept in entrepreneurship, and its relevance in modern business contexts. Through engaging exercises and thought-provoking questions, participants will explore the key principles put forth by Richard Cantillon and apply them to real-world scenarios.

Duration: 60-90 mins.

Materials: Pen/pencil and paper for each participant, Whiteboard or flip chart & Relevant examples or case studies (optional)

Instructions:

Activity	Instructions
Introduction (10 mins)	Begin by providing a brief overview of Richard Cantillon and his Theory of Cantillon. Explain how his work laid the foundation for modern entrepreneurial theory and the concept of entrepreneurship itself. Highlight the significance of Cantillon's ideas in understanding market dynamics, risk and uncertainty, and the role of the entrepreneur.
Understanding the Theory of (20 mins)	Encourage participants to read relevant excerpts from Cantillon's "Essay on the Nature of Commerce in General." If copies are available, provide them to interested participants. Alternatively, summarize the key principles of Cantillon's theory, such as the concept of the entrepreneur as a risk-bearer, the notion of market equilibrium, & the role of supply-demand.

Analyzing Real-World Scenarios (20 mins)	Present participants with a series of real-world scenarios that reflect entrepreneurial situations. These scenarios can be related to starting a new business, innovation, market disruption, or any other context where entrepreneurial decision-making is critical. Divide participants into small groups and assign each group a scenario to analyze. In their groups, participants should discuss how Cantillon's theory can be applied to the given scenario. They should identify the key actors, risks, and opportunities, as well as the potential outcomes and effects on the market.
Group Discussion (15 mins)	Bring the groups back together for a whole-group discussion. Ask each group to share their analysis of the scenario and how they applied Cantillon's theory. Encourage open dialogue and the exchange of perspectives among participants.
Reflection and Application (15 mins)	Conclude the activity by facilitating a reflection session. Ask participants to reflect on the relevance of Cantillon's theory in the current entrepreneurial landscape. How do his ideas hold up in the face of rapid technological advancements, globalization, and changing market dynamics? Encourage participants to think about how they can incorporate the theory in their entrepreneurial endeavors or decision-making processes.
Wrap-up (5 mins)	Summarize the key insights and takeaways from the activity. Provide additional resources or references for participants who wish to further explore the Theory.

Conclusion: By examining real-world scenarios and applying Cantillon's theory, participants gain a deeper understanding of the complex interplay between actors, risks, opportunities, and market outcomes. Through reflection and application, participants can incorporate Cantillon's principles into their own entrepreneurial endeavors, equipping themselves with a strategic framework for decision-making in the face of technological advancements, globalization, and changing market dynamics.

Sociological Theories

2.1 Necessity versus Opportunity

OPPORTUNITY ENTREPRENEURS

"DEVELOPS AN IDEA TO EXPLOIT AN EXISTING OPPORTUNITY"

NECESSARY ENTREPRENEURS

"LACK OF ALTERNATIVES LEADS TO THIS"

Michael T. Hannan

John H. Freeman

Scholars have divided entrepreneurship into different categories. For example, self-employed individuals are often not considered entrepreneurs. To be an entrepreneur, there has to be an organization being built. There is even a growing sense that only scalable forms of entrepreneurship should be encouraged (Shane, 2009). Another way to slice up entrepreneurs is to separate between necessity and opportunity entrepreneurs (Harding, 2002). Most entrepreneurship theories focus on opportunity entrepreneurship, but perhaps scholars should also embrace broader views that include entrepreneurship that is based on necessity, or at least consider a greater diversity of entrepreneurship (Welter et al., 2017). This approach looks at the motivations of the entrepreneurs, thus can be considered a motivational Theory. Basically, if you have one of the two motives, you are more likely to become an entrepreneur. Necessity entrepreneurs are individuals who start businesses because they cannot find a decent job (or in some cases, keep one). Opportunity entrepreneurs on the other hand, are people who leave or shun good employment to pursue even more lucrative or attractive careers as entrepreneurs. Opportunity entrepreneurship is seen as more innovative, necessity entrepreneurship, more redistributive. There is some evidence that countries that have a greater ratio of opportunity to necessity entrepreneurship have higher rates of economic growth (Wong et., 2005). Interestingly, there is more necessity entrepreneurship in societies with higher levels of income inequality (Lippman et al., 2005), suggesting that reducing necessity entrepreneurship is likely achieved by reducing overall inequality. One criticism is that sometimes necessity entrepreneurship turns into opportunity entrepreneurship. Sometimes there is also a blend of necessity and opportunity--many rags to riches stories that seem to corroborate it.

Understanding the "Necessity versus Opportunity" theory:
Necessity entrepreneurship refers to starting a business out of a need for income, usually due to a lack of employment opportunities, while opportunity entrepreneurship refers to starting a business to pursue a perceived opportunity in the market. For example.

Necessity entrepreneurship: A person who has lost their job and has been unable to find new employment may start a small business out of necessity. For example, they may start a cleaning or lawn care service to generate income to support their family.

Opportunity entrepreneurship: A person who identifies a gap in the market and sees an opportunity to fill that gap by starting a new business is an example of opportunity entrepreneurship. For example, someone who sees a growing demand for organic food may start an organic food delivery service. In both cases, the individuals are starting a business, but the motivation and circumstances are different. The person starting the business out of necessity may not have a passion for entrepreneurship or a desire to run a business long-term, but rather sees it to generate income. The person starting a business out of opportunity may have a passion for entrepreneurship and a desire to build a successful business. Understanding the difference between necessity and opportunity entrepreneurship can help policymakers and business advisors develop targeted programs and resources to support these different types of entrepreneurs. For example, programs that focus on providing access to capital and training may be more beneficial for necessity entrepreneurs, while programs that focus on market research and networking may be more beneficial for opportunity entrepreneurs.

Classroom Activity: Unleashing Entrepreneurial Perspectives

Objective: To engage readers in understanding and analyzing the concepts by exploring real-world examples and engaging in group discussions, participants will gain insights into the different motivations and challenges faced by necessity-driven and opportunity-driven entrepreneurs.

Duration: 60-90 mins.

Materials: Pen/pencil and paper for each participant, Whiteboard, or flip chart (optional) and Relevant case studies illustrating necessity-driven & opportunity-driven entrepreneurship

Instructions:

Activity	Instructions
Introduction (10 mins)	Begin by introducing the concepts of Necessity Theory and Opportunity Theory in entrepreneurship. Explain that necessity-driven entrepreneurs start businesses out of a need for survival or lack of viable alternative employment, while opportunity-driven entrepreneurs identify and exploit opportunities in the market. Highlight the different motivations, challenges, and outcomes associated with each perspective.
Real-world Examples (15 mins)	Provide participants with real-world examples of necessity-driven & opportunity-driven entrepreneurship. Ask participants to individually reflect on these examples and identify the distinguishing factors between the two types of entrepreneurships.
Group Discussion: Necessity Theory (20 mins)	Divide participants into small groups and assign each group the task of discussing necessity-driven entrepreneurship. Each group should identify and analyze the key factors that drive individuals to pursue necessity-driven entrepreneurship. Ask groups to discuss the challenges faced by necessity-driven entrepreneurs and the potential impacts on their businesses and communities. Encourage groups to share their findings with the whole group.
Group Discussion: Opportunity Theory (20 mins)	Assign another set of small groups to explore opportunity-driven entrepreneurship. In their groups, participants should discuss the factors that motivate individuals to pursue opportunity-driven entrepreneurship. Ask groups to analyze the challenges faced by opportunity-driven entrepreneurs and the potential outcomes of their ventures. Each group should share their insights and findings with the whole group, fostering discussion and debate.

Comparative Analysis (15 mins)	Bring the groups back together for a whole-group discussion. Facilitate a comparative analysis of necessity-driven & opportunity-driven entrepreneurship. Ask participants to identify the similarities, differences, and potential overlaps between the two perspectives. Encourage participants to critically evaluate the strengths and limitations of each approach and consider how they can be applied in various contexts.
Reflection and Application (15 mins)	Conclude the activity by facilitating a reflection session. Ask participants to reflect on their own entrepreneurial aspirations or experiences. Encourage participants to identify whether their entrepreneurial endeavors are driven by necessity, opportunity, or a combination of both. Participants should consider how their understanding of necessity and opportunity-driven entrepreneurship can inform their decision-making, goal setting, and overall entrepreneurial mindset.
Wrap-up (5 mins)	Summarize the key insights and takeaways from the activity. Provide additional resources or references for participants who wish to further explore the concepts of the theory.

Conclusion: Through real-world examples, group discussions, and reflective exercises, participants have gained a deeper understanding of the distinct drivers behind necessity-driven and opportunity-driven entrepreneurship. By critically analyzing the strengths and limitations of each approach, participants are better equipped to apply these insights in their own entrepreneurial endeavors, making informed decisions, setting meaningful goals, and nurturing a well-rounded entrepreneurial mindset.

2.2 Institutional

It is about conforming to the rules of the game to gain legitimacy in an institutionalized environment (North, 1991; Scott, 2001; 2005). The rules of the game may be formal, informal, or taken-for-granted assumptions about the nature of the business environment. Institutions set forth expectations that economic actors seek to conform to in order to be treated as legitimate actors in economic society. Entrepreneurs that do not heed the institutional logic of their social contexts risk failure because they may be seen as illegitimate and unworthy of support. This is related to the "liability of newness", where risk of exit or failure is higher in the earlier years of an organization. When young organizations lack legitimacy, they may not receive the vital support of their stakeholders. The main theory of the Theory may be that: Culturally varying social forces shape entrepreneurial success more than does economic efficiency, therefore, entrepreneurs should seek to align their strategies with the norms and regulations of their host societies' institutions. See Bruton, Ahlstrom and Li (2010) for a nice review that inspired me here. Institutional factors affecting entrepreneurs are numerous, including government policies that support or detract entrepreneurs (e.g., fiscal and regulatory barriers, antitrust laws, and property rights), but also more informal social attitudes toward entrepreneurship as a career choice. For instance, in countries where entrepreneurs need to bribe to get ahead, the career choice may be viewed as less attractive than engineering or medicine. Perhaps institutional voids left by inadequate government structures and support for contracts may be filled by informal arrangements, such as close social ties with government officials. However, these ties may be prohibitively expensive to maintain and assuage, forming another barrier to entrepreneurship. Legitimacy is less important for incumbents because of their past performance. Formal governmental regulations can also be prohibitively expensive, for instance, if the time taken to get a new business approved is too long or if too many permits are needed from too many government departments.

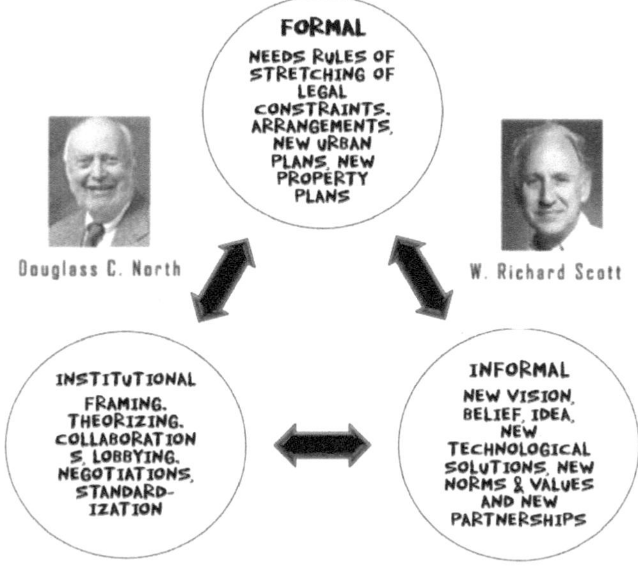

Understanding the "Institutional" theory:

Institutional theory suggests that businesses are influenced by the social and cultural norms and values that are prevalent in their environment. For an example, A company is considering implementing a new diversity and inclusion policy. This policy is designed to increase the representation of underrepresented groups in the company's workforce and create a more inclusive workplace. However, the company is in a region where there is a strong cultural norm of homogeneity in the workplace. According to institutional theory, the company is likely to face resistance to the new policy because it goes against the dominant cultural norms and values in the region. Employees may be skeptical of the policy or may resist its implementation because they do not see the value in diversity and inclusion. To overcome this resistance, the company may need to frame the policy in a way that aligns with the cultural norms and values of the region. For example, the company could emphasize the business benefits of diversity and inclusion, such as increased innovation and creativity, which may resonate with employees who prioritize economic outcomes.

Classroom Activity: Institutional Dynamics - Institutional Theory

Objective: To engage readers in understanding and analyzing the concepts of Institutional Theory by examining the influence of institutions on entrepreneurial behavior and outcomes. Participants will develop insights into the importance of institutional context and the strategies entrepreneurs employ to navigate institutional pressures.

Duration: 60-90 mins.

Materials: Pen/pencil and paper for each participant, Whiteboard or flip chart (optional) & Relevant examples or case studies illustrating institutional dynamics in entrepreneurship.

Instructions:

Activity	Instructions
Introduction (10 mins)	Begin by introducing the concept of Institutional Theory in entrepreneurship. Explain that institutions are formal and informal rules, norms, and practices that shape entrepreneurial behavior and outcomes. Highlight the importance of institutional context in shaping the opportunities, constraints, and expectations.

Real-world Examples (15 mins)	Provide participants with real-world examples or case studies that demonstrate the influence of institutions on entrepreneurship. Ask participants to individually reflect on these examples and identify the institutional factors that influenced entrepreneurial decisions and actions. Encourage participants to observe & take notes.
Group Discussion: Institutional Pressures (20 mins)	Divide participants into small groups and assign each group the task of discussing institutional pressures faced by entrepreneurs. Each group should identify and analyze the formal and informal rules and expectations that shape entrepreneurial behavior. Ask groups to discuss how entrepreneurs respond to institutional pressures and the strategies they employ to navigate them effectively. Encourage groups to share their findings with the whole group, fostering open dialogue and the exchange of perspectives.
Case Analysis: Institutional Dynamics (20 mins)	Present participants with a case study that highlights the institutional dynamics affecting entrepreneurship in a specific industry or region. In their groups, participants should analyze the case study and identify the institutional factors influencing entrepreneurial opportunities, strategies, and outcomes. Ask groups to discuss the challenges and opportunities presented by the institutional context and the strategies entrepreneurs employed to succeed. Each group should share their insights and findings with the whole group.
Reflection and Application (15 mins)	Conclude the activity by facilitating a reflection session. Ask participants to reflect on their own entrepreneurial experiences or aspirations. Encourage participants to consider the institutional context in which they operate or plan to operate. Participants should reflect on how institutional factors have influenced their entrepreneurial decisions, and how they can adapt their strategies to effectively navigate institutional pressures.
Wrap-up (5 mins)	Summarize the key insights and takeaways from the activity. Provide additional resources or references for participants who wish to further explore the theory.

Conclusion: This theory sheds light on the profound impact of formal and informal institutions on entrepreneurial behavior and outcomes. Through real-world examples, group discussions, and case analyses, participants have gained a deeper understanding of how institutions shape entrepreneurial opportunities, constraints, and strategies. By recognizing the institutional dynamics at play, entrepreneurs can better navigate and leverage the institutional context to their advantage. This activity equips participants with valuable insights into the complexities of entrepreneurship within institutional environments, empowering them to make informed decisions and adapt their strategies accordingly for sustainable success.

2.3 Emancipation

The term emancipation has roots in Roman era practices of buying, selling, and keeping slaves, but also wives and children. In Roman times, a son needed to be freed from the legal authority of the father to make his own way in the world. The term is also associated Lincoln's Emancipation Proclamation, which, in the U.S., was used to criminalize slavery. In the women's liberation movement, emancipation is associated with breaking free from bonds of marriage to a man. In a very interesting paper, Rindova and associates (2009) propose that entrepreneurship can be thought of as means of emancipation. They take a positive spin on a critical Theory perspective. They define entrepreneurship as efforts to create new economic, social, institutional, and cultural environments via the actions of groups or individuals. To bolster their arguments, they point out three key methods in which entrepreneurship resembles emancipation processes. These are seeking autonomy, authoring, and making declarations. Seeking autonomy has long been considered a motive of self-employment rather than working for an employer. Who does not want to be their own boss? Autonomy is also a goal of emancipation. Emancipation can be defined as breaking free from some authority figure or system. We may think of slave's being freed. Rindova et al. suggest that Google's founding story is consistent with 'breaking free' as Brin and Page worked to "download the internet", despite ridicule from their professors.

Breaking free can also been seen in relation to breaking down barriers to entry or other constraints. Entrepreneurs work to exploit cracks in the current system of rigid social and economic relationships to bring about change that entrepreneur deem to be desirable. Authoring is about making something one's own, or taking ownership, or becoming. Entrepreneurs must seek to build their own networks, arrangements, norms and structures to preserve their ventures. Making declarations refers to the rhetoric entrepreneurs employ to gain legitimacy for their ventures or create change. Entrepreneurs need to create meaning to hold together webs of stakeholders that support their endeavors or value their products. Rindova et al. suggest that when Amazon.com claimed to create the world's biggest bookstore, they were highlighting contradictions or being provocative in order to generate stakeholder support for the way the company was changing the status quo. Currently, research on entrepreneurship as emancipation is just beginning. Several qualitative studies seem too consistent with the Theory, but scholars have not yet started to test the Theory quantitatively. From a critical perspective, entrepreneurship may itself be a trap for those that are not able to scale. Entrepreneurship should not be viewed as easy work, in fact, it puts many people behind. We see the winners and all the rewards they get for succeeding building businesses, and we think: hey, those folks are the liberated ones, and the way out for the rest of us is to liberate ourselves by also becoming entrepreneurs.

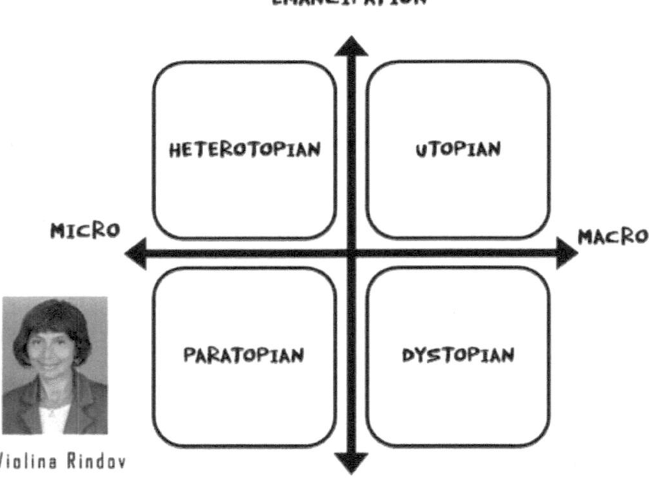

Understanding the "Emancipation" theory:

Emancipation refers to the process of empowering individuals or groups who have historically been marginalized or oppressed. Here are some examples of emancipation in a business setting:

Women's empowerment: A company implements policies and programs to support and advance women in the workplace, such as offering flexible work arrangements, providing leadership development programs, and creating a more inclusive workplace culture.

Labor rights: A company takes steps to ensure that its workers are treated fairly and have access to basic labor rights, such as safe working conditions, fair wages, and the right to unionize.

Environmental justice: A company takes responsibility for its impact on the environment and communities in which it operates and works to mitigate any negative effects. This could include investing in sustainable technologies, reducing waste and pollution, and engaging with local communities to address their concerns.

Social justice: A company takes a stand on social issues and uses its platform to advocate for social change. This could include supporting LGBTQ+ rights, racial justice, or other causes that align with the company's values.

Classroom Activity: Entrepreneurial Power – Emancipation

Objective: To engage readers in understanding and analyzing the Theory of Emancipation in entrepreneurship. By examining the concepts of empowerment, social change, and breaking free from societal constraints, participants will gain insights into how entrepreneurs drive transformative impact & challenge existing norms.

Duration: 60-90 mins.

Materials: Pen/pencil and paper for each participant, Whiteboard or flip chart (optional) & Relevant examples or case studies illustrating the Theory of Emancipation in entrepreneurship

Instructions:

Activity	Instructions
Introduction (10 mins)	Begin by introducing the Theory of Emancipation in entrepreneurship. Explain that the theory focuses on the power of entrepreneurship to empower individuals, challenge societal constraints, and drive social change. Highlight the key elements of the theory, including breaking free from traditional norms, pursuing self-determination, and creating new opportunities for marginalized groups.
Real-world Examples (15 mins)	Provide participants with real-world examples or case studies that exemplify the Theory of Emancipation in entrepreneurship. Ask participants to individually reflect on these examples and identify the elements of empowerment, social change, and breaking societal constraints within entrepreneurial endeavors. Encourage participants to take notes on their observations and insights.

Group Discussion: Elements of Emancipation (20 mins)	Divide participants into small groups and assign each group a specific element of the Theory of Emancipation (e.g., empowerment, challenging norms, social change). Each group should discuss and analyze the assigned element, sharing their understanding of how it manifests in entrepreneurship. Ask groups to identify real-world examples or case studies that exemplify the assigned element and explore their impact on individuals and communities. Encourage groups to share their findings with the whole group, fostering open dialogue and the exchange of perspectives.
Case: Entrepreneurial Transformation (20 mins)	Present participants with a case study that highlights an entrepreneurial endeavor centered around the Theory of Emancipation. In their groups, participants should analyze the case study and identify the elements of empowerment, social change, and breaking societal constraints present within the entrepreneurial context. Ask groups to discuss the transformative impact of entrepreneurial endeavors on individuals, communities, or society at large. Each group should share their insights and findings with the class.
Reflection and Application (15 mins)	Conclude the activity by facilitating a reflection session. Ask participants to reflect on their own entrepreneurial aspirations or experiences. Encourage participants to consider how they can apply the principles of the Theory of Emancipation in their own entrepreneurial endeavors to drive transformative impact and challenge existing norms. Participants should also reflect on potential barriers and strategies for overcoming them to realize emancipatory outcomes.
Wrap-up (5 mins)	Summarize the key insights and takeaways from the activity. Provide additional resources or references for participants who wish to further explore the Theory of Emancipation in entrepreneurship.

Conclusion: This activity empowers participants to reflect on their own entrepreneurial aspirations and consider how they can apply the principles of the Theory of Emancipation to drive transformative impact and challenge existing norms in their own ventures. By embracing the emancipatory mindset, entrepreneurs can become catalysts for positive change and contribute to a more inclusive and empowering society.

2.4 Withdrawal of Status Respect

Everett E. Hagen was a political scientist and economist writing at MIT in the 1950s and 1960s. He sought to explain how traditional societies changed into those with continual technological progress and hence rising incomes. Here we discuss Hagen's (1963) Theory of entrepreneurship. Hagen argues that a process eventually leading to entrepreneurship is triggered when a social group loses status in relation to other groups in a society. When members of a given social group perceive that they are given their due respected by the dominant groups in society, it triggers a creative spark that encourages entrepreneurial behaviors (Dana, 1995).

Some examples of "withdrawal of status respect" include when: 1) a formerly higher status group is displaced by a new group; 2) a social group's symbols are insulted by the dominant group; 3) a group's symbols become unaligned with their actual economic reality (e.g., elders stories reflect a more favorable past); and 4) a group's status is lowered due to migration to a new place (see misfit Theory). Hagen explains that a lowering of status may take generations before leading to the development of anxiety and the rejection of traditional values, leading to creativity and authoritarianism, as in the case of Henry Ford who was the self-made progeny of migrants to the U.S. A lowering of status is met by different reactions. An entrepreneur may acquiesce or continue to work without hope of improvement. Or they may rebel against the system by trying out innovations. Hagen used examples like the Samurai community of Japan, which had traditionally enjoyed a high status, but it was lowered when they were defeated by other groups with superior weapons. To regain their status, the Samurai pursued entrepreneurial development and contributed to the fastest growing Asian economy. Similarly, when the Russian tzar (1650s) adopted Greek practices to attain diplomatic ends, it undermined the Orthodox church and its members, triggering change processes that eventually led to revolution. Hagen's Theory emphasizes a process that generations to unfold and tends to be more dynamic than other cultural theories of entrepreneurship. The Theory also looks to the personality of the figureheads, relating to a larger class of psychological theories of entrepreneurship. In a way, Hagen's Theory is like Christensen's Theory that neglected stakeholders are the early target markets for disruptive innovations. In this case the stakeholders are those individuals who feel they are locked out of real advancement and who use entrepreneurship to get ahead--a means of social mobility.

EVERETT E. HAGEN

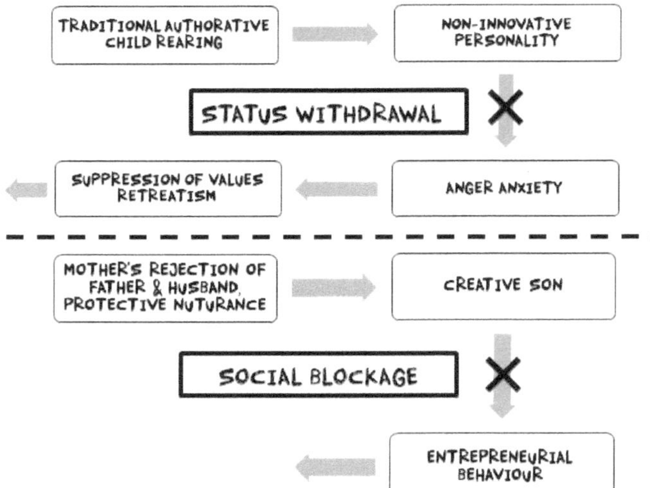

Understanding the "Withdrawal of the Status Respect" theory:
It refers to the loss of social prestige or status that an individual or group experiences when their behavior or actions no longer align with the norms and values of their community. Here are some examples of withdrawal of status respect in a business setting:

Corporate scandals: A company engages in unethical or illegal behavior, such as fraud, bribery, or insider trading. As a result, the company's reputation is damaged, and it may lose the respect of its customers, employees, and other stakeholders.

Leadership failures: A company's leadership team makes poor decisions or exhibits inappropriate behavior, such as discrimination or harassment. This can lead to a loss of respect for the leaders and the company.

Product failures: A company releases a product that is defective or unsafe, causing harm to customers. This can lead to a loss of trust and respect for the company and its products.

Environmental damage: A company engages in practices that harm the environment, such as pollution or deforestation. As a result, the company may face public backlash and a loss of respect from stakeholders who value sustainability and environmental protection.

When a company loses the respect and trust of its stakeholders, it can lead to a decline in sales, employee morale, and overall reputation. Therefore, it is important for businesses to prioritize ethical behavior, environmental sustainability, and social responsibility to maintain the respect and support of their communities.

Classroom Activity: Resilience in Adversity

Objective: To engage readers in understanding and analyzing the Theory of Withdrawal of Status Respect in entrepreneurship. By exploring the challenges of losing social status and reputation and the strategies for resilience, participants will gain insights into overcoming setbacks and thriving in the face of adversity.

Duration: 60-90 mins.

Materials: Pen/pencil and paper for each participant, Whiteboard or flip chart (optional) & Relevant examples or case studies.

Instructions:

Activity	Instructions
Introduction (10 mins)	Begin by introducing the theory & explaining that this theory focuses on the challenges faced by entrepreneurs when they experience a loss of social status, reputation, or respect. Highlight the importance of understanding & addressing these challenges for entrepreneurial resilience and success.
Real-world Examples (15 mins)	Provide participants with real-world examples or case studies that exemplify the Theory of Withdrawal of Status Respect in entrepreneurship. Ask participants to individually reflect on these examples and identify the consequences and implications of losing social status or reputation in entrepreneurial endeavors. Encourage participants to take notes on their observations and insights.

Group Discussion: Challenges & Implications (20 mins)	Divide participants into small groups and assign each group the task of discussing the challenges and implications of losing status respect in entrepreneurship. Each group should identify and analyze the potential consequences, such as loss of credibility, opportunities, and network support. Ask groups to discuss strategies for overcoming these challenges and rebuilding status respect. Encourage groups to share their findings with the whole group, fostering open dialogue and the exchange of perspectives.
Case Analysis: Resilience in Action (20 mins)	Present participants with a case study that highlights an entrepreneurial journey involving a significant loss of status respect. In their groups, participants should analyze the case study and identify the strategies employed by the entrepreneur to rebound and regain respect. Ask groups to discuss the lessons learned from the case study and the key elements of resilience exhibited by the entrepreneur. Each group should share their insights and findings with the whole group, fostering discussion and debate.
Reflection and Application (15 mins)	Conclude the activity by facilitating a reflection session. Ask participants to reflect on their own entrepreneurial experiences or aspirations. Encourage participants to consider how they would respond to a significant loss of status respect and what strategies they would employ to rebuild their reputation and resilience. Participants should reflect on importance of maintaining inner strength, seeking support, & embracing personal growth during difficult times.
Wrap-up (5 mins)	Summarize the key insights and takeaways from the activity. Provide additional resources or references for participants who wish to further explore the Theory.

Conclusion: This activity empowers participants to reflect on their own entrepreneurial journeys and consider the importance of maintaining inner strength, seeking support, and embracing personal growth in overcoming setbacks. By understanding and addressing the challenges of status respect withdrawal, entrepreneurs can cultivate resilience, bounce back from adversity, and continue their pursuit of success with renewed determination.

2.5 Social capital

Too often, entrepreneurship is viewed as a solo job. This myth is perpetuated because of the heroic status that many entrepreneurs are conferred. For instance, stories of Richard Branson, Steve Jobs, Bill Gates, Elon Musk and others reinforce the idea that entrepreneurs are individuals carving out a new world on their own. More often entrepreneurs work in social networks to get their ventures up and running, to grow and to thrive. From theory perspective, entrepreneurship is viewed as embedded in networks of enduring social relations (Walker et al., 1997).

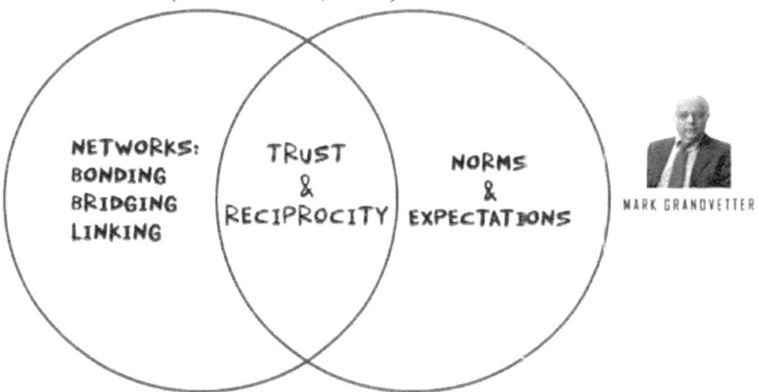

Research on entrepreneurship from a social network perspective has gained steam and evidence that networks are useful tools for gaining access to resources has emerged. Social capital is loosely defined as the value of venture founders' network resources! Networks may act as substitutes for investment capital. Private information flows over networks that can only be accessed through social interactions. An entrepreneur's ability to recognize opportunities is largely related their ability to access private information in social networks. One of the classic studies was conducted by Granovetter (1973) who concluded that weak ties are more important than strong ties for accessing opportunity-related information. Close ties usually contain high levels of redundant information, for instance, when a clique of friends or family members interact, they do so in relatively small numbers and tend to rehash many of the same experiences and information. By contrast, a single individual can establish weak ties with hundreds of individuals in disparate networks giving them access to information that would not ordinarily flow through their close ties. Social ties that bridge unconnected social networks are called bridging ties and these are particularly useful for sniffing out valuable information. Burt

(1992) noted that advantages come to those who bridge "structural holes", which are formed by a lack of social connections between large social networks. He emphasizes that it is not the number of such ties that matter, but how non-redundant they are. For instance, if an individual connects two social groups that are connected by no others, that will yield a better opportunity than if there exist others with the same connections. Moreover, if there are several links needed to connect two networks together, then being the sole direct link yields advantages. Empirical studies examine whether individuals with more structurally diverse networks are more likely to encounter opportunities that can be seized through new venture creation Greve and Salaff (2003). Entrepreneurs may also be better at accessing financial capital, tacit knowledge, and talented human resources if their networks are structurally diverse. Entrepreneurs with more structurally diverse networks may also have more influence than others. Social networks can signal legitimacy to stakeholders and investors.

Understanding the "Social Capital" theory:

Social capital refers to the network of relationships, trust, and shared values that exist between individuals and groups in a community. For example.

Networking: A business owner attends networking events and builds relationships with other professionals in their industry. Through these relationships, the business owner may gain access to new clients, suppliers, and business partners.

Employee engagement: A company creates a strong sense of community and shared purpose among its employees, fostering a culture of collaboration and teamwork. This can lead to increased productivity, innovation, and job satisfaction.

Reputation: A company has a positive reputation within its industry and community, based on its history of ethical behavior, high-quality products or services, and positive relationships with stakeholders. This reputation can attract new customers, investors, and talent to the company.

Social responsibility: A company engages in activities that benefit the broader community, such as donating to charity, volunteering, or supporting local initiatives. These activities can build goodwill and trust among stakeholders, enhancing the company's social capital.

By building and maintaining positive relationships with stakeholders and fostering a strong sense of community, businesses can gain access to new opportunities, attract top talent, and build a strong reputation in their industry and community.

Classroom Activity: Building Social Networks for Success

Objective: This activity aims to engage readers in understanding and analyzing the Theory of Social Capital in entrepreneurship. By exploring the importance of social networks and relationships, participants will gain insights into leveraging social capital to access resources, opportunities, and support for entrepreneurial success.

Duration: 60-90 mins.

Materials: Pen/pencil and paper for each participant, Whiteboard or flip chart (optional) & Relevant examples or case studies.

Instructions:

Activity	Instructions
Intro (10 mins)	Introduce the Theory & Explain that social capital refers to the value derived from social networks, relationships, and connections. Highlight the importance of social capital in accessing resources, opportunities, and support for entrepreneurs.
Real-world Examples (15 mins)	Provide participants with real-world examples or case studies that exemplify the theory. Ask participants to individually reflect on these examples and identify the social networks and relationships that played a crucial role in entrepreneurial success.
Group Discussion: Network Analysis (20 mins)	Divide participants into small groups and assign each group the task of conducting a network analysis. Each group should identify and analyze the key social networks and relationships that entrepreneurs need to cultivate for success. Ask groups to discuss the benefits and challenges associated with building and leveraging social capital. Encourage groups to share their findings with the whole group, fostering open dialogue and the exchange of perspectives.
Case Analysis: Social Capital in Action (20 mins)	Present participants with a case study that highlights an entrepreneurial endeavor where social capital played a significant role. In their groups, participants should analyze the case study and identify the specific ways in which social networks and relationships contributed to the entrepreneur's success. Ask groups to discuss the lessons learned from the case study and the strategies employed by the entrepreneur to build and leverage social capital. Each group should share their insights and findings with the whole group.

Reflection and Application (15 mins)	Conclude the activity by facilitating a reflection session. Ask participants to reflect on their own entrepreneurial experiences or aspirations. Encourage participants to consider their existing social networks and relationships and how they can be nurtured and expanded to enhance their social capital. Participants should reflect on the potential benefits of building social capital and identify strategies for cultivating valuable connections in their journey.
Wrap-up (5 mins)	Summarize the key insights and takeaways from the activity. Provide additional resources or references for participants who wish to further explore the Theory of Social Capital in entrepreneurship.

Conclusion: This activity empowers participants to reflect on their own networks and consider strategies for building and leveraging social capital in their entrepreneurial journeys. By recognizing the importance of cultivating meaningful connections, entrepreneurs can enhance their access to knowledge, support, and collaboration, ultimately increasing their chances of success. Embracing the power of social capital can foster a thriving entrepreneurial ecosystem, where networks become powerful assets for growth and innovation.

2.6 Population Ecology

Hannan and Freeman's (1977) population ecology Theory hangs on the assumption that environments can only handle a fixed number of organizations of each type. After a certain point is reached, there are diminishing returns to density that eventually balance out through the mortality of organizations. The Theory is about the tension between the need to be considered as legitimate in order to compete, but also the need to be competitive. As more organizations enter the market, they become increasingly legitimate, but this leads to greater competition making survival more challenging. Thus, the early market is dominated by the need for legitimacy, while the later market is dominated by competitive forces of selection. As environments change, often due to innovations introduced by organizations within them, mortality rates increase for organizations experiencing high levels of resistance to change. Inertial forces guarantee that most innovations will come from new entrants and not from incumbents resisting change. Organizational inertia is caused by a combination of internal (e.g., sunk costs, impaired managerial cognition, or organizational culture and history) and external restraints (e.g., government regulations, groupthink, or barriers to entry and exit).

Environmental niches are exploited by specialist organizations that risk adaptation to the requirements of a smaller number of customers. Generalist organizations span many niches, but they do so sub-optimally catering to a subset of customers in each niche in return for diversified risk. The Theory predicts mortality hazards based on the age of firms. New firms experience the liability of newness, where failure risks are high due to a lack of legitimacy. The liability of adolescence kicks in next, where firms gain stakeholder support to expand quickly, but they then reach resource constraints that raise their mortality risks. Finally, older firms face the liability of aging, where inertia kicks in making it difficult for firms to change in the face of environmental dynamism.

Understanding the "Population Ecology" theory:

Population ecology is a theoretical framework in organizational studies that examines how organizations adapt and survive in dynamic and competitive environments. Here are some examples of population ecology in a business setting:

Entry and exit of firms: In a competitive market, new firms may enter the market and existing firms may exit the market depending on factors such as demand, supply, and resource availability. This process is driven by competition & the need for firms to adapt to changing market conditions.

Resource dependence: Organizations rely on external resources such as capital, labor, and technology to operate. In a dynamic environment, firms must adapt to changes in the availability & cost of these resources, which bring changes in organizational structure, strategy, & behavior.

Selection and adaptation: In a competitive environment, firms that are best adapted to the prevailing market conditions are more likely to survive and thrive. This process of selection and adaptation is driven by the need to maximize efficiency and effectiveness in resource allocation.

Niche creation: In a crowded market, firms may differentiate themselves by creating a unique niche or market segment that is not being served by existing firms. This can involve developing new products or services, targeting new customer segments, or adopting new business models.

By understanding the factors that drive entry and exit of firms, resource dependence, selection and adaptation, and niche creation, businesses can develop strategies that allow them to thrive in a changing and uncertain world.

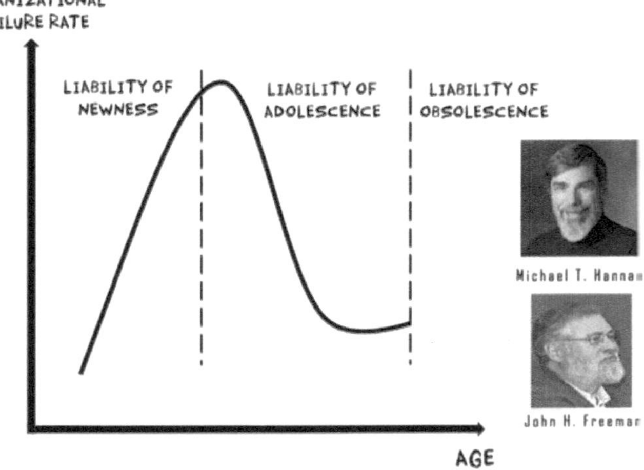

Classroom Activity: Survival of the Fittest - Population Ecology

Objective: To engage readers in understanding and analyzing the theory by exploring the dynamics of entrepreneurial ecosystems participants will gain insights into the factors influencing the survival growth, and competition among ventures.

Duration: 60-90 mins.

Materials: Pen/pencil and paper for each participant, Whiteboard or flip chart (optional) & Relevant examples or case studies.

Instructions:

Activity	Instructions
Introduction (10 mins)	Begin by introducing the Theory of Population Ecology in entrepreneurship. Explain that this theory examines the dynamics of entrepreneurial ecosystems, focusing on the interplay between startups, existing ventures, and the environment. Highlight the importance.
Real-world Examples (15 mins)	Provide participants with real-world examples or case studies that exemplify the Theory of Population Ecology in entrepreneurship. Ask participants to individually reflect on these examples and identify the factors influencing the survival and growth of ventures in competitive environments. Encourage participants to observes and to take notes

Group Discussion: Environmental Factors (20 mins)	Divide participants into small groups and assign each group the task of discussing the environmental factors influencing entrepreneurial ecosystems. Each group should identify and analyze factors such as market conditions, industry trends, technological advancements, and regulatory frameworks. Ask groups to discuss the impact of these factors on the entry, survival, and exit of ventures within the ecosystem. Encourage groups to share their findings with the whole group, fostering open dialogue and the exchange of perspectives.
Case Analysis: Competition and Adaptation (20 mins)	Present participants with a case study that highlights a competitive entrepreneurial ecosystem. In their groups, participants should analyze the case study and identify the strategies employed by ventures to compete, adapt, and differentiate themselves. Ask groups to discuss the challenges and opportunities presented by the ecosystem and the key factors contributing to the success or failure of ventures. Each group should share their insights and findings with the whole group, fostering discussion and debate.
Reflection and Application (15 mins)	Conclude the activity by facilitating a reflection session. Ask participants to reflect on their own entrepreneurial experiences or aspirations. Encourage participants to consider how they can apply the principles of Population Ecology theory to enhance their adaptability and navigate competitive environments. Participants should reflect on the importance of monitoring environmental factors, identifying opportunities, and developing strategies for survival and growth.
Wrap-up (5 mins)	Summarize the key insights and takeaways from the activity. Provide additional resources or references for participants who wish to further explore the Theory of Population Ecology in entrepreneurship.

Conclusion: By recognizing the importance of monitoring and responding to environmental changes, entrepreneurs can position themselves for success and navigate the complexities of their entrepreneurial ecosystems with resilience and agility. Embracing the principles of Population Ecology theory can guide entrepreneurs in making informed decisions, seizing opportunities, and achieving sustainable growth in their ventures.

2.7 Weak ties

The weak ties Theory was put forth by Mark Granovetter in 1969 as a Theory that explains why some people seem to access to more and better opportunities than others. He conducted a study of around 200 people who had just gotten new jobs and asked them how they got their jobs and most of them, around 75% had got them from acquaintances. The rate was even higher for the higher income earners in his sample. The core idea is that weak ties are more important than strong ties in terms of providing you with novel and actionable information. Close ties refer to individuals that we interact with on a nearly constant basis, such as roommates, nuclear family members and a few good friends. Close ties provide very little new information because most of the individuals within the clique of a close tie network share many of the same relations. Weak ties refer to social connections to individuals who are not closely related. Rather, weak ties may be part of disparate networks. These weak ties form bridges of information between networks that might otherwise never interact directly. Individuals that have many weak ties to disparate networks will encounter a greater variety of information and gain greater insights about the needs and capabilities of various networks they are connected to. This placement in the middle creates an opportunity for the entrepreneur to act to match those with needs to those with solutions and to potentially take a cut for facilitating the transaction. For instance, if I tell you about a great job opportunity that I found out about because of my network, then you might buy me lunch to thank me. Similarly, if I can connect a supplier with a client, I might ask for a finder's fee or commission. Many organizations actively manage networks to control the flow of information within them. Some regard the weak ties Theory as potentially leading to unethical practice recommendations because it seems to advocate for the active creation of weak ties at the expense of strong ties. There are also some implications about how a good set of weak ties are obtained that may have some "divide and conquer" or Machiavellian characteristics.

Understanding the "Weak ties" theory:

Weak ties refer to casual and infrequent connections between individuals, as opposed to strong ties, which are more close and frequent connections. Here is a business example of weak ties:

A salesperson attends a networking event and meets several new people. Among these people are several acquaintances, who are weak-ties. While the salesperson may not have a close relationship with these acquaintances, they still provide valuable connections and resources.

For example, one of the acquaintances might work in a complementary industry and be able to refer potential clients to the salesperson. Another acquaintance might have valuable industry insights or knowledge that can help the salesperson improve their sales pitch.
In this example, the weak ties provide access to new resources and opportunities that the salesperson might not have otherwise had. By maintaining these casual connections, the salesperson can expand their network and increase their chances of success in the industry. This illustrates the importance of weak ties in business, and the value of maintaining a diverse and extensive network of contacts.

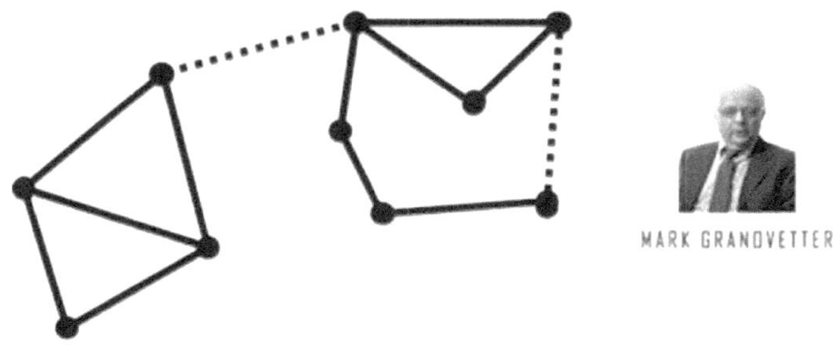

Classroom Activity: Expanding Horizons

Objective: This activity aims to engage readers in understanding and analyzing the Theory of Weak Ties in entrepreneurship. By exploring the power of weak ties in expanding networks and accessing diverse resources, participants will gain insights into leveraging weak ties for success.

Duration: 60-90 mins.

Materials: Pen/pencil and paper for each participant, Whiteboard or flip chart (optional) & Relevant examples or case studies illustrating the Theory of Weak Ties.

Instructions:

Activity	Instructions
Intro (10 mins)	Begin by introducing the Theory of Weak Ties in entrepreneurship. Explain that weak ties refer to connections with individuals outside of one's close network, such as acquaintances, colleagues, or casual contacts. Highlight the importance of weak ties in accessing diverse resources, information, & opportunities.

Real-world Examples (15 mins)	Provide participants with real-world examples or case studies that exemplify the Theory of Weak Ties in entrepreneurship. Ask participants to individually reflect on these examples and identify instances where weak ties played a crucial role in entrepreneurial success. Encourage participants to notes their observations.
Group Discussion: Leveraging Weak Ties	Divide participants into small groups and assign each group the task of discussing the ways in which weak ties can be leveraged in entrepreneurship. Each group should identify and analyze strategies for expanding weak ties, maintaining relationships, and leveraging them for accessing diverse resources and opportunities. Ask groups to discuss & share perspectives about benefits and challenges associated with building and utilizing weak ties.
Case Analysis: Weak Ties (20 mins)	Present participants with a case study that highlights an entrepreneurial endeavor where weak ties played a significant role. In their groups, participants should analyze the case study and identify specific instances where weak ties contributed to the entrepreneur's success. Ask groups to discuss the strategies employed by the entrepreneur to develop & leverage weak ties. Each group should share their insights and findings.
Reflection and Application (15 mins)	Conclude the activity by facilitating a reflection session. Ask participants to reflect on their own entrepreneurial experiences or aspirations. Encourage participants to consider their existing networks and identify opportunities to expand their weak ties. Participants should reflect on the potential benefits of cultivating & leveraging weak ties & brainstorm strategies for building connections with individuals outside their immediate network.
Wrap-up (5 mins)	Summarize the key insights and takeaways from the activity. Provide additional resources or references for participants who wish to further explore the Theory of Weak Ties in entrepreneurship.

Conclusion: This activity helps to explore strategies for expanding and leveraging weak ties, recognizing the benefits and challenges associated with building such connections. Through this activity, participants are now equipped with a deeper understanding of how to harness the power of weak ties to enhance their entrepreneurial endeavors and have been encouraged to continue expanding their networks beyond their close circles.

2.8 Social Identity

This Theory came out of Henry Tajfel and John Turner (1979) experiments showing that the slightest priming of group membership creates prejudice. "Blue eyes, a preference for the paintings of Wasily Kandinsky over those of Paul Klee and calling some people over-estimators and other under-estimators were sufficient to produce a preference for fellow group members and to elicit discrimination against outsiders" (Huddy, 2001:132). Social identity Theory has been used to explain why human personalities and behaviors seem to be context specific. A given individual may act differently depending on which groups they perceive themselves to belong. The Theory suggests that personal identity plus environmental conditions shape social identity, which in turn leads to categorization of others into in-groups and out-groups. Obschonka et al. (2012) argue that individual beliefs and attitudes are unlikely to be the main drivers of entrepreneurship. Rather, they use social identity Theory to suggest that individuals take on the norms of the groups they join. Thus, for example, if a scientist joins an entrepreneurial faculty, they are more likely to consider entrepreneurship as a career route. This is in sharp contrast to many of the psychological theories of entrepreneurship that look to individual attitudes and beliefs to predict entrepreneurial intentions. Obschonka et al. (2012) studied hundreds of German scientists & found that those that strongly identified with their peer groups were more likely to have entrepreneurial intentions if their peer group had entrepreneurial norms. In contrast, individuals that did not identify with their peers were more likely to engage in entrepreneurship if they had a high level of internal locus of control.

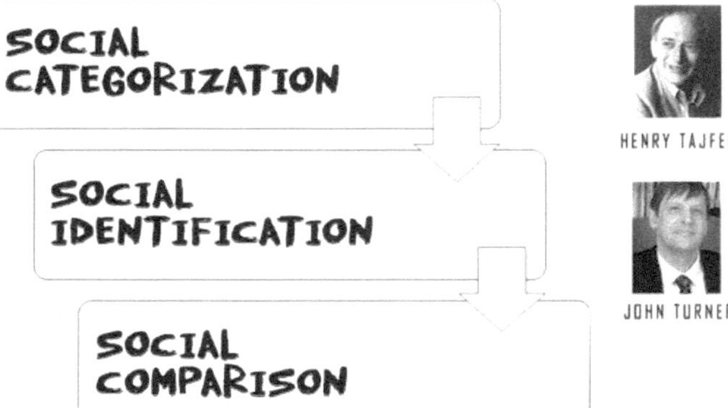

They explain that a higher level of social identification appears to be associated with lower internal locus of control, causing individuals to rely on group norms as a substitute. The Theory has interesting implications relating to entrepreneurial cultural norms in organizations such as universities, corporations, and incubators. It suggests that individuals with a weak internal locus (strong external locus) of control may become more entrepreneurial if they join a group with entrepreneurial norms. It also seems to imply that individuals with already strong internal locus of control may not experience changes in their entrepreneurial intentions as a result of joining entrepreneurial groups. Clearly, more research, in more diverse contexts is needed to draw strong conclusions.

Understanding the "Social Identity" theory:

Social identity refers to the aspects of an individual's self-concept that are based on their membership in a particular social group. For example.

Company culture: A company's culture can create a strong sense of social identity among employees, based on shared values, norms, and behaviors. For example, a company that values teamwork and collaboration might foster a strong sense of social identity among employees who see themselves as part of a high-performing team.

Brand identity: A company's brand identity can also create a sense of social identity among customers and stakeholders. For example, a luxury fashion brand might create a sense of social identity among customers who see themselves as part of a high-end, exclusive community of fashion connoisseurs.

Professional identity: An individual's professional identity can also be influenced by their membership in a particular industry or professional community. For example, a lawyer might see themselves as part of a community of legal professionals who share a commitment to upholding the law and serving their clients.

Diversity and inclusion: A company that values diversity and inclusion can create a sense of social identity among employees who feel a sense of belonging and inclusion based on their unique backgrounds and experiences.

By creating a strong sense of social identity among employees, customers, and stakeholders, businesses can foster a sense of community and shared purpose that can drive innovation, collaboration, and success.

Classroom Activity: Exploring the Theory of Social Identity

Objective: To introduce participants to the Theory of Social Identity in entrepreneurship, foster reflection on personal social identities, encourage group discussions on the influence of social identity on entrepreneurial success, analyze case studies showcasing social identity in action, and facilitate reflection on leveraging social identities for entrepreneurial endeavors.

Duration: 65 - 70 mins

Materials: Presentation or whiteboard, Case studies, Sticky notes, Markers & Handouts.

Instructions:

Activity	Instructions
Introduction (10 mins)	Begin by introducing the concept of the Theory of Social Identity in entrepreneurship. Explain that social identity refers to the part of an individual's self-concept that derives from their membership in various social groups. Highlight the relevance of social identity in shaping entrepreneurial behavior, decision-making, and outcomes. Emphasize the impact of group membership on an entrepreneur's motivation, values, goals, and network formation.
Personal Reflection (15 mins)	Encourage participants to consider their own social identities and how these identities might influence their entrepreneurial endeavors. Prompt them to reflect on questions such as: How does your social identity shape your entrepreneurial aspirations? In what ways do your group memberships impact your entrepreneurial behavior and decision-making?
Group Discussion: Entrepreneurial Success (20 mins)	Divide participants into small groups and assign each group a specific aspect of social identity to discuss, such as gender, ethnicity, nationality, or professional affiliations. Ask each group to explore how this particular social identity can influence entrepreneurial success. Encourage participants to share personal experiences, insights, and examples related to the given aspect of social identity. Facilitate a group discussion to exchange perspectives and learn from each other's unique insights.

Case Studies: Social Identity in Action (20 mins)	Present participants with case studies that highlight entrepreneurial ventures influenced by social identity. These case studies should showcase entrepreneurs who have leveraged their social identities to create successful businesses. In their groups, participants should analyze the case studies and identify specific instances where social identity played a significant role. Ask each group to discuss the strategies employed by these entrepreneurs to leverage their social identities for success. Each group should share their insights and findings with the whole group, fostering discussion and debate.
Reflection and Application (15 mins)	Conclude the activity by facilitating a reflection session. Ask participants to reflect on the insights gained from the personal reflection, group discussions, and case studies. Encourage them to consider how they can leverage their own social identities to enhance their entrepreneurial journeys. Participants should brainstorm strategies for leveraging their social identities positively and identify potential challenges or biases they may encounter. Encourage participants to share their reflections and insights with the whole group.
Wrap-up (5 mins)	Summarize the key insights and takeaways from the activity, emphasizing the significance of social identity in entrepreneurship. Provide additional resources or references for participants who wish to further explore the Theory of Social Identity in entrepreneurship. Encourage participants to continue reflecting on their social identities and actively seek ways to leverage them for entrepreneurial success while promoting inclusivity and diversity in their ventures.

Conclusion: By embracing and harnessing the power of social identity, participants are better equipped to navigate the entrepreneurial landscape and create ventures that reflect their unique perspectives while fostering an inclusive and supportive environment.

2.9 Information Processing

The Theory is explained by Allen Newell and Herbert A. Simon (1972) in their book entitled Human Problem Solving. The book focuses on how humans think and process information. They view the human system as including the sensual, memory and arousal subsystems. Hansen and Allen (1992) borrow the Theory of information processing to explain and predict the creation of new ventures. They start with the assumption that business environments produce information in varying quantities and varieties. For instance, a very simple environment might produce a small amount of very similar information, whereas a complex environment produces a large quantity of heterogeneous information. A complex environment might match a fast-paced, ever-changing high-tech industry, whereas a simple environment might match a slow-moving traditional industry such as the restaurant industry. A single individual may find it difficult or impossible to cope with the information load that a complex environment creates. Everyone can do the job of absorbing and filtering some portion of the information that complex environments produce. Then, through communication, the individuals can share the information and the network can together make sense of it. The frequency of communication between the individuals also matters, such that frequent communication between a larger number of individuals is expected to lead to the creation of an organization to take advantage of opportunities in an environment. Inter-connectivity (similar to network density) also matters, where individuals communicate with a greater share of the network rather than with just a small part of it. A key implication of the Theory is that prospective entrepreneurs seeking to start ventures in complex environments should team up with others to share the information processing load. Doing so involves creating networks that process information effectively enough to spur organization development. In support of the Theory, there is some evidence that solo entrepreneurs are less likely to survive and more likely to persist as low or no-growth ventures (Hansen, 1991). Similarly, lone inventors are more likely to invent less innovative technologies and products and do so at a slower rate than organizations.

Understanding the "Information Processing" theory:

Information processing refers to the collection, organization, and analysis of data and information to support business decision-making. For example.

Sales data analysis: A business might collect sales data from its point-of-sale systems, website analytics, and customer relationship management software. This data can be processed and analyzed to identify trends and patterns, such as which products are selling well, and which customers are most profitable.

Financial reporting: A business must process financial data in order to produce accurate financial statements and reports. This data includes information on revenue, expenses, assets, and liabilities.

Inventory management: A business might use inventory management software to track inventory levels, monitor sales trends, and forecast future demand. This data can be used to optimize inventory levels and prevent stockouts.
Human resources management: A business might use human resources information systems to collect and process data on employee performance, compensation, and benefits. This data can be used to make informed decisions about promotions, raises, and other HR-related issues.
Social media monitoring: A business might use social media monitoring tools to track mentions of its brand on social media platforms. This data can be used to identify customer feedback, sentiment, and emerging trends.
By collecting and analyzing data in a systematic way, businesses can make more informed decisions and gain a competitive edge.

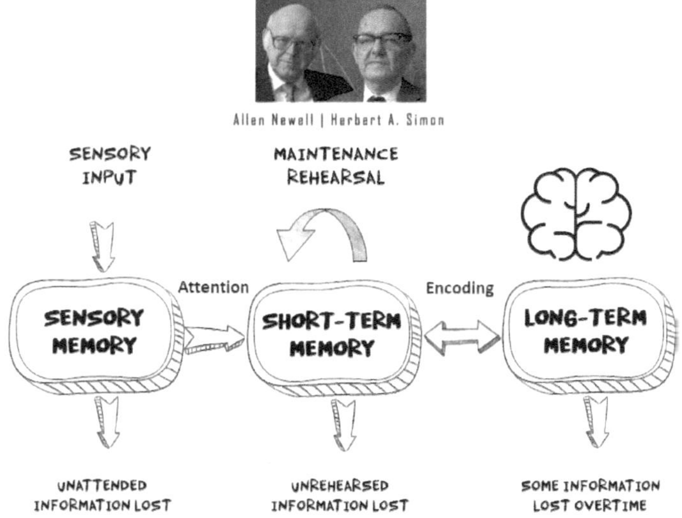

Classroom Activity: Exploring Information Processing

Objective: To familiarize participants with the Theory of Information Processing in entrepreneurship, develop their skills in acquiring, evaluating, and utilizing information for entrepreneurial decision-making, and encourage reflection on personal information processing strategies to drive entrepreneurial success.

Duration: 70 – 80 mins

Materials: Presentation or whiteboard, Case studies, Sticky notes, Markers & Handouts.

Instructions:

Activity	Instructions
Intro (10 mins)	Introduce the theory, explain that information processing refers to how entrepreneurs acquire, interpret, and utilize information to make decisions and solve problems. Highlight the importance of effective information processing in entrepreneurial success, including identifying opportunities, assessing risks, & developing innovative solutions.
Information Scavenger Hunt (20 mins)	Divide participants into small groups and provide them with a list of specific information-related tasks or questions related to entrepreneurship. Each group should work together to search for and collect relevant information from various sources, such as online databases, industry reports, or interviews. Encourage participants to utilize critical thinking skills and analyze the information they find.
Processing Information (20 mins)	Bring the groups together and facilitate a discussion on how entrepreneurs process information. Prompt each group to share their findings from the scavenger hunt and discuss the methods they used to process and evaluate the information they collected. Encourage participants to explore different techniques and approaches, such as filtering information, assessing credibility, & leveraging technology tools for information management.
Case Study Analysis (15 mins)	Present participants with a case study that showcases an entrepreneurial scenario where effective information processing played a crucial role in decision-making and success. In their groups, participants should analyze the case study and identify specific instances where information processing strategies were utilized. Ask each group to discuss the impact of these strategies on the entrepreneur's outcomes and discuss alternative approaches or improvements that could have been made.

Reflection and Application (15 mins)	Ask participants to reflect on their own experiences with information processing in entrepreneurship. Encourage them to consider how they currently acquire, analyze, and utilize information in their entrepreneurial ventures. Participants should reflect on the strengths and weaknesses of their information processing strategies and brainstorm ways to improve their effectiveness. Encourage participants to share their reflections & insights with other groups.
Wrap-up (5 mins)	Summarize the key insights and takeaways & Encourage participants to apply the knowledge gained from the activity to their entrepreneurial endeavors, focusing on enhancing their information processing skills to make informed decisions and drive success.

Conclusion: Through practical exercises and discussions, participants develop effective information processing strategies and gain insights into their own strengths and areas for improvement. By honing their information processing skills, participants are better equipped to make informed decisions, identify opportunities, and drive entrepreneurial success in today's dynamic and information-rich business landscape.

2.10 Hoselitz Theory

Burt F. Hoselitz was a professor of economics at the University of Chicago. Hoselitz argues that entrepreneurship tends to come from socially marginalized groups in a given society. This is very similar to the withdrawal of status respect Theory and the misfit Theory of entrepreneurship, which both deal with marginalized populations Hoselitz (1963) assumes that entrepreneurship can only come out of a developed cultural base. His Theory is that marginalized populations must be considered culturally developed to be considered eligible for entrepreneurship. He refers to entrepreneurship by marginalized groups as "pariah entrepreneurship". Hoselitz claimed that his Theory helps to explain to the highly entrepreneurial behaviors of Greeks and Jewish people in medieval Europe, Lebanese in West Africa, Chinese in Southeast Asia, and Indians in East Africa. The concept of cultural development is ambiguous and potentially problematic for Hoselitz Theory. The level of development of a culture may not be objectively ascertained. However, the spirit of the argument is that the culture must be perceived to be developed from the subjective perspective of the dominant groups in a society.

Hoselitz uses the term "marginal men" to mean those individuals who are both from (1) a marginalized population and (2) a developed home culture. These marginal men have a strong desire to adjust their situation by engaging in entrepreneurial behaviors. Marginalization has a way of redirecting an individual's learned culture to new ends. The Theory implies that some marginal populations are not legitimate enough to be eligible to be entrepreneurs from the perspective of the dominant population groups. One might criticize the Theory by pointing out that cultures can change and adapt in fits and spurts so that static expectations become less useful than dynamic interpretations of culture. In other words, theories like these may inadvertently contribute to stereotyping by generating self-confirming biases. It is at the very least, a controversial Theory. Perhaps a looser, but more inclusive version of the Theory is that entrepreneurs that migrate may look to aspects of their home cultures that seems in some way more effective or more efficient than the ways of the host culture(s). This avoids the problem of labeling whole cultures as more or less developed and puts the attention on the relevant routines. Routines that have evolved over many generations are likely to be better in some way on some dimensions that may not be fully appreciated by the mainstream host culture. Routines that developed under conditions of scarcity may also have efficiency advantages.

Understanding the Hoselitz theory:

A business that operates in a foreign market must consider the cultural context in which it operates to be successful. For example, a fast-food chain that expands into a new country must consider the local culture and customs when designing its menu and marketing campaigns. The company might need to modify its menu to include local flavors and ingredients and adjust its advertising to appeal to local tastes and preferences. By understanding the cultural context in which they operate, businesses can better meet the needs and preferences of local consumers and build strong relationships with local communities. This can lead to increased sales and profits, as well as enhanced brand reputation and customer loyalty.

Classroom Activity: Unleashing Entrepreneurial Spirit

Objective: Familiarize readers with the theory of Hoselitz, participants will gain a deeper understanding of the theory's core concepts and their implications for entrepreneurial endeavors.

Duration: 90 – 100 mins

Material: Pen/pencil and paper for each participant, Whiteboard.

Instructions:

Activity	Instructions
Intro (25 mins)	Provide an overview & explain how the theory explores the relationship between economic development, social change, and entrepreneurial activities. Share relevant excerpts or articles on the theory.
Reflection (45 mins)	Pose reflection questions to encourage critical thinking. • How does economic development influence entrepreneurship, & vice versa? Discuss specific mechanisms & feedback loops. • Can you identify any real-world examples that align with the theory? How do they demonstrate the theory's key principles? Analyze their impact on economic growth and societal transformation. • What are the factors that contribute to a favorable environment for entrepreneurship based on theory? Consider the role of institutions, culture, & market conditions. • How can entrepreneurs effectively adapt their strategies in response to social and economic changes, as suggested by the theory?

Discussion (25 mins)	Divide participants into small groups and allocate approximately 25 mins for each reflection question. Facilitate group discussions and encourage participants to explore different perspectives. Allow each group to present a summary of their discussions and key insights.
Application (15 mins)	Engage participants in a brainstorming session applying the theory of Hoselitz to real-world entrepreneurial scenarios. Provide case studies or entrepreneurial challenges for participants to consider. Encourage creative thinking, problem-solving, and discussion of strategies.
Wrap-up (5 mins)	Summarize the key takeaways from the theory of Hoselitz and its relevance to entrepreneurship. Encourage participants to explore further resources and continue their learning journey in the field of entrepreneurship.
Extension (Varies)	If time permits, invite guest speakers with practical entrepreneurship experience to share insights on the theory of Hoselitz. Allocate a suitable duration for the guest speaker session based on their availability & the overall session timeline.

Conclusion: By understanding the theory of Hoselitz, participants recognize the influence of factors such as culture, institutions, and market conditions on entrepreneurial opportunities. Adapting strategies in response to social and economic changes is essential for entrepreneurial success. This activity has encouraged critical thinking, reflection, and practical application of the theory, emphasizing the importance of understanding the interplay between economic development, social change, and entrepreneurship for fostering sustainable growth and making a positive impact on society.

2.11 Diffusion of Innovations

The diffusion of innovations has been studied by many scholars over the ages, but notably from 1970 onward by American sociologist Everett Rogers. Dr. Rogers was interested in trying to get farmers to adopt innovations that could better their lives and make their businesses more productive. He pondered the forces that leads some to adopt and others to abstain. Modeling adoption curves: He suggests that different types of adopters: innovators, early adoptions, early majority, late majority, and laggards have different adoption criteria.

For instance, a strategy that may attract early adopters may not attract the early majority because they want different things. The size distributions of the different types of adopters (i.e., number of members of a particular adopter category), grow and then shrink giving rise to an inverted u-shaped curve, giving rise to the famous s-curve of total adoption. Rogers noted that it is not always the best technologies that get adopted, it is often the most convenient. The learning curve involved with a product is often a much higher cost to the user than the maker anticipates. The core assumption of the Theory is that innovations do not automatically spread to large segments of a population. Instead, there are many different types of impediments to the diffusion of innovations. The diffusion of innovations is a stochastic process involving random probabilities, but it also can be influenced by strategies that change the odds. In order to cause an innovation to diffuse, an entrepreneur needs to help the innovation to surmount most of these barriers to diffusion (e.g, sunk costs, switching costs, learning costs, and material costs of buying new technologies). Other uses of the diffusion of innovations Theory include Ramani et al. (2012) who suggest that sanitation entrepreneurs use a market making strategy of education, innovation, and sanitation together to ensure the continued use of their products. They fill a void in the market for knowledge about sanitation and its technologies and maintenance. Perhaps another way to influence the diffusion of innovations is to try to regulate it with formal institutions. Mintrom (1997) suggests that policy entrepreneurs actively try to influence government to favor the adoption of their technologies. Perhaps they are key in the diffusion of innovations because of their ability to bypass the market to forces of adoption, forcing adoption and throwing the innovation into an artificial, but not necessarily unsustainable diffusion trajectory. Moore and McKenna (1999) clarified the implications of the diffusion curve for entrepreneurs. They are summarized by the idea of "crossing the chasm". Chasm refers to the space between early adopters and the early majority on Roger's chart. These two groups of adopters are different and buy based on different metrics. Moore notes that most entrepreneurs are not able to make the leap from the early adopters to the early majority. He argues that to cross the chasm, an entrepreneur must select one viable niche to cater to, thus putting all their 'eggs in one basket'. Crossing the chasm requires that the entrepreneur introduce what Moore calls the "whole product", which is 100% catered to the target customer segment.

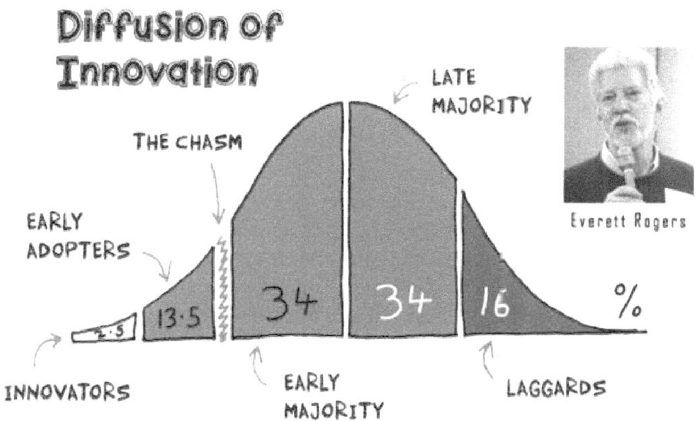

Understanding the "Diffusion of Innovations" theory:

Diffusion of innovation refers to the process by which a new product or idea is adopted and spreads throughout a population. Here is a possible business example of diffusion of innovation:

A technology company develops a new mobile payment system that allows users to pay for goods and services using their smartphones. At first, only a small group of tech-savvy consumers adopts the new payment system. However, as more people become aware of its convenience and security features, adoption begins to spread. The company invests in marketing and education campaigns to speed up the diffusion process, and partners with retailers to promote the system in-store. Over time, the mobile payment system becomes widely adopted, and eventually replaces traditional payment methods in many contexts. By understanding the factors that influence the adoption process - such as consumer awareness, ease of use, and compatibility with existing systems - businesses can develop strategies to accelerate the spread of their innovation. This can help them gain market share, increase revenue, and stay ahead of competitors.

Classroom Activity: Exploring Diffusion of Innovation

Objective: To engage readers in a hands-on exploration of the theory & helping them understand its principles and apply them to real-world entrepreneurial scenarios.

Duration: 85 – 100 mins

Materials: Flipchart or whiteboard, Markers, Sticky notes, Printed handouts or access to digital documents, Case studies & Projector or screen.

Instructions:

Activity	Instructions
Introduction (10 mins)	Introduce the concept of Diffusion of Innovation, explaining its relevance in understanding how ideas, products, or technologies spread. Provide an overview of key elements, including adopter categories and factors influencing diffusion (e.g., relative advantage, complexity). Ask participants to share their experiences.
Group Discussion (15 mins)	Divide participants into small groups to foster interaction and diverse perspectives. Provide discussion questions to stimulate critical thinking and exploration of diffusion processes across industries and innovation types. Instruct groups to discuss and develop their answers or examples based on their collective insights and experiences. Examples of questions: • Can you think of an example of a recent innovation that has diffused rapidly? What factors contributed to its rapid adoption? • How might the diffusion of an innovation differ in various industries (e.g., healthcare, technology, fashion)? • What are some challenges entrepreneurs might face in diffusing their innovations to the market?
Case Study (20 mins)	Distribute a case study illustrating the diffusion of an innovation, either real-world or fictional, to analyze and extract key insights. Participants read the case study individually or in groups, identifying adopter categories and factors influencing the diffusion process. Ask participants to share their findings and insights with others.
Interactive Exercise (30 mins)	Form pairs or small groups to facilitate brainstorming and collaborative problem-solving. Assign a scenario or product idea and challenge participants to apply the diffusion theory to develop effective strategies for diffusion. Instruct participants to consider adopter categories, influencing factors, and innovative approaches to overcome diffusion barriers. After the exercise, each pair/group presents their strategies, fostering discussion and exploration of different perspectives and insights.

Reflection (10 mins)	Facilitate a reflection session to allow participants to share their key takeaways and insights from the activity. Summarize the main concepts covered, emphasizing their relevance to entrepreneurship and innovation processes. Provide recommended readings or online articles, for participants interested in further exploring the topic. Invite speakers to share their stories.

Conclusion: The activity provides valuable insights into how new ideas, products, or technologies spread through a population over time. Understanding the different adopter categories and factors influencing the diffusion process can greatly benefit entrepreneurs in effectively bringing their innovations to the market. By considering these principles, entrepreneurs can navigate the challenges and optimize the adoption of their innovations, leading to successful diffusion and widespread impact.

Psychological & Trait Theories

3.1 Ambiguity Resistance

Ambiguity resistance theory can be followed back to Polish clinician Else Frenkel-Brunswik, whose work in 1949 zeroed in on dictatorship and ethnocentrism in kids. Vague data is all over and it can prompt the end that there is no chance to get out, no real way to comprehend, or no suitable approach. The dynamic interaction can become deadened by equivocalness that forestalls indisputable remedies. When there exist undeniable degrees of vulnerability about a specific innovative endeavor, those people that show more significant levels of resistance of Ambiguity, are bound to succeed. The capacity to endure clashing data and manage missing data has the effect. The more questionable a specific business opportunity, the more significant it is that people are fit for enduring the requests of clashing data and obscure data. We may expect those endeavors of conventional business types, like cafés, might get more reliable data, while those in new enterprises, for example, innovation organizations would have more equivocal market data. At the point when businesspeople authorize procedures to make new organizations, they normally do as such without knowing the likelihood they will succeed. They are not facing challenge; they are bearing vulnerability.

Understanding the "Ambiguity Resistance" theory:
Ambiguity tolerance refers to an individual's ability to cope with and tolerate ambiguity or uncertainty. Here is a possible business example: A startup company is founded by a group of entrepreneurs who are comfortable with ambiguity and uncertainty. They recognize that building a successful business requires taking risks, making quick decisions, and adapting to changing market conditions. They embrace

uncertainty as an opportunity for innovation and growth and are not afraid to pivot their strategy if things don't go according to plan. As the company grows, the founders hire employees who share their tolerance for ambiguity. They encourage a culture of experimentation and creativity, where employees are empowered to take risks and learn from failure. They prioritize agile decision-making, and value the ability to act quickly and decisively in the face of uncertainty. By embracing uncertainty and taking calculated risks, businesses can seize opportunities for growth and innovation, & stay ahead of competitors.

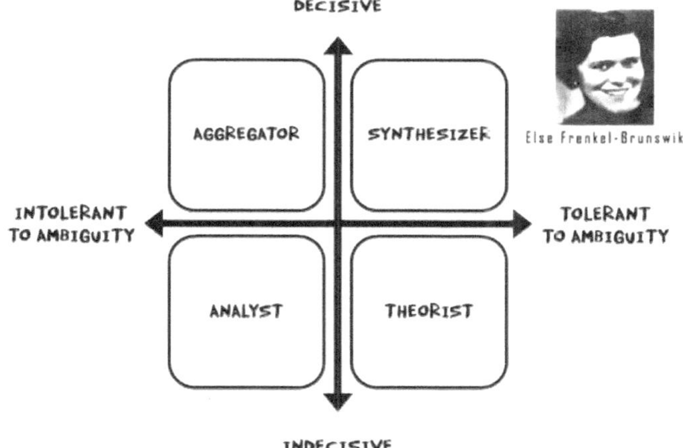

Classroom Activity: Embracing Ambiguity

Objective: To engage readers in a thought-provoking exploration of the theory of Ambiguity Resistance, helping them understand its significance in entrepreneurship and develop strategies to navigate ambiguity effectively.

Materials: Flipchart or whiteboard, Markers, Sticky notes, Printed handouts or access to digital documents, Case studies or examples.

Instructions:

Activity	Instructions
Introduction (10 mins)	Introduce the concept & provide an overview of key elements, including types of ambiguity (epistemic and ontological) and factors influencing resistance. Encourage participants to reflect on their own experiences with ambiguity & share challenges & strategies employed.

Group Discussion (15 mins)	Divide participants into small groups to foster interactive discussions and diverse perspectives on ambiguity resistance. Provide discussion questions to stimulate critical thinking and exploration of responses to ambiguity in entrepreneurial contexts. Instruct groups to discuss & develop their answers, examples, & strategies based on their collective insights & experiences.
Case Study (20 mins)	Distribute case studies or real-world examples illustrating situations involving ambiguity in entrepreneurship. Participants read the case study individually or in groups, identifying the types of ambiguity and analyzing responses to ambiguity. Encourage participants to share their findings, insights, and lessons learned from the case study to promote collective learning.
Interactive Exercise (30 mins)	Form pairs or small groups to facilitate brainstorming and collaborative problem-solving in ambiguous entrepreneurial scenarios. Assign a scenario or entrepreneurial challenge involving ambiguity and uncertainty, challenging participants to develop strategies. Instruct participants to consider the factors discussed in Ambiguity Resistance theory and innovative approaches to navigate ambiguity. After the exercise, each pair/group presents their strategies, fostering discussion and exploration of perspectives.
Reflection and Conclusion (10 mins)	Facilitate a reflection session to allow participants to share their key takeaways and insights from the activity. Summarize the main concepts covered, emphasizing the importance of embracing ambiguity in entrepreneurship and decision-making. Provide additional resources, such as recommended readings or online articles, for participants interested in further exploration. Invite guest speakers experienced in managing ambiguity in entrepreneurship to share real-world insights and experiences allowing participants to learn from them.

Conclusion: Participants have a valuable opportunity to explore ambiguity in entrepreneurship. Through discussions, case study analysis, and interactive exercises, they gained insights into navigating ambiguity effectively, fostering innovation, and making informed decisions in uncertain environments. Participants developed practical strategies and a deeper understanding of ambiguity tolerance, adaptive cognitive styles, and fostering organizational cultures that encourage exploration. Equipped with valuable knowledge and resources, they can prepare to embrace ambiguity as an integral part of the entrepreneurial journey and thrive in dynamic business landscapes.

3.2 Disagreeableness

Gladwell (2013) introduces disagreeableness as a key attribute of entrepreneurs. Not needing the social approval of peers, is explained as a psychological capability of successful entrepreneurs. It is a capability because most people might be influenced by critical feedback. If a friend or family member says, "that is a bad idea" and you stop...then you are agreeable, not disagreeable. He gives many examples, like IKEA pioneers in outsourcing production to Soviet periphery states during the Cold War, which was seen as a bad idea by many. In each case, the entrepreneurs are not afraid of being criticized (e.g., even for crossing into Eastern Europe). Disapproval should not stop an entrepreneur or keep them from trying again and again. The disagreeable entrepreneur shrugs off failure and critique and moves on. Interestingly, Gladwell uses an interpretation of the David and Goliath story that has David being the disagreeable innovator, refusing to fight with traditional weapons, and using artillery to kill the giant. The Disagreeableness Theory adds to the growing list of personality trait theories. Others include locus of control, need for achievement, impulsiveness, and self-efficacy. Gladwell says that a sense of urgency is needed to be an entrepreneur as well as a belief that the world is volatile (can and will change). These two dimensions are likely to overlap with impulsiveness and self-efficacy, respectively. This magazine article contains a video of Gladwell discussing the Theory. This one provides a transcript of his speech.

Understanding the "Disagreeableness" theory:
Disagreeableness is a personality trait characterized by a tendency to be argumentative, critical, and confrontational. While this trait may seem negative, it can be useful in certain business contexts. For example, A marketing executive is known for her disagreeable personality. She is highly critical of her team's work and is not afraid to speak her mind when she disagrees with their ideas. While this can be uncomfortable for her colleagues, it also leads to better outcomes. The executive's criticism pushes her team to improve their work and think more critically about their ideas. She is not afraid to challenge conventional wisdom and is willing to take risks to pursue new marketing strategies. As a result of her disagreeable personality, the marketing executive can drive innovation and push her team to achieve better results. Her critical thinking and willingness to challenge the status quo can help the company stay ahead of competitors and adapt

to changing market conditions. However, it is important for her to balance her disagreeable tendencies with empathy and emotional intelligence, to build strong relationss with her team & stakeholders.

Classroom Activity: Embracing Disagreeableness

Objective: To engage readers in an interactive exploration of the theory of Disagreeableness in entrepreneurship, helping them understand its significance and develop strategies to leverage disagreeableness effectively.

Duration: 85 – 100 mins

Materials: Flipchart or whiteboard, Markers, Sticky notes, Printed handouts or access to digital documents, Case studies or examples (optional) & Projector or screen (optional)

Instructions:

Activity	Instructions
Intro (10 mins)	Introduce the theory & explain its significance. Provide an overview of key elements of the theory & encourage participants to reflect & share their experiences
Case Study Analysis (20 mins)	Optional: Provide case studies or real-world examples, analyze the impact of disagreeableness in entrepreneurial contexts. Reflect on the influence of disagreeableness on decision-making, leadership, & challenging status quo.
Interactive Exercise (30 mins)	Form pairs or small groups, assign scenarios or entrepreneurial challenges, brainstorm strategies leveraging disagreeableness. Consider risks, benefits, & relationship management, present strategies, and facilitate a discussion.

Group Discussion (15 mins)	Divide participants into small groups, provide discussion questions, and instruct groups to share insights and discuss. For examples. • Can you think of a successful entrepreneur known for their disagreeableness? How did their disagreeableness contribute to their success? • What are the potential advantages and disadvantages of being disagreeable in entrepreneurial contexts? • How can entrepreneurs effectively balance disagreeableness with building strong relationships and collaborations? Explore successful entrepreneurs known for their disagreeableness, discuss advantages, disadvantages, & strategies.
Reflection (10 mins)	Facilitate a reflection session, summarize key concepts, discuss effective communication and self-awareness. Emphasize the importance of balancing disagreeableness and collaborations, provide additional resources for further exploration
Optional (Varies)	Optional: Invite guest speakers with entrepreneurial experience, share personal stories, challenges, and insights. Enhance understanding through real-world examples and strategies

Conclusion: The activity provides valuable insights into the significance of challenging norms and embracing constructive conflict. Participants explored the advantages and challenges associated with disagreeableness and developed strategies for leveraging it effectively. This activity emphasized the importance of self-awareness, communication, and finding a balance between assertiveness and collaboration. Participants left with a deeper understanding of how disagreeableness can contribute to their entrepreneurial endeavors.

3.3 Impulsivity

Impulsiveness refers to acting without thinking about it first and considering data before deciding. Wiklund Patzelt and Dimov (2016) state that "acting without thinking is characterized by rapid decision making in situations that would seem to require extensive analysis and deliberation." They go on to explain that individuals need to act impulsively in some entrepreneurial conditions because it is impossible to complete a throughout analysis due to uncertainty, ambiguity, and urgency. Rather than succumbing to analysis paralysis, entrepreneurs take leaps of faith that most others are not willing to. As it turns out, there is a way to measure impulsivity. Attention deficit and hyper-active disorder (ADHD) is usually considered a problem that need to be addressed. For instance, many parents medicate their children with drugs like Ritalin to combat the negative effects of ADHD. Interestingly, ADHD has been associated with entrepreneurial behaviors. The disorder increases the impulsiveness of the individual, which is useful for acting under uncertainty (Wiklund, Patzelt and Dimov, 2016). According to National Institute of Mental Health: "Attention-deficit/hyperactivity disorder is a brain disorder marked by an ongoing pattern of inattention and/or hyperactivity-impulsivity that interferes with functioning or development...Impulsivity means a person makes hasty actions that occur in the moment without first thinking about them and that may have high potential for harm; or a desire for immediate rewards or inability to delay gratification. An impulsive person may be socially intrusive and excessively interrupt others or make important decisions without considering the long-term consequences." Verheul et al. (2015) studied a very large sample of higher education students and find that students with more ADHD symptoms had more entrepreneurial intentions. Perhaps the lifestyle of the entrepreneur or perceived lifestyle is attractive the impulsive students.

This may be because impulsiveness may lead to failures in other aspects of life, such as math homework. Perhaps there are links here to the misfit Theory. It will be interesting to see if future research is able to distinguish whether impulsiveness is more closely linked to entry, or whether it is more closely linked with entrepreneurial performance. Perhaps impulsive people are more likely to engage in entrepreneurship, but do they actually do better over the long run? Future studies may tell. It will also be important to assess how much impulsiveness matters among other individual characteristics, like need for achievement, locus of control, and self-efficacy.

Understanding the "Impulsivity" theory:

Impulsivity is a personality trait characterized by a tendency to act quickly without thinking through the consequences. While impulsivity can sometimes lead to negative outcomes, there are certain business contexts where it can be an advantage. For example, A salesperson is known for her impulsive personality. She is not afraid to take risks and pursue new business opportunities, even if they seem unlikely or unconventional. She is quick to jump on new leads and make bold sales pitches, often without a lot of preparation or planning. While this can sometimes lead to rejection, it also helps her close deals that other salespeople might miss.

Johan Wicklund | Holger Patzelt | Dimo Dimov

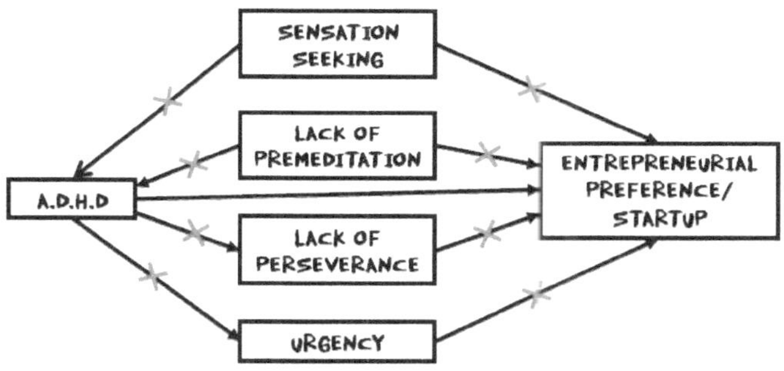

As a result of her impulsive personality, the salesperson can generate a lot of new business for her company. Her willingness to take risks and pursue unconventional leads can help the company stay ahead of competitors and identify new growth opportunities. However, it is important for her to balance her impulsivity with discipline and strategic thinking, to avoid taking unnecessary risks or damaging the company's reputation.

Classroom Activity: Journey of Self-Control

Objective: To engage readers in an interactive exploration of the theory of Impulsivity in entrepreneurship, helping them understand its impact on decision-making and develop strategies to manage impulsivity effectively.

Duration: 85 – 100 mins

Materials: Flipchart or whiteboard, Markers, Sticky notes, Printed handouts or access to digital documents, Projector & Case studies.

Instructions:

Activity	Instructions
Introduction (10 mins)	Introduce the concept & provide an overview of the theory, discussing the positive and negative aspects of impulsivity and its influence on entrepreneurial behavior. Encourage participants to reflect on their own tendencies towards impulsivity & share personal experiences in decision-making.

Group Discussion (15 mins)	Divide participants into small groups. Provide discussion questions related to the theory. For example. • Can you think of an example where impulsivity has led to positive outcomes in an entrepreneurial context? What factors contributed to the positive outcome? • How can entrepreneurs effectively manage impulsive tendencies to avoid potential negative consequences? • What strategies or can help individuals strike a balance between seizing opportunities & making thoughtful decisions? Instruct groups to discuss the questions, share insights, and develop strategies.
Case Study Analysis (20 mins)	Optional: Provide case studies or real-world examples illustrating the role of impulsivity in entrepreneurial success or failure. Participants read the case study individually or in groups. Analyze how impulsivity influenced the outcome and discuss alternative approaches. Share observations, lessons, & strategies.
Interactive Exercise (30 mins)	Divide participants into pairs or small groups. Assign a scenario or entrepreneurial challenge that requires decision-making under time pressure or high-risk situations. Brainstorm strategies and techniques for managing impulsivity while capitalizing on opportunities. Present strategies and facilitate a discussion on different perspectives and insights.
Reflection and Conclusion (10 mins)	Facilitate a reflection session where participants share key takeaways from the activity. Summarize the main concepts covered, emphasizing the importance of self-awareness and self-control in managing impulsivity. Discuss the role of reflection, deliberation, and seeking input from others in making well-informed decisions. Provide additional resources for further exploration. Invite guest speakers to share personal experiences for enriching participants' understanding of the topic.

Conclusion: The activity fosters a deeper understanding of its impact on decision-making. Participants explored strategies to manage impulsivity effectively, striking a balance between seizing opportunities and making thoughtful choices. Emphasizing self-awareness and self-control, this activity equipped participants with practical approaches for navigating impulsivity in their entrepreneurial journeys.

3.4 Passion

We have all seen motivation memes about passion. We have also witnessed entrepreneurial passion on display when entrepreneurs pitch their ideas to potential investors. TV shows like Dragon's Den and Shark Tank have helped to place passion at the center of our attributions of potential entrepreneurial success. "I like your passion" is a hallmark comment preceding made-for-TV deal-making.

Passion and entrepreneurship Theory: Over the last two decades, entrepreneurship researchers have started to unpack the concept of entrepreneurial passion, which has long been a mainstay of motivational rhetoric about entrepreneurship. "Passion inspires us to work harder and with greater effect. The irony is that we hardly notice our effort. It comes easily and enjoyably" (Chang, 2002). Perhaps entrepreneurs view their ventures as their babies and nurture them with a similar level of passion that parents feel toward their human children (Cardon et al., 2005). Perhaps entrepreneurship researchers need to pay more attention to emotions when explaining entrepreneurial behaviors. Vallerand et al. (2003) argue that there are two main types of passion:

1. "Obsessive passion (OP) refers to a controlled internalization of an activity in one's identity that creates an internal pressure to engage in the activity that the person likes."
2. "Harmonious passion (HP) refers to an autonomous internalization that leads individuals to choose to engage in the activity that they like. HP promotes healthy adaptation whereas OP thwarts it by causing negative affect and rigid persistence."

These concepts have recently been used in some empirical studies. For instance, Thorgen and Wincent (2015) find that entrepreneurial passion is greater among serial entrepreneurs than first time entrepreneurs. They find portfolio entrepreneurs (those with multiple simultaneous business interests) have the highest levels of harmonious passion. However, before we take passion too seriously, let us consider other possibilities. For example, Gielnik et al. (2015) offer a very different perspective. Their analyses suggest the potential for reverse causation where entrepreneurial effort leads to business success, which in turn feeds passion. This result suggests that nurturing passion is not so much a matter of pumping yourself up...rather it's more of a side-effect of success. There is also a selection problem in that most failed entrepreneurs would not make it into the datasets. Maybe they had passion too!

Understanding the "Passion" theory:

A passion-driven business is one that is built around the personal passions and interests of the entrepreneur or team. A couple who are avid hikers and outdoor enthusiasts decide to start a business that offers guided hiking tours. They are passionate about exploring the great outdoors, and they want to share their love of hiking with others. They spend months researching hiking trails and destinations, and create a unique tour package that emphasizes adventure, nature, and sustainability. As the business grows, the couple hires a team of guides who share their passion for hiking and the outdoors. They work hard to create a culture of enthusiasm and positivity and prioritize the customer experience above all else. Their passion for hiking is contagious, and customers often become repeat clients and refer their friends and family to the business. By building a business around something they love, the couple can create a unique and compelling value proposition that resonates with customers. Their passion drives their commitment to excellence and inspires their team to go above and beyond for their customers.

MAKE YOUR

I LIVE MY | PASSION | IS PURPOSE

YOUR

PAYCHECK

RICHARD Y CHANG

Classroom Activity: Igniting Entrepreneurial Success

Objective: To engage readers in an interactive exploration of the theory of Passion in entrepreneurship, helping them understand its significance, identify their own entrepreneurial passions, and develop strategies for harnessing passion to drive success.

Duration: 85 – 100 mins

Materials: Flipchart or whiteboard, Markers, Printed handouts or access to digital documents, Sticky notes, Case studies or examples.

Instructions:

Activity	Instructions
Introduction (10 mins)	Start by introducing the concept of Passion in entrepreneurship, explaining its meaning and implications. Provide an overview of the theory, emphasizing the role of passion in driving motivation, perseverance, and satisfaction in entrepreneurial endeavors. Encourage participants to reflect on their own passions and how they relate to entrepreneurship.

Passion Mapping (15 mins)	Ask participants to individually identify and write down their personal passions on sticky notes. Have participants place their sticky notes on a central flipchart or board, creating a passion map. Facilitate a discussion around the shared passions, allowing participants to share their motivations and how they envision integrating their passions into entrepreneurial pursuits. Encourage participants to find commonalities or areas of collaboration among their passions.
Case Study Analysis (20 mins)	Optional: Provide case studies or real-world examples that highlight individuals who have successfully pursued their passions in entrepreneurship. Instruct participants to read the case study individually or in small groups. Ask participants to analyze how passion influenced the individuals' entrepreneurial journeys, including the challenges they faced and strategies they employed. Facilitate a discussion where participants share their findings and insights, exploring how passion can impact business decisions, innovation, and perseverance.
Passion-Driven Business Ideas (30 mins)	Divide participants into pairs or small groups. Instruct each pair/group to develop a business idea that aligns with their shared passions from the passion mapping exercise. Encourage participants to think creatively, considering how their passion can solve a problem, meet a need, or create value in the market. Have each pair/group present their passion-driven business idea, highlighting the unique value proposition and market potential.
Reflection and Conclusion (10 mins)	Conclude the activity by facilitating a reflection session where participants can share their key takeaways from the session. Summarize the main concepts covered during the activity and emphasize the importance of aligning passion with entrepreneurial pursuits. Discuss how passion can fuel motivation, resilience, and innovation in the entrepreneurial journey. Provide additional resources, such as recommended readings or online articles, for participants who wish to explore the topic further. Invite guest speakers to share personal experiences for enriching participants' understanding of the topic.

Conclusion: The activity provides readers with an engaging and introspective experience. Through passion mapping, case study analysis, and the development of passion-driven business ideas, participants gained a deeper understanding of the role of passion in entrepreneurial success. They recognized the importance of aligning personal passions with entrepreneurial pursuits and discovered ways to leverage their passions to create value in the market. The activity emphasized how passion can fuel motivation, resilience, and innovation in the entrepreneurial journey. Participants left with a renewed sense of purpose and inspiration, equipped with practical strategies and resources to pursue their entrepreneurial ventures with passion and purpose.

3.5 Locus of control

What is the locus of control in entrepreneurship? Among personality theories of entrepreneurship, locus of control has received considerable attention. The concept was developed in the 1950s by Julian R otter who is an American psychologist working on social learning theories. Locus of control refers to an individual's perception about the causes of their life conditions. External locus of control describes an individual that believes that most of their life conditions are determined by forces outside of their control, such as like deities, governments, power structures, institutions, and fate or luck. Internal locus of control describes an individual that believes that they are their own master and can act to change their own life conditions. They are viewed as a continuum and most individual are situated between the two extremes of complete external control and total internal control orientations. When applied to entrepreneurs, those with an external locus might believe that their survival or success chances are determined by market and institutional forces they cannot control. Conversely, entrepreneurs with an internal locus of control believe that success is determined by his or her own efforts and abilities. The main idea is that internal locus of control is associated with intentions to become and entrepreneur, and entrepreneurial entry. Locus of control has also been deemed a cultural trait such that some countries' cultures engender more of it than others (Mueller and Thomas, 2001). This has been used to explain why some countries have more innovative entrepreneurship than others. Locus of control is believed to develop as a result of family upbringing (Schultz and Schultz, 2005). Children that receive promised rewards from their efforts and consistent discipline for wrongdoing are more likely to develop an internal locus. Some have argued that children raised by single mothers are more likely to develop an external locus of control. Locus of control tends to shift from external to internal with age. Development of the trait can be disrupted in societies experiencing unrest caused by outside forces (e.g., military occupation or economic depression). One problem with this type of Theory is that there are many individuals with an internal locus of control who choose careers other than entrepreneurship. For instance, intention theories (e.g., Theory of Planned Behavior) suggest that traits influence intentions, which fully mediate the relationship with entrepreneurial behaviors.

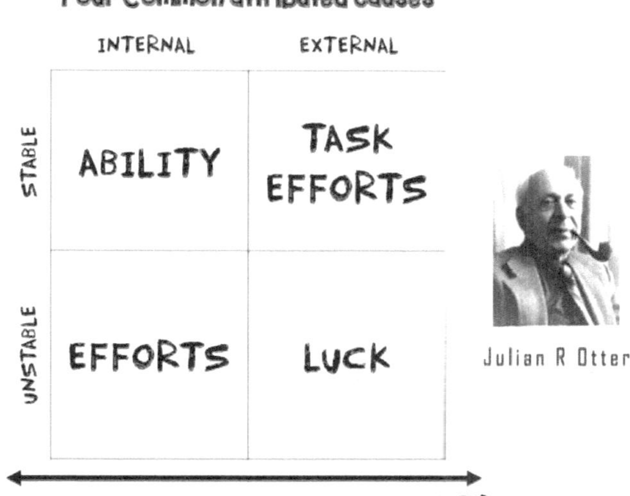

Understanding the "Locus of Control" theory:

Locus of control is a personality trait that refers to an individual's belief about the extent to which they can control events and outcomes in their lives. For example, an entrepreneur with an internal locus of control believes that they are largely in control of their own success. They believe that their own efforts, skills, and decisions are the primary factors that determine the success or failure of their business. This entrepreneur takes full responsibility for the outcomes of their business and believes that they can influence those outcomes through their actions and decisions. The entrepreneur with an external locus of control, on the other hand, believes that external factors such as luck, market conditions, and competition have a greater impact on their business success. They may feel that their actions and decisions have limited influence on the outcome and therefore may be more likely to blame external factors for any failures or setbacks. An example of an entrepreneur with an internal locus of control might be a small business owner who takes a hands-on approach to every aspect of their business, from product development to sales and marketing. They are constantly seeking feedback, learning from their mistakes, and experimenting with new approaches. They believe that their own efforts and hard work are the key to their success and are more likely to take calculated risks to drive growth and innovation. In contrast, an entrepreneur with an external locus of control may be more passive in their approach to business, relying heavily on external consultants or advisors to guide their decisions. They may be less willing to take risks or make bold moves, feeling that the outcomes of their business are largely outside of their control.

Classroom Activity: Locus of Control Simulation

Objective: To understand & apply the theory of locus of control in the context of entrepreneurship.
Duration: 60 - 70 mins
Materials: Flipchart or whiteboard, Markers, Printed handouts, or access to digital documents. Sticky notes, Case studies or examples.
Instructions:

Activity	Instructions
Intro (5 mins)	Begin by introducing the concept of the theory of locus of control. Explain that locus of control refers to an individual's belief about the extent to which they can control events and outcomes in their lives.
Share (10 mins)	Divide participants into small groups of 3-4 people. Instruct each group to discuss and share examples of situations where they have experienced an internal or external locus of control. Encourage reflection on entrepreneurship-related experiences.
Pitch (10 mins)	Ask each group to present their examples. Categorize the examples as either internal or external locus of control. Facilitate a discussion after each presentation.
Reflection and Analysis (10 mins)	Lead a reflection using following prompt questions: • What patterns or trends do you notice in the examples of internal locus of control? • What patterns or trends do you notice in the examples of external locus of control? • How do these patterns relate to entrepreneurship and its challenges? • Can you identify any advantages or disadvantages of having an internal or external locus of control in the entrepreneurial context? Encourage open discussion and ask participants questions about patterns, trends, and the relationship.

Personal Action Plan (10 mins)	Instruct participants to individually reflect on their own locus of control in the context of their entrepreneurial aspirations or endeavors. Provide prompts for identifying areas of internal and external locus of control and developing action plans, such as: • Identify one specific area where you tend to exhibit an internal locus of control. • Identify one specific area where you tend to exhibit an external locus of control. • Based on your analysis and understanding, how can you strengthen your internal locus of control in the areas where it is weak? • How can you mitigate the negative impact of an external locus of control in the areas where it is strong?
Wrap-Up (5 mins)	Invite participants to share their personal action plans with a partner or the whole group. Facilitate a brief discussion on strategies to enhance internal locus of control and support each other. Summarize insights & emphasize its importance for success.

Conclusion: Through engaging discussions, analysis of examples, and personal action planning, participants gained insights into the differences between internal and external locus of control and their implications for entrepreneurship. By recognizing patterns, identifying areas of strength and improvement, and developing strategies to enhance their internal locus of control, participants are better equipped to navigate the challenges and capitalize on opportunities in their entrepreneurial pursuits. Cultivating a strong internal locus of control is crucial for taking proactive actions, persevering through setbacks, and ultimately achieving entrepreneurial success

3.6 Alertness

Israel Kirzner, a British-American financial analyst & emeritus teacher at New York University. He is related with the Austrian school of financial aspects. Beneath, we audit Kirzner's readiness theory of business venture. Kirzner contends that business visionaries balance market interest by recognizing market defects and misusing them. Market blemishes are brought about by data deviation and limited levelheadedness. Data lopsidedness alludes to situations where various partners have differing data about an undertaking. On the off chance that one partner utilizes the data benefit to benefit from the another, it is participating in astute haggling. Limited discernment alludes to the possibility that people are not totally reasonable. Neo-old style and Classical financial aspects model the suppositions of monetary man and will in general disregard limited discernment. As indicated by Kirzner, the benefits businesspeople get from business venture are their compensation for their resistance of vulnerability as they take out exchange openings (the chance to sell a similar item at a greater cost than the person got it) made by the obliviousness or ineptitude of occupant firms. Businesspeople should be ready to have the option to see monetary freedoms that others can't yet see, like the requirement for new products or administrations. Openings are believed to exist simply because of the obliviousness of officeholders else they would as of now be abused. At the point when officeholders don't know key data or don't understand what they don't have the foggiest idea, then at that point openings for business are conceived. Obliviousness brings forth mistakes that can be amended by the activities of business visionaries. The businessperson acts under vulnerability and can't know whether their activity will return a benefit until after the move has been made. Consequently, business visionaries should acknowledge they may lose cash (or that of their financial backers) from their activities if they end up being erroneous. Kirzner accepts that innovative sharpness can't be educated. Be that as it may, this conviction has been scrutinized on the grounds that statistical surveying and client revelation can unmistakably assist with perceiving kinds of chances. In any case, an answer may be that realizing that statistical surveying was required in any case is enterprising. Kirzner doesn't see financial activities like purchasing assets or making new items as enterprising. Maybe it is just the demonstration of readiness that is pioneering.

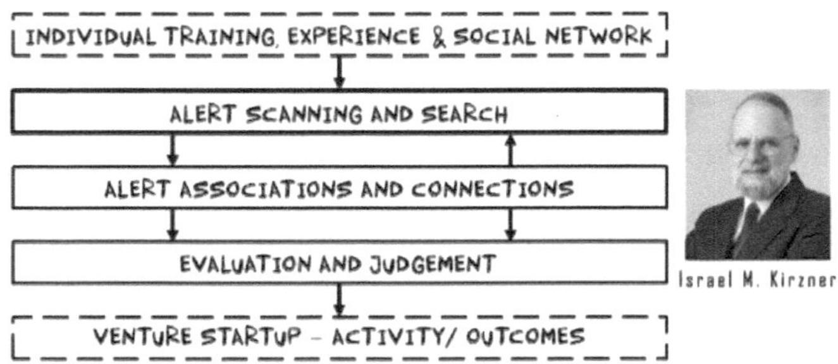

Israel M. Kirzner

Understanding the "Alertness" theory:

Alertness is a cognitive trait that refers to an individual's ability to be aware of and responsive to changes in their environment, and to identify potential opportunities and threats. For example, A tech startup founder with high alertness is constantly scanning the market for new trends and opportunities. They pay close attention to changes in consumer behavior, emerging technologies, and industry disruptors. They regularly attend conferences, networking events, and industry meetups to stay abreast of the latest developments in their field. When the founder notices a new trend or opportunity, they act quickly to capitalize on it. For example, when they noticed that more and more people were using voice assistants like Amazon's Alexa, they quickly pivoted their startup to develop a voice-enabled app. This decision paid off, as the app quickly gained traction and became a market leader in its category. The founder's alertness also helps them identify potential threats to their business. For example, when they noticed that a well-funded competitor was entering the market, they quickly made strategic changes to their product and marketing strategy to stay ahead of the competition. By staying attuned to changes in the market and the environment, alert entrepreneurs can identify new opportunities, avoid potential threats, and make strategic decisions that drive business success.

Classroom Activity for Educators: The Alertness Experiment

Objective: To explore & understand the theory of alertness & its significance in entrepreneurship.

Duration: 30-45 mins

Materials: Stopwatch or timer, Pen/pencil for each participant, Blank sheets of paper or index cards, Flipchart or whiteboard and Markers

Instructions:

Activity	Instructions
Intro (5 mins)	Begin by introducing the concept of the theory of alertness. Explain the importance of being attentive, perceptive, and responsive to opportunities and changes in the entrepreneurial context.
Team (5 mins)	Divide participants into pairs or small groups. Instruct each group to choose one member as the "observer" and the other(s) as the "performer(s)." Explain that the observers will conduct a short observation challenge while the performers engage in a simple task

Observation Challenge (15 mins)	The task: • Performers' Task: Assign a specific task to the performers, such as sorting a deck of cards, assembling a puzzle, or solving a brainteaser. Set a time limit of 3-5 mins for the task. • Observers' Task: Instruct the observers to carefully observe the performers during the task. They should pay attention to details, actions, behaviors, and any potential opportunities or challenges they notice. • Conduct the Challenge: Start the timer and let the performers begin their task while the observers focus on observing. Remind participants to be attentive and perceptive during the challenge.
Group Discussion and Analysis (10 mins)	Bring the groups together and facilitate a discussion. Encourage open dialogue where observers share their insights about performers' actions, behaviors, and any opportunities or challenges they noticed. Write down key observations and insights on the flipchart paper or whiteboard. Facilitate a collective analysis of the importance of being alert in identifying opportunities and potential challenges in an entrepreneurial context. Analyze the importance of alertness in identifying entrepreneurial opportunities.
Personal Reflection (10 mins)	Instruct participants to individually reflect on their own level of alertness in entrepreneurial situations. Provide prompts for them to rate their alertness, suggest strategies to enhance it, and explore the benefits of being more alert in their entrepreneurial journey. Provide them with a pen/pencil and a blank sheet of paper or index card to jot down their responses to the following prompts: • How would you rate your level of alertness in entrepreneurial situations? • What are some strategies or practices you can adopt to enhance your alertness? • How can being more alert benefit your entrepreneurial journey?
Wrap-up (5 mins)	Invite participants to share their reflections and action plans with a partner or the whole group. Encourage a brief discussion on strategies to enhance alertness and support each other in implementing these strategies. Summarize key insights and emphasize the importance of alertness in entrepreneurship.

Conclusion: Through the observation challenge, participants actively observed and analyzed performers' actions and behaviors, gaining insights into the importance of being alert in identifying opportunities and potential challenges. The group discussion and personal reflection segments encouraged participants to reflect on their own level of alertness and develop actionable strategies to enhance it. By cultivating alertness as an entrepreneurial skill, participants are better equipped to navigate the dynamic business environment, detect emerging trends, and seize opportunities, ultimately increasing their chances of entrepreneurial success.

3.7 Achievement Motivation

This theory was developed & explained by Harvard psychologist David McClelland in his book entitled, "The Achieving Society in 1967". McClelland looked to clarify why a few social orders are more financially effective than others. For answers, he took a gander at the innovative practices of people, which he thought were critical to the improvement. As indicated by him, business visionaries get things done in another and better manner and settle on choices under vulnerability. Business visionaries are portrayed by a requirement for accomplishment or an accomplishment direction, which is a drive to dominate, advance, and develop. By zeroing in on a specific need, he had the option to challenge the then predominant incredible man theory of business just as strict speculations of business venture. He accepted that business is learned and that such learning can be empowered productively. The requirement for accomplishment diverges from the requirement for power that is a drive to rule others in all circumstances, and with the requirement for alliance that is, a drive for close to home connections. In any case, force and member authenticity may assist with accomplishment and would thus be able to be viewed as important means or assets that can assist with fulfilling the requirement for accomplishment. He accepted that an accomplishment direction creates during center youth through family socialization stressing exclusive requirements, confidence, and less prevailing dads. It shows in practices such critical thinking, input chasing, objectives accomplishment, and hazard taking. He contended that the requirement for accomplishment is mostly socially resolved for certain social orders creating less people with accomplishment directions. Social orders ailing in accomplishment situated people are required to have below earnings. A disputable ramification of the theory is that lower-performing economies can be supported by receiving social strategies that modify socialization measures in manners that empower the advancement of more people with accomplishment inspirations. This can be censured like a sort of friendly designing however, on the grounds that a few societies may have distinctive worth constructions. For e.g., prosperity, straightforwardness, and custom might be more esteemed in certain societies than advancements prompting more longing for accomplishment. McClelland was mindful to note notwithstanding, that accomplishments are not to be mistaken for results, for example, abundance or pay as these are simply proportions of accomplishment, not accomplishments in themselves. The requirement for accomplishment is fulfilled characteristically with a sensation of individual achievement while completing something on the planet. Along these lines, the idea is very expansive and can be applied by and large. For example, in a culture that qualities prosperity or human turn of events, an individual may feel accomplishment by achieving more prominent degrees of accomplishment in others in the public. Proof for the theory appears to be genuinely impressive, with meta-examinations affirming a positive connection between need for accomplishment & innovative passage and execution (see Collins et al., 2004). There is additionally meta-logical proof that the requirement for accomplishment is more grounded in businesspeople than in supervisors (Steward and Roth, 2007). The issue with speculations like these is that while numerous businesspeople may show a requirement for accomplishment, numerous non-businesspeople may likewise have a solid requirement for accomplishment that is happy with achievement in other expert professions. Along these lines, it offers just a fractional image of the drivers of innovative passage.

Understanding the "Achievement Motivation" theory:

Achievement motivation is a personality trait that refers to an individual's desire for success and attainment of goals. For example, a sales executive with high achievement motivation is driven to meet and exceed their sales targets. They set ambitious goals for themselves and are constantly pushing themselves to improve their performance. They are highly competitive and take pride in being the top performer on their team. The executive's achievement and motivation is a key driver of their success. They are constantly seeking new challenges and are willing to take risks to achieve their goals. For example, they may be willing to try out new sales techniques or approaches, even if they are untested or unconventional. They are not afraid of failure, as they see it as an opportunity to learn and improve. The executive's achievement motivation also drives them to seek recognition and rewards for their success.

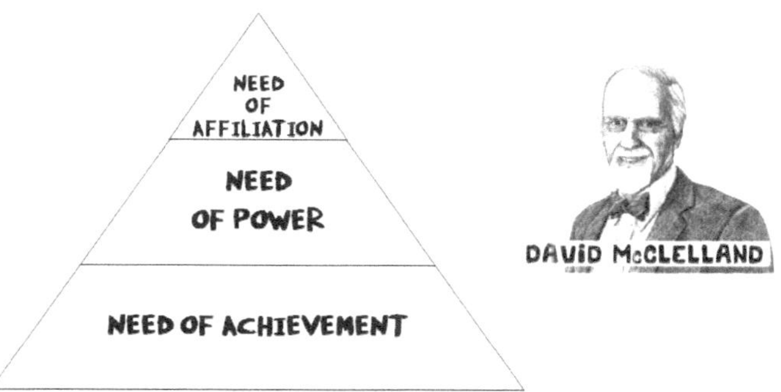

They are highly motivated by performance-based incentives, such as bonuses or promotions, and are willing to work long hours and put in extra effort to achieve these rewards. By setting ambitious goals, taking calculated risks, and seeking recognition and rewards for their success, individuals with high achievement motivation can drive performance, improve outcomes, and contribute to business success.

Classroom Activity: "Unleash Your Achievement Motivation"

Objective: To engage readers in exploring and understanding the Theory of Achievement Motivation, while also encouraging self-reflection and application of the theory to their own entrepreneurial endeavors.

Duration: 75 – 90 mins

Materials: Pen/pencil for each participant, Blank sheets of paper or index cards, Flipchart paper or whiteboard and Markers

Instructions:

Activity	Instructions
Intro (10 mins)	Provide a brief overview of the Theory & explain the concept of individuals being driven by their need for achievement. Highlight key concepts such as goal setting, intrinsic and extrinsic motivation, and the role of feedback in achievement.
Team (5 mins)	Ask readers to reflect on their personal experiences as entrepreneurs or their entrepreneurial aspirations. Provide prompts for them to consider their goals, motivations, and how they handle setbacks and failures.

Reflective Exercise (15 mins)	Use following prompts and encourage them to jot down their thoughts: • What are your current goals as an entrepreneur? Are they primarily focused on financial success, personal growth, societal impact, or a combination of these? • What motivates you to pursue these goals? Are you driven more by internal factors (e.g., passion, curiosity, personal fulfillment) or external factors (e.g., recognition, rewards, social status)? • How do you handle setbacks and failures in your entrepreneurial journey? Do they demotivate you or serve as a source of learning and motivation?
Group Discussion (20 mins)	Divide readers into small groups (if applicable) and encourage them to discuss their reflections from the previous exercise. Facilitate a discussion by asking questions about common motivations and goals, how they align with the Theory, and how the theory can enhance their entrepreneurial performance and satisfaction. Ask the following questions: • What patterns or commonalities did you notice among your motivations and goals as entrepreneurs? • How do these motivations align with the concepts discussed in the Theory? How do you think the Theory of Achievement Motivation can be applied to enhance your entrepreneurial performance and satisfaction?
Application Exercise (15 mins)	Instruct readers to select a specific goal or project they are currently working on as entrepreneurs and apply the principles of the Theory by considering the following: • Set clear & challenging goals related to the project. • Identify both intrinsic and extrinsic motivators that can drive their efforts. • Develop a plan to obtain feedback and measure progress. • Brainstorm strategies to maintain motivation in the face of setbacks or obstacles.

Sharing and Reflection (15 mins)	Invite readers to share their insights and action plans from the previous exercise with the larger group (if applicable). Encourage open discussion, provide feedback and suggestions, and prompt readers to reflect on what they have learned and how they plan to apply the Theory to their entrepreneurial journey.

Conclusion: The activity provides readers with a structured framework to analyze and apply key concepts to their entrepreneurial journey. Through self-reflection and discussions, readers gained a deeper understanding of goals, motivations, and setbacks. Applying the theory to a specific project, readers developed action plans with clear goals, motivators, feedback, and strategies to overcome obstacles. Sharing and reflection facilitated knowledge exchange and enhanced entrepreneurial performance. The activity empowered readers to leverage achievement motivation, equipping them with practical strategies for success.

3.8 Expectancy

It was developed to explain work motivation and organizational behavior (Kanfer, 1990). It has since been used to explain additional behaviors, including entry into entrepreneurship. Expectancy Theory starts with the concept of motivational forces that Vroom (1964) expressed as an equation: MF = V x I x E, where V = valence, I = instrumentality, and E = expectancy. Valence refers to the value that an individual places on the outcome of their efforts—such as the importance of financial rewards. Instrumentality refers to the belief that if an individual meets performance expectations, that they will receive the reward. Expectancy is the belief or probability that an individual's effort will result in the desired goal being achieved. Since the equation involves multiplication, it implies that if any one of the parts is zero then the motivational forces equal zero. Valance depends upon the individual's desire for material rewards or the psychic rewards of influence, ownership, power or getting things done. Expectancy is based on past experiences and feedback from others. Instrumentality may be influenced by the environment; for instance, where taxation is prohibitively high, the individual may believe that their venture, even if successful, will not yield sufficient monetary rewards. Applied to the entrepreneurial context, an individual will have the motivational force to enter entrepreneurship as a career path if they value the profits of entrepreneurship, believe that they can start a business, and believe that if they start a business, that the business will yield profits (see Renko et al., 2012). If any of these three components are not present in an individual's beliefs, then they will not start a business.

Reason to perform better

EXPECTANCY = MOTIVATIONAL FORCES / VALENCE X INSTRUMENTALITY

(PERCEIVED PERFORMANCE) (PROFIT OUTCOMES) (PERFORMANCE EXPECTATIONS)

Victor H. Vroom

Understanding the "Expectancy" theory:

This theory is a motivation theory that suggests that an individual's motivation to perform a task is influenced by their belief that their efforts will lead to a desired outcome, and that the outcome is valuable to them. For example, an employee working in a sales department has high expectancy. They believe that their efforts will lead to better performance, which in turn will lead to higher sales commissions. They are confident in their abilities to sell, and they believe that their sales efforts will lead to the desired outcome of earning more money. This employee's expectancy has a positive impact on their motivation and performance. They are motivated to work harder and smarter because they believe that their efforts will be rewarded with higher sales commissions. They are willing to put in extra effort to develop their sales skills and techniques, and to invest time and resources into building relationships with clients. The employee's expectancy is reinforced by their organization's reward system. The company has a clear and transparent commission structure that rewards top performers with higher earnings. The employee understands this reward system, and they know that their efforts will be recognized and rewarded if they perform well. By creating a transparent and effective reward system, and by supporting employees' belief that their efforts will lead to desirable outcomes, businesses can motivate and engage their employees, improve performance, and achieve their goals.

Classroom Activity: "Unlocking the Power of Expectancy"

Objective: To engage readers in exploring and understanding the Theory of Expectancy, while encouraging self-reflection and application of the theory to their entrepreneurial pursuits.

Duration: 75 – 80 mins

Materials: Pen/pencil for each participant, Blank sheets of paper or index cards, Flipchart paper or whiteboard and Markers

Instructions:

Activity	Instructions
Intro (10 mins)	Provide a brief overview of the Theory & explain key concepts such as expectancy, instrumentality, and valence and how they shape motivation & behavior in entrepreneurship.
Reflective Exercise (15 mins)	Prompt readers to reflect on their entrepreneurial experiences or aspirations. Ask them to consider their expectations regarding the outcomes of a significant goal or project, and how those expectations influenced their motivation and actions. Encourage reflection on instances where expectations were met or not met, and how it impacted their future motivation and decision-making. Use following questions: • Think about a significant goal or project you've pursued as an entrepreneur What were your expectations regarding outcomes of your efforts? • How did these expectations influence your motivation and the actions you took to achieve the desired outcomes? • Reflect on instances where your expectations were met or not met. How did it affect your future motivation and decision-making?
Group Discussion (20 mins)	Divide readers into small groups (if applicable) to discuss their reflections from the previous exercise. Facilitate a discussion by exploring patterns and commonalities in their expectations and their impact on entrepreneurial pursuits. Use following questions: What patterns or commonalities did you notice among your expectations and their impact on your entrepreneurial pursuits? • How do these patterns align with the concepts discussed in the Theory of Expectancy? • How can understanding the Theory of Expectancy help you set more effective goals, enhance your motivation, and make better decisions as an entrepreneur? Connect these patterns with the concepts discussed in the Theory of Expectancy. Discuss how understanding the theory can enhance goal setting, motivation, and decision-making in entrepreneurship.

Application Exercise (15 mins)	Instruct readers to choose a specific entrepreneurial goal or project and apply the principles of the Theory of Expectancy. They should identify desired outcomes, assess their confidence in achieving them (expectancy), evaluate the instrumentalities (link between efforts and outcomes), and determine the valence (importance) of the outcomes and their impact on motivation.
Sharing (15 mins)	Encourage readers to share their insights and action plans from the application exercise with the larger group (if applicable). Foster an open discussion and provide feedback and suggestions. Finally, ask readers to reflect on their learnings from the activity and discuss how they plan to apply the theory to their entrepreneurial journey.

Conclusion: The readers develop a deeper understanding of how expectations influence their entrepreneurial pursuits. Through self-reflection and group discussions, readers have gained insights into the impact of expectations on motivation, decision-making, and goal achievement. By applying the principles of the Theory of Expectancy to their specific entrepreneurial goals or projects, readers have developed action plans that consider confidence in achieving desired outcomes, instrumentalities, and the value attached to those outcomes. The sharing and reflection phase has allowed for knowledge exchange and the identification of strategies to enhance goal setting, motivation, and decision-making. Equipped with this understanding, readers are now better prepared to navigate their entrepreneurial journey with a heightened awareness of the power of expectations and how to harness them effectively for success.

3.9 Self-efficacy

Bandura (1977) proposed that an individual's belief in their ability to perform a given task can be conceptualized as self-efficacy. Self-efficacy is viewed as an antecedent to the formation of intentions. If an individual believes that they can achieve a goal, they are more likely to develop the intention to achieve the goal. By contrast, if an individual believes that they do not have the ability to achieve a goal, then they will not form intentions to purse the goal. Individuals develop self-efficacy over time as they obtain a variety of skills (cognitive, social, linguistic, or physical) through life experiences. Past achievements (e.g., mastery of a given task) reinforce self-efficacy, thus leading to more ambitious intentions (i.e., higher aspirations). Self-efficacy can also be gained via modeling the behaviors of others through close observation (i.e., vicarious, or social learning), self-reflection, and social persuasion (positive feedback). Thus, if an individual performs well at a task as compared with similar others that they observe and are told they are performing well by others, they may decide that they indeed have the skills necessary to pursue the next, more challenging task. Self-efficacy Theory suggests that entrepreneurs will only pursue an entrepreneurial venture if they believe they have the skills and abilities necessary to tackle the challenges that a particular opportunity presents. If the potential entrepreneur deems the challenge to be too difficult, he or she may then consider other options, such as salaried employment. Scherer et al. (1987) finds that individuals who perceived that their own parents were high performers are more likely to think they will themselves start a business when compared to those who perceived their parents as lower performing or who did not have any such role models. Entrepreneurs' offspring also tend to view themselves as having a higher level of competence about performing entrepreneurial tasks needed to start a business.

ALBERT BANDURA

Understanding the "Self-Efficacy" theory:

Self-efficacy is a belief in one's ability to succeed in a specific situation or task. For example, an employee who works in a marketing department has high self-efficacy. They believe that they have the skills and abilities to create effective marketing campaigns. They are confident in their ability to research, analyze data, and develop creative ideas that will resonate with customers. This employee's self-efficacy has a positive impact on their motivation and performance. They are willing to take on challenging tasks and projects and are not deterred by setbacks or obstacles. They approach their work with a sense of enthusiasm and optimism, knowing that they can succeed. The employee's self-efficacy is reinforced by their supervisor and team members. They receive positive feedback on their work and are recognized for their contributions to the team's success. This feedback helps to strengthen their belief in their abilities and motivates them to continue to perform at a high level. By creating an environment that supports and reinforces employees' belief in their abilities, businesses can help to build a motivated and high-performing workforce.

Classroom Activity: "Building Self-Efficacy Vision Board"

Objective: To help participants develop and enhance their self-efficacy, which is the belief in their ability to accomplish tasks and achieve their goals.

Materials: Poster board or large sheets of paper, Magazines, newspapers, or printed images, Scissors, Glue sticks or tape & Markers, or colored pencils. Optional: Personal photos or images.

Instructions:

Activity	Instructions
Intro (5 mins)	Provide a brief introduction to the concept of self-efficacy. Explain the definition of self-efficacy and its importance in entrepreneurship and personal growth. Share examples of successful entrepreneurs with high levels of self-efficacy. Encourage participants to reflect on their own self-efficacy beliefs and challenges they've faced.
Discussion (10 mins)	Engage participants in a group discussion about self-efficacy. Encourage them to share their own experiences and challenges related to believing in their abilities. Discuss the impact of self-efficacy on entrepreneurial success and personal development. Explore strategies for building and maintaining self-efficacy.
Vision Board Explanation (5 mins)	Introduce the concept of a vision board as a tool for visualizing and reinforcing self-efficacy. Explain that a vision board is a collage of images, words, and phrases representing goals, aspirations, and belief in one's abilities. Discuss the power of visualization and provide examples of successful vision boards.
Identify Goal (10 mins)	Instruct participants to reflect on their personal and entrepreneurial goals. Ask them to write down their goals on a separate sheet of paper. Emphasize setting SMART goals - specific, measurable, achievable, relevant, and time-bound.

Image and Word Gathering (15 mins)	Distribute magazines, newspapers, or printed images to participants. Instruct them to search for visuals that resonate with their goals and reflect their self-belief and abilities. Encourage creativity and finding images, words, and phrases that inspire them.
Vision Board Creation (20 mins)	Provide each participant with a poster board, scissors, glue sticks, and markers. Instruct them to arrange and glue their chosen images, words, and phrases onto the board, creating a visually appealing and meaningful collage. Encourage the addition of personal photos or images representing past achievements or future aspirations.
Sharing and Reflection (15 mins)	Allow participants to share their vision boards with the group. Invite each participant to explain the significance of their chosen visuals and their relation to self-efficacy and goals. Encourage positive feedback and support from the group to foster a sense of community and inspiration.
Action Plan (10 mins)	Guide participants in developing an action plan based on their vision boards. Ask them to identify specific steps they can take to enhance self-efficacy and work towards their goals. Emphasize breaking down goals into actionable tasks and setting up deadlines.
Wrap-up and Discussion (5 mins)	Facilitate a brief discussion on how vision boards can help strengthen self-efficacy. Encourage participants to reflect on their experiences and share insights or realizations from the activity. Prompt them to consider how they will integrate their vision boards into their daily lives and leverage self-efficacy beliefs to overcome challenges and achieve goals.

Conclusion: The activity provides participants with a valuable opportunity to reflect on goals, beliefs, and abilities. By visualizing aspirations and engaging in discussions, participants gained a deeper understanding of self-efficacy's role in entrepreneurship and personal growth.

3.10 Regulatory focus

Regulatory focus Theory was developed by psychologist E. Tory Higgins of Columbia University in the 1990s. At the core of regulatory focus Theory is the idea that individuals change between two states dubbed a promotion focus and a prevention focus. When in the promotion focused state, individuals attempt to bring themselves into alignment with their need for growth and advancement (their ideal self), causing them to focus on potential gains from risk-taking. By contrast, when individuals are in the prevention focused state, they tend to succumb to their needs for security and safety (their ought self), causing them to focus on potential losses from risk-taking. A recent meta-analysis confirms that regulatory focus is associated with several organizational outcomes. Brockner et al., (2004) borrow regulatory focus Theory to explain entrepreneurial phenomena. They argue that entrepreneurial process requires a greater promotion focus during the idea-generating phase, and a greater prevention focus during the idea filtering stage. Their research suggests that if entrepreneurs can match their promotion and prevention focus phases to the demands of the entrepreneurial stage they are encountering, then they should perform better. Some research suggests that entrepreneurs with a promotion focus perform better in dynamic environments, whereas those with a prevention focus perform better in stable environments (Hmieleski and Baron, 2008).

Understanding the "Regulatory Focus" theory:

Regulatory focus theory suggests that people have two different motivational orientations: a promotion focus, which emphasizes the pursuit of positive outcomes, and a prevention focus, which emphasizes the avoidance of negative outcomes. For example, an entrepreneur starting a new business has a promotional focus. They are excited about the possibilities of success and growth and are motivated by the potential rewards of starting their own business. They are focused on achieving positive outcomes, such as increasing sales and expanding their customer base. This entrepreneur's promotion focus has a positive impact on their motivation and performance.

They are willing to take risks, experiment with new ideas, and pursue opportunities for growth and innovation. They are not deterred by setbacks or failures and remain focused on their goals. In contrast, another entrepreneur starting a new business has a prevention focus. They are more concerned about avoiding negative outcomes, such as financial loss or reputational damage. They are focused on avoiding mistakes and minimizing risks, rather than pursuing opportunities for growth. This entrepreneur's prevention focus has a different impact on their motivation and performance. While they may be more cautious and risk-averse, they may also be less willing to take the kinds of bold and innovative steps that can lead to growth and success. By understanding their own regulatory focus and that of their employees, business leaders can create an environment that is conducive to success and motivate their employees to achieve their goals.

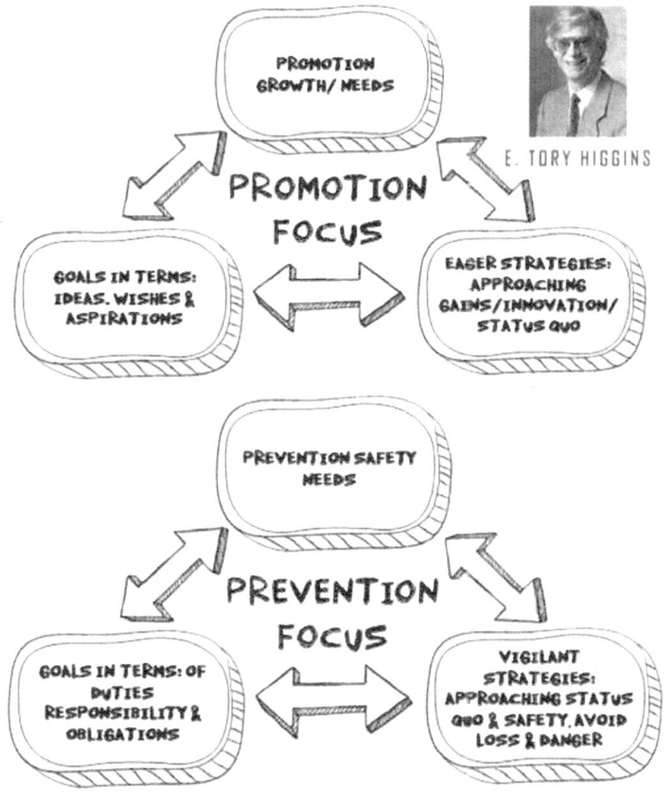

Classroom Activity: "Navigating Regulatory Focus for Success"

Objective: The objective of this activity is to help readers understand and apply the concept of regulatory focus in the context of entrepreneurship. By engaging in various exercises and self-reflection, readers will gain insights into their own regulatory focus tendencies and learn how to leverage them for entrepreneurial success.

Duration: 175 – 180 mins

Materials: Pen and paper or a digital device for notetaking, Access to online resources and articles on regulatory focus in entrepreneurship.

Instructions:

Activity	Detailed Instructions
Introduction (15 mins)	Provide a brief overview of regulatory focus theory and its relevance to entrepreneurship. Explain the concepts of promotion focus and prevention focus. Share real-world examples of entrepreneurs who embody each focus type. Encourage readers to reflect on their initial impression of which focus type they relate to more and why.
Understanding Promotion and Prevention Focus (30 mins)	Ask readers to explore online articles, research papers, or case studies on promotion and prevention focus in entrepreneurship. Provide a set of questions or prompts for readers to consider while reading: What are the key characteristics of individuals with a promotion focus? What are the key characteristics of individuals with a prevention focus? How do these focus types influence decision-making and risk-taking in entrepreneurship? Can individuals exhibit a combination of both focus types? If so, how does that impact their entrepreneurial journey?
Self-Reflection and Assessment (30 mins)	Ask readers to complete a self-assessment questionnaire or survey to identify their dominant regulatory focus type. Provide a list of reflective questions to help readers understand their dominant focus type and how it manifests in their entrepreneurial endeavors: In what situations do you feel more inclined towards a promotion focus? In what situations do you feel more inclined towards a prevention focus? How does your dominant focus type influence your goal setting and risk management strategies? Can you identify any challenges or limitations associated with your dominant focus type in entrepreneurship?
Applying Regulatory Focus (40 mins)	Present readers with a series of entrepreneurial scenarios or case studies. Ask readers to analyze each scenario from the perspective of both a promotion-focused and prevention-focused entrepreneur. Encourage readers to identify the advantages and disadvantages of each focus type in those scenarios and reflect on which approach they find more effective.

Action Plan & Implementation (20 mins)	Based on their self-reflection and understanding of regulatory focus, ask readers to develop an action plan for leveraging their dominant focus type in their entrepreneurial pursuits. The action plan should include specific strategies, tactics, or mindset shifts that align with their focus type and can be implemented in their entrepreneurial journey.
Reflection and Discussion (40 mins)	Invite readers to share their reflections and insights from completing the activity. Facilitate a discussion, either in person or online, where readers can engage with each other, and exchange experiences & ideas related to regulatory focus theory.

Conclusion: The theory provides valuable insights into the role of mindset and decision-making in entrepreneurial success. By understanding the concepts of promotion focus and prevention focus, individuals can gain a deeper understanding of their own inclinations and tendencies when it comes to goal pursuit and risk management. The action plan created based on this understanding can serve as a roadmap for aligning their focus type with their goals and aspirations. Engaging in reflection and discussion further enhances the learning experience by facilitating the exchange of ideas and experiences among participants. By embracing regulatory focus, entrepreneurs can enhance their decision-making abilities, optimize their approach to risk, and maximize their chances of entrepreneurial success.

3.11 Cognitive Evaluation

This is a Theory in psychology (part of self-determination Theory) where it has been used to explain how external factors affect an individual's intrinsic or internal motivation. Events that increase (decrease) perceived confidence increase (decrease) intrinsic motivation. Keh et al. (2002) borrow the Theory to conduct a study of entrepreneurs and find that: "illusion of control and belief in the law of small numbers are related to how entrepreneurs evaluate opportunities." These authors propose that individuals that perceive a lower level of risk associated with an opportunity are more likely to judge it positively. Entrepreneurs exhibiting an illusion of control will have higher overconfidence and will perceive less risk. This is related to the hubris Theory of entrepreneurship. Another finding is that entrepreneurs with stronger beliefs in "the law of small numbers" perceive lower risks. The law of small numbers refers to the fallacy that motivates some people to buy lottery tickets. It is a cognitive bias that leads to hasty generalizations based on too little information anecdotal evidence and mere gossip. Incidentally, there is an interesting anecdote provided by successful entrepreneur David Daneshgar who won his startup capital by playing poker. The same kind of logic that drove him to gamble helped him in his entrepreneurial career.

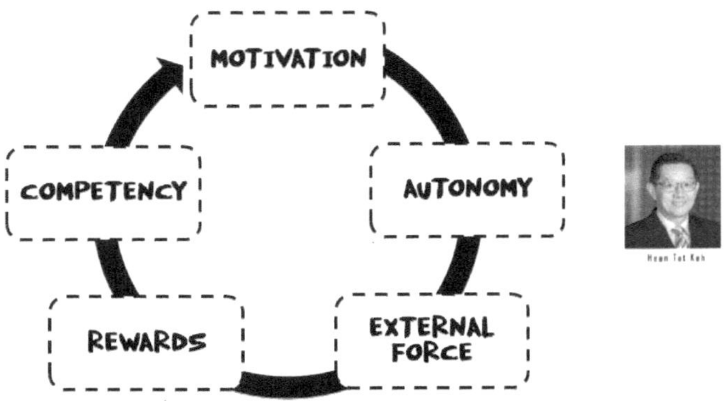

Understanding the "Cognitive Evaluation" theory:

The theory suggests that people are motivated by different types of rewards and that the presence of extrinsic rewards can either enhance or undermine intrinsic motivation. For example, a company decides to introduce a new incentive program to reward employees for achieving sales targets. The program offers bonuses to employees who meet or exceed their targets. The company hopes that this program will motivate employees to work harder and increase their sales performance. However, the introduction of this extrinsic reward may have unintended consequences on employee motivation. Some employees may see the reward as a signal that their work is not inherently interesting or valuable, and that they need to be bribed to perform well. This can decrease their intrinsic motivation and result in a decrease in their overall performance.

On the other hand, other employees may view the incentive program as a recognition of their hard work and dedication. This can increase their intrinsic motivation and lead to improved performance. By designing incentive programs that align with employees' intrinsic motivations, businesses can enhance their overall performance and productivity.

Classroom Activity: "Mind Your Evaluation"

Objectives: To help readers understand and apply the principles of Cognitive Evaluation Theory (CET) in the context of entrepreneurship & explores the influence of intrinsic and extrinsic motivators on an individual's level of intrinsic motivation and subsequent performance. By engaging in this activity, readers will gain insights into how motivation and evaluation impact entrepreneurial behavior and decision-making.

Duration: 100 – 120 mins

Materials: Pen and paper or digital note-taking tool, Access to relevant resources on Cognitive Evaluation Theory (books, articles, online sources)

Instructions:

Activity	Instructions
Introduction (10 mins)	Begin by introducing the concept of Cognitive Evaluation Theory (CET) and its relevance to entrepreneurship. Provide a brief overview of the theory, focusing on the impact of intrinsic & extrinsic motivation on individual performance, creativity, & satisfaction.
Reading & Reflection (20 mins)	Ask participants to read selected articles or sections from books that explain Cognitive Evaluation Theory. Provide them with a list of recommended resources & encourage notetaking. Allocate time for individual reflection on CET's application in entrepreneurship.
Group Discussion (30 mins)	Divide participants into small groups (3-4 members per group) and facilitate a discussion. Encourage sharing of reflections and dialogue about the practical implications of CET for entrepreneurs. Prompt with questions related to intrinsic motivation, extrinsic motivators, and external evaluation. Prompt them with questions such as: • How can intrinsic motivation be fostered in the entrepreneurial journey? • What are the potential challenges & benefits of relying on extrinsic motivators? • How might the presence of external evaluation or rewards influence an entrepreneur's creativity and decision-making?
Case Study Analysis (30 mins)	Provide participants with a real-world case study involving motivation & evaluation in entrepreneurship. Ask them to analyze it through the lens of theory. Identify motivators, evaluate impact, & propose strategies based on CET principles.

Presentation & Reflection (20 mins)	Each group presents their case study analysis and recommendations. Encourage feedback and open discussion. Facilitate a reflection session where participants share key takeaways and discuss how they can apply CET insights in their entrepreneurial endeavors.

Conclusion: By engaging in this activity, readers will develop a deeper understanding of Cognitive Evaluation Theory and its implications for entrepreneurship. They will gain practical insights into how motivation and evaluation can influence entrepreneurial behavior, creativity, and decision-making. Encourage participants to continue exploring the topic further and apply CET principles to their entrepreneurial journeys.

3.12 Planned Behavior

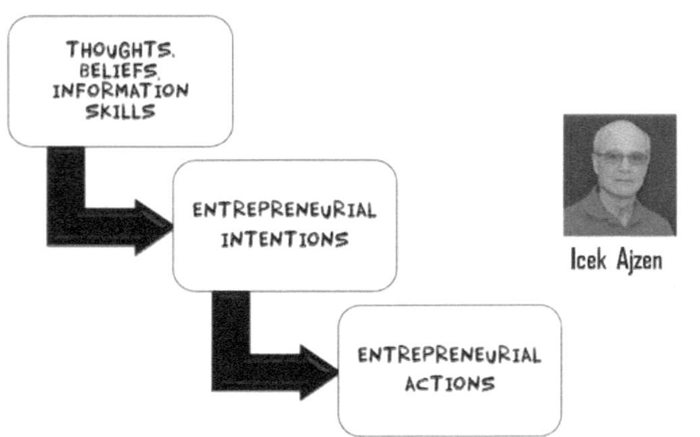

It was developed by Polish social psychologist Icek Ajzen (1991) to predict a variety of social behaviors in different fields including consumer behavior, politics, and healthcare. According to the Theory, the most important determinants of an individual's behaviors is their intention to engage in the behavior—not their attitudes toward behaviors as these are only expected to affect intentions. Thus, for example, if a potential voter has the intention to vote they are more likely to vote than if they merely think voting is a good thing to do. The Theory hangs on the concept of intentions, which are defined as an individual's motivation and conscious decision or plan to expend effort to bring about a behavior. The link between intention and action is expected to be stronger when there is a short time gap between them and when there is an appropriate level of specificity between the intention and the action to be taken. Continuing our example, if a voter has an intention to vote in a nearing election at a specified location and for a specified party and level of government, they are more likely to carry out their intention. When applied to entrepreneurship, the Theory suggests that engaging in entrepreneurship is intentional and therefore is better predicted by intentions as opposed to personality, demographic characteristics, attitudes, or beliefs. It suggests full mediation, such that studies should always use exogenous factors to predict an individual's intention to become an entrepreneur & not propose models that link exogenous factors directly to entrepreneurial behaviors.

Understanding the "Planned Behaviour" theory:
The theory of planned behavior suggests that individuals' behavior is shaped by their attitudes, subjective norms, and perceived behavioral control. For example, a company wants to encourage its employees to participate in a company-wide sustainability initiative to reduce the organization's carbon footprint. The company believes that its employees' attitudes, perceived social norms, and perceived behavioral control will play a critical role in whether they choose to participate in the initiative. The company creates a survey to assess employees' attitudes towards sustainability and the initiative, their perceptions of what others in the organization think about sustainability, and their perceived ability to make a difference. Based on the results of the survey, the company designs a campaign to promote the initiative that addresses any negative attitudes, highlights the positive social norms within the organization, and provides support and resources to help employees make a meaningful contribution. By using the theory of planned behavior, the company can better understand what drives employees' behavior and design interventions that are more likely to be effective. By promoting positive attitudes, social norms, and perceived behavioral control, the company can increase the likelihood that employees will participate in the initiative and help achieve the company's sustainability goals.

Classroom Activity: Application of Theory of Planned Behaviour

Objective: To help readers understand and apply the Theory of Planned Behaviour (TPB) in the context of entrepreneurship. By engaging in this activity, readers will gain a deeper understanding of the factors that influence entrepreneurial intentions and behavior.
Duration: 130 – 150 mins
Materials: Pen and paper or digital note-taking tool, Access to relevant resources on TPB (books, articles, online sources)

Instructions:

Activity	Instructions
Introduction (10 mins)	Begin the session by providing a brief introduction to the (TPB). Explain that TPB is a well-established psychological theory that helps predict & understand human behavior in various contexts. Emphasize TPB's three key factors: attitudes, subjective norms, & perceived behavioral control. Describe how these factors shape an individual's intentions & ultimately their behavior with real-world examples.
Small Group Discussions (20 mins)	Assign small groups consisting of 3-5 members a specific entrepreneurial scenario or case study each. Scenarios could include starting a tech startup, opening a local coffee shop, or launching an e-commerce business. Provide clear instructions on the objectives of the discussions, emphasize on the analysis of attitudes, subjective norms, and perceived behavioral control in relation to the given scenario.
Analyzing the Entrepreneurial Scenario (40 mins)	Groups analyze assigned entrepreneurial scenarios based on TPB's three key factors. For attitudes, groups will discuss and identify the various attitudes & beliefs individuals might have towards starting a business in the given scenario. Consider the positive & negative aspects associated with the venture, such as potential risks, rewards, personal values, & motivations. Regarding subjective norms, groups delve into social influences impacting an individual's decision to start a business in the specific context. For e.g., Opinions, expectations, and norms set by family, friends, mentors, or society at large. Lastly, for perceived behavioral control, groups discuss and identify factors (knowledge, skills, resources, external constraints, & potential barriers) influencing an individual's perception of their ability to perform the entrepreneurial behavior successfully.
Group Presentations (40 mins)	After discussions, allocate time for each group to present their analysis of the entrepreneurial scenario based on the TPB factors. Each group should explain their reasoning behind their analysis and provide relevant examples to support their points. Encourage active listening and facilitate a constructive question-and-answer session after each presentation to promote further engagement & understanding among participants.

Reflection and Application (15 mins)	Allow readers to reflect on the insights gained from applying the TPB. Facilitate a conversation on how the theory can help entrepreneurs better understand their own intentions and behaviors, as well as those of potential customers, employees, and stakeholders. Encourage participants to share their key takeaways and discuss practical applications of the theory in real-world entrepreneurial contexts.
Optional Extension (Varies)	Further, encourage readers to apply the TPB to their own entrepreneurial aspirations or experiences. Prompt them to reflect on their own attitudes, subjective norms, and perceived behavioral control in relation to their entrepreneurial goals & discuss how the theory can help decision-making process & potentially influence their future actions and outcomes.

Conclusion: Through small group discussions, analysis of entrepreneurial scenarios, and reflective discussions, readers gained a deeper understanding of attitudes, subjective norms, and perceived behavioral control. The TPB framework offers entrepreneurs a powerful tool to better understand their own motivations and make informed decisions in their entrepreneurial journeys.

3.13 Resilience

Resilience is the ability to get up after you fall, whether it be physically, psychologically, cognitively, financially, socially, or economically. Resilience is expected to be an important capability of entrepreneurs because they typically face numerous failures on their way to eventual success. The idea of resilience as a virtue for entrepreneurs is appealing because it soothes the failed or failing entrepreneur. It involves a belief that continuing on despite setbacks is better than withdrawing from entrepreneurial activities. For example, the popular idea of the pivot implies the need to change directions as reality comes into focus. Ayala and Manzano (2014) find that Spanish small business owners are more resilient than the general population, highlighting the sub-construct of resourcefulness. Bullough, Renko and Myatt (2014) focus on entrepreneurs during times of war, who show great resilience in the face of danger. Entrepreneurial resilience is a borrowed Theory, arguably from evolutionary theories, where resilience increases survival and reproductive success. Like all borrowed theories, it suffers from the limitation that while it may apply to entrepreneurs, they do not monopolize it. Even if there is a strong link between entrepreneurship and resilience, there is likely also a link between resilience and other things, like success in battle, or managerial effectiveness. Entrepreneurial intentions are now widely studied with many researchers trying to predict intention formation with a wide variety of antecedents such as self-efficacy and human capital. However, there is still some skepticism about the Theory because entrepreneurial intentions do not always translate into entrepreneurial action. Sometime entrepreneurial action is not called for, and promoting entrepreneurial intentions may not be helpful if other factors are not in place.

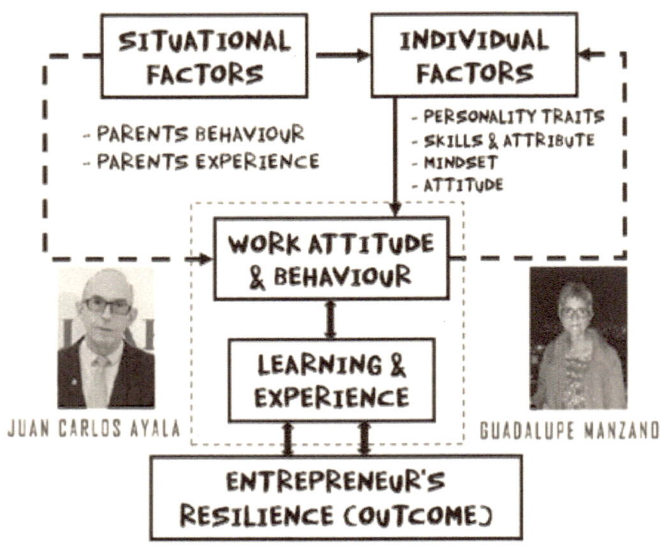

Understanding the "Resilience" theory:

Resilience is the ability of a business to withstand and adapt to challenging situations, such as economic downturns, natural disasters, or unexpected disruptions. For example, a small retail store faces a sudden drop in sales due to the COVID-19 pandemic. The store owner realizes that continuing to operate as usual is not feasible and decides to pivot the business to an online platform. The owner invests in e-commerce infrastructure, creates a website, and promotes the store's products on social media. By taking swift action and adapting to the new circumstances, the store can maintain a steady stream of revenue and even expand its customer base. The store also continues to offer curbside pickup and delivery options to accommodate customers who prefer to shop in person. By being proactive and adaptable, businesses can remain relevant and competitive in changing markets.

Classroom Activity: Building Resilience in Entrepreneurship

Objective: To help readers understand, develop & build resilience strategies in the context of entrepreneurship. Resilience is a crucial trait for entrepreneurs to possess. It enables us to navigate challenges, adapt to changing circumstances, and bounce back from failures.

Duration: 105 – 120 mins

Material: Pen/pencil for each participant, Blank sheets of paper or index cards, Flipchart paper or whiteboard and Markers

Instructions:

Activity	Instructions
Intro (10 mins)	Explain how resilience relates to the ability to persevere, handle setbacks, and maintain a positive mindset in the face of challenges. Highlight the importance of resilience in startup journey.
Case Study Analysis (20 mins)	Provide participants with a case study that showcases a successful entrepreneur who faced significant obstacles and setbacks but managed to overcome them. Ask participants to read the case study individually and identify the specific challenges the entrepreneur encountered and the strategies they employed to overcome them.
Group Discussion (20 mins)	Create groups and facilitate a discussion about the case study. Ask them to share their observations and insights. Use following guiding questions: • What key challenges did the entrepreneur face in the case study? • What actions or strategies did the entrepreneur employ to overcome those challenges? • How did the entrepreneur's resilience contribute to their success? • Can you relate any of the challenges or strategies to your own entrepreneurial experiences?
Personal Resilience Assessment (15 mins)	Provide a resilience assessment tool or questionnaire focused on entrepreneurship. Ask participants to individually assess their own resilience levels by answering the questions honestly. The assessment can cover areas such as emotional resilience, adaptability, problem-solving skills, & self-belief.

Reflection and Action Planning (20 mins)	After completing the assessment, encourage participants to reflect on their results and identify areas where they would like to improve their resilience. Ask them to think about specific strategies or actions they can take to enhance their resilience in those areas. Provide a worksheet or template for participants to document their reflections and action plans.
Group Sharing (15 mins)	Invite participants to share their reflections and action plans with the larger group. Encourage participants to learn from each other's insights & offer suggestions or support where applicable.
Wrap-up (5 mins)	Conclude the activity by summarizing the key points discussed during the session. Remind participants that building resilience is an ongoing process and encourage them to implement their action plans in their entrepreneurial journey. Invite guest speakers who have experienced entrepreneurship challenges and demonstrate resilience to share their stories and insights.

Conclusion: Resilience is a vital trait for entrepreneurs, enabling them to overcome challenges, maintain a positive mindset, and achieve success. Through case studies, discussions, and personal assessments, participants gained insights into the qualities and strategies that contribute to resilience. The activity emphasized that building resilience is an ongoing process and encouraged participants to implement action plans in their entrepreneurial journeys.

Managerial Theories

4.1 Stakeholder

The stakeholder Theory is being developed by (Laplume, Walker, Zhang & Yu, 2020) authors and associates, but has roots in a debate that had occurred between professors Ron Mitchell and S. Venkataraman in 2002, over the connections between stakeholder Theory (Freeman, 1984) and entrepreneurship. Stakeholder Theory had largely been born out of studies of large corporations managing their stakeholders to improve firm performance (i.e., between incumbent competitors), and had not been fully applied to the entrepreneurship area to explain entrepreneurial behaviors, processes, or outcomes. They were discussing how entrepreneurship and strategy research tends to be about how new wealth is created, whereas stakeholder Theory is more about how that wealth should be distributed. For the latter author, the value creation and distribution issues were separate problems, complementary perhaps, but requiring different logics. The theory seeks to integrate the wealth creation and redistribution problem. Developed economies feature some degree of competition among incumbents of innovations that can become valuable. Many of the best (read: most profitable) business opportunities are being vigorously explored. Let us adopt the premise that from the entrepreneurial new entrant's perspective, entrepreneurial opportunities emerge from the appearance of a marginalized stakeholder. The cause of this stakeholder's marginalization is the set of strategic choices that incumbent firm managers have made to balance stakeholder interests optimally. Entrepreneurial opportunities are born out of stakeholder imbalances, as entrepreneurs discover business models for marginalized stakeholders. There are often strategic reasons behind investments in stakeholders, such as focusing on the set of stakeholders that contribute resources to the firm that combine into a self-reinforcing bundle that is valuable, rare & hard to imitated (Barney, 2018). Therefore, entrepreneurial opportunities are a natural part of economic processes involving the pursuit of competitive advantage. The theory has interesting implications for entrepreneurship practice because it suggests broadening the customer discovery process into a stakeholder discovery process. The shift is important because the theory recognizes the sources of entrepreneurial opportunities as catering to under-served stakeholders in the current incumbent regime. Customers are just one of the several key stakeholders that entrepreneurs should pay attention to.

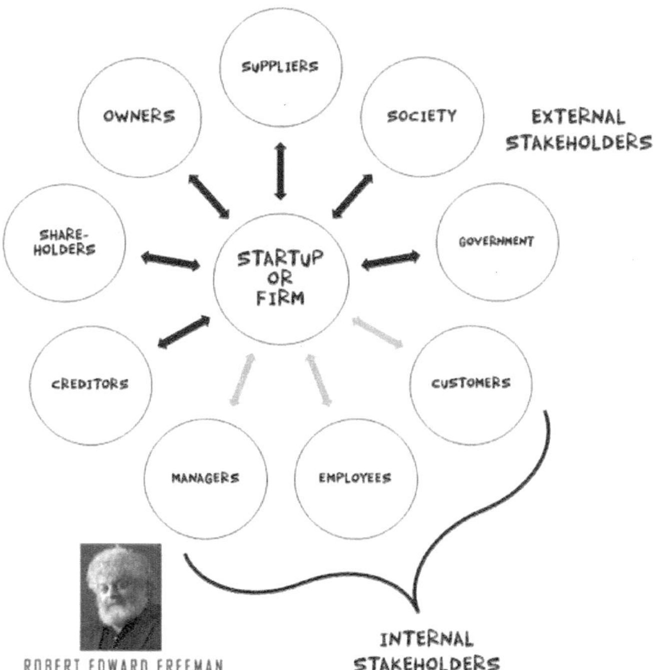

ROBERT EDWARD FREEMAN

Understanding the "Stakeholder" theory:
Stakeholders are individuals or groups who have an interest or concern in a business, such as employees, customers, investors, suppliers, and the community. For example, a food company recognizes that its products have an impact on the health of its customers and the environment. The company decides to engage with stakeholders to understand their concerns and incorporate their feedback into its business practices. The company starts by conducting surveys and focus groups with customers to better understand their dietary

preferences and concerns. Based on this feedback, the company develops new products that meet customer demand for healthier and more sustainable food options. The company also works with suppliers to ensure that the ingredients used in its products are sourced responsibly and sustainably. Additionally, the company partners with community organizations to promote healthy eating and support local food banks. The company also provides training and development opportunities for its employees to enhance their skills and advance their careers. By engaging with stakeholders, the company can create value for both its customers & society.

Classroom Activity: Stakeholder Impact Mapping

Objective: To deepen the understanding of stakeholders and their impact on a business or entrepreneurial venture through mapping.
Duration: 65 – 90 mins
Materials: Large whiteboard or flip chart paper, Marker pens in different colors, Sticky notes or index cards & Pens or pencils for participants
Instructions:

Activity	Instructions
Intro (5 mins)	Introduce the concept of Stakeholder Theory, explaining that stakeholders are individuals or groups who have a vested interest in or are affected by a business or venture. Emphasize how it is crucial for the success of any entrepreneurial endeavor.
Brain-storming (10 mins)	Ask participants to brainstorm and write down as many stakeholders as they can think of for a hypothetical or real-life entrepreneurial venture. Encourage them to think beyond the obvious stakeholders such as customers and investors. Provide examples if needed (e.g., employees, suppliers, community, government, etc.).
Groups (10 mins)	Divide the participants into small groups (3-4 people per group) and provide each group with a large whiteboard or flip chart paper and marker pens. Instruct each group to create a stakeholder impact map by drawing a large circle in the center of the whiteboard/paper and labeling it as the "Entrepreneurial Venture." Next, ask each group to choose one stakeholder from their brainstormed list and draw a smaller circle around the central circle, connecting it with a line. Inside the smaller circle, they should write the name of the stakeholder.

Stakeholder Mapping (15 mins)	Then, ask the groups to discuss and identify the potential impact that stakeholders could have on the venture. They should write down the positive and negative impacts around the smaller circle, using different colors to differentiate between positive and negative impacts. Encourage them to think about both direct and indirect impacts. Repeat this process for each stakeholder the group identified, connect & map them.
Presentations and Discussion (15 mins)	Ask each group to present their stakeholder impact map to the rest of the participants. Each group should explain their mapping choices and discuss the potential positive and negative impacts identified for each stakeholder. Encourage the participants to ask questions, provide feedback, and engage in a discussion about the stakeholder impact maps & how their impacts can influence each other.
Reflection & Application (10 mins)	Conclude the activity by facilitating a group reflection. Ask participants to share their key insights and takeaways from the stakeholder impact mapping exercise. Discuss how this activity can be applied to real-life entrepreneurial scenarios and decision-making processes.
Optional Extension (Varies)	To deepen the learning experience, you can provide participants with real-life case studies or scenarios and ask them to create stakeholder impact maps based on the specific context provided. This will help participants apply their knowledge of stakeholder theory to practical situations & analyze the potential impacts critically.

Conclusion: The activity proves to be an engaging and insightful exercise in understanding the importance of stakeholders in entrepreneurial ventures. Through brainstorming, mapping, and group discussions, participants gain a deeper understanding of stakeholder impacts and the interconnectedness between various stakeholders. This activity highlights the significance of considering stakeholder needs and perspectives in decision-making processes, providing valuable insights applicable to real-life entrepreneurial scenarios.

4.2 Contingency

This theory proposes that an organization's performance is determined by the fit between its resources, structure, and strategies on one hand, and the external environmental conditions on the other hand (e.g., political, economic, social, technological). A core concept in contingency Theory is fit. Fitness is viewed as a match between the organization's characteristics and the characteristics of the environments around them. At the heart of the Theory is the assumption of equifinality, that is, that there are many ways to achieve performance and that the right way depends upon the conditions in the environment of the firm in question (Lawrence and Lorsch, 1967). This also implies that a one-size-fits-all approach to strategy is doomed to fail. For example, when a firm's technological environment is characterized by rapid change or turbulence, then a firm may perform better with a more organic structure (flatter hierarchy, less formal control, etc...), whereas when a firm's technological environment is stable, then a more mechanistic structure (top down, centralized, formal) may be better (Miller and Toulouse, 1986). Entrepreneurship researchers have found support for contingency Theory in new ventures too. For instance, Chowdhury (2011) finds that new ventures dealing with complex customer environments should avoid high levels of formalization as compared with those facing simpler customer environments. Wiklund and Shepard (2005) had demonstrated that CEOs with an entrepreneurial orientation help the firms to greater success in dynamic environments with low capital availability.

Understanding the "Contingency" theory:

The theory suggests that there is no single best way to manage a business, and that the most effective management style depends on the specific situation. For example, a manufacturing company is considering implementing a new management system to improve efficiency and reduce costs. The company's leadership team recognizes that there is no one-size-fits-all approach, and that the best management system will depend on the specific characteristics of the organization. To determine the most effective management system, the company conducts a thorough analysis of its internal and external environment, including its organizational structure, culture, technology, and competitive landscape. Based on this analysis, the company identifies several potential management systems that could be effective in improving efficiency and reducing costs. To determine the most appropriate management system, the company tests each system in a small pilot program, measuring the results and gathering feedback from employees and stakeholders. After analyzing the results and feedback, the company selects the management system that is most effective in its specific context. By using a contingency approach, the company can tailor its management system to its unique organizational context, which can lead to improved performance and competitiveness. The company recognizes that what works for one organization may not work for another, and by taking a contingency approach, it is able to find the management system that is most effective in its specific context.

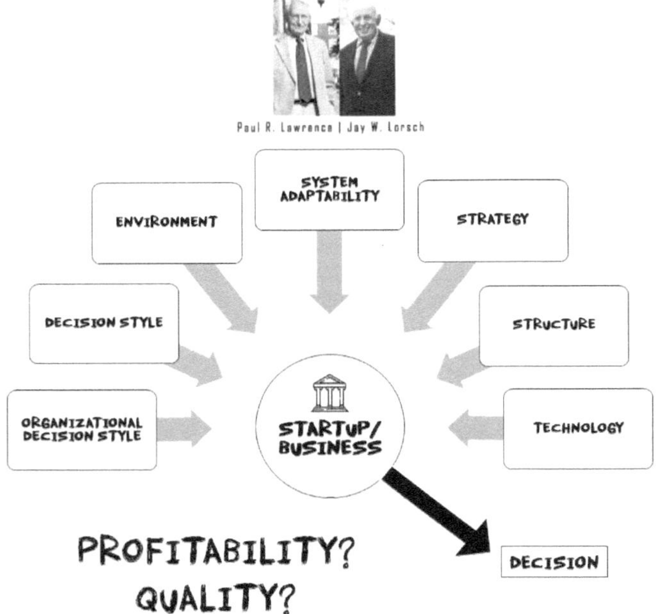

Classroom Activity: Contingency Theory Challenge

Objective: To deepen participants' understanding of contingency theory, a key concept in entrepreneurship, and apply it to real-world scenarios. By engaging in this challenge, they will develop critical thinking skills and explore the importance of adapting your entrepreneurial approach based on different situational factors.

Duration: 60 – 90 mins

Material: Large whiteboard or flip chart paper, Marker pens in different colors, Sticky notes & Pens or pencils.

Activity	Instructions
Intro (5 mins)	Begin by providing a brief overview of the theory, explaining its significance in entrepreneurship. Highlight the key idea that there is no universal approach to entrepreneurship, & success depends on adapting strategies to match the specific circumstances.

Scenario Selection (5 mins)	Divide participants into small groups or pairs. Assign each group a specific scenario related to entrepreneurship. Scenarios can be based on industry-specific challenges, market conditions, or organizational contexts. Examples of scenarios: • Launching a tech startup in a highly competitive market. • Starting a small retail business during an economic recession. • Expanding an existing business into a new international market. Dealing with disruptive technological advancements in an established industry.
Analysis and Discussion (20 mins)	In their respective groups, participants should analyze the given scenario from a contingency theory perspective. Encourage participants to discuss the various situational factors that could influence their entrepreneurial approach, such as competition, resources, market conditions, technological advancements, and regulatory factors. Participants should identify specific aspects of the scenario that require adaptation & discuss potential strategies for each situation.
Presentation and Debate (15 mins)	Each group will present their findings and recommendations to the other participants. After each presentation, encourage open discussion and debate among all participants, allowing for the exchange of ideas and alternative perspectives. Facilitate a conversation on the benefits and challenges of adopting a contingency approach in entrepreneurship.
Reflection and Conclusion (5 mins)	Wrap up the activity by summarizing the main takeaways from the discussions and presentations. Emphasize the importance of recognizing that there is no one-size-fits-all approach to entrepreneurship, and success depends on adapting strategies to align with the specific context. Encourage participants to reflect on how they can apply contingency theory principles in their own entrepreneurial endeavors.
Role-playing Element (30 mins)	For a more interactive experience, you can introduce a role-playing element where participants take on the roles of entrepreneurs facing the given scenarios. They can engage in a simulated decision-making process, discussing and negotiating their strategies based on the principles of contingency theory.

Conclusion: The theory provides valuable insights into the dynamic nature of entrepreneurship and the significance of adapting strategies to match specific circumstances. We learned that there is no one-size-fits-all approach to entrepreneurship, and success depends on the ability to identify and adapt to the unique challenges and opportunities presented by each situation. By applying the principles of contingency theory, we gained a deeper understanding of how flexibility, adaptability, and strategic decision-making play crucial roles in entrepreneurial success. As we reflect on this activity, let us carry forward the lessons learned and apply them in our own entrepreneurial endeavors, recognizing that our ability to adjust and tailor our strategies to specific contexts will ultimately shape our journey towards success.

4.3 Disruptive Innovation

This Theory of was developed by Harvard Business School professor Clayton Christensen in his famous book entitled The Innovator's Dilemma (2003). Christensen's core argument is that new entrants succeed when they pursue disruptive innovation whereas incumbents tend to pursue sustaining innovations. Disruptive innovations are technologies, products and business models that are lower performing than incumbent offerings along traditional dimensions of performance, but compensate with increased simplify, convenience, customizability, or affordability. For example, the Nintendo Wii disrupted the Xbox and Sony Playstation by offering lower quality graphics in exchange for the simplicity in the intuitive movements offered by gyroscopic technology added to the controllers. This allowed younger children, game novices, and older gamers to be able to learn to play with a minimal learning curve. Sustaining innovations, on the other hand, improve technologies, products, and business models along traditional performance dimensions. For instance, the movie theater incumbents are pushing 3D movies, which offer increased stimuli over the visual sense. New entrants, such as startups, are able to defeat incumbents with disruptive innovations because they come in at the bottom of the market, offering marginal customers solutions that are good enough for them, but not yet good enough for expert users. For instance, while the Wii attracted many new users to console gaming, it did not affect the market share of PC games catering to hard core gamers. Incumbents typically respond to disruptive innovations by moving up-market, pursuing higher margin customers rather than competing on the low end. This is often a mistake, however, because new entrants quickly improve their innovations until they start to challenge the incumbents in mainstream markets. One suggestion is that incumbents should create new divisions to compete along disruptive dimensions, but this approach is difficult because it implies a certain level of self-cannibalization. While the Theory has gained popularity, empirical studies have found mixed support for the Theory (Markides, 2006). There is some evidence that incumbent firms are becoming increasingly willing to be the disruptors, and even to self-disrupt. This may be a result of the Actor's widespread use in teaching in business school with curricula around managing innovations. Perhaps after two decades of grads with exposure to the Theory penetrating the ranks of management, organizations are learning to harness disruption rather than being disrupted by newcomers.

Understanding the "Disruption" theory:

Disruptive innovation theory, popularized by Clayton M. Christensen, refers to the process by which new technologies, products, or services enter the market and eventually disrupt and replace established products or services.

Global Examples of disrupted industries:

Personal Computers (PCs): They disrupted the mainframe computer industry. PCs were smaller, more affordable, and user-friendly compared to mainframes, which were large and expensive. This disruption led to the decline of many mainframe computer companies.

Digital Photography: The advent of digital cameras disrupted the traditional film photography industry. Digital cameras offered instant results, easier editing, and the ability to store and share photos digitally. This disrupted film manufacturers, photo labs, and companies associated with the analog photography ecosystem.

Mobile Phones: They revolutionized the telecommunications industry. Initially, they were bulky and expensive, but over time, they became smaller, more affordable, and packed with features.

Indian Examples disruptive companies:

Paytm: It disrupted the traditional cash-based economy in India. It offered a convenient way for people to make digital transactions using their smartphones. Paytm's success led to a surge in digital payments and compelled traditional banking institutions to enhance their digital offerings.

Ola and Uber: It disrupted the traditional taxi industry in India. They provided a user-friendly app-based platform for booking rides, offering competitive pricing, and convenient payment options. This disrupted traditional taxi services and created a new market for on-demand transportation.

Jio: It disrupted the telecom industry by offering affordable 4G data services. Jio's entry into the market led to a drastic reduction in data prices, making internet access more accessible to a larger population. This disruption forced other telecom operators to revise their pricing and data plans.

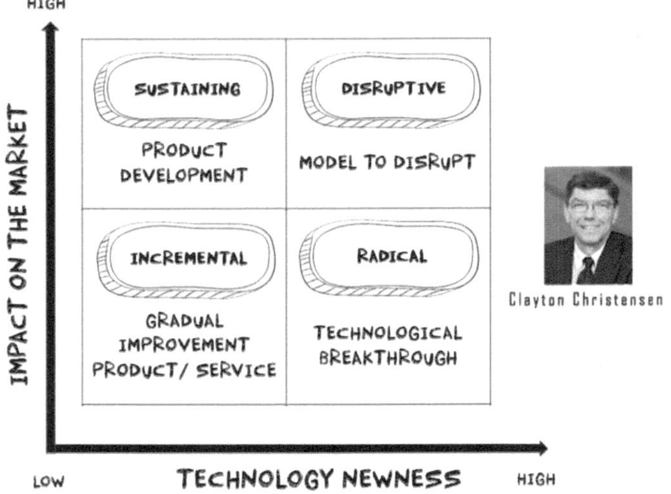

Classroom Activity: Unleashing Creative Solutions

Objective: To engage readers in exploring the concept of disruptive innovation and its implications for entrepreneurship. By participating in a simulation, readers will develop a deeper understanding of the theory and apply it to real-world scenarios.

Duration: 130 – 150 mins

Material: Large whiteboard or flip chart paper, Marker pens in different colors, Sticky notes or index cards & Pens or pencils for participants

Instructions:

Activity	Instructions
Intro (15 mins)	Provide a brief overview of disruptive innovation theory, explaining core concepts like disruptive vs. sustaining innovation, understanding customer needs, and potential for industry disruption. Share examples of successful disruptive innovations (e.g., Uber, Airbnb) to illustrate the theory in action.

Selecting an Industry (10 mins)	Divide readers into small teams of 4-5 participants, encouraging diverse backgrounds and skill sets to foster a broader perspective. Instruct each team to select an industry of interest or relevance, such as transportation, healthcare, education, or entertainment. This industry will be the focus for the remainder of the activity.
Identifying Existing Solutions (15 mins)	Ask teams to identify and analyze existing solutions within their chosen industry. Consider dominant players, their products/services, and the customer needs they address. Encourage critical thinking about potential gaps or unmet needs.
Discuss Disruptive Ideas (20 mins)	Instruct teams to brainstorm disruptive ideas that could reshape their chosen industry. Encourage creative thinking and exploration of alternative approaches to solving existing problems. Remind them that disruptive innovations often start by targeting underserved or overlooked customer segments.
Develop a Concept (20 mins)	Teams select one compelling concept from their disruptive ideas and refine and develop it further. Consider feasibility, potential impact, and sustainability. Encourage thinking beyond incremental improvements and embracing radical changes.
Pitch & Discuss (20 mins)	Each team presents their disruptive innovation concept to the other participants. Facilitate a discussion where teams provide feedback, ask questions, and evaluate the viability and potential challenges of each concept.
Reflection and Discussion (15 mins)	Conclude the activity with a reflection and discussion session. Participants share key takeaways from the simulation and discuss how disruptive innovation theory can be applied to real-world entrepreneurial endeavors. Encourage consideration of the potential risks, opportunities, and ethical implications of disruptive innovations.

Conclusion: The activity provides readers with an immersive and engaging experience to understand the theory and its application in entrepreneurship. Through team collaboration, industry analysis, and creative ideation, participants gained practical insights into identifying disruptive opportunities. The reflection and discussion session deepened their understanding of the potential impacts and ethical considerations of disruptive innovations, equipping them with valuable knowledge for real-world entrepreneurial endeavors.

4.4 Strategic Disagreements

Steven Klepper (2007) was an American economist at Carnegie Mellon University. He introduced the used the concept of strategic disagreements to explain a particular type of entrepreneurship commonly referred to as spinout (or employee spinoff) entrepreneurship. Klepper credited spinouts with the creation of clusters like Silicon Valley and Detroit. A spinout occurs when an employee of a firm leaves to start a new business. Most spinout entrepreneurs create ventures that compete indirectly with their employers by pursuing new strategies or going after new markets with differentiated products. However, the seeds of spinout ventures often originate in parent firms. For instance, many entrepreneurs report that they are exploiting ideas that were generated inside of the organizations of their previous employers (Bhide, 1994). Strategic disagreements refer to disagreements between employees and managers regarding the prospects of new ideas or new projects. For instance, an employee may believe that the firm should pursue a new technology, but the management of the firm may choose not to do so (Thompson and Chen, 2011). Conversely, the management of a firm may choose to exploit new technology, but the employee may not want to do so, believing instead that continued exploitation of the current technology is more efficient or effective. These types of disagreement encourage employees to leave to start their own ventures. Strategic disagreements are viewed as inevitable because firms often produce many more ideas than they can exploit. Firms that narrow their strategies and encourage their employees to explore within them may produce fewer spinouts (Stieglitz and Heine, 2007), whereas more diversified firms may encourage the pursuit of an excessively broad set of ideas and projects that can multiply the potential for strategic disagreements.

Understanding the "Strategic Disagreements" theory:

Strategic disagreements can arise in a business when different stakeholders have different views on how the company should be run or what direction it should take. For example, a large retail company is facing declining sales and increased competition from online retailers. The company's CEO believes that the best way to compete is to invest heavily in the development of an online presence, including a new e-commerce platform and marketing campaign. However, the CFO is concerned about the cost of this investment and believes that the company should focus on cutting costs and improving the efficiency of its existing brick-and-mortar stores. Meanwhile, the head of marketing believes that the company should invest more in traditional advertising campaigns to build brand awareness and drive foot traffic to stores. These strategic disagreements can create tension and uncertainty within the organization. To address these disagreements, the company convenes a series of meetings to facilitate open and honest discussion about each stakeholder's position. The company also hires an outside consultant to provide an objective perspective and help find common ground. Through this process, the company can develop a new strategic plan that incorporates the perspectives of each stakeholder. The plan includes investments in the online platform, cost-cutting measures in the physical stores, and a new marketing campaign that leverages both digital and traditional channels. By addressing strategic disagreements in a constructive and collaborative manner, the company can develop a more comprehensive and effective strategy that leverages the strengths of each perspective.

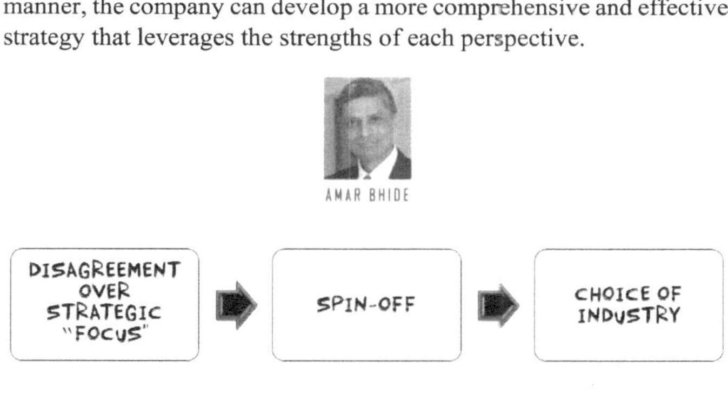

Classroom Activity: Strategic Disagreements Simulation

Objective: To explore the concept of the theory & its implications in entrepreneurship and business decision-making.

Duration: 85 – 100 mins

Material: Large whiteboard or flip chart paper, Marker pens in different colors, Sticky notes or index cards & Pens or pencils for participants

Instructions:

Activity	Instructions
Intro (5 mins)	Introduce the theory & explain that it focuses on how strategic disagreements among individuals or groups within an organization can lead to better decision-making and innovation. Highlight the importance of diverse perspectives and constructive conflicts in shaping strategic choices and outcomes.

Group (5 mins)	Divide participants into small groups of 4-5 members each. Encourage participants to form diverse groups by considering their different backgrounds, experiences, and perspectives.
Case Study (10 mins)	Provide each group with a case study that presents a strategic decision-making scenario. The case study should include multiple viable options and potential pros and cons for each option. Emphasize that the goal is not to find a single "correct" solution but to encourage differing opinions and perspectives within the group.
Self-View (10 mins)	Ask each participant to spend a few mins individually reviewing the case study and selecting the option they believe is the best. Encourage participants to write down their reasons for selecting that option.
Group Discussion (15 mins)	Instruct the groups to discuss the case study and their individual choices within their group. Encourage participants to share their perspectives, reasoning, and any potential concerns or disagreements with the other group members. Emphasize the importance of active listening, respecting diverse viewpoints, and fostering a constructive and open-minded environment.
Strategic (10 mins)	Facilitate a group discussion on the concept of strategic disagreements. Ask the groups to reflect on the benefits and challenges of strategic disagreements within an organization. Encourage participants to consider how strategic disagreements can lead to better decision-making, innovation, and avoiding groupthink.
Consensus Building (10 mins)	Challenge the groups to find common ground and reach a consensus on the best option for the case study. Encourage participants to consider the insights gained through the strategic disagreements and how they can be leveraged to improve the decision-making process.
Pitch (15 mins)	Ask each group to present their consensus decision to the rest of the participants. Allow time for questions and comments from the other groups, fostering further discussions and reflections.
Wrap-up (5 mins)	Summarize the main takeaways from the activity, emphasizing the value of strategic disagreements in entrepreneurship and decision-making. Encourage participants to apply the principles of the Theory of Strategic Disagreements in their future endeavors and to embrace diverse perspectives and constructive conflicts.

Conclusion: By embracing disagreements, participants discover how they can foster innovation, avoid group thinking, and make better strategic choices. The activity culminates in consensus building and reflections, empowering participants to apply these principles in their entrepreneurial journeys.

4.5 First Mover Advantage

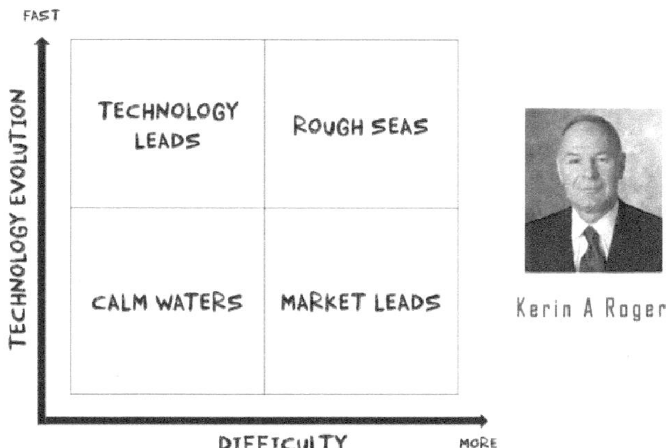

Should entrepreneurs strive to be first? This is an important question that is relevant to myriads of decisions that entrepreneurs make involving commitments of resources and attention. For instance, given the option to implement two ideas, one with early entry potential and the other with late entry potential, which should an entrepreneur run with? According to Kerin et al. (1992), "studies purport to demonstrate the presence of a systematic direct relationship between order of entry for products, brands, or businesses and market share." First mover advantage Theory posits that new entrants that are earliest to a new market niche get several advantages, such as brand awareness and a reputation for innovativeness. Followers can build great brands too, though at a greater cost. Another first movers' advantage is the ability to tie up factor markets by engaging in long term contracts with key suppliers, which makes it harder for followers to acquire the necessary complementary assets to compete. Tying up suppliers only works if there are few quality suppliers available. First movers may also ride down the experience curve ahead of rivals creating barriers to entry. In general, this advantage is only sustainable if followers have fewer resources to be able to speed down the experience curve even faster, then catch up and surpass the leader. There are some reasons to question the notion of first mover advantage. Startups usually occur in clusters where more than one entrepreneur independently pushes a business model, product, or technology. After a technological discontinuity, many individuals independently pursue the next logical business innovation, forming a cohort of competing new ventures known as the fermentation stage (Tushman and Anderson, 1986). Interestingly, evolutionary theories of technological innovation tend to discount the first mover, arguing instead that the first mover takes on extra costs (e.g., training customers and basic research) that the second mover does not need to bear. Followers can benefit from the leader's wake of supplier training and research and development spillovers and use reverse engineering to save on development time. This cost advantage is enough in the early stages of an industry to make the difference between winning and losing. Teece (1986) suggests that first movers usually win only if followers don't have access to the intellectual property needed to imitate, or when the followers lack the complementary assets (manufacturing, distribution, & marketing) needed to compete effectively. Entrepreneurs need to compare themselves with the incumbent firms & size up their ability to compete.

Understanding the "First Mover" theory:
A first mover in the business context refers to a company that is the first to enter a particular market or introduce a new product or service. For example, Amazon is a prime example of a first mover in the e-commerce market. In the mid-1990s, Amazon was one of the first companies to sell books online, a market that was previously dominated by brick-and-mortar bookstores. Amazon's early success in this market allowed the company to expand into other retail categories, such as electronics, clothing, and home goods. By being the first mover in the e-commerce space, Amazon was able to establish a dominant position in the market and build a loyal customer base. The company also invested heavily in infrastructure, such as warehouses and distribution centers, which helped to further solidify its competitive advantage. As a first mover, Amazon also faced several challenges, such as developing the technology and logistics necessary to sell products online and building trust with customers who were hesitant to shop online. However, by successfully navigating these challenges, Amazon was able to establish itself as a major player in the e-commerce market and pave the way for other online retailers.

Classroom Activity: Analyzing the First Mover Advantage

Objective: To engage readers in understanding and critically analyzing the concept of the First Mover Advantage in entrepreneurship.

Duration: 80 – 90 mins

Material: Large whiteboard or flip chart paper, Marker pens in different colors, Sticky notes or index cards & Pens or pencils for participants

Instructions:

Activity	Instructions
Introduction (5 mins)	Begin the session by introducing the concept of First Mover Advantage. Explain that it refers to the competitive advantage a business gains by being the first to enter a specific market or introduce a new product/service. Highlight the potential benefits and challenges.
Case Study (5 mins)	Select a relevant case study that illustrates the theory of First Mover Advantage. Choose a real-life example of a business that achieved success or faced challenges as a first mover.
Case Study (15 mins)	Present the selected case study to the participants. Provide relevant details about the company, industry, and the specific product/service. Discuss the factors that contributed to the company's decision to be a first mover and the strategic choices they made.
Group Discussion (20 mins)	Divide participants into small groups. Assign discussion questions related to the case study, prompting analysis of advantages, disadvantages, and outcomes of being a first mover. Example discussion questions: • What were the main advantages the company gained as first mover? • What were the challenges or risks the company faced as a first mover? • How did the company differentiate itself from potential competitors? • What impact did being a first mover have on the company's long-term success?
Pitch (15 mins)	Ask each group to present their findings and insights from the discussion. Encourage participants to engage in a constructive dialogue about the case study.

Take-aways (5 mins)	Summarize the key takeaways from the case study and group discussions. Reiterate the importance of understanding First Mover Advantage in entrepreneurial decision-making.
Reflect (5 mins)	Encourage participants to reflect on how they can apply the concept of First Mover Advantage to their own entrepreneurial ventures or business ideas. Provide additional resources for further exploration.

Conclusion: Exploring the theory of First Mover Advantage through a case study and group discussions helps entrepreneurs understand the strategic implications and potential benefits of being the first to enter a market, fostering informed decision-making in their own ventures.

4.6 Upper Echelons

The underlying assumptions of this theory are that top managers' decision-making processes determine competitive strategies, and that strategies affect firm performance (Hambrick and Mason, 1984). Further, decision-making processes are expected to be affected by the characteristics of individuals in top management as well as the composition of teams. Competitive strategies may include the choice of business strategy, such as low cost, differentiation, and focus strategies. They may also affect corporate strategy such as vertical and horizontal integration, as well as diversification. Business and corporate strategies are well-known to affect the financial performance of firms and new ventures. When applied to entrepreneurial teams, characteristics that have been examined include age, formal education, length of job tenure, and functional experience. Heterogeneity, such as the diversity of functional backgrounds, age and experience, has been found to affect new venture strategy-making (Vanaelst et al., 2006).
Team cohesion and conflict have also been found to affect strategy and performance of new ventures. Because the upper echelons Theory posits that the characteristics of individuals and teams influence their decision-making, it is viewed as a counterbalance to population ecology and institutional perspectives that tend to view individuals as unimportant.

Understanding the "Upper Echelons" theory:
Upper echelons theory suggests that the decisions made by top managers are influenced by their personal characteristics, experiences, and values. For example, Tesla, the electric vehicle and renewable energy company, is often cited as an example of Upper Echelons

theory. CEO Elon Musk has a unique set of personal characteristics, experiences, and values that have influenced the company's decisions and strategy. Musk has a strong passion for sustainable energy and has made it his mission to accelerate the world's transition to electric vehicles and renewable energy. This passion has translated into Tesla's focus on developing cutting-edge electric vehicles, solar panels, and energy storage systems. Musk's personal characteristics and experiences have also influenced Tesla's strategy. For example, he has a strong background in technology and engineering, which has driven Tesla's focus on innovation and developing new technologies. Additionally, Musk's entrepreneurial spirit and willingness to take risks has led Tesla to pursue ambitious goals, such as building a network of Supercharger stations and launching the first electric vehicle to travel 400 miles on a single charge.

DONALD C HAMBRICK | PHYLLIS A. MASON

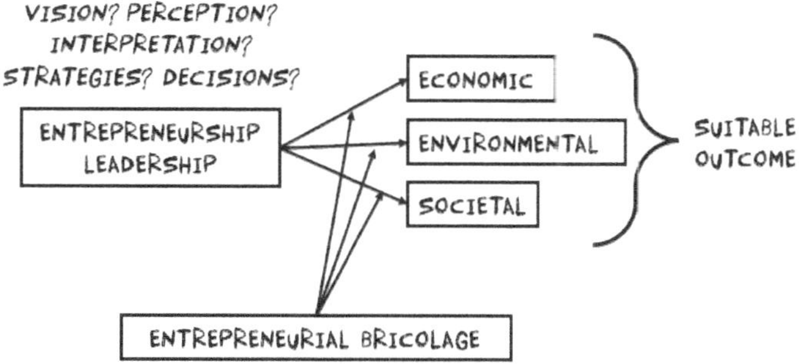

Classroom Activity: "Upper Echelons Decision-Making"

Objective: The objective of this activity is to simulate the decision-making process at the upper echelons of an organization and explore the theory of Upper Echelons in entrepreneurship.

Duration: 75 – 90 mins

Material: Large whiteboard or flip chart paper, Marker pens in different colors, Sticky notes or index cards & Pens or pencils for participants

Instructions:

Activity	Instructions
Intro (5 mins)	Introduce the concept of Upper Echelons theory, explaining how top-level executives' characteristics, experiences, and values influence strategic decision-making in organizations. Emphasize the significance of understanding this theory for entrepreneurs.
Group (5 mins)	Divide participants into small groups (4-5 members per group) and assign roles (CEO, CFO, CMO, COO). Explain that each group will simulate decision-making scenarios at the upper echelons level (fictional company)
Scenario (10 mins)	Provide each group with a decision-making scenario related to a critical strategic issue faced by the company. Give time for groups to read and understand the scenario and background information about the company.
Decision-Making (20 mins)	Instruct each group to discuss the scenario and make a collective decision based on their assigned roles. Encourage consideration of how characteristics and experiences influence decision-making. Remind them to assess potential implications and consequences.
Group Pitch (15 mins)	Ask each group to present their decision and rationale to the participants. Encourage other groups to ask questions and engage in constructive discussions about the decision-making process and the influence of upper echelons.
Reflection & Analysis (15 mins)	Facilitate a group discussion on the findings and insights from the simulation. Encourage reflection on the influence of upper echelons' characteristics, experiences, and values on decision-making outcomes. Discuss advantages & limitations of the theory.
Take-aways (5 mins)	Summarize key takeaways, emphasizing the role of top-level executives in shaping organizational strategies and the importance of considering upper echelons in entrepreneurship.

Conclusion: The decision-making simulation highlights the influence of top-level executives' characteristics on strategic decisions, offering entrepreneurs insights into the importance of understanding and leveraging upper echelons in driving organizational success. By examining these dynamics, entrepreneurs can make more informed decisions and enhance their leadership effectiveness.

4.7 Stewardship

Lex Donaldson and James Davis in the late 1980s came up with Stewardship theory as an alternative to agency theory, which they viewed as having negative assumptions about managers. In contrast to agency theory, stewardship theory posits that managers and entrepreneur are motivated to act in the interests of their organizations and principals. The core idea is that the rewards from pro-social behavior have greater utility than individualistic or self-serving behaviors. The steward receives greater personal satisfaction when the organization is successful and therefore acts accordingly. Since stewards can be trusted to act in accordance with the principals' interests, they should be afforded greater autonomy to act in ways that further the organization's success. Accordingly, there is little need to waste resources monitoring, bonding, or creating incentives for stewards, such controls may reduce the stewards' pro-social behaviors by reducing motivation (Argyris, 1964). Mechanisms that give stewards greater autonomy and discretion include making the CEO the chairman of the board of directors (Donaldson and Davis, 1991). Other studies have, however, found that boards with non-executive chairmen have higher corporate financial performance (Rechner and Dalton, 1991). Recently, Elon Musk was fired as chairman of Tesla Motors' board for tweeting that he planned to take the company private, when he did not have such intentions. This punishment was intended to reduce agency problems.

Understanding the "Stewardship" theory:

Stewardship theory suggests that managers are entrusted with resources and are responsible for managing those resources for the benefit of all stakeholders. For example, the outdoor clothing and gear company Patagonia is often cited as an example of stewardship theory. The company's founder, Yvon Chouinard, has long been committed to environmental and social responsibility, and this commitment is reflected in the company's approach to business. Patagonia has been a leader in using sustainable materials and manufacturing processes and has taken a strong stance on issues like climate change and public lands conservation. The company has also taken steps to reduce its carbon footprint and has pledged to donate 1% of its sales to environmental causes. In addition to its environmental commitments, Patagonia has also been recognized for its employee-focused policies and practices. The company offers on-site childcare, paid time off for volunteering, and other benefits aimed at promoting work-life balance and employee well-being. From Patagonia we can learn how stewardship theory can be put into practice in a business context with a focus on using resources in a responsible and sustainable way and managing the company for the benefit of all stakeholders.

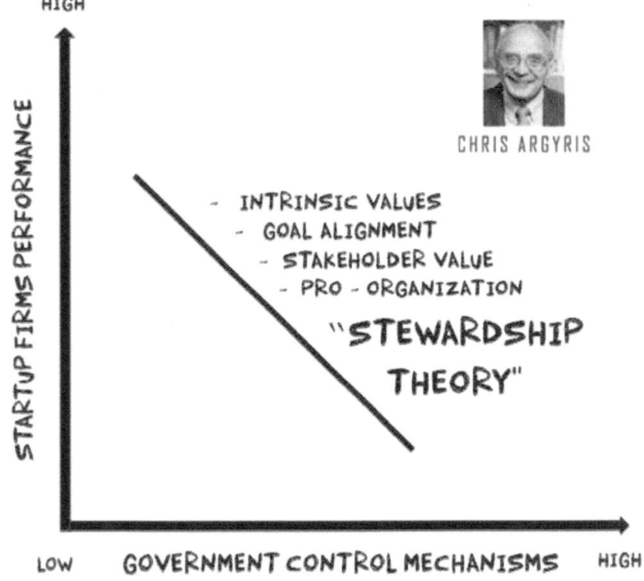

Classroom Activity: "Stewardship Leadership Workshop"

Objective: To explore the theory of Stewardship in entrepreneurship and develop an understanding of the principles and practices of stewardship leadership.

Duration: 90 – 100 mins

Material: Large whiteboard or flip chart paper, Marker pens in different colors, Sticky notes or index cards & Pens or pencils

Instructions:

Activity	Instructions
Intro (5 mins)	Begin the workshop by introducing the concept of Stewardship as a leadership theory emphasizing leaders' responsibility to care for and protect the organization's resources and stakeholders. Explain the importance of stewardship in entrepreneurship.

Steward-ship Principles (10 mins)	Present the key principles of stewardship leadership: accountability, service, trust, empowerment, and long-term orientation. Discuss each principle and provide examples of their manifestation in entrepreneurial contexts.
Case Study Analysis (20 mins)	Divide participants into small groups. Provide each group with a case study of a successful entrepreneurial venture exemplifying stewardship leadership. Instruct the groups to analyze the case study, focusing on identifying instances of stewardship principles.
Group Discussion (15 mins)	Bring groups together for a discussion on the case study analysis. Encourage participants to share observations, insights, and reflections on how stewardship principles influenced the venture's success.
Leadership Exercise (20 mins)	Conduct a role-playing exercise where participants take turns as stewardship leaders in various scenarios. Provide leadership challenges, and participants demonstrate the application of stewardship principles in decision-making and interactions.
Reflection and Sharing (15 mins)	Allow participants time to individually reflect on their experiences and challenges as stewardship leaders. Facilitate a group sharing session where participants discuss lessons learned and the importance of stewardship leadership in entrepreneurship.
Key Take-aways (5 mins)	Summarize key takeaways, emphasizing the role of stewardship in entrepreneurial leadership and its impact on success and sustainability. Highlight the importance of practicing stewardship principles in decision-making and fostering a culture of stewardship.

Conclusion: The Stewardship Leadership Workshop highlights the importance of leaders acting as stewards, fostering a culture of accountability, trust, and long-term orientation in entrepreneurial ventures. By embracing stewardship principles, entrepreneurs can create sustainable organizations that prioritize the well-being of stakeholders and drive long-term success.

4.8 Resource-Based

Jay Barney developed the resource-based view of the firm, which is a strategic management Theory designed to explain why some firms perform better than others even when they occupy a very similar business environment. The resource-based view seeks to explain why some firms perform better than others by looking to the firms' resources. This contrasts with earlier perspectives, such as Porter's five forces, which focus on the external environment as sources of threats and opportunities. The core idea behind the resource-based view is that competitive advantage comes from a firm's effective use of tangible and intangible resources or assets. Tangible assets include plant, equipment, and even human resources, whereas intangible assets include things like trade secrets and corporate reputation.

VRIO: Resources that are valuable, rare, and difficult to imitate or substitute are sources of sustained competitive advantage (Barney, 1991). When such resources are bundled or combined, they can be mutually reinforcing, further differentiating the firm's capabilities.

Resources and entrepreneurship: The Theory has important implications for entrepreneurship research. Entrepreneurial opportunities can be expressed as an entrepreneur's unique insight into the value of resources that established firms may not yet possess. This perspective places emphasis on striving for uniqueness rather than trying to be the best company across all metrics. Alvarez and Barney (2007) suggest that if an entrepreneur has all the resources needed to take advantage of an opportunity, then there is little need for organizing, just coordinating, and executing. They consider this situation to be akin to exploiting arbitrage opportunities created by changes in the environment. By contrast, much more entrepreneurial organizing is needed to take advantage of an arbitrage opportunity when the entrepreneur is lacking one or more key resources. Resources that might be important for entrepreneurs include: special information, leadership capabilities, education, and experience (explicit and tacit knowledge) embodied in the entrepreneurs or their social networks, all of which may help to make their ventures difficult to imitate. The resource-based perspective has been combined with the stakeholder perspective in recent writings by Barney (2018). This gives rise to a view of stakeholders as means to resources. It suggests that entrepreneurs care more about the interests of stakeholders that control access to the resources comprising a firm's self-reinforcing VRIO resource bundle. Other stakeholders deserve only minimal attention to attain competitive parity.

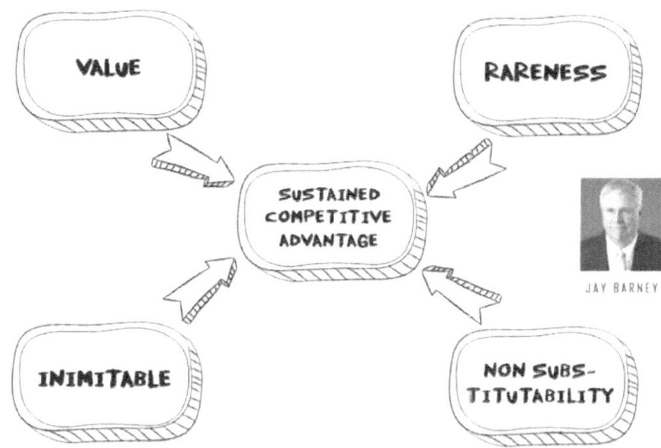

Understanding the "Resource-Based" theory:

Resource-based theory suggests that a company's resources and capabilities are key determinants of its success. For example, the technology giant Apple is often cited as an example of resource-based theory. Apple has a range of valuable resources & capabilities that create a sustainable competitive advantage in the technology industry to contribute to its success, including:

Strong brand: Apple is one of the most recognizable and valuable brands in the world, with a reputation for quality and innovation.

Design expertise: Apple is known for its sleek, user-friendly designs, which have helped the company establish a unique identity and create a competitive advantage.

Intellectual property: Apple holds numerous patents and trademarks, including key patents related to its iPhone and iPad products.

Supply chain management: Apple has a complex global supply chain that enables it to efficiently produce & distribute its products.

Human capital: Apple's employees are highly skilled and passionate about the company's products, which contributes to the company's ability to innovate and stay ahead of the competition.

Classroom Activity: "Resource-Based Strategy Game"

Objective: To understand and apply the principles of resource-based theory in entrepreneurship by participating in a resource-based strategy game.

Duration: 90 – 100 mins

Material: Large whiteboard or flip chart paper, Marker pens in different colors, Sticky notes or index cards & Pens or pencils for participants

Instructions:

Activity	Instructions
Intro (5 mins)	Begin the activity by introducing the concept of resource-based theory, explaining the importance of unique and valuable resources in gaining a competitive advantage in entrepreneurship. Discuss the relevance of resource-based theory in decision-making & planning.
Identifying Resource (10 mins)	Divide participants into small groups. Instruct each group to identify critical resources for a successful entrepreneurial venture. Encourage participants to consider tangible & intangible resources.
Strategy Game (30 mins)	Introduce a strategy game that simulates the competitive landscape. Provide groups with scenarios & assign specific roles. Groups make strategic decisions based on available resources.
Resource Allocation (20 mins)	Instruct groups to discuss and make strategic decisions based on assigned roles and resources. Encourage consideration of leveraging unique resources for a competitive advantage. Emphasize effective resource allocation.
Game Simulation (15 mins)	Conduct the game simulation. Evaluate outcomes based on factors like market share and profitability. Facilitate a discussion on the results, allowing participants to reflect on the influence of resource-based strategies on their performance.
Reflection & Analysis (15 mins)	Engage group discussion to analyze game results and reflect on employed strategies. Encourage sharing of insights, lessons learned, & challenges faced during decision-making. Discuss the role of resource-based theory in gaining a competitive edge.
Key Take-aways (5 mins)	Summarize key takeaways, emphasizing the importance of identifying and leveraging unique and valuable resources in entrepreneurial ventures. Highlight the role of resource-based theory in strategic decision-making and competitive advantage.

Conclusion: The activity provides participants with a hands-on experience in applying resource-based theory to gain a competitive advantage in entrepreneurship. By understanding the significance of identifying and effectively utilizing unique resources, entrepreneurs can make informed decisions and drive long-term success in their ventures.

4.9 Resource Dependency

Jeffrey Pfeffer and Gerald R. Salancik (1978) proposed the resource dependency Theory as a way to explain the behavior of organizations by looking to the contexts in which they operate. Organizations are influenced by numerous external contingencies; thus, the Theory views the role of the manager as acting to reduce dependencies, especially the power of other actors to exert control over vital resources, often by increasing the power of the focal organization.

The assumptions of the Theory are that organizations are the main units of analysis for understanding society. Organizations are viewed not as autonomous, but rather, they are seen as constrained by webs of dependence relationships with other organizations that can exercise power.

Success and survival are uncertain because of the ever-changing power relations among organizations. Organizations manage inter-dependencies creating new patterns of inter-dependence and inter-organizational power. Power is typically exerted in a way that reduces the profits of the less powerful determinant, while increasing the profits of the more powerful determinant. Managers take strategic actions to reduce environmental dependence, such as mergers (especially vertical integration), joint ventures, changes to boards of directors, political activities, and executive changes. For instance, Netflix vertically integrated into content creation to gain market power over content price setters.

How does resource dependency Theory relate to entrepreneurship? The Theory suggests that new ventures need to be weary of the power of other actors and should try to ensure that they are not too dependent on any one outside determinant that might try to take advantage of their power. New ventures tend to be careful not to become too dependent on powerful outside actors unless they have defensive mechanisms at their disposal, or the resources provided are critical for survival (Katila et al. 2008). The presence of resource dependencies with powerful actors may also make it difficult for new ventures to acquire subsequent resources as such dependencies may act as negative signals. New ventures manage relationships with powerful actors in special ways, such as using formal contracts, embeddedness, and strategic alliances (Yli-Renko et al., 2001). For example, if a new venture forms a joint venture with a powerful incumbent, then the incumbent may resist wielding power over the venture because it might reduce the value of their own ownership shares in the venture. Similarly, embeddedness through close ties allows social sanctions and reputation effects to constrain the behavior of powerful actors.

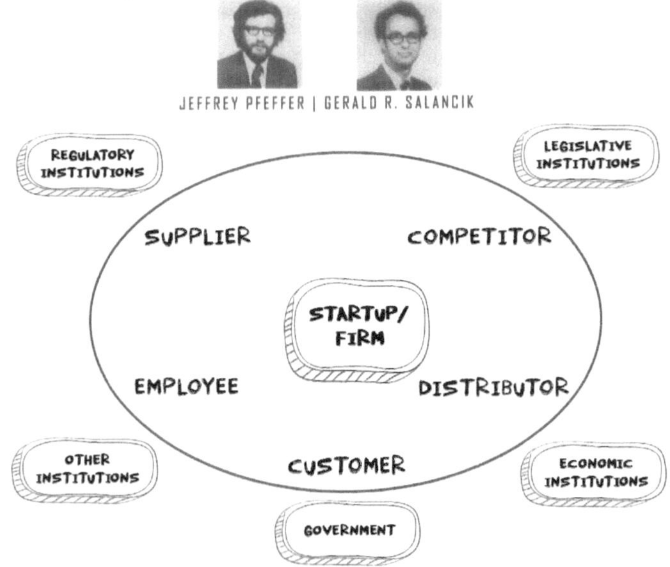

Understanding the "Resource Dependency" theory:
The theory suggests that organizations rely on external resources to function and survive, and that managing those dependencies is key to organizational success. For example, the American automotive company General Motors (GM) is often cited as an example of resource dependency theory. GM relies heavily on a range of external resources to operate, including suppliers for raw materials, distributors for sales, and financial institutions for loans and investments. Any disruption or change in these external resources can have a significant impact on GM's ability to operate.
During the 2008 financial crisis, GM was heavily reliant on loans and investments from financial institutions. When the credit markets froze,

GM was unable to secure the financing it needed to continue operating, and the company ultimately filed for bankruptcy. To manage its external dependencies, GM has worked to build strategic relationships with key suppliers, distributors, and financial institutions. For example, the company has established long-term contracts with key suppliers to ensure a steady supply of raw materials and has formed joint ventures with distributors to ensure access to key markets. We can learn that companies that are able to manage their external dependencies effectively are more likely to survive and thrive in the long term. By building strategic relationships with key external partners, companies like GM can ensure that they have the resources they need to operate, even in challenging market conditions.

Classroom Activity: "Resource Dependency Simulation"

Objective: To explore the concepts of resource dependency theory in entrepreneurship and gain insights into managing external resource dependencies through a simulation exercise.

Duration: 80 – 90 mins

Material: Large whiteboard or flip chart paper, Marker pens in different colors, Sticky notes or index cards & Pens or pencils for participants

Activity	Instructions
Intro (5 mins)	Begin the activity by introducing the concept of resource dependency theory, explaining its relevance in understanding the influence of external resources on organizational behavior and decision-making in entrepreneurship.
Resource Mapping (10 mins)	Divide participants into small groups. Instruct each group to identify and map the key external resources their ventures depend on, considering suppliers, customers, partners, investors, or government support. Encourage reflection on the significance and vulnerabilities of each resource
Simulation (30 mins)	Introduce a simulation exercise replicating resource dependency scenarios. Assign roles representing stakeholders. Present resource-related scenarios for decision-making. Instruct groups to discuss and address the scenarios based on their assigned roles.

Decision-Making and Negotiation (20 mins)	Facilitate decision-making and negotiation within each group to address the resource dependency scenarios. Encourage consideration of strategies like diversification, strategic alliances, and contingency plans. Remind participants to assess the impact of decisions on performance and sustainability.
Simulation Debrief and Discussion (15 mins)	Conduct a debriefing session for groups to share experiences, strategies, and outcomes from the simulation. Facilitate a group discussion analyzing challenges, insights, and lessons learned. Discuss the implications of resource dependency theory for decision-making and strategic planning.
Reflection and Application (15 mins)	Allocate time for individual reflection on the simulation's relevance to participants' ventures. Encourage identification of external resource dependencies and the development of effective management strategies. Facilitate a group discussion to share insights and practical applications.
Takea-ways (5 mins)	Summarize the key takeaways, emphasizing the importance of recognizing and managing external resource dependencies in entrepreneurship. Highlight the strategies and considerations discussed during the simulation and debriefing.

Conclusion: The activity offers participants a practical understanding of managing external resource dependencies in entrepreneurship. By exploring resource mapping, engaging in decision-making, and reflecting on the implications of resource dependency theory, entrepreneurs can enhance their ability to strategically manage resources & navigate external dependencies for long-term success.

4.10 Machiavellian

Niccolo Machiavelli (born 1479) in Italy is an infamous strategist who wrote extensive letters teaching cunning strategies to "princes" that ruled over fiefdoms throughout feudal Europe at the time. 16th century Europe was very divided compared to today, especially in and around Italy, which was composed of many small autonomous and semi-autonomous territories. Although Machiavelli is often considered as a figure in the history of political science, fiefdoms were ruled by what Baumol describes as entrepreneurs. Thus, Machiavelli's letters can be thought of as elaborating entrepreneurial strategies to get ahead in feudal times. Many regard Machiavelli's strategies as unethical, yet his famous book "The Prince" continues to be cited and read within the business school community and by business and military practitioners. That work, along with Sun Tzu's Art of War, are considered classic works on strategy, but they also have much to say about entrepreneurship. If a young prince wants to achieve, he needed to topple another or an older incumbent. The core ideal of the Theory is that the ends justify the means, as the end is total power over a territory and its resources. For example, he recommended strategies including the use of killing to eliminate competitors. He viewed this strategy as superior to imprisonment or exile because these alternatives could allow a return to be staged by the competitor and their networks. Axioms credited to Machiavelli include:

1. It is better to be feared than to be loved.
2. Loyalty must be strong, and resistance crushed.
3. The ends justify the means.

Perhaps Machiavellian was a realist writing during a time of weak institutions. Today, entrepreneurs often find themselves in trouble with the law when they pursue Machiavellian strategies to usurp incumbent firms. The modern institutional systems that are in place regulate Machiavellian behaviors, act as a barrier to entry However, these types of barriers may be considered desirable because they prevent what is now understood to be a destructive form of entrepreneurship, in terms of its effects on society or network.

Understanding the "Machevellian" theory:
A business example of Machiavellianism could be a CEO who uses manipulative tactics to gain power and influence within the organization. They may be willing to deceive and exploit others in order to achieve their goals, and they may be more focused on their own self-interest than the overall success of the company.

Niccolo Machiavelli

For example, they may use unethical business practices to increase profits, or they may undermine or sabotage their colleagues in order to advance their own career. Ultimately, a Machiavellian leader can create a toxic work environment and damage the reputation and profitability of the business.

Classroom Activity: "Ethics: Exploring the Machiavellianism"

Objective: To engage readers in a discussion about the theory of Machiavellianism and its implications for ethics in entrepreneurship.

Duration: 95 – 105 mins

Material: Large whiteboard or flip chart paper, Marker pens in different colors, Sticky notes or index cards & Pens or pencils for participants.

Instructions:

Activity	Instructions
Intro (5 mins)	Begin the activity by introducing the concept of Machiavellianism as a psychological theory focusing on manipulative behavior in pursuit of self-interest and power. Explain its relevance in understanding ethical decision-making in entrepreneurship.
Case Study (15 mins)	Divide participants into small groups. Instruct each group to select a facilitator who will guide the discussion. Provide each group with a case study presenting a moral or ethical dilemma faced by an entrepreneur or business. Instruct groups to analyze the case study considering the actions and behavior of the entrepreneur in relation to Machiavellian traits.
Group Discussion (20 mins)	Facilitate group discussions, allowing participants to share insights and perspectives on the ethical implications of Machiavellian behavior in entrepreneurship. Encourage critical examination of ethical consequences and discussion of alternative approaches.
Ethical Decision-Making (20 mins)	Introduce an ethical decision-making exercise, presenting challenging scenarios to each group. Instruct groups to discuss and make decisions based on ethical considerations, considering the potential influence of Machiavellian principles.

Group Pitch and Debate (15 mins)	Ask each group to present their decisions and rationale to the rest of the participants. Encourage constructive debate among groups, discussing the ethical implications of different approaches and the role of Machiavellianism in entrepreneurial decision-making.
Reflection & Analysis (10 mins)	Allocate time for individual reflection on the discussions and activities. Engage participants in a group reflection, discussing the complexities of ethical decision-making in entrepreneurship and the balance between self-interest and ethical behavior.
Key Takeaways (5 mins)	Summarize key takeaways, emphasizing the importance of considering ethical implications and values in entrepreneurial decision-making. Highlight potential risks and consequences associated with Machiavellian behavior and the importance of fostering an ethical culture.

Conclusion: The exploration of Machiavellianism in entrepreneurship sheds light on the ethical implications of strategic behavior and self-interest. By critically examining ethical dilemmas and fostering ethical decision-making, entrepreneurs can cultivate a culture that balances ambition with integrity for long-term success and stakeholder trust.

4.11 Born Global Startups

Conceived worldwide new companies are adventures that begin thinking and acting universally in their beginning phases of improvement, which use global business sectors and assets to scale their development. Consideration regarding conceived worldwide new companies comes from a flood of theory and exploration that looks at how new businesses quickly internationalize their new pursuits (Knight and Cavusgil, 2004). Customarily, business visionaries would zero in on homegrown business sectors first and afterward seek after internationalization slowly as they foster the essential abilities through experimentation. Current advances in web advances, worldwide ability streams, and global stockpile chains have significantly brought the expense for businesspeople down to internationalize (McCormick and Somaya, 2020). They have additionally made it workable for new businesses to address worldwide business sectors from the earliest starting point of their reality. Businesspeople would now be able to sidestep large numbers of their nation of origin limitations like government failures and actual area (McCormick and Somaya, 2020).

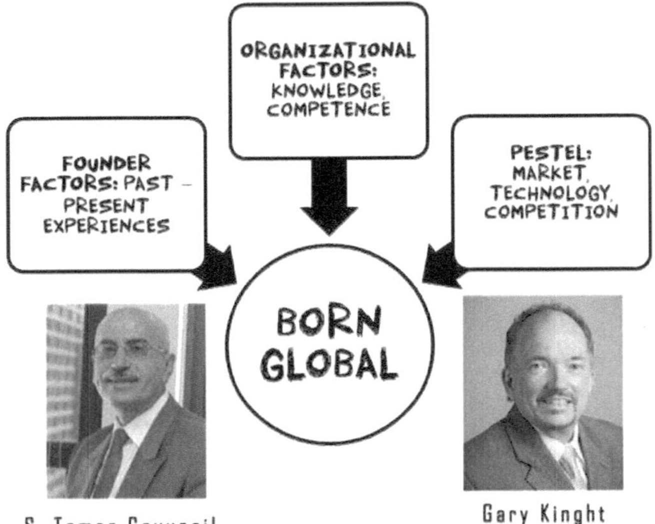

S. Tamer Cavusgil

Gary Kinght

For instance, an expense programming startup may choose to address the Australian market as opposed to the over-immersed U.S. market, regardless of whether it is situated in the U.S., or in Europe. Since the entirety of the connections are intervened by the web, there is less requirement for actual vicinity of creation and deals. We would anticipate that born global startups should be more common in more modest nations as businesspeople search for bigger business sectors or creation abilities. Bilingualism and biculturalism of the populace may likewise be significant; accordingly, we may hope to see a greater amount of this kind of business among people from assorted foundations or with admittance to variety through their organizations. For example, 1/3 of individuals living in Toronto were brought into the world external Canada. Global encounters (counting travel, schooling, and living abroad encounters) increment the intellectual intricacy needed to flourish in worldwide organizations (Leung and Chiu, 2008; Pidduck, 2019) and gives expanded comprehension of unfamiliar societies which can be helpful in producing business thoughts. Moreover, businesspeople and groups with earlier worldwide experience will have information and set up networks that they can use in their worldwide endeavors. Perhaps the best illustration of conceived worldwide new companies are outsourcing organizations. Outsourcing is a strategy for web-based business retail deals where the store doesn't hold the items it sells. The business buys things from an outsider provider and works with its shipment straightforwardly to the shopper. This model takes out the requirement for warehousing, B2B delivering, retail facade costs (lease, utilities and so on), and empowers the organization to have a generously more extensive reach from the beginning. One region that appears to be ready for future examination is to take a gander at the arbitrators of the propensity to begin worldwide. For instance, how do factors like pay disparity, strength of protected innovation rights, or nature of establishments overall reinforce or debilitate the impact of variety of involvement on the probability of being conceived worldwide as opposed to following customary steady internationalization way.

Understanding the "Born Global" theory:

Born global startups are companies that from their inception seek to operate globally and enter international markets quickly. One example of a born global startup is TransferWise, a financial technology company that provides international money transfer services. TransferWise was founded in Estonia in 2011 and immediately set its sights on global expansion. Within its first year of operation, TransferWise had customers in over 30 countries, and it has since grown to serve over 10 million customers across the world. Another example of a born global startup is Hootsuite, a social media management platform. Hootsuite was founded in Canada in 2008 and quickly expanded into international markets, with offices in 13 countries and users in over 175 countries. By focusing on global growth from the outset, these born global startups were able to establish themselves as key players in their industries and capture market share in a rapidly changing global marketplace.

Classroom Activity: "Born Global Simulation Game"

Objective: To engage readers in a simulation game that explores the concepts and strategies associated with the Born Global theory in entrepreneurship.

Duration: 100 - 120 mins

Material: Large whiteboard or flip chart paper, Marker pens in different colors, Sticky notes or index cards & Pens or pencils for participants.

Instructions:

Activity	Instructions
Intro (5 mins)	Introduce the theory and its relevance in the context of globalization. Discuss the potential advantages and challenges for entrepreneurs.

Scenario Presentation (15 mins)	Divide participants into small groups and designate a team leader for each group. Present a fictional scenario representing a Born Global venture, including industry, target market, product/service, and competitive landscape. Highlight the opportunities and challenges of internationalization from the beginning.
Strategic Decisions (30 mins)	Instruct groups to discuss and make strategic decisions based on the scenario. Encourage consideration of market entry strategies, international expansion plans, marketing & distribution approaches, and resource allocation.
Simulation Round (30 mins)	Conduct a simulation round where each group implements their strategic decisions. Simulate market conditions, competitors' actions, and customer responses. Evaluate outcomes based on predefined success metrics such as market share, profitability, & international presence.
Reflection 15 mins)	Engage participants in a group discussion to analyze simulation outcomes and reflect on the challenges, successes, and lessons learned. Discuss the implications of the Born Global theory for entrepreneurial decision-making and internationalization strategies.
Key Take-aways (5 mins)	Summarize key takeaways, emphasizing the unique opportunities and challenges faced by Born Global ventures. Highlight the importance of strategic decision-making, market entry strategies, & resource allocation in achieving international success.

Conclusion: This activity demonstrates the importance of strategic decision-making, market entry strategies, and resource allocation for entrepreneurs aiming to seize global opportunities. By encouraging further exploration of Born Global ventures and providing additional resources, participants are empowered to delve deeper into this topic and apply the principles of internationalization to their own entrepreneurial journeys.

Process Theories

5.1 Harvard School

This one is a bit of a stretch to call a Theory, but we can perhaps think of it as a process Theory or a discovery Theory. Pradhan and Nath (2011) discuss the Harvard School Theory of entrepreneurship. They say the Theory views entrepreneurship as involving "all such activities that initiates, maintains and results in a profit-oriented enterprise for production or distribution of economic goods or services and which is consistent with internal and external forces." Mohanty (2005) suggests that the Harvard school Theory involves internal analysis (e.g., assessing resources and capabilities) and external analysis (e.g., conducting political, economic, social, technological, environmental, and legal analyses and five forces analysis) and the selection among types of entrepreneurial activities (alternatives and recommendations). The Theory resembles the common SWOT analysis, but applies specialized analysis techniques (e.g., PESTEL, P5Fs and VRIO). The Theory is like a contingency Theory in that the right entrepreneurial activity must fit the internal and external environmental conditions. Thus, there is not a right answer for all ventures, but different right and wrong answers for each venture. It is interesting to see what the Harvard case process is basically applied to entrepreneurial opportunities as a Theory. It is in the same bucket as experiential learning, human capital Theory, and other approaches that assume that students can learn to be entrepreneurs by doing a set of things.

Understanding the "Harvard School" theory:
The Harvard Business School (HBS) is one of the most prestigious business schools in the world and has had a significant impact on the development of management theory and practice. One business example of the Harvard School is the Balanced Scorecard approach, which was developed by Robert Kaplan and David Norton, both of whom are affiliated with the Harvard Business School. The Balanced Scorecard is a strategic management framework that helps organizations to align their activities with their mission and strategy. It

provides a set of measures and targets that can be used to evaluate organizational performance and to communicate progress to stakeholders.

Another example of the Harvard School's impact on business is its case method, which is a teaching technique that uses real-world business cases to help students develop critical thinking and decision-making skills. The case method has been widely adopted by business schools around the world, and it has become an important tool for developing future business leaders. In addition to these examples, the Harvard Business School has contributed to a wide range of management theories and practices, including the concept of disruptive innovation, the resource-based view of the firm, and the concept of shared value. Many of these concepts have become widely accepted and have had a significant impact on the way that businesses operate and compete in today's global economy.

PAPRI NATH | RABINDRA KUMAR PRADHAN

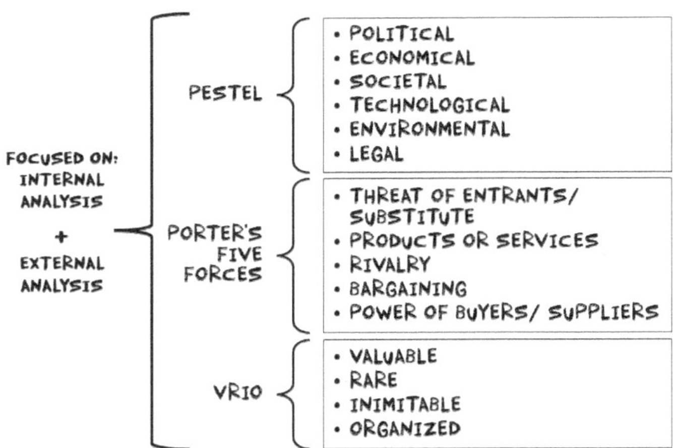

Classroom Activity: "Strategic Thinking - Harvard School"

Objective: To engage readers in strategic thinking exercises inspired by the Harvard School of Entrepreneurship theory, enabling them to analyze and apply key concepts to real-world scenarios.

Duration: 105 - 120 mins

Material: Large whiteboard or flip chart paper, Marker pens in different colors, Sticky notes & Pens or pencils for participants.

Instructions:

Activity	Instructions
Intro (5 mins)	Introduce the Harvard School of Entrepreneurship theory and its relevance in strategic thinking and planning. Emphasize the importance of developing a competitive advantage and achieving long-term success in dynamic business environments.
Case Study Analysis (20 mins)	Provide participants with a real-world case study and instruct them to analyze it using the Harvard School theory. Focus on competitive positioning, value proposition, and resource allocation. Encourage participants to identify strategic choices and discuss their implications.
Group Discussion (15 mins)	Divide participants into small groups and facilitate a discussion on the case study analysis. Encourage the exchange of perspectives on strategic decisions made by entrepreneurs. Foster a constructive dialogue about the effectiveness of the strategies employed.
Strategic Framework Exercise (25 mins)	Introduce a strategic framework exercise, such as SWOT analysis or PESTEL analysis. Instruct groups to apply the chosen framework to assess external and internal factors influencing the venture. Guide participants in identifying strengths, weaknesses, opportunities, and threats.
Strategy (20 mins)	Instruct each group to develop a strategic plan based on the case study analysis and insights gained. Encourage alignment between the venture's vision, mission, and objectives. Remind participants to identify competitive advantage and value proposition.
Group Pitch (15 mins)	Ask each group to present their strategic plan to the rest of the participants. Encourage constructive feedback and a meaningful discussion on the strengths and potential areas for improvement in each plan. Reflect on key learnings and the application of the Harvard School theory.

Key Takeaways (5 mins)	Summarize the key takeaways, highlighting the significance of strategic thinking and planning in entrepreneurship. Emphasize the importance of considering competitive positioning, value proposition, and resource allocation in developing effective strategies.

Conclusion: The activity underscores the importance of strategic thinking & planning in entrepreneurial ventures. Participants gained insights into competitive positioning, value proposition, and resource allocation through case study analysis *& strategic decision-making exercises. It emphasizes the significance of the Harvard School theory in achieving long-term success & encourages participants to apply strategic principles in their entrepreneurial pursuits.

5.2 Effectuation

Dr. Saras Sarasvathy is an Indian born business school professor researching strategy, entrepreneurship, and business ethics, currently appointed at the University of Virginia. Sarasvathy proposed the Theory of effectuation in the early 2000s after studying a sample of expert entrepreneurs with diverse backgrounds. Effectuation Theory is often considered a process Theory because it explains the process that entrepreneurs use to create new ventures. Effectuation Theory stems from the way that expert entrepreneurs think about problems and how they go about solving them. Effectuation logic contrasts with what Sarasvathy calls "causation theories" of entrepreneurship, where it is proposed that entrepreneurs start with a goal and then acquire the resources needed to achieve the goal, in a linear fashion. Each resource acquisition is a step toward the goal. In stark contrast, effectuation logic involves evaluating resources that are available to use today and then deriving goals out of what can be made from the recombination of those resources. Thus, entrepreneurs do not just recombine resources to meet goals, they accept floating goals within a set of limits and allow the resources that are available now to guide the evolution of their strategies.

By forgoing the need for expensive resources like large sums of startup capital, effectuators do in kind deals that achieve their desired effects. Elaborating on the Theory, Sarasvathy suggested that effectuation involves five core principles.

1) The bird in the hand principle: A bird in the hand beats two in the bush—This refers to maximizing the use of what an entrepreneur knows (i.e., their background and experience), who they know (e.g.,

friends, family and others around them), and aligning options based on who they are (i.e., what are the entrepreneur's abilities).
2) The affordable loss principle: Only take on affordable losses—Don't obsess about windfall profits but do try to minimize potential losses. This involves taking low probability bets, but only with a small investment of resources lost with each failure.
3) The crazy quilts principle: Make crazy quilts—Weave potential deals with potential partners until something sticks. Many iterations are often required.
4) The lemonade principle: Make lemonade means to see potential in depressed or under-utilized resources. This is like the alertness principle.
5) The pilot in the plane principle—Focus on today, not next year. Effectuation Theory continues to gain research attention from entrepreneurship scholars and has made its way into entrepreneurship textbooks. There is some evidence that expert entrepreneurs use effectuation logic more often than causal logic, providing some support for the Theory. One meta-analysis suggests that most of the core effectuation behaviors are positively related to venture performance (Read, Song and Smit, 2009).

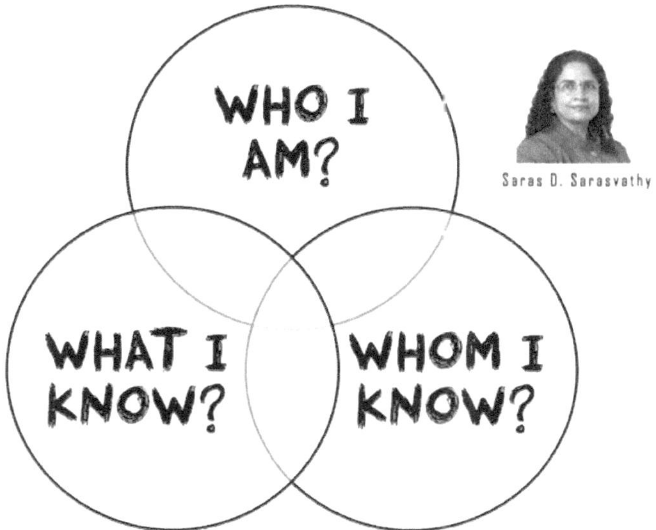

As an example, a chef using causal logic decides to cook a particular meal recipe and then gathers the requisite ingredients to do so. A chef using effectuation logic looks in the fridge to see what ingredients are available, then improvises a meal using what is there. Causation logic is rational and may be best employed in situations that do not involve too much uncertainty. By contrast, effectuation logic is useful when there is uncertainty about the goals of the entrepreneur, and therefore, no definable selection environment to analyze (Chandler, DeTienne, McKelvie, and Mumford, 2011). Effectuation Theory is rising fast in academic teaching because it offers a Theory-rich complement to experiential courses such as Lean Launch Pad.

Understanding the "Effectuation" theory:
Effectuation is a decision-making framework used by entrepreneurs to identify and pursue opportunities. A good example of effectuation in practice is the story of Sara Blakely, the founder of Spanx, a popular brand of women's shapewear. Blakely started Spanx with just $5,000 in savings and no experience in the fashion industry. Rather than conducting market research or seeking outside investment, Blakely used effectuation principles to grow her business. She started by designing a prototype and then tested it on herself and her friends. When she realized there was demand for her product, she used her existing network to find a manufacturer and a patent attorney. Blakely also used effectuation principles to market her product. Rather than spending money on advertising, she sent her product to influential people in the fashion industry, who then spread the word to their friends and colleagues. This helped to build buzz around Spanx and attract new customers. Today, Spanx is a hugely successful business, with a wide range of products and a global customer base. Blakely's use of effectuation principles helped her to build a successful business from scratch, without relying on outside investment or traditional market research.

Classroom Activity: "Building a Startup"

Objective: To engage readers in a hands-on exercise that explores the principles of Effectuation & its application in building a startup.
Duration: 125 - 140 mins
Material: Large whiteboard or flip chart paper, Marker pens in different colors, Sticky notes or index cards & Pens or pencils for participants.
Instructions:

Activity	Instructions
Intro (5 mins)	Introduce the theory & highlight its focus on entrepreneurial decision-making under uncertainty. Explain key principles such as means-driven, affordable loss, and partnerships.

Scenario Presentation (10 mins)	Divide participants into small groups and designate a team leader for each group to guide decision-making. Present a startup scenario to each group, setting the context of the problem or opportunity they will address. Simulate limited resources and uncertain market conditions.
Analysis (55 mins)	Instruct groups to adopt a means-driven approach, leveraging available resources and brainstorming solutions. Discuss the affordable loss principle, emphasizing risk management and achievable goals. Instruct groups to define their affordable loss in terms of resources, time, and effort. Explain the significance of partnerships and instruct groups to identify potential stakeholders & analyze their value and feasibility.
Startup idea and Pitch (30 mins)	Instruct groups to develop their startup concept, integrating Effectuation principles to create a compelling pitch to communicate value proposition, means-driven approach, and potential partnerships.
Share (15 mins)	Facilitate a group discussion on learnings, insights, and the influence of Effectuation principles. Reflect on advantages and challenges in applying Effectuation in building a startup.
Take-aways (5 mins)	Summarize key takeaways, emphasizing the value of Effectuation in decision-making under uncertainty for startups.

Conclusion: The activity provides participants with hands-on experience in applying Effectuation theory to startup creation. Through scenario analysis, means-driven approaches, stakeholder analysis, and pitch development, participants gained insights into managing uncertainty and leveraging available resources. Activity emphasizes the value of Effectuation in entrepreneurial decision-making and highlights the principles of means-driven action, affordable loss, and partnerships as key tools for startup success.

5.3 Bricolage

Ted Baker

Bricolage Theory is credited to Levi-Strauss (1962) who was a French anthropologist who introduced the concept of bricolage entrepreneurship as he tried to show that "savage" (aboriginal) peoples were just as entrepreneurial as "civilized" peoples. He compared the "bricoleur" to the "engineer" in his book entitled *The Savage Mind*. Unlike the engineer, the bricoleur would "make do" with the material at hand to concoct whatever tools he/she needed to accomplish a particular project as it develops. By contrast, the engineer plans, gains access to all that is needed to complete a project before starting. Thus, the bricoleur is seen as contrasting with the rational view as projects are accomplished by solving problems as they emerge, with whatever is available rather than what is really needed. The bricoleur practices radical experimentation rather than planning. Bricolage Theory is mainly focused on explaining how entrepreneurship emerges in economically depressed, or resource-poor areas. The concept of making something out of nothing is the key driver of the Theory. "Nothing" refers to under-utilized resources that can be recombined into productive resources. Baker and Nelson (2005) give the example of retrofitting machines or software to be used for purposes they were not intended for, with the creation of appendages and hacks. Resources at hand are those resources that are readily available in the environment of the entrepreneur, such that their acquisition and use does not require great effort or extensive capital. Entrepreneurs that make use of resources at hand are viewed as individuals that refuse to accept the limitations of their environments. Instead, they act despite socially constructed limitations, and shun standards or traditional definitions of legitimate inputs. Bricolage may be used in different domains such as physical inputs, human resources, markets, human capital, and institutional, however, there is limited empirical research examining the Theory.

Understanding the "Bricolage" theory:

Bricolage refers to the process of creating something using the resources that are readily available or that have been accumulated through experience. For an example, an entrepreneur is trying to start a new restaurant, but they do not have the funds to purchase all of the expensive equipment and hire a full staff. Instead, they use their personal savings to purchase a few key pieces of equipment, such as a grill and refrigerator, and they hire a small staff of family and friends who are willing to work for lower wages. They also get creative with their menu, using affordable and locally sourced ingredients to create unique and delicious dishes. By utilizing the resources that they have available and being resourceful with their approach, the entrepreneur can create a successful restaurant without a significant upfront investment.

Classroom Activity: "Creativity in Entrepreneurship"

Objective: To engage readers in a hands-on exercise that explores the concept of bricolage and its application in entrepreneurship, fostering creativity and resourcefulness.

Duration: 125 - 140 mins

Material: Large whiteboard or flip chart paper, Marker pens in different colors, Sticky notes or index cards & Pens or pencils for participants.

Instructions:

Activity	Instructions
Intro (5 mins)	Introduce the concept of bricolage as an entrepreneurial approach that fosters creative problem-solving using existing resources. Explain its significance in overcoming constraints & fostering innovation.
Resource Scavenger Hunt (20 mins)	Divide participants into small groups and assign a team leader to facilitate the creative process. Provide a list of accessible resources and instruct groups to go on a scavenger hunt to collect items within a specified time. Encourage creative thinking in gathering resources for entrepreneurial use.
Test (30 mins)	Present a challenge that requires creative problem-solving and the use of collected resources. Instruct groups to brainstorm and develop innovative solutions using the bricolage approach.
Develop Solution and Pitch (30 mins)	Instruct groups to further develop their solutions considering feasibility, market potential, and resource utilization. Prepare a presentation highlighting their bricolage-based solution & value proposition.
Reflection and Discussion (15 mins)	Facilitate a group discussion on the insights gained, including the stimulation of creativity, resourcefulness, and problem-solving skills through bricolage. Discuss the advantages and challenges of using bricolage in entrepreneurship.

Conclusion: The bricolage activity provided participants with practical experience in applying the principles of creative problem-solving and resourcefulness in entrepreneurship. Through the resource scavenger hunt, bricolage challenge, and solution development, participants learned to leverage existing resources and think outside the box to develop innovative solutions. The activity emphasized the importance of bricolage in overcoming constraints, fostering innovation, and encouraging adaptive thinking in entrepreneurial endeavors.

5.4 Experiential Learning

Learning involves the transformation of experience into potential knowledge, cognition, behaviors, and/or actions (Kolb, 1984). Experiential learning can be differentiated from rationalist (e.g., cognitive theories). Rather than emphasize the role of acquiring, manipulating, and recalling, experiential learning Theory embraces subjective experience. Subjective experience can be of many different types. However, the concept of 'know-how' is useful here. Unlike knowledge, which is learned by language, know-how is acquired through experience, for instance, actually doing something in the real world, like taking entrepreneurial action. Building on Kolb's experiential learning model, Corbett (2005) argues that entrepreneurship requires several different types of learning (convergent, assimilative, divergent, accommodative) at different stages of the entrepreneurial process (preparation, incubation, evaluation, elaboration, respectively)..The Theory perhaps helps to explain spinouts. Experiential learning within parent organizations may enable employees to learn skills and knowledge, identify opportunities, absorb values and beliefs, and develop social capital (Sørensen and Fassiotto,2011). They can then use some of these resources or capabilities in their spinout ventures. Experiential learning helps to explain why serial entrepreneurs are so successful& how each experience produces a learning outcome that affects the odds of success in the next round.

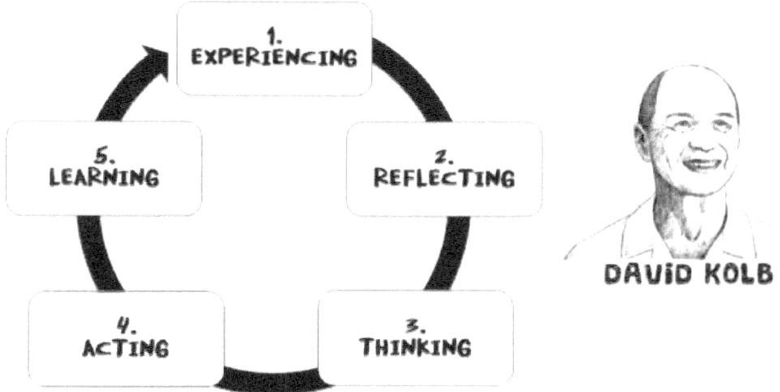

Understanding the "Experiential Learning" theory:

A company wants to improve its customer service, so it decides to send a group of employees to a customer service training program that uses experiential learning techniques. The program includes role-playing exercises where employees are given scenarios to practice their customer service skills and receive immediate feedback. The program also includes case studies and simulations to help employees understand different customer situations and how to respond appropriately. After completing the training program, the employees return to the company and apply what they have learned to their customer interactions. The company monitors customer feedback and sees a significant improvement in customer satisfaction ratings. The employees also report feeling more confident and capable in their customer service roles, which leads to increased job satisfaction and retention.

Classroom Activity: "Entrepreneurship: Experiential Learning"

Objective: To engage readers in an experiential learning journey that immerses them in real-life entrepreneurial experiences, fostering hands-on learning, critical thinking, and reflection.

Duration: 185 - 200 mins

Material: Large whiteboard or flip chart paper, Marker pens in different colors, Sticky notes or index cards & Pens or pencils for participants.

Instructions:

Activity	Instructions
Intro (5 mins)	Introduce the concept of experiential learning as a powerful approach to entrepreneurship education that emphasizes learning through firsthand experiences. Explain its value in developing entrepreneurial mindsets, skills, and decision-making capabilities. Discuss how experiential learning differs from traditional classroom-based learning and its benefits in fostering creativity, problem-solving, & adaptability.
Groups (5 mins)	Divide participants into small groups (3-4 members per group). Instruct each group to select a team leader who will facilitate the group's learning process. Encourage diversity in group composition to foster collaboration and different perspectives.
Real-Life Case Study Analysis (20 mins)	Provide each group with a real-life case study of an entrepreneurial venture or entrepreneur. Instruct groups to analyze the case study, focusing on the entrepreneurial journey, challenges faced, strategic decisions made, and lessons learned. Encourage participants to critically evaluate the entrepreneurial experiences presented in the case study, discussing both successes and failures.

Entrepreneurial Immersion (60 mins)	Instruct each group to design and plan an experiential learning adventure for themselves, simulating an entrepreneurial experience. Participants can choose from options such as creating a mock startup, conducting a business simulation, or participating in a mini-pitch competition. Each group should consider the key elements of entrepreneurship, including idea generation, market analysis, customer validation, resource allocation, and marketing strategies. Encourage creativity and innovation in their approach.
Experiential Learning Journey (60 mins)	Allocate time for each group to execute their planned experiential learning adventure. Participants should immerse themselves in the experience, applying their entrepreneurial skills, making decisions, and adapting to challenges in real-time. Encourage participants to document their experiences, challenges faced, and key learnings throughout the journey. Emphasize the importance of reflection during the experiential learning process.
Reflection and Discussion (30 mins)	Facilitate a group discussion where each group shares their experiential learning journey and reflects on the process and outcomes. Encourage participants to discuss the insights gained, challenges encountered, and lessons learned from their entrepreneurial immersion. Guide the discussion to explore the connections between the experiential learning adventure and real-world entrepreneurial experiences. Encourage active listening and open dialogue among participants.

Conclusion: The activity highlights the vital role of experiential learning in entrepreneurship, enabling participants to grow and develop as entrepreneurs. By immersing themselves in hands-on experiences, participants gain valuable skills and adaptability needed for success in the unpredictable entrepreneurial journey. Encouraging a continuous pursuit of experiential learning and providing additional resources empowers participants to further expand their knowledge and expertise in this transformative approach to entrepreneurship.

Discovery Theories

6.1 Individual-Opportunity Nexus

There is a long-standing debate about the origins of entrepreneurial opportunities. There is a divide between scholars that think entrepreneurs create opportunities, and those that believe they merely discover them. Scott Shane and Jonathan Eckhardt (2003) make the case that opportunities are found and discovered, not made or created. They propose that the foundation of the field of entrepreneurship relies upon the objectiveness of opportunities and would otherwise be on shaky ground. *"[W]e define entrepreneurial opportunities as situations in which new goods, services, raw materials, markets, and organizing methods can be introduced for profit." - Eckhardt and Shane (2010).* The Theory suggests that it is the constant pivoting of the entrepreneur that lands him or her on an opportunity that exists out there, objectively. Although it resembles a process of search it appears from the outside to be a creative activity, which may explain the incorrect association that entrepreneurs create opportunities. That would be like saying that if Tesla had never launched, no one else would ever have filled the space they hold today. Surely another would have come along, eventually. Therefore, first, opportunities exist, then individuals discover the opportunities, then entrepreneurs exploit the opportunities.

The Theory highlights that both enterprising individuals and entrepreneurial opportunities are needed for entrepreneurial ventures to develop, hence the nexus occurring at two different levels of analysis. This olive branch to the individual's role highlights the need for a certain mix of personality, skills, and abilities, as well as access to resources within a network. More broadly thought, there must be someone digging for anything to get dug up. The Theory makes no prediction about the role of effort by entrepreneurs. It also assumes that different entrepreneurs might be involved in opportunity recognition and exploitation (i.e., specialization). The Theory acknowledges a role for creativity, but only in the process of opportunity exploitation. Finally, success in entrepreneurship is subjective and may be informed by motivations other than profit.

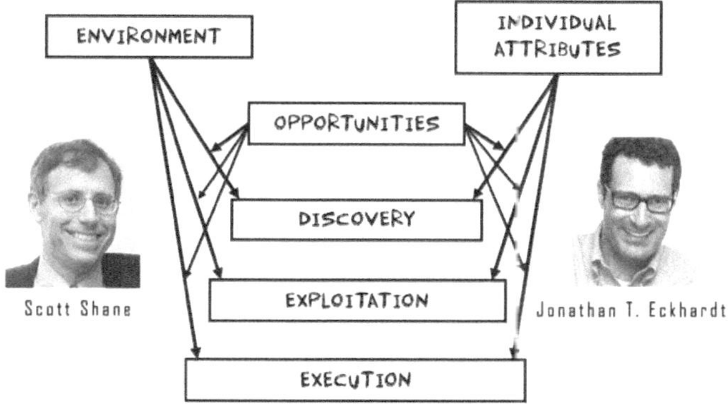

Understanding the Individual-Opportunity Nexus theory:
Individual opportunity nexus is a concept that describes the relationship between an individual's opportunities and their ability to take advantage of those opportunities. For an example, A talented software engineer who lives in Silicon Valley has many opportunities to work for successful startups and tech companies. However, if they lack the necessary skills or experience, they may not be able to take advantage of those opportunities. A small business owner who has a unique product or service may have opportunities to expand their business and enter new markets. However, if they lack the financial resources or knowledge to scale their business, they may not be able to take advantage of those opportunities. An aspiring musician who has a great voice and songwriting skills may have opportunities to perform at local gigs and events. However, if they lack the confidence or stage presence to perform in front of large audiences, they may not be able to take advantage of those opportunities. A recent college graduate who has a degree in marketing may have opportunities to work for top advertising agencies. However, if they lack the necessary networking skills or industry connections, they may not be able to take advantage of those opportunities. The individual's opportunities are contingent upon their ability to take advantage of them, highlighting the importance of personal development, resources, & skills to achieve success.

Classroom Activity: "Opportunity Exploration Challenge"

Objective: To enhance participants' understanding of the Individual-Opportunity Nexus theory and develop their skills in identifying and evaluating entrepreneurial opportunities.

Duration: 100 - 120 mins

Material: Large whiteboard or flip chart paper, Marker pens in different colors, Sticky notes or index cards & Pens or pencils for participants.

Instructions:

Activity	Instructions
Introduce (10 mins)	Start by introducing the Individual-Opportunity Nexus theory, explaining its key concepts and importance in entrepreneurship. Provide examples of successful entrepreneurs who effectively identified & capitalized on opportunities. Emphasize role of creativity, observation, & problem-solving to identify new opportunities.
Opportunity Brainstorming (15 mins)	Divide participants into small groups of 3-4 members. Provide each group with flip charts, markers, and sticky notes. Instruct each group to brainstorm as many potential entrepreneurial opportunities as possible within a specific time frame (e.g., 10 minutes). Encourage them to think outside the box and consider various sectors and industries. Instruct them to conduct a preliminary evaluation of the selected opportunity using the following criteria: a) Market demand and potential profitability b) Feasibility and available resources c) Competitive landscape and differentiation d) d) Personal fit and passion
Opportunity Evaluation (25 mins)	After the brainstorming session, ask each group to select one opportunity from their list for evaluation. Instruct them to conduct a preliminary evaluation of the selected opportunity using criteria such as market demand, feasibility, competition, and personal fit. Each group should document their evaluation on flip charts, highlighting the key points.
Opportunity Pitch (20 mins)	Instruct each group to prepare a brief pitch for their chosen opportunity. Encourage them to address the key evaluation criteria and highlight the unique selling proposition. Allocate 5 minutes for each group to present their pitch to the entire audience.

Group Discussion and Feedback (20 mins)	Facilitate a group discussion to gather feedback from participants. Encourage constructive criticism, highlight the strengths & weaknesses of each opportunity. Discuss the challenges faced during the evaluation & pitch process. Allow participants to ask to questions & help in exploration of the opportunities presented.
Wrap-up (10 mins)	Ask participants to share their key takeaways and insights gained about the Individual-Opportunity Nexus theory. Summarize the main points discussed during the session. Provide additional resources or readings for participants who wish to delve deeper into the topic.

Conclusion: The activity provides participants with a hands-on experience in understanding and applying the Individual-Opportunity Nexus theory for identifying and assessing entrepreneurial opportunities. The group discussions and feedback foster collaborative learning and enhance critical thinking. It reflects that encourages participants to share their key takeaways and further explore the topic. Overall, this activity promotes an entrepreneurial mindset and empowers individuals to recognize and capitalize on opportunities in their own ventures.

6.2 Actualization

The realization theory of pioneering openings presented by Ramoglou and Tsang (2016) is planned to overcome any barrier among disclosure and creation speculations of enterprising freedom. The disclosure viewpoint sees pioneering openings as existing out there in target reality holding on to be found and abused by business visionaries. This infers that assuming a chance doesn't exist, no measure of exertion to abuse it will be productive. One would waste their time! Denying the target presence of chances is somewhat like contending that if Edison had kicked the bucket early, we probably won't have the electric world we flow insight as maybe no one but he could abstractly build the thought of electric light. Unmistakably it is a stretch to have so little confidence in numerous free developments. The creation viewpoint takes the contrary view, recommending that chances don't exist outside of businesspeople themselves and are made by their perceptions and activities. This view recommends that Edison might have prevailed in any field of innovative undertaking had he coordinated his endeavors there. There is some proof that he fiddled with dark advances, however all appear to be employments of power, which is the broadly useful innovation. This is likewise somewhat near the incredible man theory. Completion theory takes the center ground, suggesting that chances are genuine, however that they are simple penchants that are useless except if they are found and misused with the right consideration and ability (Ramoglou and Tsang, 2016). Like blossom seeds covered up under the outside of the ground, they may stay unborn for quite a while before the conditions are perfect. Example: The business visionary comes around to discover the seed, water it, and guarantee it gets sufficient manure and light. Hence, the significant differentiation gives off an impression of being that although chances may appear to exist impartially, it isn't clear on the off chance that they will be misused at all and assuming this is the case all around ok to ultimately turn them productive.

Eric Tsang

Stratos Ramoglou

"PLANT A SEED, MANURE IT, WATER IT & GIVE IT SOME LIGHT TO GROW"

Understanding the "Actualization" theory:

In the context of business, actualization refers to the process of realizing one's full potential or achieving one's goals. A good example of actualization in business is an entrepreneur who starts a business with a vision to create a product or service that will change the world in some way. Through hard work, determination, and the ability to overcome obstacles, the entrepreneur can turn their vision into a successful business that has a positive impact on society. For instance, Steve Jobs, co-founder of Apple, had a vision to create a computer that was accessible and easy to use for everyday people. He believed that technology should be user-friendly, and design driven. Jobs was able to actualize his vision by leading Apple to develop the Macintosh computer, which revolutionized the computer industry and changed the way people interacted with technology. His relentless pursuit of excellence and commitment to his vision enabled him to actualize his full potential as a business leader and innovator.

Classroom Activity: Unleashing Your Full Potential

Objective: The readers understand and apply the principles of actualization in their lives to unlock their full potential through self-reflection & action-oriented exercises.

Duration: 100 - 120 mins

Material: Large whiteboard or flip chart paper, Marker pens in different colors, Sticky notes or index cards & Pens or pencils for participants.

Instructions:

Activity	Instructions
Intro (10 mins)	Begin by providing a brief overview of actualization theory, explaining its key concepts and principles. Emphasize the importance of self-actualization as a lifelong pursuit of personal growth and fulfillment.
Understanding Current State (20 mins)	Ask participants to reflect on their current state of being and their aspirations for personal and professional growth. Provide guiding questions to assess strengths, passions, values, & areas for improvement. Encourage participants to note their thoughts.
Visioning Your Ideal Self (15 mins)	Ask participants to imagine their ideal self, describing personal traits, achievements, relationships, and lifestyle. Encourage them to write down a vivid and inspiring vision of their ideal self.
Identifying Barriers and Limiting Beliefs (15 mins)	Help participants identify barriers and limiting beliefs that hinder their potential. Provide a list of common limiting beliefs and prompt participants to reflect on resonating beliefs. Encourage challenging these beliefs and considering alternative perspectives.

Action Planning (20 mins)	Guide participants in creating an action plan to bridge the gap between their current state and their ideal self. Ask them to set specific goals, milestones, and actionable steps, breaking them down into manageable tasks with realistic timelines.
Sharing (10 mins)	Create a supportive environment for participants to share their vision, goals, and action plans. Encourage finding accountability partners or forming small groups for support and progress tracking. Emphasize regular check-ins & celebrating milestones.
Reflection and Closure (10 mins)	Allow participants to reflect on their experience and insights gained. Ask them to write down key takeaways & commit to integrating actualization theory principles into their lives. Provide additional resources for further exploration.

Conclusion: This activity offers participants a transformative journey of self-discovery and growth. By reflecting on their current state, envisioning their ideal self, and creating actionable plans, participants are empowered to overcome barriers and unlock their full potential. With accountability and reflection, they can integrate the principles of actualization theory to lead a more fulfilled and purposeful life.

Financial Theories

7.1 Liquidity

Founding a new venture is more common among individuals with greater access to financial capital because financial capital makes it easier to acquire the resources needed to start ventures. For instance, Evans and Jovanovic (1989) find that wealthier individuals are more likely to enter into entrepreneurship because they can risk their own capital. There is some evidence that many employees make the leap to entrepreneurship during liquidity events such as initial public offerings and acquisitions of their parent firms which can put significant financial resources into the hands of employees that own shares or options in the company. These employees, now flush with cash, have the financial freedom to spin out new ventures from their parent firms into independent companies (Stuart and Sorenson, 2003). Hurst and Lusardi (2004) find some evidence for liquidity constraints however only at the top of the range, suggesting that only very wealthy individuals are more likely to become entrepreneurs, whereas increase access to capital among less wealthy individuals may not make a difference. New ventures that are founded with a large pool of capital available to them can scale much more easily than those that enter with scarce capital. Scaling is considered key to financial performance through efficiency (economies of scale).

Recent developments in crowdfunding and now ICOs, have made available larger pools of capital for startups in some sectors. The Theory would predict that crowdfunded startups would outperform those that receive no funding or just nominal funding. The Theory would also predict that unicorns, that start with large investments of private capital should outperform all other startup types. The jury is out on this theory. Some research suggests that ventures that receive VC funds gain more employees, which is positively associated with equity value growth (Davila, Foster and Gupta, 2003), at least in Silicon Valley. Some scholars point out that starting a business does not necessarily require significant resources, rather, access to financial capital may be more important for firm growth (Davidsson and

Honing, 2003). The Bricolage & Effectuation theories help to explain how entrepreneurs go through to start their ventures with minimal financial capital.

Understanding the "Liquidity" theory:
A common example of liquidity in business is having enough cash on hand to cover short-term obligations, such as payroll, rent, and other operating expenses. If a business does not have enough liquidity, it may struggle to meet its financial obligations and risk defaulting on its loans or other debt. For instance, suppose a small retail store does not have enough cash reserves to meet its monthly rent and payroll expenses. In that case, it may need to rely on short-term loans or credit lines to cover the costs until it generates enough revenue to cover the expenses. However, if the business cannot access financing or generate enough revenue, it may face bankruptcy or closure due to insufficient liquidity. Thus, managing liquidity is critical for businesses to maintain their operations and meet their financial obligations.

David S. Evans | Boyan Jovanovic

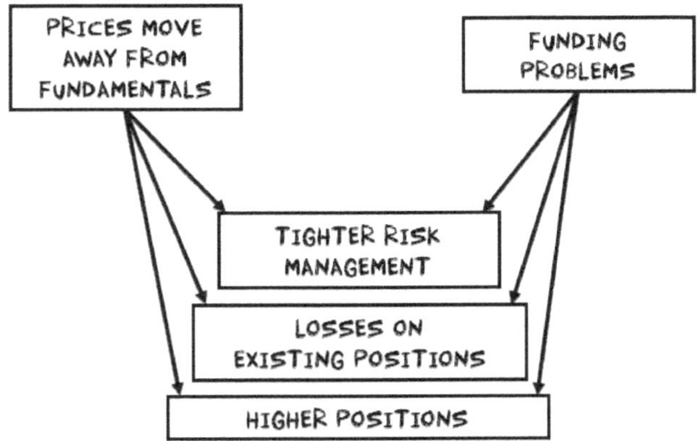

Classroom Activity: "Navigating Financial Fluidity"

Objectives: Participants delve into the concept of liquidity and its significance for entrepreneurs in managing their financial resources effectively. Through interactive exercises and discussions, participants will explore strategies for optimizing liquidity, understanding cash flow management, and making informed financial decisions to support the growth and sustainability of their ventures.

Duration: 100 - 120 mins

Material: Large whiteboard or flip chart paper, Marker pens in different colors, Sticky notes or index cards & Pens or pencils for participants.

Instructions:

Activity	Instructions
Intro (10 mins)	Start by providing an overview of liquidity theory, explaining its key principles and relevance to entrepreneurial ventures. Discuss the importance of liquidity in maintaining financial stability, seizing growth opportunities, & mitigating risks.
Understanding Liquidity (20 mins)	Engage participants in a discussion about different dimensions of liquidity, such as cash on hand, accounts receivable, and short-term investments. Explain the concept of liquidity ratios and their significance in assessing the financial health and stability of a business. Illustrate the trade-offs between liquidity and other financial objectives, such as profitability and asset management.
Assessing Liquidity Needs (15 mins)	Guide participants through an exercise to assess their venture's liquidity needs based on their industry, business model, and growth plans. Encourage them to identify potential liquidity risks and challenges specific to their ventures. Discuss various factors that can impact liquidity, such as seasonality, market volatility, and changes in customer behavior.
Cash Flow Management Strategies (20 mins)	Introduce participants to effective cash flow management techniques, including cash flow forecasting, monitoring, and optimization. Share practical tips for accelerating cash inflows, such as offering incentives for early payments or implementing efficient invoicing processes. Discuss strategies for managing cash outflows, such as negotiating favorable payment terms with suppliers and optimizing inventory levels.

Mitigating Liquidity Risks (15 mins)	Facilitate a brainstorming session where participants identify potential liquidity risks and develop risk mitigation strategies. Discuss the importance of building contingency plans and establishing emergency funds to address unforeseen challenges. Highlight the role of financial reserves and lines of credit in managing liquidity shocks and maintaining business continuity.
Financial Decision-Making (15 mins)	Explore key financial decisions that entrepreneurs face, such as investment prioritization, capital structure choices, and debt vs. equity financing. Discuss how liquidity considerations should inform these decisions and strike a balance between short-term liquidity needs and long-term growth objectives. Encourage participants to analyze real-world scenarios and make informed financial decisions considering liquidity implications.
Reflection and Action Planning (10 mins)	Allow participants to reflect on the insights gained from the activity and identify specific actions they can take to enhance liquidity management in their ventures. Provide a framework or template for participants to create their liquidity management plan, including key metrics to monitor and strategies to implement. Encourage participants to set measurable goals, establish checkpoints for reviewing progress, and seek ongoing education or resources to further enhance their liquidity management skills.

Conclusion: This activity on liquidity theory equips entrepreneurs with essential knowledge and practical strategies to navigate financial fluidity effectively. By understanding liquidity dimensions, optimizing cash flow management, and mitigating risks, participants can make informed financial decisions, maintain stability, and foster the growth and sustainability of their ventures. Empowered with these skills, they can confidently tackle liquidity challenges and seize opportunities for long-term success.

7.2 Pecking order

The pecking order Theory was developed in the 1980's by finance scholars & made famous by Stewart Myers and Nicolas Majluf seeking to understand the financing preferences of firms. Pecking order Theory also relates to entrepreneurs' preferences about financing choices. Financing options include using one's own personal funds, reinvesting profits back into the business, selling equity to outside investors, and bank debt or loans. At the core of the Theory are information asymmetries between the entrepreneur or the startups' executive team, and the prospective sources of funds for the business—that is, the financiers. Entrepreneurs and other insiders have better information about the business' operations and potential than do prospective financiers because the former deal with stakeholders and problems on a day-to-day basis. Financiers usually have to rely on secondhand information provided by the leadership team of the startup and the financial statements they provide. While corporate officers have a fiduciary duty toward shareholders, that is, they are legally required to be truthful, there is still plenty of room for understatement, overstatement, and obfuscation (see agency Theory for more on this). To make up for their informational disadvantages, financiers typically demand higher interest rates or more favorable terms to protect themselves against what they do not know (Paul, Whittam and Wyper, 2007). As a result, entrepreneurs tend to prefer to fund their ventures using their own funds and profits of the business rather than submitting to the costly demands of outside investors and lenders. New equity investors will typically demand a higher rate of return on their investment than the founding investors, thus entrepreneurs will typically prefer loans. Entrepreneurs also prefer short-term loans to long-term loans, as these will typically have lower interest rates (Paul et al., 2007). The information asymmetries are more acute for some types of firms than for others. For instance, firms with complex business models that are difficult for outsiders to understand will typically have greater asymmetries than simple or conventional business models that are easy to understand. Warren Buffett is famous for stating that he only invests in simple businesses that he understands. Presumably, he would require a much higher rate of return to invest in more complex businesses.

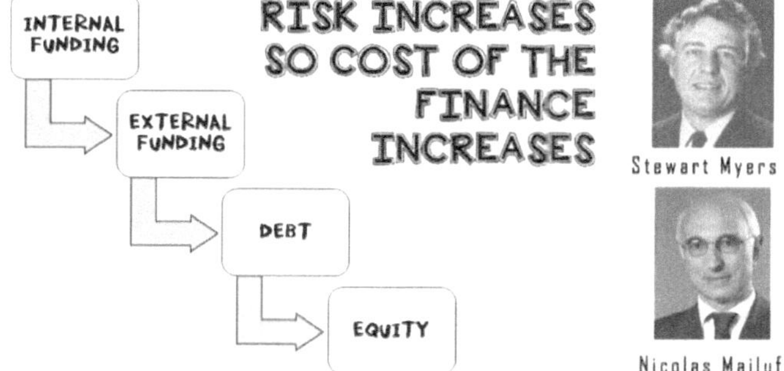

Understanding the "Pecking" theory:

Pecking order theory is a theory in corporate finance that explains the financing behavior of companies. The theory states that companies prefer to finance their projects using internal funds, then debt, and lastly, equity. Companies tend to follow this "pecking order" because of the asymmetric information problem that arises when a company tries to raise funds externally. For example, suppose a company has a new project that requires funding. The management will first try to finance the project using its internal funds, such as retained earnings. If that is not enough, they will try to borrow money from banks or other financial institutions. Only when the first two options are not feasible, they will consider issuing new equity to raise capital. The pecking order theory suggests that companies prefer to use internal funds over external financing sources because of the higher costs of external financing and the negative signal it sends to the market about the company's financial health.

Classroom Activity: "Exploring Hierarchy in Entrepreneurship"

Objective: To help readers understand and analyze the concept of "pecking order" in the context of entrepreneurship. By engaging in this activity, participants will gain insights into the dynamics of power, influence, and decision-making within entrepreneurial ecosystems.

Duration: 100 - 120 mins

Material: Large whiteboard or flip chart paper, Marker pens in different colors, Sticky notes & Pens or pencils for participants.

Instructions:

Activity	Instructions
Intro (10 mins)	Present the concept of pecking order in entrepreneurship. Explain the emergence of an informal hierarchy where individuals or groups establish positions of power and influence. Emphasize the importance of understanding the pecking order for entrepreneurial success.
Case Study (20 mins)	Select a real-life case study illustrating the pecking order in entrepreneurship. Provide participants with the case study and ask them to analyze key individuals or groups, power dynamics, the evolution of the pecking order, and lessons learned.

Case Analysis (20 mins)	Encourage group discussions. Ask them to analyze and identify the following: • Key individuals or groups involved in the venture. • Power dynamics and the influence each individual or group exerted. • How the pecking order evolved and its impact on decision-making.
Personal Reflection (15 mins)	Ask participants to reflect individually on their experiences with pecking orders in entrepreneurial environments. Provide guiding prompts for participants to describe scenarios, evaluate the impact of the pecking order, discuss their role, and extract lessons for future endeavors. For example. • Describe a specific scenario where you observed a pecking order within an entrepreneurial setting. • How did the theory affect decision-making, resource allocation, or team dynamics in that scenario? • What role did you play within the pecking order, & how did it influence your experience or outcomes? • What lessons can you extract from that experience and apply to your future entrepreneurial endeavors?
Group (15 mins)	Facilitate a group discussion where participants share their reflections, insights, challenges, and strategies for navigating pecking orders in entrepreneurial environments. Encourage an open conversation and learning from each other's experiences.
Key Take-aways (10 mins)	Summarize the key takeaways from the discussion, emphasizing strategies to navigate and manage pecking orders effectively in entrepreneurship. Encourage participants to apply their understanding of the pecking order to enhance their entrepreneurial journey. If time permits, invite a guest speaker—an experienced entrepreneur or an organizational behavior expert—to share insights and experiences related to pecking orders in entrepreneurship, providing additional perspectives, and enriching the activity.

Conclusion: By engaging in this activity, readers will develop a deeper understanding of the pecking order in entrepreneurship and its impact on decision-making, power dynamics, and team collaboration. This knowledge will equip them with valuable insights and strategies to navigate and manage pecking orders effectively as they pursue their entrepreneurial ventures.

7.3 Signaling

Signaling Theory has been used to explain how firms communicate their quality and intentions to investors. For instance, debt and dividends signal quality because low quality firms presumably cannot keep up interest payments over the long run (Bhattacharya, 1979).

Signaling Theory is used to explain which startups get funded by investors and which do not raise capital. The typical study identifies a set of signals sent by a firm around the time of an initial public offering (IPO). Signals may include top management team characteristics, founder involvement, or the presence of venture capitalists or angel investors. Signaling Theory predicts how these signals will affect the signal receiver's decisions. The next step is to characterize the signals as either positive or negative in terms of their effects on subsequent investments or valuations by public or private investors (see review by Connelly, Certo, Ireland and Reutzel, 2011). For example, founder involvement may be viewed as a positive signal by investors in an IPO because it demonstrates commitment to the venture. Most of the research looks only at deliberate positive signals because of the tendency to suppress negative signals (Connelly et al., 2011). Yet, some negative signals are communicated unintentionally as a by-product of some other action (i.e., issuing new shares can signal that shares are over-valued). The best signals are costly and observable because costly signals are difficult to fake, especially if the signal cost is lower for higher quality firms (e.g., ISO9000 certification).

Signals can correct information asymmetries, such as when entrepreneurs' private (insider) information about their own ventures' prospects (unobservable quality) are superior to that of outsiders. For example, entrepreneurs may be privy to the early results of research and development projects or early sales data of a new product. They may also learn about impeding lawsuits or union troubles earlier than outsiders. This type of information can also shape entrepreneurs' intentions about the business, such as whether they will sell out their share or stay for the long haul (Connelly et al., 2011).

One of the key assumptions of the Theory is that the signalers and signal receivers have somewhat conflicting interests, otherwise the signaler would have no reason not to fully divulge their private information. Outsiders, such as investors, could make better decisions if they had access to the entrepreneur's private information, but since they often do not have such access, at least not without considerable costs, signals are the next best thing. Signaling Theory poses a special challenge to the "perfect information" assumption of economists. It also challenges human capital theories, because individuals may seek education and training to signal their abilities in areas that are hard to observe directly rather than acquiring the knowledge.

SUDIPTO BHATTACHARYA

SIGNALING THE INVESTORS

PROFITABLE/ PERFORMANCE	DIVIDEND POLICY/ PROFIT SHARE	EXPANSION/ NEW PRODUCT
CAPITAL STRUCTURE/ FINANCING	ENVIRONMENTAL/ ETHICAL	PRACTICE

Understanding the "Signaling" theory:

One example of signaling theory in business is the use of high prices as a signal of quality. This theory suggests that consumers will often associate higher prices with higher quality, even if there is no objective evidence to support this belief. As a result, businesses may use high prices as a way to signal to consumers that their products are of high quality. For example, luxury brands like Louis Vuitton or Chanel are known for their high prices, which often signals to consumers that their products are of superior quality compared to less expensive brands. Similarly, high-end restaurants may charge higher prices for their food and wine to signal to customers that they offer a superior dining experience. Another example of signaling theory is the use of credentials and certifications to signal expertise or credibility. For instance, a financial advisor may earn a professional certification, such as a Certified Financial Planner (CFP), to signal to potential clients that they have expertise and experience in the field. In both cases, businesses are using signals to convey information to consumers or stakeholders that may be difficult to observe or evaluate objectively. These signals can be powerful tools for building brand reputation and establishing a competitive advantage in the marketplace.

Classroom Activity: "Decoding Business Language"

Objective: To familiarize readers with the concept of Signaling Theory in entrepreneurship and help them understand how businesses use various signals to convey information and build trust.

Duration: 80 – 90 mins

Materials: Whiteboard or flip chart, Markers, Handouts or printed materials with case studies or examples & Sticky notes.

Instructions:

Activity	Instructions
Intro (10 mins)	Emphasize its importance in communicating characteristics, capabilities, and intentions to external stakeholders. Highlight its impact on building trust, attracting investors, securing partnerships, and differentiation in the market.
Teams (5 mins)	Divide participants into small groups or pairs. Provide each group with a whiteboard or flip chart and markers. Instruct them to brainstorm and list various signals used by businesses to convey information.
Think (15 mins)	Encourage thinking beyond traditional marketing and branding signals. After 15 mins, have each group share their lists with the larger group.
Case Studies Discussion (20 mins)	Distribute case studies/examples of businesses that effectively used Signaling strategies. Participants read the case studies individually or in pairs and highlight key signals used. Facilitate a group discussion by asking questions the following questions: • What signals did the businesses use to communicate their characteristics and capabilities? • How did these signals contribute to building trust and attracting stakeholders? • Were there any signals that surprised you or stood out as particularly effective? • Are there any signals that you think could be improved or additional signals that could have been used?
Signaling Strategy Design (25 mins)	Divide groups to choose a business scenario or hypothetical situation. Ask them to design a Signaling strategy, identifying key characteristics, capabilities, or intentions to signal, and brainstorm specific signals to effectively communicate them. Encourage creativity and innovative thinking. After 20 mins, have each group present their strategies to the larger group for feedback.

Wrap-up & Reflection (10 mins)	Summarize key learnings from the activity. Ask participants to reflect on the importance of Signaling in entrepreneurship and its impact on business success. Invite them to share additional insights or ask questions related to Signaling theory.

Conclusion: The activity allows participants to explore crucial role of effective communication in entrepreneurship. Through brainstorming, case study analysis, and strategy design, participants gained insights into various signals used by businesses to convey information and build trust. By understanding the power of signaling, participants are better equipped to navigate the entrepreneurial landscape and make informed decisions to optimize their business's success.

7.4 Agency

This theory was created during the 1980s by business analyst Michael C. Jensen at the Harvard Business School for the reasons of clarifying and anticipating the practices of financial backers and directors. It recognizes administrators and specialists, the previous being parties that delegate duty regarding some arrangement of activities to the last mentioned. For example, businesspeople and chiefs are regularly the specialists of financial backers, who delegate the duty over a business association. The theory' hidden supposition that will be that the two players are self-intrigued and that the interests of chiefs and specialists veer or are in struggle. In this way, specialists may settle on choices for directors that are not to the administrators' advantage, which is called an organization issue. For example, specialists may face more noteworthy challenges than chiefs would need them too on the grounds that specialists are wagering with the directors' capital. Organization issues are exacerbated when there is data deviation among head and specialists. Specialists normally have preferable data over chiefs since they are responsible for everyday choices and are generally nearer to the association than directors, who are commonly financial backers fairly eliminated from the business. Data imbalance makes it hard for administrators to screen the activities of specialists (directors and businesspeople), and it is unthinkable for chiefs to configuration ideal agreements to deal with every conceivable situation. Data imbalance & deficient agreements create organization dangers called unfavorable determination & good risk. Antagonistic choice is the issue of choosing specialists that are inappropriate, though upright danger is the issue of choosing specialists that misuse assets. Misappropriation comes in numerous structures, including free riding, evading, & the exorbitant utilization of advantages. Organization scholars propose result bases motivations as answers to adjust the interests of specialists to those of administrators.

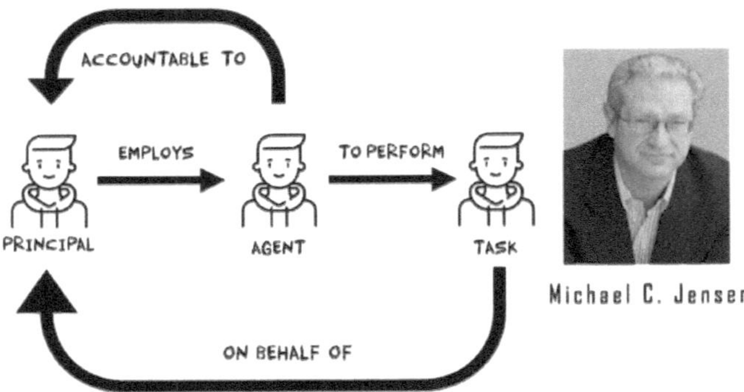

Michael C. Jensen

Understanding the "Agency" theory:

One example of agency in business is the relationship between a company's shareholders and its management team. In this case, the shareholders are the principals, and the management team is the agent. The shareholders entrust the management team with the responsibility of running the company and making decisions that are in the best interest of the shareholders. However, the management team may have their own interests and goals that are not necessarily aligned with those of the shareholders. For example, the management team may be more concerned with maximizing their own compensation or job security than with maximizing shareholder value. To mitigate this agency problem, companies may implement various mechanisms to align the interests of the management team with those of the shareholders. For example, they may link executive compensation to the company's performance, such as tying bonuses to earnings per share or stock price. They may also appoint independent directors to the board who can provide oversight and accountability for management decisions. Another example of agency in business is the relationship between a company and its suppliers. In this case, the company is the principal, and the suppliers are the agents. The company relies on its suppliers to provide goods or services that meet certain quality, price, and delivery standards. However, the suppliers may have their own interests and goals, such as maximizing their own profits or avoiding risk. To mitigate this agency problem, companies may implement various mechanisms to ensure that their suppliers meet their expectations. For example, they may use performance metrics and regular audits to monitor supplier performance and quality. They may also negotiate contracts with clear terms and incentives to encourage suppliers to meet their expectations.

Classroom Activity: "Balancing Stakeholder Interests"

Objective: To enhance & engage participants in a role-playing exercise to explore the dynamics between business owners & their appointed managers & how agency conflicts can arise.

Duration: 70 – 80 mins

Materials: Whiteboard or flip chart, Markers, Handouts or printed materials with case studies or examples & Sticky notes or index card.

Instructions:

Activity	Instructions
Create Groups (5 mins)	Participants are divided into groups of three, with one person assigned as the business owner (principal), one as the appointed manager (agent) and one as an observer/note-taker.
Provide a case scenario! (10 mins)	Each group receives a case scenario that describes a fictional company's background, ownership structure, & specific challenges related to agency conflicts. The scenarios may involve performance evaluation, risk-taking behavior, or diverging goals between owners and managers. Participants understand case scenario, taking notes on key points, conflicts, & potential solutions.
Role-playing (15 mins)	The owner (principal) and manager (agent) within each group engage in a role-playing dialogue, addressing the challenges presented in the case scenario. Observer/note-taker documents the conversation, noting areas of agreement, disagreement, & potential agency conflicts arising during the discussion.
Group discussion (15 mins)	The groups reconvene & facilitated discussion takes place focusing on topics as followed: • What were the main sources of conflict between the owner and manager? • How did the conflicting interests of various stakeholder's impact decision-making? • What strategies could be employed to align the interests of the owner and manager? • What mechanisms that could be implemented to reduce agency problems in this scenario? • What lessons can be drawn from this exercise for real-world entrepreneurship?

Group pitch (20 mins)	Each group presents their case scenario, role-playing dialogue, and key takeaways to the larger group. Participants are encouraged to ask questions, provide feedback, and engage in a broader discussion on agency theory and its implications for entrepreneurial ventures. The instructor facilitates the discussion reflecting on the presented scenarios & lessons learned during the activity.
Key Takeaways (5 mins)	Highlight the main insights gained from the role-playing exercise and the subsequent discussion. Include the challenges of aligning stakeholder interests, strategies to mitigate agency conflicts, the importance of effective communication and monitoring, and the significance of designing appropriate incentive structures. Participants are given the opportunity to ask questions and share their own reflections on the topic.

Conclusion: By actively engaging in this role-playing exercise, participants will gain a deeper understanding of the complexities of agency theory and its relevance to entrepreneurship. They will also develop practical strategies for addressing agency conflicts and ensuring the alignment of stakeholder interests within their own ventures.

Biological Theories

8.1 Birth Order

Birth order Theory is the development of 1950's psychoanalysts (think Sigmund Freud, Carl Jung, and Alfred Adler) who placed that when (the circumstance) an individual is conceived, corresponding to the introduction of kin, shapes encounters and characters. Birth request is loaded down with so much social importance both inside families and in social orders as a rule, that it guides mental turn of events. Robinson and Hunt (1992) quote Rychlak (1981:145) outline the normal rationale behind birth request theory as follows: "In a various kid family, the firstborn youngster turns into an extraordinary adherent to control, however as a grown-up the person is almost certain than different kids in the home to have a moderate, adjusting standpoint, to be a 'standard resident' and a customary person. The second-conceived kid is probably going to feel a feeling of challenge in the family star grouping. . . If a second-conceived kid has any ability, we are bound to see this posterity foster it than the others in view of the kid's plausible way of life of attempting to dominate here and there... Regardless, we hope to see a great deal of drive in the second-conceived and less authority-inclination than in the firstborn kid. The wild child sibling, who will 'accept any challenge' and likes to disrupt the guidelines, pleasantly meets the image of a second-conceived kid." The birth order Theory of business venture has endured in spite of reactions (Hirsric and Brush, 1983; Robinson & Hunt, 1992; Watkins & Watkins, 1983).

No observational help for the theory once family pay and size are thought of. Since various societies give various implications to birth request, the theory is probably not going to anticipate anything diversely. The theory is futile for aiding business teachers and experts. It is entirely yet debilitating, as people have no power over their introduction to the world request.

Alfred Adler | Sigmund Freud | C. G. Jung

WHAT CAME FIRST?

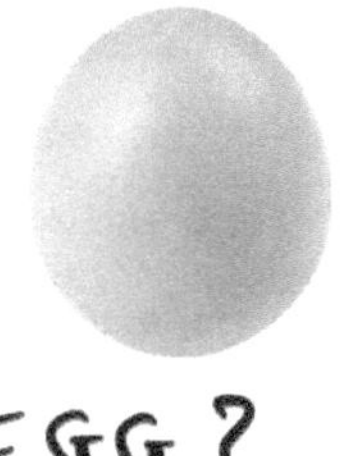

EGG? HEN?

Understanding the "Birth Order" theory:

Birth order is a psychological concept that refers to the order in which children are born in a family and how this may influence their personality traits, behavior, and decision-making. While birth order is not a direct factor in business, it can influence the way people interact with their colleagues, employees, and customers. For example, first-born children are often described as natural leaders, responsible, and goal oriented. They may be well-suited for management positions or entrepreneurship, as they tend to be decisive and focused on achieving success. On the other hand, youngest children are often described as more creative, social, and adaptable. They may be well-suited for roles that require collaboration, networking, or innovation, as they tend to be more comfortable with risk-taking and experimentation. In the context of a family-owned business, birth order can also play a role in succession planning and leadership transitions. For example, the eldest child may be expected to take over the family business, while the younger siblings may have different career aspirations or interests. However, it is important to note that birth order is just one factor that can influence a person's behavior and personality. Other factors such as genetics, environment, and upbringing can also play a role. It is important not to make assumptions about someone' abilities or potential based solely on their birth order.

Classroom Activity: "Birth Order Entrepreneurship Challenge"

Objective: To explore the impact of birth order on entrepreneurial traits and behavior, fostering self-awareness & promote discussions on how birth order theory may influence entrepreneurial success.

Duration: 80 – 90 mins

Materials: Whiteboard or flip chart, Markers. Handouts or printed materials with case studies or examples & Sticky notes.

Instructions:

Activity	Instructions
Intro (10 mins)	Introducing the concept and its potential influence on individual characteristics and behavior. Explain that the theory suggests that the order in which individuals are born within their families can have a significant impact on their personalities, traits, and tendencies.
Group Discussion (15 mins)	Divide the participants into small groups and ask them to discuss their own birth order (e.g., oldest, middle, youngest) and how they believe it has influenced their entrepreneurial traits and behavior. Encourage participants to share personal stories or observations about themselves or people they know.
Personal Reflection (10 mins)	Provide a worksheet to all with guiding questions, as: • How do you think your birth order has influenced your personality traits and behaviors? • Do you identify with any characteristics commonly associated with your birth order? • In what ways do you think your birth order might impact your entrepreneurial journey? • Are there any challenges or advantages you perceive based on your birth order?
Share (20 mins)	Facilitate a discussion by asking follow-up questions as: • Do you see any patterns among different birth orders in terms of entrepreneurial traits? • How might birth order influence team dynamics within a startup or entrepreneurial venture? • Can you think of any successful entrepreneurs who exemplify characteristics associated with their birth order?

Group Pitch (15 mins)	Invite each group to prepare a short presentation summarizing their discussions and insights on the topic. Each group should highlight key points, interesting anecdotes, and any divergent perspectives they encountered.
Key – Takeaways (10 mins)	Summarize the key findings from the discussions and presentations. Emphasize that birth order is just one factor among many that can influence entrepreneurial traits and behaviors. Encourage participants to reflect on their own unique qualities and leverage them in their entrepreneurial endeavors.

Conclusion: By exploring the potential influence of birth order on entrepreneurial traits and behavior opens intriguing discussions and self-reflection among participants. While birth order is just one factor among many, it encourages individuals to consider how their unique experiences within their families may shape their entrepreneurial journey. Ultimately, embracing & leveraging one's distinctive qualities can contribute to entrepreneurial success regardless of birth order.

8.2 Brain Parasite

As usual, we should think about new theory while taking other factors into consideration. For this situation, you may get somewhat netted out! The Toxoplasma gondii parasite is conveyed by cats (felines) and has been found to taint their human experts as well. The parasite can be gotten through contact with the creatures and their organic liquids and solids. The parasite causes mind sores that endure forever and lead to practices including bipolar turmoil, decreased dread, and lower IQ. Some have assessed that more than 2 billion people have been contaminated, however disease rates vary enormously by country. For example, the U.S. contamination rate is around 3%, while it could be just about as high as 50 to 70% in France and Mexico. Petr Houdek at University of Economics in Prague investigated the writing in a 2017 paper distributed in the Academy of Management Perspectives. Exploration by Stefanie Johnson (Leeds School of Business) and partners (a posse of non-researcher) proposes that those contaminated by the infection are 1.7 occasions bound to pick pioneering vocation ways. They guineas pigs for disease by taking spit swabs. They discover critical positive relationship among disease and pioneering action and goal, and a huge negative relationship with dread of disappointment. The clarification for this adjustment of conduct is because of the relationship between a Toxoplasma Gondii and an expansion in testosterone levels (Zouei et al., 2018). Exploration recommends that higher testosterone levels is related with more danger taking conduct and pioneering plan in people (Bönte et al., 2016). A new benchmark group concentrate by Lerner et al. (2020), was led on 16,068 female organizers from 11,433 new companies and found that there were various connections between the Toxoplasma Gondii and business venture accordingly reproducing the aftereffects of Johnson's (2018) study. Lerner et al., proceed to express that the contamination of the parasite goes before innovative endeavors implying that people are fundamentally bound to seek after another endeavor following a Toxoplasma Gondii disease. This examination is quite new and ought to be duplicated a few times prior to growing businesspeople choose to open themselves to cats deliberately. This examination is new and ought to be imitated a few times prior to sprouting business visionaries choose to uncover themselves deliberately.

Stefanie K Johnson

Understanding the "Brain Parasite" theory:

Brain parasites are organisms that can infect the brain and alter the behavior of their hosts, and they are not typically associated with business activities or operations.

In the context of business, it is important to maintain a safe and healthy work environment for employees, customers, and other stakeholders. This includes implementing measures to prevent the spread of infectious diseases and providing access to healthcare resources for those who may become ill. However, brain parasites are not a typical concern in the workplace. It is important to seek medical attention if you suspect that you have been infected with a brain parasite or any other type of infection or illness. Consult with a healthcare provider for appropriate diagnosis and treatment.

Classroom Activity: "Unleashing Innovative Solutions"

Objective: To engage readers in an interactive activity that stimulates critical thinking, creativity, and problem-solving skills while exploring the concept of the Brain Parasite Theory.

Duration: 140 – 150 mins

Materials: Whiteboard or flip chart, Markers, Handouts or printed materials with case studies or examples & Sticky notes.

Instructions:

Activity	Instructions
Intro (15 mins)	Start by introducing the workshop and its objectives. Provide a brief overview of the Brain Parasite Theory, explaining how it suggests that parasites can manipulate human thoughts and actions. Encourage participants to approach the theory with an open mind, embracing creativity and curiosity.
Brainstorming (20 mins)	Divide participants into small groups (3-5 people per group) and provide each group with flipchart paper, markers, and sticky notes. Instruct each group to brainstorm potential ways in which the Brain Parasite Theory could impact society, individuals, or businesses. Encourage participants to think broadly and explore both positive and negative implications of the theory.
Group Discussion (30 mins)	Ask each group to present their ideas and insights to the whole group. Ask thought-provoking questions, such as: • How might the Brain Parasite Theory influence consumer behavior? • What industries or sectors could be most affected by this theory? • Are there any potential positive outcomes that could arise from this concept?
Ideation (40 mins)	Instruct participants to focus on developing innovative solutions to address the challenges or opportunities presented by the Brain Parasite Theory. Each group should identify a specific problem or scenario related to the theory and brainstorm potential entrepreneurial solutions. Encourage participants to think creatively, considering technological advancements, social interventions, or business models.
Solution Pitch (20 mins)	Ask each group to present their proposed solutions to the entire group. Provide constructive feedback and encourage further discussion and refinement of the ideas.

Wrap-up (15 mins)	Facilitate a reflection session, allowing participants to share their thoughts on the activity and what they have learned about entrepreneurship, problem-solving, and creativity.

Conclusion: Through group discussions and solution presentations, participants gained insights into potential impacts and entrepreneurial responses. The activity encourages critical thinking, collaboration, and reflection, leaving participants with a deeper understanding of entrepreneurship and the power of imaginative problem-solving.

8.3 Genetic

The genetic approach to entrepreneurship looks to biological inheritance to explain the tendency for an individual to become an entrepreneur and succeed in entrepreneurial ventures. Research on genetic links is spurred on by considerable anecdotal evidence that the children of entrepreneurs are more likely to become entrepreneurs than the children of non-entrepreneurs. Genetic research tries to tease out family and environmental factors (learning, role modeling, and resources) from genetic factors. Nicolaou et al. (2008) concludes that when one twin becomes an entrepreneur then the other twin is more likely to, even when controlling for family upbringing and other environmental factors. They suggest that testosterone levels are inherited and related to the decision to become an entrepreneur. Later studies have added more depth to the analysis, looking to personality traits as mediators. For instance, Shane et al. (2010) study twins (with 50% and 100% similar genes) and conclude that the personality traits (openness to experience and extroversion) associated with entrepreneurial entry are indeed inheritable. The study finds limited support though, because the effect sizes were rather small. Genetic theories are controversial because they tend to downplay the potential for entrepreneurial preparation and education to spur individuals toward the career path with success. However, the small effect sizes suggest that nature matters, but nurture matters much more. To date, no studies have demonstrated a genetic effect on entrepreneurial success, which seems to be logical step for genetic Theory research.

Nicos Nicolaou

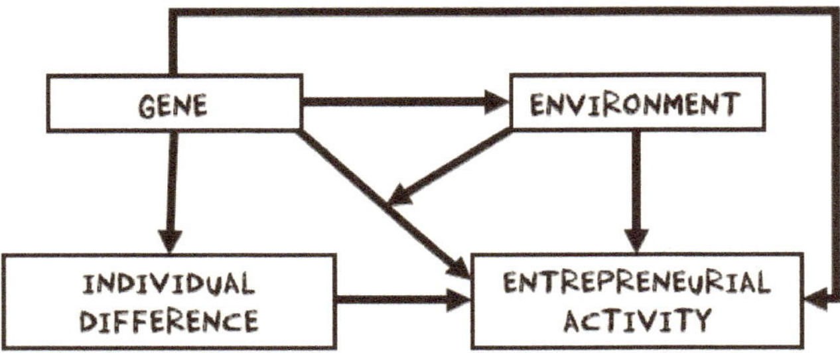

Understanding the "Genetic" theory:

Genetic theory, also known as the theory of inherited traits, suggests that certain characteristics, abilities, and behaviors can be passed down from parents to their offspring through genetic inheritance. While genetic theory is not typically directly applicable to business operations, it can be relevant in the context of certain industries or business activities.

For example, genetic theory may be relevant in the field of biotechnology, where companies may be involved in research and development related to genetic engineering or genetic testing. In this context, understanding genetic theory and the mechanisms of inheritance may be essential to developing new products or technologies. In addition, genetic theory may also be relevant in the context of human resources and talent management. Some companies may use genetic testing or other types of genetic information to evaluate job candidates or employees for certain traits or abilities that may be relevant to their job performance. However, the use of genetic information in employment decisions can raise ethical and legal concerns, and many jurisdictions have regulations in place to protect against discrimination based on genetic information. While genetic theory may not be directly applicable to all aspects of business operations, it can be relevant in certain industries or contexts where genetic information is important. It is important for businesses to be aware of the ethical and legal considerations surrounding the use of genetic information in employment or other business decisions.

Classroom Activity: "Unleashing Power of Genetic Theory"

Objective: To explore the principles of genetic theory and apply them to entrepreneurial scenarios. Participants will learn how to adapt genetic concepts to their entrepreneurial endeavors and discover new perspectives for business development.

Duration: 110 – 120 mins

Materials: Whiteboard or flip chart, Markers. Handouts or printed materials or examples & Sticky notes or index cards (optional). Internet access for research.

Instructions:

Activity	Instructions
Intro (10 mins)	Start by providing a brief overview of genetic theory. Explain the fundamental concepts, such as genes, inheritance, DNA, mutations, and genetic variation. Highlight the connection between genetics and the evolution of life.
Identify Traits (15 mins)	Discuss how genetic traits can be analogous to entrepreneurial traits. Ask participants to identify characteristics like risk-taking, adaptability, creativity, resilience, & persistence. Encourage them to think about how these traits influence entrepreneurial success.
Genetic Variation Ideas (20 mins)	Explain the concept of genetic variation and how it leads to diversity in organisms. Now, challenge participants to apply this concept to their entrepreneurial ideas. Ask them to brainstorm different variations or adaptations of their existing business ideas or products. How can they introduce innovative features or target different customer segments?
Mutation and Innovation (15 mins)	Introduce the idea of genetic mutations and how mutations can lead to beneficial changes and open new opportunities. Encourage participants to think about their existing business models or processes and identify areas that could benefit from a "mutation" or radical change. How can they disrupt their industry by introducing innovative practices or technologies?
Genetic Cross-Pollination (20 mins)	Explain the concept of genetic cross-pollination, where genetic material is exchanged between different organisms. Relate this concept to entrepreneurship by encouraging participants to seek inspiration and ideas from diverse industries or disciplines. Ask them to think about how they can combine different elements, concepts, or technologies to create unique business opportunity.

Group Discussion and Reflection (15 mins)	Facilitate a group discussion to share the ideas generated during the activity. Encourage participants to reflect on how the principles of genetic theory can enhance their entrepreneurial mindset and practices. Prompt them to consider the potential impact on their business strategies, innovation processes, and problem-solving approaches. Prompt them questions such as: • What are some examples of genetic traits that could be advantageous or disadvantageous for founders? • How might genetics interact with other factors, such as environmental influences or learned behaviors? • How has this exploration of the Genetic Theory influenced your perception of entrepreneurship?
Key Take-away (15 mins)	Help participants summarize the key takeaways from the activity, emphasizing the application of genetic theory principles in entrepreneurship, such as leveraging traits for success, embracing variation and mutation for innovation, and cross-pollinating ideas from diverse fields. Encourage participants to apply these insights to their entrepreneurial journey for enhanced problem-solving, creativity, and adaptability.

Conclusion: Exploring genetic theory in the context of entrepreneurship provides valuable insights into adapting and evolving in the business landscape. By identifying entrepreneurial traits, applying genetic variation to ideas, embracing mutation and innovation, and fostering genetic cross-pollination, participants gain a fresh perspective on problem-solving and innovation, empowering them to navigate challenges and seize new opportunities. By harnessing the power of genetic theory, entrepreneurs can unlock their potential for transformative growth and success.

8.4 Great Man

One of the most popular 19th century theories of entrepreneurship is the "great man Theory". The Actor's popularity is probably owing to the historian Thomas Carlyle. Yes, I know, it sounds sexist from the start, but let us stretch the meaning and say it's the Great Man Theory and try to move it along from there. Great people theories are often heard in historical tales of Mahabharat – Arjuna, Abhimanyu, etc. WW2 - Hitler, Stalin, Churchill, Eisenhower, Roosevelt, and a few others leading the way. Tens of millions of people were involved in the war and a myriad of events occurred over time that may have impacted the outcomes of the war. The same is done with entrepreneurs, pitting

Bill Gates against Steve Jobs in the battle for the PC, for instance. The great people Theory holds that most of the important decisions about how the economic and political world works today were made by just a handful of people. These gifted individuals are the heroes and heroines of every age. Another popular assumption among great people theories is that great people are born, not made. They are born with a special gift or power that allows them to ascend above others and assume positions of influence and power. This assumption is quite problematic too, because it basically means that most of us just need to accept our low lots in life. There is an elitism built into the Theory, that a few should be great and others not great and thus not impactful in the world. If greatness cannot be learned, then why try hard? Finally, another critique is that entrepreneurship is not really about individuals, rather it is about groups of individuals who form a network together in the pursuit of common goals (Drakopoulou and Anderson, 2007). Thus, over-emphasizing individuals downplays the importance of networks.

Understanding the "Great Man" theory:

The Great Man Theory suggests that certain individuals possess innate qualities, such as intelligence, charisma, and leadership skills, that make them natural-born leaders. This theory has been applied to various fields, including business. One example of the Great Man Theory in the business world is Steve Jobs, the co-founder and former CEO of Apple Inc. Jobs was known for his visionary ideas, strong leadership skills, and ability to inspire and motivate his team. He was seen as a charismatic and innovative leader who was able to turn Apple into one of the most successful and influential companies in the world.

Jobs' ability to make bold decisions and push the boundaries of technology was crucial to the success of Apple, and many credit his leadership style as a major factor in the company's growth. His leadership and vision helped Apple revolutionize the computer, music, and mobile phone industries, and his impact can still be felt in the company's products and culture today. While there are certainly other factors that contributed to Apple's success, Jobs' leadership style is often cited as a prime example of the Great Man Theory in action.

Classroom Activity: "Unveiling Individual Leaders"

Objective: To delve into the theory and encourage readers to critically analyze its relevance and implications to gain a deeper understanding of the theory and engage in a discussion about the role of individual leaders in shaping organizations and societies.

Duration: 110 – 120 mins

Materials: Whiteboard or flip chart, Markers, Handouts or printed materials or examples & Sticky notes or index cards (optional). Internet access for research.

Instructions:

Activity	Description
Reading (15 mins)	Provide participants with reading material on the Great Man Theory, including scholarly articles, books, and online resources. The material should delve into the theory's historical context and key principles.
Individual Reflection (20 mins)	Participants spend time reflecting on the Great Man Theory and its implications. They are encouraged to ponder historical examples supporting or challenging the theory and its relevance to entrepreneurship and leadership. They should also critically assess the theory's strengths and weaknesses.
Group Discussion (25 mins)	Organize a group discussion to explore participants' perspectives on the Great Man Theory. Facilitate an open dialogue where participants share their reflections, discussing whether they find the theory convincing or problematic. Encourage the exploration of contemporary examples of leaders who align or contradict the theory and alternative theories challenging it.

Case Study Analysis (30 mins)	Provide case studies featuring prominent leaders or entrepreneurs for analysis through the lens of the Great Man Theory. Participants discuss whether the leaders' actions and characteristics align with the theory or if other factors played a significant role in their success. This exercise encourages critical thinking and the examination of multifactorial influences on leadership.
Personal Reflection (20 mins)	Conclude the activity by prompting participants to reflect on their leadership aspirations and how the Great Man Theory might impact their thinking. Encourage them to develop an action plan outlining specific steps to enhance their leadership skills while considering alternative theories and perspectives. This exercise fosters self-awareness and an open-minded approach to leadership development.

Conclusion: Participants discuss the role of individual leaders in entrepreneurship and leadership. They examine historical examples, evaluate its strengths & weaknesses, to develop a broader understanding of multifactorial influences on leadership & to chart their own leadership journey.

8.5 Life -Cycle Stages

The entrepreneurial process is often conceptualized as stage-based or as a life cycle. These theories are borrowed from biology where life cycles of flora and fauna are studied extensively. Thus, perhaps it is alright to think of this borrowing as a kind of analogy - imperfect, but potentially interesting. In ecology and biology, there are stages of development or decay present in many phenomena. These theories start with the assumptions of birth, growth, maturity, and decline. The Instructions, explanation and prediction of cycles is one of the mainstays of the hard sciences. By definition, a life has a beginning and an end, which provides initial boundary conditions for the Theory. What happens in between, or those inner transitions, are where we are going to find most of the action in terms of debate. Kazanjian and Drazin (1990) suggest four stages to explain how an entrepreneurial opportunity becomes a business. They propose that the drivers and resistors of entrepreneurship are different at each stage of venture development. Probably only the first stage or two is really about entrepreneurship, whereas growth and stability are managerial issues after a certain point. Such as 1. Conception and Development, 2. Commercialization, 3. Growth & 4. Stability. Bhave (1994) put forward four stages. In this case, the transitions were ordered but one can easily imagine cases where these stages overlap temporally or are happening simultaneously. While the stages proposed by each Theory do not perfectly line up, there is a pattern between them. However, the length of each stage and the emphasis on indicators of stage transition differ. Perhaps there are stages, but these would be too context-specific to replicate: 1. Opportunity, 2. Technology set-up, 3. Organization-creation & 4. Exchange stage. The pattern in academia seems to be to define the stages and check that they are there, especially across contexts. There are many stage-based models out there and new ones are continually popping up. A critic might wonder if a four-stage Theory is a great way to kill an hour-long paid keynote - it's a story with a nice progression, after all.

Understanding the "Life-Cycle Stages" theory:

The business life cycle is a model that describes the stages that a business goes through from its inception to its eventual decline or exit. The stages of the business life cycle include:

Startup: The entrepreneur is developing the concept, creating a business plan, and launching the business. Example: A tech startup developing a new software application.

Growth: The business experiences rapid growth in revenue, customer base, and market share. Example: A small clothing boutique that has expanded to several locations and an online store.

Maturity: The business has stabilized and is generating consistent revenue and profits. Example: A well-established chain of fast-food restaurants that has been in business for several decades.

Decline: The business starts to experience a decline in revenue, market share, and profits. Example: A video rental store that is struggling to compete with digital streaming services.

Turnaround/Revival: Business attempts to reverse the decline & revive growth. E.g.: A struggling electronics retailer introduces a new product line & marketing strategy to regain market share.

Exit: The business owner decides to exit the business, either through a sale or closure. Example: A family-owned restaurant that is sold to a larger restaurant chain.

Life cycle understanding prepares for the challenges and opportunities that arise at each stage. By identifying which stage their business is in, they can make informed decisions about strategy, financing, & operations to maximize growth and profitability.

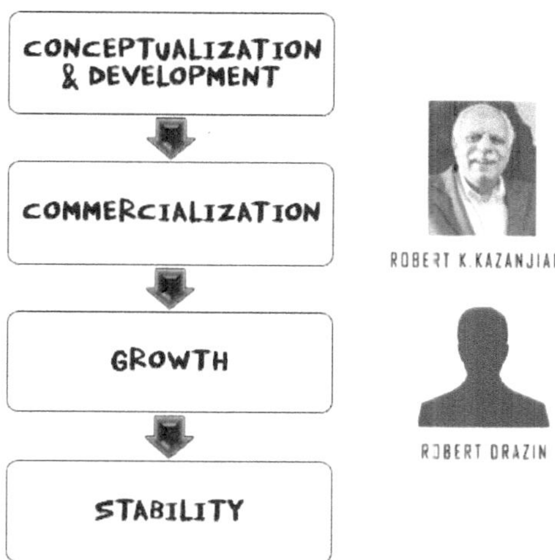

Classroom Activity: "Life-Cycle Journey for Startup Success"

Objective: To help readers understand the concept of life-cycle stages theory in entrepreneurship and how it applies to their own entrepreneurial journeys. By reflecting on the different stages of the entrepreneurial life cycle, participants will gain insights into the challenges, opportunities, and strategies associated with each stage.

Duration: 30-45 mins

Materials: Pen or pencil, Paper or notebook & Whiteboard or flipchart for group activities

Instructions:

Activity	Instructions
Intro (5 mins)	Introduce the concept of life-cycle stages theory in entrepreneurship, highlighting its relevance and discussing the common stages such as idea generation, startup, growth, maturity, and exit.
Individual Reflection (15 mins)	Participants reflect on their own entrepreneurial journeys or aspirations, considering the stage they are currently in or envision themselves in, identifying the main challenges, and exploring opportunities and strategies specific to their stage. Use following prompts: • Which stage of the entrepreneurial life cycle are you currently in or envision yourself in? • What are the main challenges you face or expect to face in this stage? • What opportunities & strategies can be leveraged at given stage?

Small Group Discussion (15 mins)	Divide participants into small groups and assign a facilitator to each group. Participants share their reflections from Step 2, engage in a discussion about their experiences and perspectives, and explore alignment, resources, skills, and successful strategies for navigating their current or future stage. Facilitators should encourage open dialogue and pose additional questions, such as: • How do your experiences align or differ from others in group? • What resources, skills, or support do you believe are crucial in navigating your current or future stage? • Are there any strategies or approaches that have worked well for you or others you know in a similar stage?
Group Pitch (10 mins)	Each small group presents a summary of their discussion to the larger group, highlighting common themes, key insights, and unique perspectives that emerged during their small group discussions. This session promotes learning from one another and broadens understanding of the various life-cycle stages.
Wrap-up and Application (5 mins)	Encourage participants to apply the insights gained to their own entrepreneurial endeavors or future ventures. Recommend further exploration and seeking additional resources to deepen their understanding of the life-cycle stages theory. If time permits, invite guest speakers who have experienced different stages of the entrepreneurial life cycle to share their stories and insights of the challenges & opportunities associated with each stage.

Conclusion: The activity offers participants a valuable opportunity to explore and understand the different stages of the entrepreneurial life cycle. By reflecting on their own experiences, engaging in group discussions, and sharing insights, participants gain valuable knowledge and strategies to navigate the challenges and leverage the opportunities associated with each stage. Armed with these insights, participants are better equipped to navigate their entrepreneurial journeys with confidence and adaptability.

8.6 Niche

In ecology, a niche refers to a space with specific necessary environmental conditions that may guide the evolution and existence of species (Hardesty, 1972). This is closely related to the concept of convergent evolution, where two or more species develop similar adaptations because they occupy similar evolutionary niches. For example, the marsupial wolf is adapted to forests, plains, and preys on other mammal herbivores, just like the placental wolf. In entrepreneurship lingo, a niche refers to a narrow market space. Hutchinson (1978) suggests that much like animal species, competitors rarely occupy the same niche because if they do then they compete directly and would result in frequent fights (e.g., price wars). Rather, each species tends to specialize, for instance, one might evolve to prey at night, while the other preys during the day. Similarly, businesses can cater to distinct customer segments by offering differentiated products and services. The Theory of population ecology is used to elaborate on the role of entrepreneurship, so we point the reader there (Hannan and Freeman, 1977). Nonetheless, the basic idea is that each niche can only accommodate a fixed population size and mix and that entrepreneurs compete for space in niches with incumbents and other entrepreneurs. The Theory points to the need for unique niche exploitation strategies in order to carve out unique space. This is related to blue ocean strategy & disruptive innovation theory, both of which focus on the concept of unique market spaces.

Understanding the "Niche" theory:

A niche is a specialized segment of the market that targets a specific customer group with specific needs or interests. Here are some examples of businesses that operate in niche markets:

A vegan bakery: It specializes in producing baked goods that are entirely plant-based and free from animal products. They cater to customers who follow a vegan lifestyle or have dietary restrictions that prohibit them from consuming animal products.

Luxury pet accessories: It specializes in creating high-end, designer pet products such as collars, leashes, and beds. They cater to customers who pamper their pets & are willing to pay a premium.

Personalized stationery: It creates customized stationery items, such as invitations, notepads, and cards, with a personal touch for customers who reflect & value uniqueness (one-of-a-kind items).

Gluten-free bakery: It specializes in producing baked goods that are free from gluten, catering to customers who have celiac disease or gluten sensitivity.

Sustainable fashion: It focuses on creating clothing & accessories made from environmentally friendly materials and sustainable production methods for eco-friendly & customers.

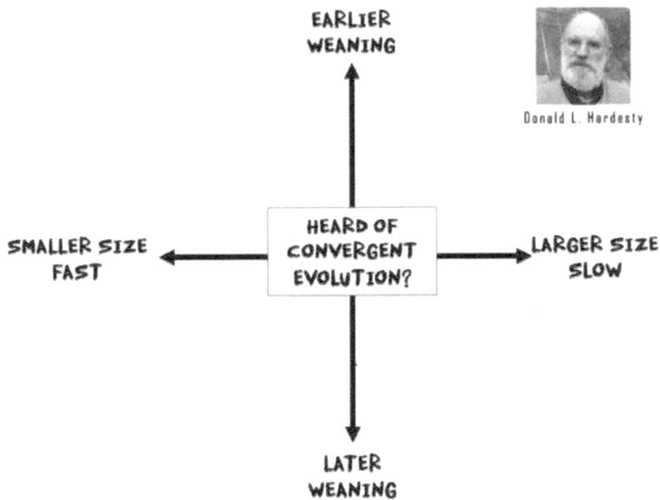

Classroom Activity: Niche Discovery Exercise

Objective: To help readers understand the concept of niche theory & apply it to their entrepreneurial endeavors.

Duration: 75 – 80 mins

Materials: Pen or pencil, Paper or notebook & Whiteboard or flipchart for group activities

Instructions:

Activity	Instructions
Intro (5 mins)	Introduce the concept of niche theory. Explain that a niche refers to a specialized segment of the market that a business targets to differentiate itself from competitors. Emphasize that finding a unique and profitable niche is crucial for entrepreneurial success.

Brain-storming (10 mins)	Ask readers to brainstorm potential niches that they find interesting or have expertise in. Encourage them to think about specific industries, customer segments, or unique needs that are currently underserved in the market.
Research (15 mins)	Instruct readers to choose one or two niche ideas from their brainstorming session & conduct basic research. • **Market demand:** Is there a need for products or services within the chosen niche? Are there any existing competitors? • **Target audience:** Who are the potential customers within the niche? Their demographics, preferences & pain points? • **Trends and opportunities:** Are there any emerging trends or untapped opportunities within the niche?
Evaluation & Selection (10 mins)	Based on their research, ask readers to evaluate the potential viability and profitability of each niche idea. They should consider factors such as market size, competition, barriers to entry, and their own resources and expertise. Encourage them to choose the most promising niche idea for further development.
Niche Statement (15 mins)	Instruct readers to create a niche statement that clearly defines their chosen niche with target audience, the specific needs, or problems they aim to address, the unique value proposition they plan to offer.
Group (15 mins)	Divide readers into small groups and ask them to share their chosen niche and niche statement with their group members. Each participant should provide feedback and suggestions.
Wrap-up (5 mins)	Wrap up the activity by asking readers to reflect on what they have learned about niche theory and how it applies to their entrepreneurial journey.

Conclusion: Through brainstorming, research, and evaluation, participants learn how to identify viable niches and develop concise niche statements. The group discussions and reflections foster critical thinking and empower readers to leverage their chosen niches for entrepreneurial success.

Cultural Theories

9.1 Misfit

GEERT HOFSTEDE

ARE YOU AN IMMIGRANT?

DISSATISFIED WITH YOUR JOB?

WELCOME TO THE MISFITS CLUB

Hofstede et al. (2004) suggest that misfit individuals attempt to start ventures because they do not share the dominant cultural values. The assumption is that misfit individuals are dissatisfied with their job prospects and are more likely to attempt entrepreneurial careers as alternatives. The misfit Theory of entrepreneurship has been used to explain why immigrants are often more entrepreneurial than native born populations. Immigrants' credentials may not respect in their new home countries. Their skills may be undervalued, their certifications and degrees may not be trusted or considered invalid or inadequate. Moreover, immigrants from countries with a different language and culture find it more difficult to integrate and find it more difficult to find lucrative employment (Kahn et al., 2017). In sum, imperfect information from foreign experience and education coupled with lingual and cultural differences make it more difficult to enter the workforce as salaried employees. This necessitates an alternative occupation like entrepreneurship. Where immigrants find it difficult to find employment in their areas of expertise, they may pursue entrepreneurial ventures as an alternative to working in low paying jobs outside their fields. Others have argued that pirates, hackers and gangsters also represent a type of misfit entrepreneurship (Clay and Phillips, 2016) though at times a potentially unproductive or destructive type. Overall, it is interesting to think of entrepreneurs as rule breakers. Perhaps there exists some potential for crossovers with informal entrepreneurship and institutional Theory.

Understanding the "Misfit" theory:

Misfit is a term used to describe businesses that don't fit neatly into a traditional industry or market category. Here are some examples of businesses that operate in a misfit market:

Casper: It sells mattresses and bedding products online. While this may seem like a typical retail business, Casper disrupted the traditional mattress industry by offering a direct-to-consumer model and by creating a new category of "bed-in-a-box" products.

Tesla: It disrupted the industry by focusing on electric cars and creating a luxury brand that appeals to environmentally conscious consumers.

Airbnb: It disrupted the traditional hotel industry by offering an alternative to traditional hotels and creating a new category of "home-sharing" accommodations.

Etsy: It disrupted the traditional retail industry by creating a platform for independent sellers to reach a global customer base.

These businesses are successful because they identified a gap in the market and created a unique value proposition that sets them apart from their competitors to build a loyal customer base and achieve significant growth.

Classroom Activity: The Misfit Mindset Workshop

Objective: To introduce and explore the concept of the "Theory of Misfits". Participants will understand the potential of misfit thinking and learn how to harness it to foster innovation and create unique business opportunities.

Materials: Whiteboard or flip chart, Markers, Sticky notes, Index cards & Pen/pencil for each participant

Duration: 60-90 mins

Instructions:

Activity	Instructions
Intro (10 mins)	Provide an overview of the "Theory of Misfits" as a tool for entrepreneurial success. Explain the concept of misfits and how their unique perspectives lead to innovative solutions & disruptive ideas.
Celebrate Differences (15 mins)	Divide participants into small groups and ask them to identify a member who thinks differently. Groups discuss and share the unique qualities and strengths of their chosen misfit.
Case Study Discussion (20 mins)	Present a case study of a successful entrepreneur or company that embraced misfit thinking. Facilitate a group discussion on the key characteristics and actions that contributed to their success. Explore how misfit thinking generated unique business opportunities and overcame challenges.
Ideation Exercise (25 mins)	Distribute sticky notes and index cards. Participants write down a personal or professional problem they face. Encourage them to think innovatively and consider how a misfit mindset could solve the problem. Give time for generating ideas on sticky notes.
Group Sharing (15 mins)	Participants share their ideas and engage in a discussion on the potential impact of misfit thinking on problem-solving and entrepreneurship. Reflect on how the misfit mindset can be applied to entrepreneurial endeavors or daily lives. Summarize key insights and takeaways.
Wrap-up (5 mins)	Express gratitude for participation, provide additional resources or recommended readings on misfit thinking, and encourage participants to embrace their unique perspectives and experiment with misfit thinking in their entrepreneurial pursuits.

Conclusion: By embracing the misfit mindset in entrepreneurship opens doors to innovative solutions and disruptive ideas. By celebrating our differences and thinking outside the box, we can create unique business opportunities and drive entrepreneurial success.

9.2 Cultural

Thomas Cochran (1965) proposed that entrepreneurs are influenced by their own attitudes toward their occupation, and the expectations of groups facilitating new ventures, as well as the difficulty level of the operational requirements of the career. He argues that both attitudes of potential entrepreneurs and the expectations of investors are "culturally determined". He looked to evidence in historical cases such as the entrepreneurial prominence of Protestants in America, Samurais in Japan, the Yoruba in Nigeria, the Kikuya in Kenya, Christians in Lebanon, the Halai Memon in Pakistan, and the Parsis in India. Each of these cases can be considered interpretations derived from cultural biases. Hofstede (1980) proposed that culture captures the set of values, beliefs and expectations about behaviors that are shared by a social group. Cultural values can be unconscious or conscious, rational or irrational, but either way, they influence the social, political and technological institutions of a society. These institutions then serve to reinforce the values in a virtuous or vicious circle. Cultural values influence the entrepreneurial behaviors in a society, such as the propensity take risks, or to pursue innovations that deviate from norms. Some cultures may value conformity, which discourages innovation. For instance, Shane (1992) finds that individualism is positively related with innovation whereas power-distance is negatively related with innovation. Davidsson and Wiklund (1997) find that societies that value autonomy, have a higher level of need for achievement and greater self-efficacy tend to have higher rates of new venture founding. Low uncertainty avoidance may also play a role in new venture creation.

Understanding the "Cultural" theory:

Cultural theory is a perspective that views organizations and management practices as shaped by broader cultural values and beliefs. For an example, Patagonia is a clothing company that specializes in outdoor clothing and gear. The company has built its brand around environmental and social responsibility, emphasizing the importance of sustainability and activism. Patagonia's mission statement reads, "Build the best product, cause no unnecessary harm, use business to inspire and implement solutions to the environmental crisis." Patagonia's commitment to environmental and social responsibility is deeply ingrained in its culture and management practices. The company has implemented a range of sustainability initiatives, such as using recycled materials in its products, reducing waste and energy use in its operations, and supporting grassroots environmental activism through its Patagonia Action Works program. Patagonia's management practices reflect its cultural values, such as offering flexible work arrangements and paid time off for employees to engage in activism and environmental volunteering. By embodying its cultural values in its products, operations, and management practices, Patagonia has been able to differentiate itself from competitors and build a loyal customer base. The company's commitment to sustainability and activism also resonates with consumers who prioritize environmental and social responsibility in their purchasing decisions.

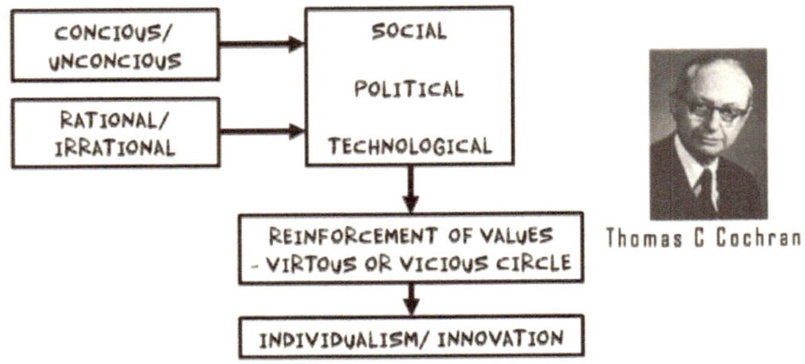

Classroom Activity: Cultural Theory Simulation

Objective: To explore & understand cultural theory concepts and apply them to real-life scenarios.

Materials: Whiteboard or flip chart, Markers, Sticky notes, Index cards & Pen/pencil for each participant

Duration: 75-90 mins

Activity	Instructions
Intro (5 mins)	Introduce the concept of cultural theory, explaining how different cultures shape beliefs, values, and behaviors. Inform participants about the activity and group formation.
Overview (10 mins)	Provide a brief overview of the four cultural theory perspectives: egalitarian, individualist, hierarchical, and fatalist. Explain their core beliefs and characteristics, emphasizing that they are analytical tools rather than generalizations.

Scenario Preparation (10 mins)	Distribute sticky notes. Instruct groups to choose one cultural theory perspective. Explain that they will analyze an assigned case study scenario from their chosen perspective. For example: a) A multinational company expanding operations to a new country with a different cultural background. b) A startup team composed of individuals from diverse cultural backgrounds facing conflicts due to different work styles and communication approaches. c) A company struggling to market its product to a specific cultural group due to mismatches in messaging and values. Encourage them to consider how the chosen perspective would influence decision-making, communication, teamwork, and overall success in the given scenario.
Scenario (25 mins)	Provide each group with a case study scenario related to cultural challenges in entrepreneurship or business. Instruct groups to discuss and analyze the scenario based on their chosen cultural theory perspective. Encourage consideration of decision - making, communication, teamwork, & success factors.
Pitch (20 mins)	Ask each group to present their analysis and insights to the whole group. Encourage discussion, questions, and exploration of different perspectives' implications in the scenarios. Facilitate a conversation on how cultural theory understanding informs entrepreneurship strategies and addresses cultural challenges.
Wrap-up (5 mins)	Summarize key takeaways & emphasize the importance of cultural awareness and understanding in entrepreneurship. Provide additional resources for further exploration of cultural theory.

Conclusion: By analyzing case study scenarios through various cultural theory lenses, participants gain insights into decision-making, communication, teamwork, and success factors in diverse cultural contexts. Cultivating cultural awareness and embracing the nuances of cultural theory equips entrepreneurs to navigate global business environments more effectively and build inclusive and successful ventures.

9.3 Religious

Max Weber was a German sociologist writing in the early 1900s who theorized that religious beliefs are a key determinant of entrepreneurial development. He argued that entrepreneurial energies are driven by beliefs about causes and consequences. In particular, he emphasized how religions encourage investment in economic growth and development (and compound interest). A religious belief in saving for the future was key, he believed, to the capitalistic spirit. Weber distinguished between religions that encourage capitalism from those that do not. Weber noted that Hinduism, Buddhism and Islam may not be conducive to entrepreneurship. Hinduism and Buddhism purportedly have a focus on the present moment and tend to shun materialism, making them problematic to the pursuit of entrepreneurial goals. He suggested that Islam's focus on the rewards of the afterlife make material accumulation problematic. By contrast, he argued that the protestant work ethic prevalent in Northern Europe at the time was highly compatible with entrepreneurial development. For example, among Quakers, cultural frugality and savings were hallmarks of the good life, and as a means of gaining the power to do God's work through enterprise. Weber's Theory is not widely accepted by sociologists, who argue that it was used as a tool to justify colonial rule in India. One of the propositions implied by the Theory was that pre-capitalist labour should not be offered higher wages with the expectation that they will work more because these folks' religion guides them to work less and enjoy more leisure as a response. The Theory also dismisses the variety of sub-traditions within major religions that come along with different views on material views. It ignores the local innovations of religious workers. The usefulness of the Theory is also challenged by the numerous counterexamples that are out there. The phenomenon of an emerging market multinationals seems to put the main tenets of the Theory in dispute.

Understanding the Religious theory:

Religious theory in the context of business suggests that organizations and management practices are influenced by religious values and beliefs. For example.

Chick-fil-A: It's a fast-food chain that is known for being closed on Sundays. This policy is rooted in the Christian beliefs of the company's founder, who prioritized faith & family over profits.

Hobby Lobby: A craft store chain that is closed on Sundays and observes Christian holidays. The company's founders are devout Christians, and they have incorporated their religious values into the company's operations, such as providing health insurance coverage that excludes certain forms of contraception.

Islamic banking: This is a type of banking that is based on Islamic principles and is compliant with sharia law. The principles of Islamic banking include a prohibition on interest-based transactions and a focus on socially responsible investments.

Kosher food production: The food production is a type of food production that follows Jewish dietary laws. This includes strict guidelines on the types of food that can be consumed and the way in which food is prepared.

Faith-based investing: This investing is based on religious values and beliefs. This can include investing in companies that align with specific religious values or avoiding companies that engage in practices that are considered immoral or unethical.

These businesses have been influenced by religious values and beliefs and have been able to build a loyal customer base and differentiate themselves from competitors.

Classroom Activity: Intersection of Entrepreneurship & Religion

Objective: In this activity, we will delve into the fascinating topic of the theory of religion and its potential impact on entrepreneurship. We will explore how religious beliefs, values, and practices can influence entrepreneurial behavior and decision-making. This activity aims to stimulate critical thinking, encourage open discussions, and broaden participants' perspectives on the relationship between entrepreneurship and religion.

Materials: Whiteboard or flip chart, Markers, Sticky notes, Index cards & Pen/pencil for each participant

Duration: 100 – 120 mins

Instructions:

Activity	Instructions
Intro (10 mins)	Introduce the topic of the theory of religion and its relevance to entrepreneurship. Highlight the role of religion in shaping individuals' values, ethics, and worldview. Explain the purpose of the activity.
Brain-storming (15 mins)	Divide participants into small groups or pairs. Provide flip charts or whiteboards and markers to each group. Instruct them to brainstorm ways in which religious beliefs and practices could influence entrepreneurial activities.

Group (20 mins)	Bring the groups together and facilitate a discussion. Each group presents their ideas and participants can add or build upon them. Encourage open dialogue and sharing of personal experiences related to the topic.
Case Analysis (25 mins)	Provide participants with case studies of entrepreneurs influenced by their religious beliefs. Divide participants into smaller groups for analysis and discussion. Identify ways religion influenced decisions and business models.
Personal views (15 mins)	Allow participants time for individual reflection on the discussion and case studies. Prompt them to consider how their own religious beliefs might impact their entrepreneurial aspirations or actions.
Wrap-up (15 mins)	Invite participants to share their reflections and insights. Facilitate a group discussion to explore common themes or differences in experiences and viewpoints. Summarize key takeaways and emphasize respecting diverse perspectives.

Conclusion: Through this activity, we explore the dynamic relationship between entrepreneurship and religion, recognizing how religious beliefs and practices can influence entrepreneurial behavior, motivations, and decision-making. By analyzing real-world case studies and engaging in open discussions, participants gain a deeper understanding of the diverse ways in which religion can shape and impact the entrepreneurial landscape. This activity highlights the importance of recognizing and respecting the role of religion in entrepreneurship, promoting a more inclusive and comprehensive approach to understanding the motivations and actions of entrepreneurs from various religious backgrounds.

Technological Theories

10.1 Marshall McLuhan's

"The crossing or hybridizations of the media release great new force & energy as by fission or fusion" (1964:48). Marshall McLuhan was a Canadian academic and celebrity who famously coined the phrase "the medium is the message" back in the 1960s to express his thesis about the effect of new technologies (extensions of ourselves) on culture and society. He and his son are known together for the McLuhan Tetrad, which suggest that careful analysis of the extensions, amputations, retrievals and reversals inherent in innovations help to reveal their effects. At a time when critics railed against sex, violence, and blasphemy on vacuum tube televisions, McLuhan claimed that the content of television was irrelevant, as it is the medium of television that really changes us by creating new audio/visual tribes, and seating us passively in front of the tube. New environments! He also suggested that the radio is the preferred of violent agitators--wonder what he would say today about social media. The implication of McLuhan's Theory is that new technologies shape environments and perceptions, by making accessible new dimensions of time and space. My shirt is an extension of my skin, my car is an extension of my legs, and my computer is an extension of my legs. To help us understand the difference between the medium and the message, he gave the example of the light bulb, which is a medium devoid of any content (or message), yet it creates an environment by its mere presence, illuminating the dark, extending our ability to make use of time and space, increasing our productivity and possibly our enjoyment of evenings. The lightbulb retrieves the day during the night, it reverses into insomnia and a blurred sky. It extends our eyes, while it amputates the candle. Marshal McLuhan is known for many things, but it is perhaps his concepts of "cold" and "hot" innovations that is most relevant to entrepreneurship scholars. Entrepreneurs exist in ecosystems with incumbent organizations and therefore should be selective about the innovations they pursue. The core idea here is that hot innovations (improvements along existing dimensions) are for incumbents whereas cold innovations are for new entrants (new combinations). This is very similar to Tushman and Anderson (1986) who argue that incumbents/entrants have the advantage with competence enhancing/destroying innovations. It is also similar to disruptive innovation Actor's distinction between disruptive and sustaining innovation. Let's examine McLuhan's concepts of hot and cold innovations in turn: Hot innovations increase performance along an existing dimension. McLuhan relates hot innovations to the word "hot", which is used to express an attachment to local and popular cultures. By increasing stimulus over one sense, a deeper connection to the environment created by the technology is achieved. The 3D movie is a great example of this: it adds more stimuli over the visual sense while not affecting any of the other senses. The large screen already offers more pixels than can be processed by the audience. With the 3D movie, this idea is taken to the extreme, where the visuals are so dense that one must continually choose where to focus attention. At the extreme, heating up a technology makes it hypnotic--similar to what Christensen called over-serving with products that do more and cost more than wanted by niche customers and those at the bottom of the market. Innovations that get too hot are soon challenged by the emergence of cold innovations. McLuhan's Cold innovations add some new dimension of performance for the senses, while compromising performance for senses along existing dimensions. This new combination of stimulus creates opportunities for newcomers to get positioned in a new but growing industry. This is very similar to Christensen's idea that disruptive innovations compensate for lower performance along traditional dimensions of performance by adding convenience, simplify, & affordability.

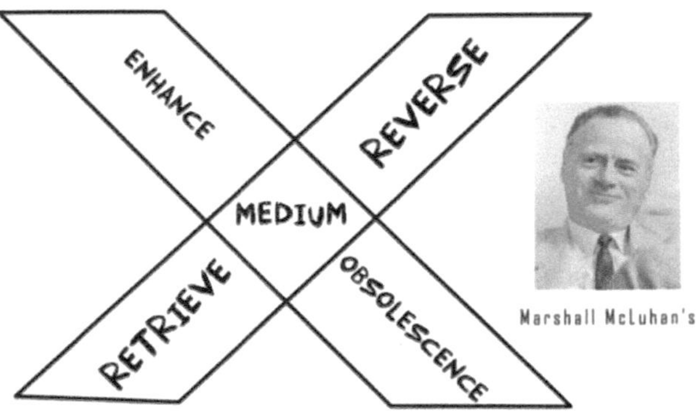

Cold innovations eventually get heated up giving rise to new cold innovations. McLuhan relates cold innovation to the word "cool" where a person or object is detached from the currents of popular thought. Unlike hypnotic hot innovation, cold innovations are more akin to hallucination--the user has to fill in the blanks. For e.g. the comic book requires the reader to fill in the joke--today it is the meme. For entrepreneurs, there is perhaps nothing more important than understanding media (technology) and its effects on people. It can help them to shape their ventures to take advantage of trends toward overheating and reversal.

Understanding the Marshall McLuhan's theory:

Marshall McLuhan's theory suggests that media and communication technologies shape our culture and society. For example.

Social media platforms: Facebook, Twitter, and Instagram have transformed the way we communicate and connect with one another. McLuhan's theory suggests that these platforms are not simply tools for communication but are also shaping our culture and society in profound ways.

Video streaming services: Netflix, Hulu, and Amazon Prime have disrupted the traditional media industry and changed the way we consume entertainment. McLuhan's theory suggests that these platforms are not just a new way to watch TV shows and movies but are also changing our relationship to media and technology.

E-commerce: Amazon and Alibaba have transformed the way we shop and do business. McLuhan's theory suggests that these platforms are not just a new way to buy goods and services but are also changing the way we think about commerce and the economy.

Virtual reality and augmented reality: VR & AR) technologies are changing the way we experience the world and interact with one another. McLuhan's theory suggests that these technologies are not just new tools for entertainment and communication but are also shaping our understanding of reality and our relationship to technology.

Smartphones: They have become an integral part of our daily lives, changing the way we communicate, work, and socialize. McLuhan's theory suggests that these devices are not just new tools for communication but are also shaping our relationship to technology and our understanding of the world around us.

These businesses have been influenced by McLuhan's theory, which suggests that media and communication technologies are shaping our culture and society in profound ways. By understanding these technologies and their impact on our culture and society, businesses can better adapt to the changing needs and expectations of their customers and stakeholders.

Classroom Activity: Media Tetrad: Impacts Entrepreneurship

Objective: In this activity, we will delve into Marshall McLuhan's Media Tetrad, a framework that explores the effects of media on society & four key aspects of the tetrad and their implications for entrepreneurship. This activity aims to stimulate critical thinking, foster lively discussions, and encourage participants to apply McLuhan's theories to their entrepreneurial endeavors.

Materials: Whiteboard or flip chart, Markers, Sticky notes, Index cards & Pen/pencil for each participant

Duration: 100 – 110 mins

Instructions:

Activity	Instructions
Intro (10 mins)	Introduce participants to Marshall McLuhan, his background, and contributions to media theory. Explain the concept of the Media Tetrad, consisting of enhancement, obsolescence, retrieval, and reversal. Emphasize that the activity will explore the impact of these elements on entrepreneurship and how they shape communication and innovation in the digital era.
Small Group Discussions (20 mins)	Divide participants into small groups or pairs. Assign each group one aspect of the Media Tetrad. Instruct groups to discuss and analyze their assigned aspect, considering its effects on entrepreneurship in the modern media landscape. Encourage the sharing of relevant examples and case studies that illustrate the application of the Tetrad to entrepreneurial ventures.
Group Presentations and Analysis (25 mins)	Bring groups together and allow each group to present their analysis of their assigned aspect of the Media Tetrad. Facilitate a discussion after each presentation, encouraging questions and feedback. Promote critical thinking by asking participants to identify specific ways in which their assigned aspect could impact entrepreneurial behavior, business models, or communication strategies.
Reflection and Application (15 mins)	Provide questions related to the Media Tetrad and its implications for their entrepreneurial pursuits. Encourage participants to share their reflections and insights with the group, promoting collaboration and a deeper understanding of the concepts.

Group Brainstorming and Action Planning (20 mins)	Facilitate a brainstorming session where participants collectively explore practical applications of the Media Tetrad in their entrepreneurial endeavors. Encourage creative thinking and the identification of opportunities to leverage the Tetrad for enhancing products, adapting to changing markets, retrieving valuable elements, or challenging established norms. Guide groups in developing action plans, emphasizing concrete steps & potential obstacles.
Group Sharing and Conclusion (10 mins)	Invite each group to share their action plans and ideas with the entire group. Facilitate a group discussion to discuss common themes, differences in approaches, and potential synergies. Summarize the key takeaways from the activity, emphasizing the significance of the Media Tetrad in guiding entrepreneurial strategies and fostering innovative thinking.

Conclusion: The activity has allowed participants to explore Marshall McLuhan's Media Tetrad and its direct relevance to entrepreneurship in the digital era. Through critical analysis and reflective discussions, participants have gained valuable insights into how the Tetrad's elements impact entrepreneurial behavior, communication strategies, and innovation, fostering a deeper understanding of media's influence on business ventures. By applying McLuhan's theories to their own entrepreneurial pursuits, participants are better equipped to navigate the dynamic media landscape and seize opportunities for creative and innovative growth.

Ethical Theories

11.1 Utility

JOHN STUART MILL

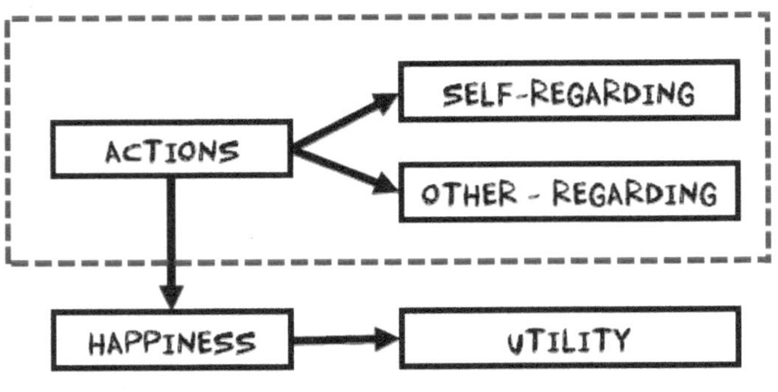

Utility Theory was developed by moral philosophers in the early 1900s, including John Stuart Mill. The core concept is that individuals make (or should make) decisions that maximize utility. Utility includes value for oneself and for others (society). Mill's book Utilitarianism sets forth several principles and argues that happiness has utility, as does justice. All sentient beings can experience utility, thus maximizing utility can consider the interests of animals. But it brings forth a debate about how much utility to give to a deer versus a driver in the decision to construct an expensive nature fence and land bridge. Moreover, there might be "more sentient" beings, such as gifted humans, which some might want to give a higher utility in their calculations. Another problem is that we might give little weight to things that affect many people but only a little bit. For example, if one may litter and affect many people (who will see the trash), but this has little negative impact on them by itself. Douglas and Shepard did a study of entrepreneurs to see if they really think in ways that are compatible with utilitarian thinking. They emphasize the desire for independence as having utility in addition to income. "Significant relationships were found between the utility expected from a job and the independence, risk, and income it offered. Similarly, the strength of intention to become self-employed was significantly related to the respondents' tolerance for risk and their preference for independence."

Understanding the "Utility" theory:

It is a theory of economics that suggests that individuals make decisions based on the expected utility or satisfaction that they will receive from their choices. Here are some examples of businesses that have been influenced by utility theory:

Airlines: They use utility theory to determine their pricing strategies. By understanding how consumers make decisions based on factors such as price, convenience, and travel time, airlines can optimize their pricing strategies to maximize revenue and profitability.

Insurance companies: They use utility theory to calculate the risk of insuring a particular individual or business. By understanding the expected utility or satisfaction that a policyholder will receive from their insurance coverage, insurance companies are able to determine the appropriate premiums to charge.

Investment firms: They use utility theory to help their clients make investment decisions. By understanding the expected utility or satisfaction that clients will receive from their investment choices, investment firms are able to provide personalized investment advice & recommendations.

Marketing firms: They use utility theory to understand consumer behavior and preferences. By understanding the expected utility or satisfaction that consumers will receive from a particular product or service, marketing firms are able to design effective advertising campaigns and promotional strategies.

Energy companies: They use utility theory to determine their pricing strategies and to evaluate the potential profitability of new energy projects. By understanding the expected utility or satisfaction that consumers will receive from different energy sources and pricing models, energy companies are able to make informed decisions about their business strategies.

Theory clearly suggests individuals make decisions based on their expected utility or satisfaction. By understanding factors influencing consumer behavior & decision-making, businesses can optimize their pricing strategies, product offerings, & marketing efforts to customers' centricity.

Classroom Activity: Exploring Utility - From Theory to Practice

Objective: Participants will delve into the fascinating world of the "Theory of Utility" by exploring the concept of utility and its practical implications for entrepreneurs. By engaging in thought-provoking exercises and discussions, readers will gain a deeper understanding of utility theory and its relevance in the business world.

Materials: Whiteboard or flip chart, Markers, Sticky notes, Index cards & Pen/pencil for each participant

Duration: 90 – 100 mins

Activity	Instructions
Intro (10 mins)	Explain core concepts with relevance in economics & decision-making. Highlight the distinction between total utility and marginal utility, emphasizing their significance in understanding consumer behavior.
Real-Life Utility Assessment (15 mins)	Ask readers to reflect on their recent purchase decisions and identify three products or services they have bought or considered buying. Have readers list the reasons why they believed the purchase would provide utility or satisfaction, considering emotional, social, and psychological factors.
Utility Ranking & Comparison (10 mins)	Instruct readers to create a utility ranking list for the three products they previously identified. Ask them to assign a score to each product based on perceived utility, considering both total utility and marginal utility. Prompt readers to reflect on any patterns or differences they notice in their utility rankings.
Group Discussion (20 mins)	Organize readers into small groups to facilitate a discussion on utility theory. Encourage participants to share their individual utility rankings and the reasoning behind their choices. Prompt participants to explore how utility theory can be applied in entrepreneurial contexts, such as product development, pricing, & marketing campaigns.

Case Study Analysis (25 mins)	Provide a case study or scenario where readers can apply utility theory to analyze business decisions. Ask readers to identify key stakeholders, potential trade-offs, and utility considerations in the given situation. Facilitate a group discussion or have readers share their analysis to encourage critical thinking and practical application of utility theory.
Take aways (10 mins)	Ask readers to reflect on their understanding of utility theory and its implications for entrepreneurship. Encourage them to identify at least one actionable insight or lesson they can implement.

Conclusion: Through the exploration of utility theory and real-life assessments, participants gain valuable insights into consumer behavior and its application in entrepreneurial contexts. This activity empowers them to make informed decisions, prioritize utility considerations, and leverage utility theory for business success.

11.2 Procedural Justice

This Theory was introduced by John Thibaut and Laurens Walker (1975) and has then been applied to the organizational strategy context (e.g., Kim and Mauborgne, 1991), and most recently to help explain entrepreneurial success from a financing-availability perspective. Thibaut and Walker propose that procedural justice focuses on the processes of justice rather than the outcomes of such processes (i.e., distributive justice), because the processes are more important in the evaluations of participants. Processes take place over time, whereas outcomes are more like events For example, a client may be more willing to accept concessions suggested by a lawyer that assures him or her that the negotiation process is normal and offers are within the bounds of acceptable behavior for an opponent's council. According to Sapienza and Korsgaard, we do not yet know much about how entrepreneurs manage their relationships with investors. Entrepreneurs want to build trust to attain continuous support for their ventures and a boost to their reputations, but how do they do it? They look to information sharing between the entrepreneurs and their investors. While entrepreneurs benefit from sharing information with investors, they also may benefit from withholding information. Providing information builds trust while withholding information increases relative power. They find that procedural justice optimizes information flows in order to gain inventor trust, support, growth financing, and imparted reputation. Procedural justice may help explain how entrepreneurs successfully manage their investor relationships. More generally, entrepreneurs may aim for procedural justice in the application of their decision-making power in all stakeholder relationships.

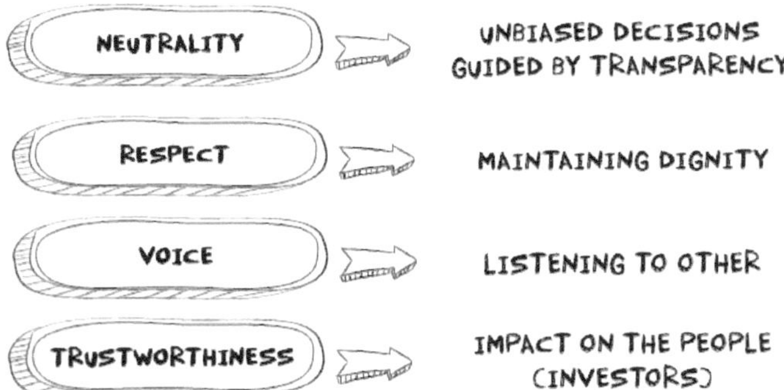

Understanding the "Procedural Justice" theory:

Procedural justice theory is a framework that examines how fairness and justice are perceived by individuals in organizations. It focuses on the processes and procedures used to make decisions, rather than the outcomes themselves. Here are some business examples of procedural justice theory:

Performance evaluations: Procedural justice theory suggests that employees are more likely to perceive performance evaluations as fair when they are provided with clear and specific performance standards, given ample opportunity to provide feedback, and are evaluated by unbiased and trained evaluators.

Hiring and promotion: When organizations follow transparent and objective procedures for hiring and promoting employees, employees are more likely to perceive the process as fair. This can include using objective criteria such as skills and experience, providing clear communication about the selection process, and offering feedback to unsuccessful candidates.

Pay and compensation: Fairness in pay and compensation can be achieved by using objective and transparent criteria, such as market rates or performance metrics, and offering opportunities for negotiation and feedback.

Dispute resolution: Procedural justice theory suggests that organizations can promote a sense of fairness in dispute resolution by offering clear and objective procedures for addressing conflicts, such as mediation or arbitration, and ensuring that all parties are treated equally and with respect.

Layoffs and terminations: When organizations follow clear and objective procedures for layoffs and terminations, such as using seniority or performance metrics to determine who is affected, and providing clear communication and support to affected employees, the process is more likely to be perceived as fair.

The theory emphasizes the importance of fairness and transparency in organizational decision-making processes, which can lead to greater employee satisfaction, commitment, and trust in the organization.

"Classroom Activity: Fair & Inclusive Environments"

Objective: Participants delve into the theory and its significance in entrepreneurship. Participants will explore the principles of fairness, transparency, and inclusivity in decision-making processes. Through engaging exercises and discussions, readers will gain a deeper understanding of procedural justice and its application in fostering a supportive entrepreneurial ecosystem.

Materials: Whiteboard or flip chart, Markers, Sticky notes, Index cards & Pen/pencil for each participant

Duration: 100 – 120 mins

Instructions:

Activity	Instructions
Intro (10 mins)	Provide a concise introduction to the theory of procedural justice, emphasizing its relevance in organizational settings and entrepreneurship. Explain the core principles of procedural justice, such as fairness, transparency, participation, and voice.
Personal Reflection (15 mins)	Ask readers to reflect on a time when they felt a sense of fairness or unfairness in a decision-making process within an entrepreneurial context. Prompt them to identify and describe the specific elements that contributed to their perception of procedural justice or injustice.

Case Study Analysis (20 mins)	Provide a case study or scenario that highlights a decision-making process in an entrepreneurial setting. Instruct readers to analyze the case study from the perspective of procedural justice, considering factors such as impartiality, inclusion, opportunity for input, and transparency. Encourage them to identify any potential shortcomings and propose alternative approaches to enhance fairness & inclusivity.
Designing a Fair Decision-Making Process (20 mins)	Ask readers to imagine they are starting a new entrepreneurial venture and need to design a decision-making process that prioritizes procedural justice. Instruct them to outline the key steps, guidelines, and mechanisms they would incorporate to ensure fairness, transparency, and inclusivity. Encourage them to think beyond traditional approaches and consider innovative methods or technologies that can enhance procedural justice.
Group Discussion (25 mins)	Organize small groups to facilitate a discussion on procedural justice in entrepreneurship. Prompt participants to share their personal reflections and case study analyses, encouraging dialogue and the exchange of diverse perspectives. Discuss the challenges faced in procedural justice propagation within entrepreneurial environments & brainstorm strategies to overcome these obstacles.
Reflection and Takeaways (10 mins)	Conclude the activity by asking readers to reflect on their understanding of procedural justice and its implications for entrepreneurship. Encourage them to identify at least one actionable insight or strategy they can implement to promote procedural justice in their entrepreneurial endeavors. Emphasize the importance of creating an inclusive and supportive environment that nurtures diverse perspectives and fosters fair decision-making processes.

Conclusion: Participants reflect on personal experiences and analyze case studies to identify specific elements that contribute to their perceptions of fairness or injustice in decision-making processes. Through engaging group discussions and innovative brainstorming, participants design fairer decision-making approaches that prioritize inclusivity and diverse perspectives, aiming to create an environment of transparency and ethical entrepreneurship.

Other Startup Theories

12.1 Actor-Network

This theory was made by Bruno Latour, Michel Callon, and John Law. It portrays a "material-semiotic" technique for investigation that is unmistakable from standard organization examination in that it remembers non-human articles for networks as almost similarly significant as human Actors.

As indicated by Latour (1999): "You are diverse with the weapon in your grasp; the firearm is distinctive with you holding it. You are another subject since you hold the weapon; the firearm is another item since it has gone into a relationship with you."

As indicated by Korsgaard (2011), Latour's point is that neither the firearm nor the individual kills alone, however the mix of individual and weapon can execute the evil demonstration. The end is that human organization isn't just a human wonder, since it depends on non-human components also be executable. Korsgaard applied Theory network theory (ANT) to business. He contends that ANT is better than the more established 'disclosure speculations' that have overwhelmed business writing, particularly research on enterprising freedoms. Office is presented in an organization and isn't housed in a solitary Theory. Actors follow a vague and non-direct interaction subject to consistent interpretation. Connection impacts are made by conversational and material communications. Business makes advertises that are brief the business sectors are not there; it is the business venture that makes them and they are along these lines transient. The innovative capacity is along these lines on one of making events to activate Actors in a briefly steady organization. The construction of the organization shapes Theory personalities and likely cooperation or activities. The center thought is the idea of interpretation which is the cycle through which an organization is addressed by a solitary element.

Bruno Latour, Michel Callon, & John Law

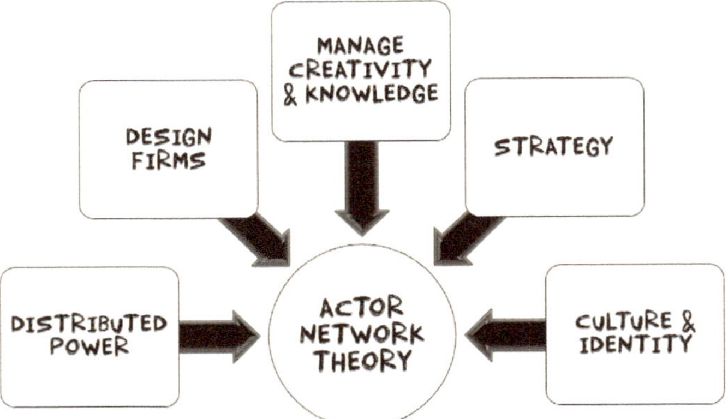

Understanding the Actor-Network theory:

Actor-network theory (ANT) is a framework that examines the relationships between actors, objects, and technologies in the formation of social networks. Here are some business examples:

Supply chain management: To analyze the relationships between various actors involved in the production and distribution of goods. For example, a manufacturer may work with suppliers, distributors, and retailers to bring a product to market. ANT can be used to examine how each actor and technology involved in the supply chain influences the overall network.

Innovation and new product development: To analyze the relationships between actors involved in the development and commercialization of new products. For example, a company may work with scientists, engineers, marketers, and regulatory agencies to bring a new product to market. ANT can be used to examine how each actor and technology involved in the innovation process influences the overall network.

Corporate social responsibility: To analyze the relationships between a company and its stakeholders, including customers, employees, communities, and the environment. For example, a company may work with non-governmental organizations, government agencies, and local communities to address social and environmental issues. ANT can be used to examine how each actor and technology involved in the CSR network influences the overall network.

Project management: To analyze the relationships between actors involved in project management. For example, a project manager may work with team members, stakeholders, vendors, and customers to complete a project. ANT can be used to examine how each actor and technology involved in the project management network influences the overall network.

Example: Even though Apple enterprise, its items, and its kin, are assorted, perplexing and extensive, Steve Jobs came to address the entire organization. The objective of the business visionary is help to shape networks including both human and non-human components to empower preparation. By understanding the network and the relationships between actors, companies can better manage their resources and achieve their goals.

Classroom Activity: Entrepreneurial Network Maps: ANT

Objective: Participants will explore the key concepts of ANT and its application in mapping and analyzing the complex relationships between actors in entrepreneurial ecosystems. Through interactive exercises and discussions, readers will gain a deeper understanding of ANT and its implications for entrepreneurial success.

Materials: Whiteboard or flip chart, Markers, Sticky notes, Index cards & Pen/pencil for each participant

Duration: 100 – 120 mins

Instructions:

Activity	Instructions
Intro (10 mins)	Provide a concise introduction to ANT, explaining its origins, key principles, and its application in understanding networks and associations. Highlight the notion of non-human actors, the role of intermediaries, & the dynamic nature of relationships in ANT.
Mapping the Network (15 mins)	Instruct readers to identify an entrepreneurial network they are familiar with and create a visual representation (e.g., a diagram or network map) of the key actors and their relationships within the chosen network. Encourage consideration of both human and non-human factors that influence the network.

Analyzing Interactions (15 mins)	Prompt readers to reflect on the connections and interactions between actors in their mapped entrepreneurial network. Ask them to identify key relationships, power dynamics, and influence flows. Encourage consideration of the role of intermediaries & factors that shape their success or failure.
Group Discussion (20 mins)	Organize readers into small groups to discuss ANT and entrepreneurial networks. Participants share their mapped networks and insights gained from analyzing actor-network interactions. Engage in a group discussion exploring the implications of ANT for entrepreneurship, such as strategic partnerships, resource flows, and power dynamics.
Case Study Analysis (25 mins)	Provide a case study or scenario showcasing an entrepreneurial endeavor or network. Instruct readers to apply ANT concepts and principles to analyze the case study, identifying key actors, relationships, and factors contributing to success or failure. Encourage critical thinking and alternative perspectives.
Reflection & Takeaways (10 mins)	Ask readers to reflect on their understanding of ANT and its implications for entrepreneurship. Encourage identification of at least one actionable insight or lesson applicable to their entrepreneurial endeavors. Emphasize leveraging relationships within networks to foster collaboration, innovation, and success.

Conclusion: By delving into the realm of Actor-Network Theory (ANT) and mapping entrepreneurial networks, participants gain valuable insights into the intricate relationships and dynamics within entrepreneurial ecosystems. This activity empowers them to analyze actor-network interactions, identify strategic opportunities, and leverage diverse actors and resources for entrepreneurial success. Armed with ANT principles, participants get equipped to navigate complex networks, foster collaboration, and drive innovation in their entrepreneurial endeavors.

12.2 Architectural Innovation

This theory centers around changes in item engineering and their benefits/inconveniences for officeholders and new participants (Henderson and Clark, 1990). The reality of the theory for businesspeople is that a kind of development called "design advancement", is a promising road for new participant to seek after on the grounds that it is hard for occupant to seek after. The theory begins with the essential thought that an item or administration is comprised of segments that fit together as per some sort of configuration called "item design" (Ulrich, 1995). For example, a transport design utilizes a solitary resource for every one of the segments to associate with. An opening engineering has a special connector for each sort of part. In a sectional engineering, parts can be genuinely masterminded in various distinctive manners. Distinctive designs are those which make it conceivable to detach the improvement of segments by normalizing their interfaces. Measured designs make it conceivable to trade segments later on or to change it up. Design developments are those which include blends of similar segments, just they are coordinated in another way, as per another item engineering. For example, a change from an opening engineering to a transport design. There is a differentiation with coordinated or fundamental designs, where the linkages between segments are not balanced.

For instance, a roof fan producer may think that it's hard to begin making standing fans. Even though standing fans are like roof fans, standing fans address an adjustment of item design that requires what is possibly a totally different worth chain, or set of partner connections. Firms foster skills with the hierarchical designs that create around item engineering. For instance, a firm with a measured item design is bound to reevaluate the greater part of the segments. The firm creates abilities around overseeing associations with segment providers through the organized interfaces managed by the item design. Firms then, at that point become exhausted about changing to another item design since they would prefer not to annihilate their current abilities (Tushman and Anderson, 1986). The creators sum up away from segments to ideas, so one could likewise say that Netflix is presenting similar parts as link and Blockbuster did yet utilizing another item engineering. Though the Blockbuster experience was face to face, the Netflix experience is on the web. The substance, in any case, is something similar.

Understanding the "Architectural Innovation" theory:

Architectural theory is a framework that examines the structure and design of organizations and how it affects their performance. Here are some business examples of architectural theory:

Organizational structure: The organizational structure of a company is an important aspect of architectural theory. It refers to the way in which the company is organized, including the hierarchy of authority, the allocation of resources, and the division of labor. An example of architectural theory in action could be seen in a traditional hierarchical organizational structure, where decision-making power flows from the top-down and employees have clearly defined roles and responsibilities.

Workflows and processes: Architectural theory can be applied to analyze workflows and processes within a company. For example, a manufacturing company may use architectural theory to analyze the layout of its production line, the allocation of resources, and the flow of materials through the manufacturing process to improve efficiency.

Information systems: Architectural theory can be applied to analyze the design and implementation of information systems within a company. For example, a software company may use architectural theory to design its software architecture, including the allocation of resources, the division of labor, and the communication protocols between different components of the system.

Business models: Architectural theory can be applied to analyze the structure and design of business models. For example, a subscription-based business model may be designed with architectural theory in mind, including the pricing structure, the delivery of products or services, and the management of customer relationships.

The theory emphasizes the importance of the structure and design of organizations, workflows, and processes in achieving business goals. By understanding the principles of architectural theory, companies can optimize their performance and improve their bottom line.

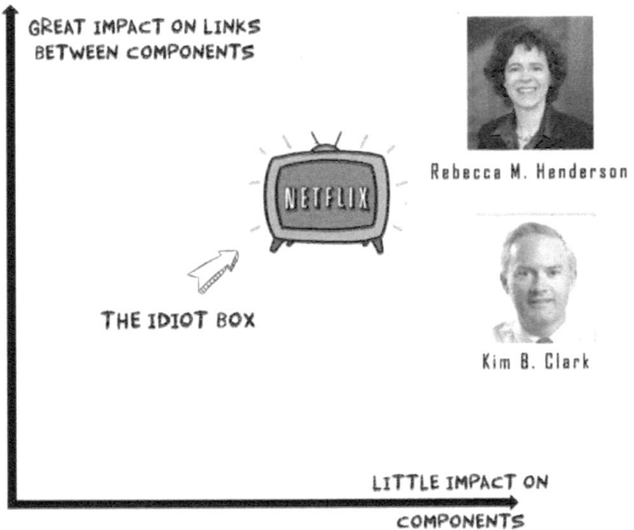

Classroom Activity: Ecosystems – Architectural Innovation

Objective: Participants will delve into the key principles and frameworks of architectural innovation theory and examine how it shapes the development of innovation ecosystems. Through interactive exercises and discussions, readers will gain a deeper understanding of architectural innovation and its role in fostering entrepreneurial success.

Materials: Whiteboard or flip chart, Markers, Sticky notes, Index cards & Pen/pencil for each participant

Duration: 100 – 120 mins

Instructions:

Activity	Instructions
Intro (10 mins)	Provide a concise introduction to architectural innovation theory, explaining its origins, core concepts, and relevance in understanding innovation ecosystems. Highlight the distinction between architectural and incremental innovations, emphasizing their transformative nature.
Case Study Analysis (15 mins)	Present a case study or scenario showcasing an industry or market disrupted by architectural innovation. Instruct readers to analyze the case study through the lens of architectural innovation theory, identifying key architectural changes, value reconfigurations, and impacts on existing players and business models. Encourage consideration of ecosystem-wide implications.
Mapping Innovation (15 mins)	Ask readers to identify an innovation ecosystem (e.g., technology cluster, startup hub) and create a visual map or diagram highlighting key actors, organizations, and interconnections. Encourage consideration of visible and hidden components, such as funding sources, research institutions, and regulatory bodies.
Analyzing (20 mins)	Prompt readers to analyze the identified innovation ecosystem through the lens of architectural innovation theory. Ask them to identify and assess the presence of architectural innovations, considering transformative changes in technology, business models, and value creation. Encourage reflection on interdependencies and interconnections.

Group Discussion (20 mins)	Organize readers into small groups for a discussion on architectural innovation and innovation ecosystems. Participants share their mapped ecosystems and identify architectural innovations. Engage in a group discussion exploring implications for entrepreneurship, such as disruption opportunities, collaboration, and navigating ecosystem dynamics.
Reflection (10 mins)	Conclude the activity by asking readers to reflect on their understanding of architectural innovation theory and its implications for entrepreneurship. Encourage identification of at least one actionable insight or strategy applicable to their entrepreneurial endeavors. Emphasize leveraging architectural innovations for entrepreneurial success & industry transformation.

Conclusion: Through exploring Architectural Innovation Theory, participants gained insights into the transformative nature of architectural innovations and their impact on innovation ecosystems. This activity empowered them to analyze case studies, map innovation ecosystems, and identify opportunities for disruption and collaboration. Armed with knowledge of architectural innovation, participants are equipped to navigate dynamic ecosystems, foster innovation, and drive entrepreneurial success in an ever-evolving marketplace.

12.3 Attribution

Attribution theory was created by Austrian clinician Fritz Heider during the 1950s. The crucial presumption of attribution theory is that individuals are persuaded to discover foundations for their own prosperity and disappointment occasions just as the practices of others. People are bound to ascribe the reasons for an effective occasion to themselves or their in-bunch, while they are bound to credit the reasons for disappointment occasions to distal powers or out-bunch individuals. This is known as a self-serving inclination. Also, when we see others come up short, we are probably going to credit their inability to inner causes, for example, lethargy or ineptitude instead of thinking about ecological conditions. This is called key attribution blunder. In this manner, when we see a business visionary fizzle in business, we expect that the disappointment is on the grounds that they accomplished something incorrectly. This may prompt a faith in wrong causes on the grounds that the businessperson might have fizzled for reasons outside of their control. Assuming, attribution theory clarifies how partners perceive business visionaries. It implies that when businesspeople fail, they may be perceived negatively by partners within the business. However, partners have the capacity to overcome these perceptions and seek the true causes, including internal and external factors, to gain a more comprehensive understanding of the situation. It might likewise assist with clarifying the normal heuristic of an environment or field, to heap the compensations onto a known champ to such an extent that the victor continues winning in a prudent circle. Attribution theory assists us with accounting for unavoidable outcomes, not simply molds. The table underneath gives the regular 3-dimensional portrayal of attribution theory. If the factor is inward, stable, and controllable, we characterize the achievement or inability to exertion. On the off chance that the factor is outer, wild and unsteady, we trait the achievement or inability to karma. There are 8 mixes altogether.

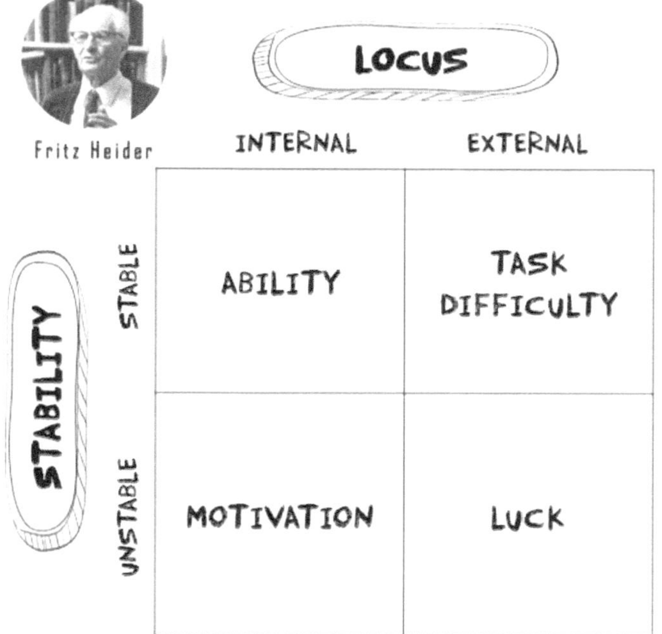

Understanding the theory of "Attribution":

Attribution theory is a framework that examines how individuals explain the causes of events, behavior, and outcomes. For example.

Performance evaluation: A manager may attribute an employee's poor performance to their lack of effort or ability, or to external factors such as a lack of resources or a difficult work environment.
Customer service: Attribution theory can be used to analyze how customers explain their satisfaction or dissatisfaction with a company's products or services. For example, a customer may attribute their satisfaction with a product to the quality of the product itself or to the helpfulness of customer service representatives.
Sales performance: A salesperson may attribute their success to their own persuasive abilities or to external factors such as the quality of the product or the customer's budget.
Project management: Attribution theory can be used to analyze how project managers explain the success or failure of a project. For e.g., a project manager may attribute the success of a project to their own leadership abilities or to external factors such as the quality of the team or resources.
Leadership: Attribution theory can be used to analyze how individuals perceive and explain the behavior of leaders within an organization. For e.g., employees may attribute a leader's success to their charisma, vision, or strategic thinking, or to external factors such as luck or the support of their team. The principles of attribution theory, companies can improve their communication, decision-making, and performance evaluation processes, leading to greater success and satisfaction.

Classroom Activity: Attribution Theory in Entrepreneurship

Objective: To help readers understand the concept of attribution theory and its application in entrepreneurship. It aims to foster critical thinking and reflection on how entrepreneurs interpret and attribute success or failure.

Materials: Whiteboard or flip chart, Markers, Sticky notes & Pen/pencil for each participant

Duration: 90 – 100 mins

Instructions:

Activity	Instructions
Intro (5 mins)	Provide a brief overview of attribution theory in the context of entrepreneurship. Explain its focus on how individuals interpret and explain the causes of events, including success and failure. Emphasize the impact on motivation and decision-making.

Case Study Analysis (20 mins)	Present a case study or real-life example of an entrepreneur facing challenges and ask readers to analyze potential attributions for success or failure. Encourage them to consider internal factors (e.g., skills, effort, strategy) and external factors (e.g., market conditions, competition, luck).
Group Discussion (15 mins)	Facilitate a discussion to share and compare attributions with questions about internal and external attributions, their influence on future actions, and the presence of biases or cognitive traps. Ask the following questions to guide the discussion: • What internal attributions might the entrepreneur make for their success or failure? • What external attributions might the entrepreneur make for their success or failure? • How might these attributions influence the entrepreneur's future actions & decision-making? • Are there any biases or cognitive traps that could influence attributions?
Self-views (5mins)	Prompt readers to reflect individually on their entrepreneurial experiences. Ask them to identify attributions made for a specific success or failure & reflect on the fairness in those attributions.
Adjusting (15 mins)	Encourage readers to identify biases or distortions in their initial attributions. Prompt them to consider alternative explanations and challenge their initial attributions to promote a more balanced perspective.
Application Exercise (20 mins)	Provide a hypothetical entrepreneurial scenario with a challenge or setback. Ask readers to analyze their attributions for the situation & suggest how adjusting attributions could impact mindset & subsequent actions.
Wrap-up (5 mins)	Summarize the key points discussed, emphasizing the importance of understanding attribution theory for entrepreneurs and its impact on motivation, decision-making, and resilience

Conclusion: By analyzing and adjusting attributions, entrepreneurs can gain a more balanced perspective, challenge biases, and make informed choices. Applying this knowledge empowers entrepreneurs to navigate challenges with a growth-oriented mindset, ultimately enhancing their entrepreneurial journey.

12.4 Baumol's

William J. Baumol was an American financial specialist at New York University. His theory of business venture begins with the suspicion that each general public is blessed with a lot of business visionaries. In any case, how business visionaries utilize their energies relies on the foundations—the principles of the game—set up in each society. It is additionally occasionally called a political theory because the system in each nation or domain may have gigantic impact on motivators. He contends that businesspeople may take part in useful (i.e., development) or ineffective (lease chasing and wrongdoing) types of business venture contingent upon what a country's organizations empower. Baumol contends that the thought of a "feeling of business venture" is futile for policymakers on the grounds that there is nothing they can do to further develop it. He recommends that by adjusting the principles of the game, policymakers can effectively stimulate useful business in their social orders and lessen useless or damaging types of business venture. Changes to the standards of the game can shift yet incorporate changes to burden rules, guidelines, appropriations and backing programs. The thought is to sharpen the principles over the long run until a greatest constructive outcome on innovative results is recognized. Baumol utilizes a few verifiable accounts to back up his theory. For example, in Feudal Europe, business venture was generally dangerous or redistributive. At that point, the vast majority of Europe was coordinated into little independent domains, for example, a palace securing two or three thousand sections of land of farmland. Young fellows with desire (rulers) could assemble a military and endeavor to sack a close by fiefdom. The outcome was some proportion of death and annihilation, and nothing was useful was refined. No new abundance was made - it just changed hands and for an extreme price. He additionally utilizes the case of business being attached to calligraphy in old China and afterward of sexual subjugation in antiquated Rome as is displayed in the model beneath. All the model share for all intents and purpose a bunch of pathways of adequate lead that are utilized to direct pioneering energies. "A shrewd (and attractive) individual from the lower requests may purposely mastermind to be sold into bondage to an affluent and incredible expert. Then, at that point, with karma, ability, and drive, he would develop near his proprietor, maybe dealing with his monetary issues (and at times taking part in some gay movement with him). The expert then, at that point acquired cachet, after an appropriate period, by conceding opportunity to the slave, setting him up with his very own fortune."

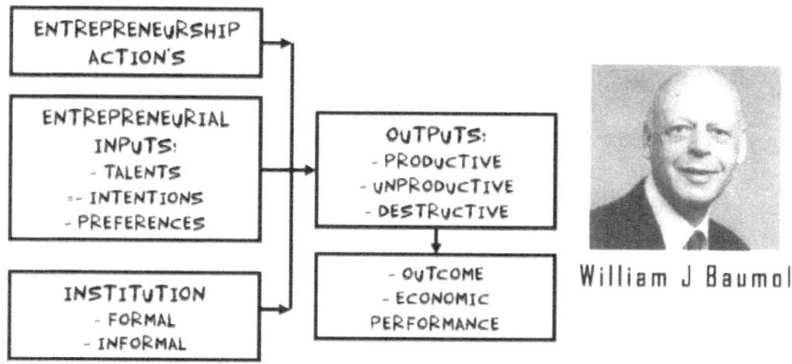

Understanding the Baumol's theory:

Baumol's theory of cost disease is a framework that examines the effect of rising wages in industries with low productivity growth, resulting in increased costs for goods and services. Here is a business example

Performing Arts: The cost of putting on a live theater performance or a symphony concert has increased dramatically over the years due to the rising wages of performers and support staff, even though the productivity of these industries has not increased significantly. This has led to higher ticket prices for consumers, making it more difficult to attract new audiences and stay competitive.

Healthcare: The cost of healthcare services has increased significantly due to rising wages for healthcare professionals and support staff, despite relatively low productivity growth. This has led to higher healthcare costs for consumers and businesses, making it more difficult to provide affordable healthcare to all.

Education: The cost of education has increased dramatically due to rising wages for teachers and support staff, even though productivity growth has remained relatively low. The cost of education has increased dramatically due to rising wages for teachers and support staff, even though productivity growth has remained relatively low. This has led to higher tuition costs for students and increased financial pressure on educational institutions.

Legal Services: The cost of legal services has increased significantly due to rising wages for lawyers and support staff, despite relatively low productivity growth. This has led to higher legal fees for clients, making it more difficult for individuals and small businesses to access legal services.

With the help of the principles of Baumol's theory, businesses can better manage their costs and pricing strategies, and develop strategies to improve productivity growth and stay competitive in the market.

Classroom Activity: Exploring Baumol's Theory for Startups

Objective: To familiarize readers with Baumol's theory of entrepreneurship and its implications for economic growth and innovation. It aims to stimulate critical thinking and discussion on the role of entrepreneurship in the economy.

Materials: Whiteboard or flip chart, Markers, Sticky notes, Index cards & Pen/pencil for each participant

Duration: 75-90 mins

Instructions:

Activity	Instructions
Intro (5 mins)	Introduce Baumol's theory & explain the division of entrepreneurial efforts between innovative and unproductive activities due to sector constraints.
Group (15 mins)	Divide readers into small groups and assign each group a specific industry or sector. Ask them to identify examples of innovative & unproductive entrepreneurial activities within their assigned sector, considering constraints that impact entrepreneurial efforts.
Pitch (15 mins)	Have each group present their findings to the audience. Facilitate a discussion comparing examples across sectors, analyzing factors that impact innovative entrepreneurship & economic growth.
Case Study Analysis (20 mins)	Provide a case study of a successful entrepreneur or company exemplifying Baumol's theory. Ask readers to analyze the entrepreneurial activities leading to economic growth and innovation, considering how constraints influenced the allocation of efforts & outcomes achieved.
Imply (5 mins)	Engage readers in a reflective discussion on the implications of Baumol's theory for entrepreneurship and economic development. Explore challenges, opportunities, and strategies for creating an environment that encourages productive entrepreneurship.
Reflection (15 mins)	Understand the theory & dynamics of entrepreneurship & its impact on economic growth? • What are the potential challenges & opportunities entrepreneurs face in balancing innovative and unproductive activities? • How can policymakers & institutions create an environment to encourage entrepreneurship? • Are there any real-world examples or current trends that align with or challenge Baumol's theory?

Takeaways (5 mins)	Summarize key points discussed, emphasizing the relevance of Baumol's theory in understanding the role of entrepreneurship in economic growth and innovation. Encourage readers to apply this knowledge to their own entrepreneurial endeavors for sustenance.

Conclusion: The activity sheds light on the crucial role of entrepreneurs in driving economic growth and innovation. By understanding the constraints and trade-offs they face in allocating their efforts, we can better support and foster an environment that encourages productive entrepreneurship. Applying the insights gained from this activity empowers individuals to contribute to sustainable economic development through entrepreneurial endeavors.

12.5 Biculturalism

Biculturalism alludes to an individual trademark that creates because of openness to two societies. The ordinary case is the outsider who should get familiar with the host country's nearby culture and in doing as such embrace's components of a subsequent culture. The Al-Shammari group inspects people with bi-social abilities and encounters: "the individuals who are presented to various societies and conditions will encounter various sorts of encounters in their social collaborations and subsequently will gather rich information that is assorted". They speculate that biculturalism gives benefits in the chance acknowledgment, assessment, choice and abuse stages. They find that bicultural people enjoy benefits in the previous stages, however battle with abuse (because of institutional imperatives), except if they can construct networks in the host country. This is an intriguing theory, however, clearly fits an expansion to multiculturalism, which would be a name given to those people presented to at least two different societies. A multicultural individual would be presented to at least three societies and collect a considerably more assorted arrangement of encounters that could assist with perceiving, picking and misusing openings. Maybe, notwithstanding, the lavishness melts away with each extra layer of lore.

There is the undeniable issue as well, of separating between societies, making instances of between country movement simplest to gauge, when contrasted with state or commonplace social contrasts. It likewise can be reached out to the incredible assortment that exists inside the subcultures of some random culture, and the possibility to encounters numerous such subcultures. Maybe social distance matters to such an extent that people with openness to different societies that are more far off from one another advantage more (or less). Maybe there is a rearranged U-molded relationship where eventually more openings (or more prominent contrasts) have unavoidable losses. The theory additionally may supplement different speculations like the nonconformist theory, which takes a gander at the detriments that settlers face in the work market to clarify why foreigners are bound to picked business venture as a lifelong way. They are likewise a few similitudes with Hoselitz's theory, which recommends that people from profoundly created societies are especially well-suited to begin new pursuits in their host nations. It additionally resounds to some degree with the withdrawal of status regard theory that recommends business visionaries come from the offspring of beforehand high-status bunches that is sad. It is intriguing to have the option to plan a test that would separate people (specifically, workers) in view of the different speculations to see which theory is upheld and which are invalidated.

Understanding the "Biculturalism" theory:

Biculturalism is a framework that examines the cultural identities and practices of individuals who are exposed to and incorporates two different cultures. For example.

Marketing and Advertising: A company targeting the Hispanic market in the U.S.A may use bicultural marketing strategies to effectively engage with customers who are fluent in both Spanish and English, & who have cultural values that are a blend of both Hispanic and American cultures.

Workforce Diversity: A company that values diversity may seek to hire employees who are bicultural and can bridge the gap between different cultural groups within the organization. This can improve communication and collaboration between employees from different backgrounds and enhance the company's overall performance.

Global Business: A company that is expanding into new markets in Asia may hire employees who are bicultural and can effectively navigate the cultural differences between the company's home country and the new market. This can help to build relationships with customers & partners & increase its chances of success in the new market.

Cross-Cultural Training: A company that sends employees to work in different countries may provide bicultural training to help them understand the cultural differences between their home country and the country they are working in. This can improve the employee's ability to communicate effectively and build relationships with colleagues and clients in the new culture.

Biculturalism can help businesses can develop strategies to promote cultural understanding and effectively engage with diverse cultural groups.

Classroom Activity: Exploring Biculturalism in Startups

Objectives: To highlights the unique advantages & challenges that bicultural individuals bring to entrepreneurship.

Materials: Whiteboard or flip chart, Markers, Sticky notes, & Pen for each participant

Duration: 100 – 120 mins

Instructions:

Activity	Instructions
Intro (5 mins)	Introduce biculturalism theory in entrepreneurship, emphasizing the integration of two distinct cultural identities and its impact on mindset, creativity, and cross-cultural communication.

Personal Reflection (10 mins)	Ask readers to reflect individually on their own cultural background and experiences, considering if they have a bicultural identity or have interacted with individuals who do. Discuss potential benefits and challenges in an entrepreneurial context.
Group Discussion (15 mins)	Divide readers into small groups to share personal reflections on biculturalism. Facilitate a discussion on the advantages, challenges, and how biculturalism can contribute to innovation and cross-cultural understanding in the entrepreneurial context. Facilitate a discussion by asking questions such as: • What are the advantages of having a bicultural identity in entrepreneurship? • What are the challenges or conflicts that bicultural individuals may face in entrepreneurial contexts? • How can biculturalism contribute to innovation and cross-cultural understanding in entrepreneurship?
Case Study Analysis (20 mins)	Provide a case study of a successful bicultural entrepreneur. Ask readers to analyze how the entrepreneur leveraged their biculturalism for success, considering market insights, cultural adaptation, & networking advantages.
Cross-Cultural Skilling (20 mins)	Engage readers in a skill-building exercise on cross-cultural competence. Present scenarios where bicultural entrepreneurs face cultural challenges and ask readers to brainstorm strategies to navigate these situations effectively using their bicultural identity.
Implication & Execute (15 mins)	Lead a discussion on the implications of biculturalism theory for entrepreneurship, emphasizing its contribution to success, innovation, and inclusive business environments. Encourage practical steps for leveraging bicultural identity in their pursuits.
Wrap-up Takeaways (5 mins)	Summarize key points, highlighting the significance of biculturalism in entrepreneurship. Encourage readers to embrace their bicultural identity, fostering diversity and cross-cultural exchange in their entrepreneurial journeys.

Conclusion: Embracing a bicultural identity fosters innovation, cross-cultural understanding, and the ability to navigate diverse business environments. By leveraging their biculturalism, entrepreneurs can unlock new opportunities and contribute to inclusive and dynamic entrepreneurial ecosystems.

12.6 Competence Destruction

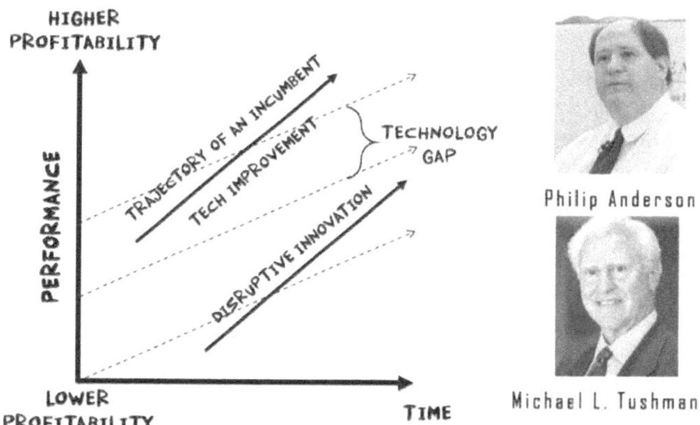

Philip Anderson

Michael L. Tushman

Competence destroying innovations are expected to be brought to market more successfully by new entrants than competence enhancing innovations (Tushman & Anderson, 1986). Competence = abilities + resources. An incumbent firm's competence is destroyed when a technological innovation obsolesces the abilities and or resources that previously composed the competences of the firm. For instance, Blockbuster's retail competence was undermined by Netflix's online model. The theory goes that incumbent are reluctant to adopt competence destroying innovations because they prefer to preserve and enhance their existing competences. Besides, developing new competences often means shedding the old and that can involve painful layoffs or divestitures. These difficult organizational changes and the coalitions that form within organizations to try to stop them, create a friction that impairs adoption. Instead, the new entrant benefits from adopting competence-destroying innovations because they to some extent inoculate against incumbents' competitive responses. While the incumbents struggle to make shrew and painful decisions, the entrepreneurs can develop new ventures with the technology. Therefore, competence-destroying innovations are ways for entrepreneurs to fly under the radar. By contrast, if a new entrant comes to market with a competence-enhancing innovation, then they are at a disadvantage. There is nothing stopping an incumbent from adopting a competence-enhancing innovation. Given that incumbents usually have more resources and experience, the best course of action for a new entrant might be to try to secure intellectual property rights & to license technology to the incumbents. Interestingly, Christensen and Bower (1996) positioned the disruptive innovation Theory as an alternative to the competence-destroying Theory. They argued that managers have become increasingly willing to make shrew decisions allowing them to respond to competence-destroying innovations.

Understanding the "Competence Destruction" theory:

Competence destruction, also known as disruptive innovation, is a phenomenon where an existing technology, product or service is replaced by a new technology, product or service that offers greater value to customers. Here is a business example of competence destruction:

Photography Industry: Digital photography disrupted the traditional photography industry, which relied on film-based cameras and printing services. It offered several advantages, including instant feedback, lower costs, and greater flexibility. Many traditional photography companies went out of business, & new digital photography companies emerged, such as Canon, Nikon, and Sony.

Streaming Media: It disrupted the traditional media industry, which relied on cable television and physical media such as DVDs and Blu-rays. It offered several advantages over traditional media, including on-demand access to a wide range of content, lower costs, and greater flexibility. As a result, many traditional media companies went out of business, and new streaming media companies emerged, such as Netflix, Amazon Prime, and Hulu.

Ride-Hailing Services: It disrupted the traditional taxi industry, which relied on physical taxi stands and dispatching services. Ride-hailing services offered several advantages over traditional taxi services, including lower costs, greater convenience, and the ability to track and rate drivers. As a result, many traditional taxi companies went out of business, and new ride-hailing companies emerged, such as Uber, Lyft, and Didi Chuxing.

E-commerce: It offered several advantages over traditional retail, including greater convenience, lower costs, and the ability to access a wider range of products. As a result, many traditional retail companies went out of business, & new e-commerce companies emerged, such as Amazon, Alibaba, and eBay.

With the help of principles of competence destruction, businesses can better anticipate and respond to disruptive technologies, products, and services, and develop strategies to stay competitive in the market.

Classroom Activity: Exploring Competence Destruction

Objective: To introduce readers the concept of competence destruction theory and its implications for entrepreneurship. It aims to foster critical thinking and reflection on the importance of adaptability and continuous learning in entrepreneurial endeavors.
Materials: Whiteboard or flip chart, Markers, Sticky notes, Index cards & Pen/pencil for each participant
Duration: 100 – 120 mins
Instructions:

Activity	Instructions
Intro (5 mins)	Introduce the theory in entrepreneurship, explaining how established knowledge, skills, or capabilities can become obsolete due to rapid technological advancements & changing market dynamics. Highlight the importance of adaptability & continuous learning.
Case Study Analysis (20 mins)	Provide a case study or real-life example of a company or industry that faced competence destruction. Ask readers to analyze the factors contributing to competence destruction, explore the consequences of failing to adapt, & identify opportunities for entrepreneurs embracing competence destruction.
Group Discussion (15 mins)	Facilitate a group discussion to share and compare findings from the case study analysis. Prompt discussions on the key factors leading to competence destruction, better preparation and response strategies, implications for entrepreneurs, and cultivation of adaptability and continuous learning. Ask the following questions: • What key factors led to competence destruction? • How could the company or industry be prepared for or responded to competence destruction? • What are the implications of competence destruction for entrepreneurs and their businesses? • How can entrepreneurs cultivate adaptability and continuous learning to thrive in the face of competence destruction?

Personal Reflection (10 mins)	Ask readers to reflect individually on their own entrepreneurial aspirations or experiences. Prompt them to consider their existing competencies and their vulnerability to competence destruction. Encourage brainstorming on proactive adaptation and competence upgrading strategies.
Competence Exercise (20 mins)	Provide readers with a list of emerging trends, technologies, or skills relevant to their entrepreneurial interests. Ask them to choose one area and develop a plan for upgrading their competence in that domain. Encourage specific actions, resources, & timelines for acquiring new skills or knowhow
Strategies (15 mins)	Engage readers in a discussion on practical strategies for applying and adapting their upgraded competencies in entrepreneurial pursuits. Encourage exploration of how to leverage newfound knowledge and skills for innovation, value creation, & staying ahead of competence destruction.
Wrap-up Takeaways (5 mins)	Summarize key points discussed during the activity, emphasizing the importance of adaptability, continuous learning, & proactive competence upgrading in entrepreneurship. Encourage embracing change, fostering a growth mindset, & lifelong learning for entrepreneurial success.

Conclusion: The activity underscores importance of adaptability & continuous learning in entrepreneurship. It highlights the factors contributing to competence destruction and the need for entrepreneurs to embrace change. By proactively upgrading their competencies and applying adaptive strategies, entrepreneurs can navigate dynamic business landscapes, stay competitive, & seize new opportunities for growth & innovation.

12.7 Critical

Critical Theory may be attributed to Max Horkheimer's 1937 essay *Traditional and Critical Theory*. The Frankfurt School of sociology has developed critical Theory from a combination of Marxian and Kantian ideas about critiquing traditional theories. Alvesson and Willmot (1992: 89) state that: *"Emancipation describes the process through which individuals and groups become freed from repressive social and ideological conditions, in particular those that place socially unnecessary restrictions upon the development and articulation of human consciousness".* Most entrepreneurship literature takes a functionalist (rational or empirical) perspective, where there is an objective reality that can be measured and theory that can be tested against that reality. However, there are many problems with scientific methods in the social sciences. For one, theories that work in one temporal-spacial context may not work in another. Very few studies have adopted alternative approaches (Jennings, Perren, and Carter, 2005), but one important alternative perspective comes from critical Theory. Critical theorists aim to liberate humans from the circumstances that enslave them. For instance, critical Theory dissects something like Disney World amazement park as a class struggle about emotional labor and low pay. Ogbor (2000) argues that most of the rhetoric of entrepreneurship reflects a heroic white male bias. She frames the entrepreneurial discourse as ethnocentric, pointing out that most of the literature examining entrepreneurship among minorities is aimed at helping those minorities to improve (i.e., become more like whites). This practice "reinforced the prevailing myth that non-dominant groups have psychological and racial characteristics which inhibit entrepreneurial development.".

The consequences of these biases include discrimination against women seeking venture capital investment and women or minorities seeking loans. Perren and Jennings (2005) argue that government rhetoric tends to simultaneously legitimize and subjugate entrepreneurship, first by affirming the importance of small business, then by seeking to unify their voices into just one. Possibly, political rhetoric about entrepreneurship may take a back seat to the broader (macro) forces unleashed by ideologically motivated economic policies affecting the population.

Critical Theory is related to the emancipation Theory of entrepreneurship, however, emancipation Theory has a more positive (optimistic) spin on entrepreneurship, where entrepreneurship is a means of emancipation from the ideological slavery of employment. Many critical theorists might question if entrepreneurship is really a great career choice for most, who may have to endure several difficulties and sacrifices to get a business going. Perhaps entrepreneurship is yet another ideological trap the convince people that the status quo is up to them to change with business rather than political activism.

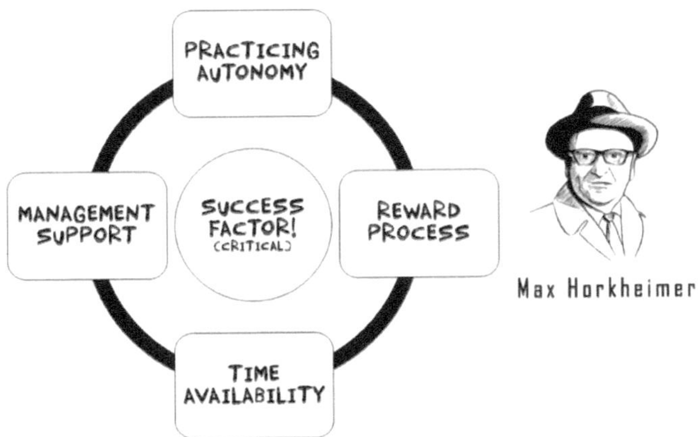

Understanding the "Critical" theory:

Critical theory is a framework that examines the power dynamics and inequalities present in society, including in the business world. Here is a business example of critical theory:

Gender Pay Gap: Some companies have implemented pay transparency policies or conducted pay equity audits to identify and address gender-based pay disparities.

Environmental Sustainability: To examine the power dynamics between businesses and the environment, and advocating for policies and practices that prioritize environmental sustainability. For example, some companies have implemented sustainability initiatives such as reducing carbon emissions or using environmentally friendly materials in their products.

Diversity and Inclusion: To examine the power dynamics between different social groups and advocating for policies and practices that promote diversity, equity, and inclusion. For example, some companies have implemented diversity and inclusion training programs or established employee resource groups to support underrepresented groups in the workplace.

By using critical theory to examine these issues, businesses can develop policies and practices that promote fairness, equity, and sustainability in their operations, and contribute to a more just and equitable society.

Classroom Activity: "Analyzing Perspectives"

Objective: To introduce readers to the concept of critical theory and engage them in a thoughtful analysis of various perspectives.
Materials: Whiteboard or flip chart, Markers, Sticky notes & Pen/pencil for each participant.
Duration: 65- 80 mins
Instructions:

Activity	Instructions
Intro (5 mins)	Provide a brief overview of critical theory, explaining its purpose & its emphasis on questioning established norms and power structures. Highlight that theory encourages a deeper understanding of social, political, and cultural issues by examining the underlying power dynamics and assumptions.
Reading Selection (10 mins)	Select a short excerpt or article that can be analyzed from a critical theory perspective on topics such as inequality, discrimination, power imbalances, or social justice. Provide the reading material to the participants and give them sufficient time to read and reflect on the content.
Group Discussion (20 mins)	Divide the participants into small groups of 3-5 people. Instruct each group to discuss the reading material & explore following aspects: • Identify the main power dynamics and hierarchies at play in the given context. • Discuss the assumptions or ideologies that underpin these power dynamics. • Analyze the potential consequences or implications of these power dynamics for various individuals or groups involved. Encourage participants to challenge their own assumptions and explore alternative perspectives.
Presentations and Reflection (15 mins)	Each group to present a summary of their findings and key insights to the rest of the participants. Facilitate a reflective discussion by encouraging questions, comments, and alternative viewpoints from the participants. Emphasize the importance of critical thinking, questioning established norms, and considering multiple perspectives when analyzing complex social issues.

Application Exercise (10 mins)	Provide a hypothetical scenario or a real-world case study related to the topic discussed in the reading. Ask participants to individually brainstorm ways in which critical theory can be applied to understand and address the issues presented in the scenario. Allow participants to share their ideas and insights with the larger group, fostering a collaborative learning environment.
Wrap-up (5 mins)	Summarize the key takeaways from the activity, emphasizing the value of critical theory in understanding and addressing social issues. Encourage participants to continue exploring critical theory in their personal and professional lives and to actively challenge power imbalances and assumptions in society.

Conclusion: This activity allows participants to delve into the intricacies of power dynamics and assumptions in society, fostering a deeper understanding of social issues. By encouraging critical thinking and alternative perspectives, participants gain valuable insights into the impact of power imbalances and the importance of questioning established norms. This activity will inspire participants to continue applying critical theory in their lives, challenging power structures, and actively working towards a more equitable and just society.

12.8 Dynamic Capabilities

David J. Teece

At the core of the Theory of dynamic capabilities is the assumption that an organization's current resources and capabilities, which may be optimally suited to the current environmental conditions, will not likely be relevant under future conditions. Recognizing that changes in technologies, policies, and tastes make for a continuously evolving landscape of needs and wants, an organization needs to be able to respond. Organizations need to be able to transform their capabilities over time as needed to seize new opportunities. They also need to be continually sensing new opportunities. According to Teece (2007): *"the competitive advantage of firms stems from dynamic capabilities rooted in high performance routines operating inside the firm, embedded in the firm's processes, and conditioned by its history".* How do they respond effectively to changes on the order of converging industries and internet-based or machine learning-based disruption? Dynamic capabilities are organizational abilities that can accommodate change in the environment, including those that emerging from inside the organization. Organizational leaders shift emphasis between what they view as their core business, and initiatives that act as footholds into future business opportunities requiring different competencies. The underlying idea is that an organization's activities can be broken up into different types. For instance, Zahra et al. (2006) propose that entrepreneurial companies "create, define, discover, and exploit opportunities" early. According to Teece, dynamic capabilities are defined as a "firm's ability to integrate, build, and reconfigure internal and external competences to address changing environments". Dichotomous typologies suggest that exploration and exploitation are concepts that maximally differentiate between types of activities with very different risk/reward profiles. Exploration involves placing cheap bets early on to get foothold investments in potentially valuable future initiatives. Most of the bets fail to pay off, but a few of them provide big wins providing the firm with two options. First, the firm can seek to license out the innovation to another firm with more suited competences. Second, the firm can choose to exploit the opportunity internally as a new business. Third, an organization can hold and do nothing. The ability of an organization to shift from exploiting a self-reinforcing resource bundle that is becoming obsolete with a new one that is less tested, but which seems to be the way of the future is a dynamic capability. Dynamic capability Theory has been used to critique other theories such as the resource-based view. Resource perspectives, including concepts like core competence, are flawed when applied firms in dynamic environments. The prescription of those approaches is to invest in and leverage competences within a definable core business area, and to essentially contract out whatever is non-core or peripheral. According to Eisenhardt (2000): *"At the level of RBV, we conclude that traditional RBV misidentifies the locus of long-term competitive advantage in dynamic markets, overemphasizes the strategic logic of leverage, and reaches a boundary condition in high-velocity markets."*

Understanding the "Dynamic Capabilities" theory:

Dynamic capabilities refer to a company's ability to adapt and respond to changing market conditions and emerging opportunities by leveraging its resources and capabilities.

Apple: It has a history of adapting to changing market conditions and emerging opportunities by leveraging its resources and capabilities. For example, when the company saw the potential of the smartphone market, it leveraged its existing capabilities in hardware design and software development to create the iPhone, which became a game-changer in the mobile phone industry.

Similarly, when Apple saw the potential of the wearable technology market, it leveraged its existing capabilities in design and miniaturization to create the Apple Watch.

Amazon: It has a history of adapting to changing market conditions and emerging opportunities by leveraging its resources and capabilities. For example, when Amazon saw the potential of the e-commerce market, it leveraged its existing capabilities in logistics and supply chain management to create an online marketplace that revolutionized the way people shop. Similarly, when Amazon saw the potential of the cloud computing market, it leveraged its existing capabilities in data storage and processing to create Amazon Web Services (AWS), which has become one of the leading cloud computing platforms in the world.

Toyota: It has a history of adapting to changing market conditions and emerging opportunities by leveraging its resources and capabilities. For example, when Toyota saw the potential of the hybrid car market, it leveraged its existing capabilities in manufacturing and engineering to create the Prius, which became one of the best-selling hybrid cars in the world. Similarly, when Toyota saw the potential of the electric car market, it leveraged its existing capabilities in battery technology and manufacturing to create the Toyota Mirai, a hydrogen fuel cell vehicle.

By leveraging their existing resources and capabilities to adapt to changing market conditions and emerging opportunities, companies can stay ahead of the competition and maintain their position as industry leaders.

Classroom Activity: "Building Dynamic Capabilities"

Objective: To introduce readers to the concept of Dynamic Capabilities theory and engage them in a practical exploration of its application in an entrepreneurial context.

Materials: Whiteboard or flip chart, Markers, Sticky notes & Pen/pencil for each participant.

Duration: 80 - 90 mins

Instructions:

Activity	Instructions
Intro (5 mins)	Provide a brief overview of Dynamic Capabilities theory, explaining its significance in entrepreneurship and strategic management. Highlight that Dynamic Capabilities theory focuses on an organization's ability to adapt, learn, and innovate in response to changing market conditions.
Case Study (15 mins)	Present a case study of a real or hypothetical entrepreneurial venture facing a significant market disruption or competitive challenge. Describe the company's background, industry context, and the specific problem or opportunity they encounter. Explain how it can help to navigate & capitalize on the situation.
Small Group Analysis (20 mins)	Divide participants into small groups of 3-5 people. Assign each group to analyze and discuss the case study through the lens of Dynamic Capabilities theory. Instruct groups to identify the key dynamic capabilities that the company should develop or enhance to address the challenge effectively. Encourage participants to consider factors such as resource allocation, knowledge acquisition, organizational flexibility, and strategic agility.
Group Presentations (15 mins)	Ask each group to present their analysis and recommendations to the rest of the participants. Facilitate a discussion by encouraging questions, feedback, and alternative viewpoints from the participants. Emphasize the importance of strategic thinking, adaptability, and innovation in building dynamic capabilities within an entrepreneurial context.

Application Exercise (15 mins)	Provide participants with a different case scenario or ask them to reflect on their own entrepreneurial experiences. Instruct individuals to identify and brainstorm potential dynamic capabilities that they can develop or strengthen in their ventures to navigate a specific challenge or seize an opportunity. Encourage participants to think creatively and consider both internal and external factors influencing their dynamic capabilities.
Wrap-up and Reflection (10 mins)	Summarize the key insights from the activity, emphasizing the role of Dynamic Capabilities theory in fostering entrepreneurial adaptability and innovation. Encourage participants to reflect on how they can apply the principles of dynamic capabilities to their own entrepreneurial endeavors. Highlight the importance of continuous learning, strategic experimentation, and the ability to adapt to changing market conditions.

Conclusion: By analyzing real-world case studies & engaging in group discussions, participants have learned how to identify and develop key dynamic capabilities crucial for addressing challenges in a dynamic business landscape. It is our hope that this activity inspires participants to apply the principles of dynamic capabilities in their entrepreneurial ventures, fostering continuous growth and resilience in the face of evolving market conditions.

12.9 Embeddedness

Karl Polanyi was an Austrian-Hungarian economic sociologist in the middle years of the twentieth century. He coined the term 'embeddedness' to mean the extent that economic activity is constrained by institutions that are non-economic. Non-economic institutions may include:
1) kinship or family, 2) religious or cultural, 3) power & politics. Embeddedness can also be thought of as the nature, depth, and extent of an individual's ties into the environment (Jack and Anderson, 2002). Patterns of economic exchange become embedded in webs of social relations that over time leading to the development of trust and reciprocity (Uzzi, 1997). Embeddedness affects decisions about who to transact with including potential investors and customers of entrepreneurs' ventures. For instance, someone that graduates from Stanford may be more likely to get investment from someone in the Stanford venture capital network, but they may also be more likely to get funding from outside that network because they have access to the high-status network. Startups may accumulate supportive resources

from existing or new ties (Hite and Hesterly, 2001). Entrepreneurs that do not have the right ties to access network resources may use various strategies to overcome this barrier. It is interesting to think about how an entrepreneur goes about developing the right stakeholder networks to get funded. For instance, founders that have worked for prestigious firms may be deemed investment worthy, thus entrepreneurs can seek to work for prestigious firms as an in. Another possibility is to spin out an idea from a prestigious firm, or to find partners from or hire from the desired networks.

Understanding the "Embeddedness" theory:

Embeddedness is the idea that businesses are not isolated entities, but are rather embedded within social, economic, and political networks. Here is a business example of embeddedness:

Silicon Valley: The success of technology companies in Silicon Valley is often attributed to the close relationships and networks between entrepreneurs, venture capitalists, and academia in the area. The business community in Silicon Valley is highly interconnected, with individuals and organizations collaborating, sharing knowledge and resources, & supporting each other's ventures.

Supply Chain Networks: Companies that are part of a supply chain are embedded within a network of suppliers, distributors, and customers. The success of a company in a supply chain is often dependent on its ability to build and maintain strong relationships with other actors in the network, as well as its ability to adapt to changes in the network.

Corporate Social Responsibility (CSR): Companies that engage in CSR activities are embedded within the larger social and political context in which they operate. The success of these initiatives is often dependent on the company's ability to build relationships with stakeholders, including customers, employees, and local communities. By recognizing and leveraging these relationships, companies can build stronger networks, improve their social and environmental impact, and ultimately contribute to the well-being of society.

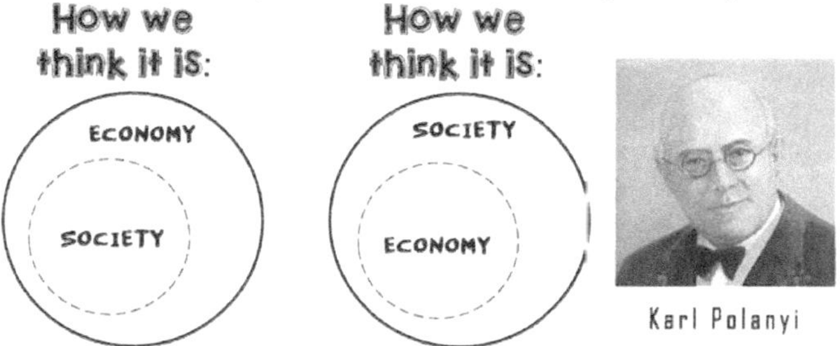

Classroom Activity: "Unveiling Startup Network"

Objective: The aim of this activity is to introduce participants to the concept of "Embeddedness Theory" in entrepreneurship and help them understand the significance of social networks and relationships in the entrepreneurial process.

Duration: 60 minutes

Material: Whiteboard or flip chart, Markers, Sticky notes & Pen/pencil for each participant.

Instructions:

Activity	Instructions
Intro (10 mins)	Introduce the theory & explain that the primary focus of this activity is to explore the concept of "Embeddedness Theory" in the context of entrepreneurship. Describe "Embeddedness Theory" as a framework that examines how entrepreneurs are embedded in social networks and relationships, influencing their behavior, decisions, and overall success in their entrepreneurial journey.
Understanding Embeddedness (15 mins)	Distribute the handout on Embeddedness Theory to participants. Take time to go through key concepts: a. Social Embeddedness: The extent to which entrepreneurs are connected to and influenced by their social networks. b. Structural Embeddedness: The patterns and configurations of relationships in the social network. c. Relational Embeddedness: The quality and strength of relationships between entrepreneurs & other actors in the network. d. Normative Embeddedness: The shared norms, values, and expectations within the entrepreneurial network. Encourage participants to ask questions for better clarity.
Groups (5 mins)	Divide participants into small groups (3-5 people per group). Provide each group with an entrepreneurial case study (or examples of real entrepreneurs) showcasing the significance of embeddedness in their journey.
Real-life Examples (20 mins)	Instruct the groups to analyze the case study, identifying: a. The entrepreneur's social network & key relationships. b. How these relationships influenced the entrepreneur's decisions and actions. c. The role of shared norms & values within the network. Each group presents their findings to the rest of the participants.

Interactive Discussion (10 mins)	Facilitate a group discussion on the insights gained from the case studies and examples. Encourage participants to share their thoughts on the importance of social networks and embeddedness in entrepreneurial success. Discuss potential challenges and benefits of being embedded in a network.
Application Exercise (5 mins)	As a wrap-up activity, ask participants to reflect on their own entrepreneurial journey or business idea. Have them jot down: a. The key individuals or groups in their social network relevant to their entrepreneurial venture. b. How these connections could positively or negatively impact their business decisions. c. Strategies they can use to strengthen their social embeddedness for better entrepreneurial outcomes.
Wrap-up (Varies)	Summarize the main takeaways from the activity, emphasize the significance of the theory & encourage participants to continually nurture and develop their social networks to enhance their entrepreneurial journey. Provide additional resources or reading materials for further exploration of the topic.

Conclusion: The activity has revealed the vital role of social networks and relationships in shaping entrepreneurial success. Nurturing strong connections and adhering to shared norms can empower entrepreneurs to make informed decisions and thrive in their ventures.

12.10 Feminism

For the most part, women entrepreneurs are in the minority, and they are less likely to be funded by venture capitalists. This naturally leads to criticism of the old boys' club in venture capital investment that tends to invest less in women led ventures. There are some indications that these trends are changing but it's far from over. Much of the feminist literature that discusses entrepreneurship tends to look at differences between entrepreneurial entry rates and opportunities for women entrepreneurs as well as the systems and structures that cause the disparities between men and women. Hurley (1999): *"Traditional anthropological theories stated that the key factor in human evolution was the male's hunting activities. The men developed the important social skills of communication, co-operation and tool making, while women contributed little...Feminist theories showed that women's activities were the key factors in human evolution. The activities of gathering, childbearing, and childrearing developed the social skills of co-operation, sharing, and tool making."* Most feminist approaches advocate for equal or even greater rights for women given their unequal position in society. Greer and Green (2003) propose that different streams of feminist Theory have different implications for entrepreneurs.

- The liberal feminist approach views men and women as equals, which critics say undermines women in their special roles as mothers.
- The Marxist feminist approach views parenting as a form of productive but unpaid labor that affect entrepreneurial behaviors of women. It advocates for women coming out of the home to do productive work & for programs like maternity that should be mother-friendly.
- The radical feminist perspective calls for men to be equally involved in parenting. They also propose separatist measures such as programs dedicated and tailored to women entrepreneurs given their unique biology and related life experiences.

Another take, which is sometimes called a positive approach is to see that entrepreneurship is a means to overcome inequality, it can be used to advance women's rights (Hurley, 1999). Women entrepreneurs bring themselves out of disadvantage, but also face unique challenges.

Understanding the "Feminism" theory:

Feminist theory in business is concerned with addressing gender inequalities and promoting equal opportunities for women. For e.g., The 2021 Women in the Workplace study: McKinsey & Company, a management consulting firm, partnered with LeanIn.Org to produce an annual report on the state of women in the workplace. The 2021 report highlights the challenges faced by women during the COVID-19 pandemic and provides recommendations for companies to promote gender equality. The report encourages companies to prioritize diversity, equity, and inclusion efforts, provide flexible work arrangements, and address the gender pay gap.

The #MeToo movement: The #MeToo movement is a feminist movement that has had a significant impact on the business world. The movement has led to increased awareness and action around sexual harassment and assault in the workplace. Many companies have implemented policies and training programs to address these issues and promote a safe and inclusive work environment.

Gender diversity initiatives: Many companies are implementing gender diversity initiatives to increase the representation of women in leadership positions. For example, companies may set targets for the number of women in leadership roles, implement mentoring programs, and provide training and development opportunities for women.

Feminist theory in business is about promoting gender equality and addressing gender inequalities. By recognizing and addressing these issues, companies can create a more inclusive and equitable work environment, which can lead to improved employee engagement, productivity, and overall business performance.

Classroom Activity: "Feminism in Startups"

Objective: To introduce readers to Feminism theory & its relevance in the entrepreneurial context, encouraging a meaningful discussion on gender equality and diversity in business.

Materials: Whiteboard or flip chart, Markers, Sticky notes for each participant.

Duration: 75 - 90 mins

Instructions:

Activity	Instructions
Intro (5 mins)	Explain core principles and how it relates to issues of gender equality, representation, & empowerment. Highlight considering feminist perspectives in entrepreneurship for inclusivity & diversity
Group Brainstorming (15 mins)	Divide participants into small groups of 4-6 people. Ask each group to brainstorm and list the potential challenges and barriers faced by women and other marginalized genders in the entrepreneurial ecosystem. Encourage participants to consider both external (societal) and internal (structural and cultural) factors that contribute to these challenges.

Case Study Analysis (20 mins)	Provide a case study of a successful feminist entrepreneur or a business that has effectively incorporated feminist principles into its operations. Instruct each group to analyze the case study, identifying specific strategies and practices that foster gender equality and empowerment. Encourage participants to discuss how these strategies could be adapted in other entrepreneurial ventures.
Group Presentations (15 mins)	Ask each group to present their findings and insights from the case study analysis to the rest of the participants. Facilitate a collaborative discussion by encouraging questions, feedback, and diverse perspectives on the presented strategies. Emphasize the importance of fostering an inclusive and supportive environment in entrepreneurial settings.
Personal Reflection (10 mins)	Individually, ask participants to reflect on how they can apply feminist principles in their own entrepreneurial journey or in their workplaces to promote gender equality and inclusivity. Encourage participants to consider concrete action steps they can take to support & empower women and marginalized genders in entrepreneurship.
Wrap-up (10 mins)	Conduct an open discussion where participants can share their reflections and experiences related to feminism in entrepreneurship. Summarize the key takeaways and emphasize the importance of creating a supportive and inclusive entrepreneurial ecosystem. Provide additional resources and reading materials for participants interested in delving deeper into feminism theory & its application.

Conclusion: The activity empowers participants to understand the significance of Feminism theory in entrepreneurship & its potential to create more inclusive & diverse business environments. Through collaborative discussions, participants identified challenges faced by women and marginalized genders in entrepreneurship, while also exploring actionable strategies to promote gender equality and empowerment. This exploration of Feminism theory will inspire participants to apply its principles in their entrepreneurial journeys, fostering a more equitable and supportive ecosystem for all entrepreneurs.

12.11 Hubris

Mathew Hayward and colleagues (2006) introduce a hubris Theory of entrepreneurship. Their aim is to explain why so many new ventures are started despite a very high background failure rate. After all, most businesses fail within the first few years of founding. So why do entrepreneurs keep trying to create new ones? Individuals overestimate the personal wealth they may attain by starting new ventures. The Theory assumes that individuals have information about their likelihood of success but think that they can beat the odds. Hayward and colleagues suggest that overconfident individuals may harm their ventures by depriving them of resources. Thus, while overconfidence may help in starting a venture, it does not help much with operating a business. Cassar (2010) finds empirical evidence that prospective entrepreneurs are indeed overconfident. Hogarth and Karelaia (2012) find that overconfident entrepreneurs have lower success chances. Thus, overall, there is some support for the Theory, and it does help explain the higher-than-expected entry rates we see in practice. The Theory hangs on the idea of confidence. More confident individuals have the bravado to be able to start businesses and allocate resources in challenging situations, while less confident individuals may not be moved to start ventures or grow them. According to Sundermeier (2017), hubristic founders exhibit certain traits that help them excel in their startups including having increased resilience in the implementation of original ideas which often carries potential for creative destruction, having a high internal locus of control, possessing the ability to be persuasive and secure strategic partnerships. They are also driven by their feelings of invulnerability.

Understanding the "Hubris" theory:

Hubris refers to excessive pride and self-confidence, which can lead to risky and harmful decision-making in the business world. Here are few business examples of hubris:

Enron: It collapsed in 2001 due to accounting fraud and corporate mismanagement. The company's leadership, including CEO Jeffrey Skilling and Chairman Ken Lay, were known for their hubris and arrogance, which led them to engage in risky financial schemes and unethical behavior. Enron's collapse resulted in the loss of thousands of jobs and billions of dollars for investors.

WeWork: The real estate company was valued at $47 billion in early 2019, but its value plummeted after the company's IPO was cancelled later that year. The company's leadership, including CEO Adam

Neumann, were known for their hubris and unconventional management style, which included expensive personal investments and a lack of financial transparency.

Uber: The company's former CEO, Travis Kalanick, was known for his hubris and aggressive leadership style, which led to several controversies and legal issues. Kalanick ultimately resigned in 2017 amid pressure from investors.

Hubris can be a dangerous trait in the business world, leading to risky decision-making and negative consequences for companies and their stakeholders. It is important for business leaders to recognize and address their own hubris, and for boards of directors and investors to hold leaders accountable for their actions.

H	HIGH CONFIDENCE
U	UNSUCCESSFUL
B	BRAVADO
R	RESILIENCE
I	INTERNAL FOCUS
S	STRATEGY

Mathew Hayward

Classroom Activity: "Hubris in Startups"

Objective: To introduce readers to the concept of Hubris theory and its implications in entrepreneurship, encouraging critical thinking about the role of overconfidence and its potential impact on decisions.

Materials: Whiteboard or flip chart, Markers, Sticky notes & Pen/pencil for each participant.

Duration: 75 - 90 mins

Instructions:

Activity	Instructions
Intro (5mins)	Explain how excessive pride, overconfidence, or self-belief that can lead to risky decision-making. Highlight, where bold decisions & ambition are prevalent but can also carry inherent risks.
Case Study Pitch (15 mins)	Present a case study of a well-known entrepreneurial venture that experienced both success and failure due to the impact of hubris on decision-making. Describe the company's background, the key decisions influenced by overconfidence, and the subsequent consequences. Explain how hubris affected the company's trajectory and long-term sustainability.

Small Group Analysis (20 mins)	Divide participants into small groups. Ask them to analyze and discuss the case study, focusing on identifying signs of hubris-driven decisions and their effects on the business. Encourage participants to explore potential measures which have been taken to mitigate the negative impact of hubris.
Group Pitch (15mins)	Ask groups to present their analysis & recommendations to the rest of the participants. Facilitate a discussion by encouraging questions, critiques, and alternative viewpoints on how to recognize and address hubris tendencies in entrepreneurship. Emphasize the value of open discussions and diverse perspectives.
Personal Views (10 mins)	Individually, ask participants to reflect on times they may have experienced overconfidence or witnessed it in others in their entrepreneurial journey. Encourage them to consider the potential consequences of unchecked hubris & how they develop self-awareness to avoid falling into hubris-driven decision traps.
Discussion Learnings (10 mins)	Conduct an open discussion where participants can share their reflections and insights on hubris theory in entrepreneurship. Summarize the key learning points and discuss strategies for fostering a balanced entrepreneurial mindset that embraces ambition while mitigating the risks of hubris-driven decision-making.
Wrap-up (5 mins)	Reiterate the importance of recognizing and addressing hubris in entrepreneurship to ensure sustainable growth and long-term success. Encourage participants to continue exploring the topic of hubris theory and apply the lessons learned to their own entrepreneurial endeavors. Provide additional resources & reading materials for further study.

Conclusion: The valuable insights into the consequences of unchecked hubris & importance of self-awareness in entrepreneurship from this activity will encourage participants in the future to approach business challenges with humility & critical thinking, fostering a more balanced and sustainable approach to entrepreneurial decision-making.

12.12 Human Capital

Human capital Theory was developed by Dr. Gary Becker, an American economist at the University of Chicago, and others. According to Becker (1994), human capital is different kind of capital from physical and financial resources. Education, technology and etiquette training, and health expenditures are capital too because they improve wellbeing, health, earnings, and appreciation. Expenditures on education, training, and health care are investments in human capital. Human capital also refers to an individual or group's stock of knowledge, routines, personality characteristics and social habits. Human capital even includes creativity that can be usefully applied to an economic purpose, and thus is a type of wealth. Countries, organizations, and groups with greater human capital are expected to be better able to accomplish goals to bring about economic improvement. Several studies have found a positive association between human capital and economic development, including innovation and productivity growth. These associations have been used as evidence to justify government subsidies for education and training. Human capital attributes, such as education and experience, may also be critical for entrepreneurial success. The human capital of founders attracts investors (Stuart and Abetti, 1990), especially venture capitalists (Zacharakis and Meyer, 2000). Some have argued that human capital Theory is problematic because individuals often seek education and training in order to signal their quality to employers and investors rather than aiming to attain knowledge and skills (Spence, 1973).

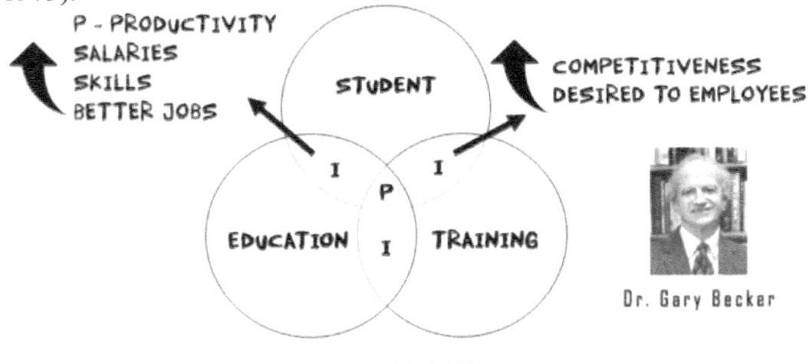

Understanding the "Human Capital" theory:

Human capital refers to the knowledge, skills, and abilities that employees bring to a business, which can increase its productivity and profitability. For example.

Google: It offers a range of training and development programs, including leadership training, mentoring, and skills development workshops. It also provides its employees with a range of benefits, including free meals, on-site gyms, and generous vacation time. These investments in human capital have helped Google attract & retain top talent & have contributed to its success.

Starbucks: It provides its employees with extensive training on topics such as coffee brewing, customer service, and sales techniques. Starbucks also offers its employees a range of benefits, including health insurance and stock options. These investments in human capital have helped Starbucks create a strong corporate culture and attract and retain employees who are passionate about the company's mission and values.

Procter & Gamble: It offers a range of training and development programs, including leadership development, mentoring, and on-the-job training. Procter & Gamble also provides its employees with a range of benefits, including flexible work arrangements and opportunities for career advancement. These investments in human capital have helped P&G attract and retain top talent and have contributed to its success as a company.

Apple: Its success can be attributed in part to the knowledge and skills of its employees. Apple invests in employee training and development programs, and the company is known for its rigorous hiring process, which seeks out the best and brightest talent in the technology industry.

McKinsey & Company: It places a high value on human capital. The company hires top talent from leading universities and business schools, and the company invests heavily in employee training and development programs. McKinsey & Company is known for its rigorous and challenging work environment, which attracts ambitious and talented individuals.

Investing in human capital can help businesses attract and retain top talent, improve productivity and profitability, and create a strong corporate culture. By prioritizing employee development and growth, businesses can build a competitive advantage and position themselves for long-term success.

Classroom Activity: " Skill Assessment Class"

Objective: To introduce readers to Human Capital theory and its significance in entrepreneurship. Participants will engage in a skill assessment workshop to identify and leverage their unique human capital for business success.

Materials: Whiteboard or flip chart, Markers, Sticky notes & Pen/pencil for each participant.

Duration: 90 – 100 mins

Instructions:

Activity	Instructions
Intro (5 mins)	Provide an overview of Human Capital theory, explaining how it refers to the skills, knowledge, experiences, and attributes that individuals bring to the workforce. Highlight the importance of human capital in entrepreneurial ventures and how it can be an asset for business growth and innovation.
Self-Assessment (20 mins)	Ask participants to create a list of their own skills, talents, and expertise relevant to entrepreneurship. Encourage them to reflect on both technical skills (e.g., coding, marketing, finance) and soft skills (e.g., leadership, communication, problem-solving). Provide a self-assessment questionnaire or worksheet to help participants evaluate their proficiency in each skill and identify areas for improvement.
Skill Exchange (15 mins)	Divide participants into small groups of 3-5 people. Instruct each group to share their skill inventory and self-assessment results with one another. Encourage group members to discuss potential collaborative opportunities where their combined human capital can create synergetic advantages.
Identifying new areas (20 mins)	Ask each participant to individually brainstorm entrepreneurial opportunities that align with their unique human capital and expertise. Challenge them to think creatively about how their skills can address market needs and solve specific problems.
Group Idea Pitching (15 mins)	Have each participant present their entrepreneurial opportunity to their group. Encourage constructive feedback & suggestions from group members to further refine & strengthen each idea.
Reflective Discussion (10 mins)	Conduct an open discussion with all participants, allowing them to share insights gained from the skill assessment workshop. Facilitate a conversation on how human capital can be leveraged to create a competitive advantage & contribute to success.

Wrap-up Action Plan (5 mins)	Summarize the key takeaways & encourage participants to develop an action plan for further developing and applying their skills in their entrepreneurial journey. Provide additional resources and reading materials on Human Capital theory and skill development for those interested in exploring the topic further.

Conclusion: This activity empowers participants to recognize the significance of their human capital in entrepreneurial endeavors, promoting self-awareness and skill development. Through collaborative exploration, participants discovered how their unique skillsets can be leveraged to identify entrepreneurial opportunities and create a competitive advantage. This activity will inspire & continue nurturing their human capital, fostering success & innovation in their Startup journeys.

12.13 Hybrid

Most entrepreneurs work for organizations before or while they start their businesses. There is macho entrepreneurship dogma that says you have to go all in, experience "the fear" and dedicate yourself for 80 hours a week to your venture. Implicit in this is the notion that an entrepreneur cannot succeed if they hedge their bets by keeping one foot in employment. Why go all in to a startup if startups are probabilistic events, not givens. Many employers and regulators allow employees the freedom to pursue new ventures on the side, especially those that do not directly compete with their employers (and therefore not breaching a duty of loyalty). Hybrid entrepreneurship refers to entrepreneurship whereby an employee starts a business on the side and keeps their day job until the startup reaches a certain size. Once the business is large enough to command the founder's full attention, then the employee makes their exit. However, it is important to note that many attempts will also be halted at some point along the way, delaying the probability of exit. There might usually be an equal or sequential balance of emphasis between them, but both the startup and the employer's job, get done. Folta et al. (2014) argue that: *"In contrast to previous efforts to model the individual 's movement from wage work into entrepreneurship, we consider that individuals might transition incrementally by retaining their wage job while entering into self-employment."* Their research on Swedish wage earners in the knowledge sector demonstrates that hybrid entrepreneurs represent a large minority of entrepreneurial activity.

Raffiee and Feng (2014) say: Don't quit your day job! *"Hybrid entrepreneurs who subsequently enter full-time self-employment (i.e., quit their day job) have much higher rates of survival relative to individuals who enter full-time self-employment directly from paid employment"*

Perhaps if more employers knew that hybrid entrepreneurs are more successful, they would be more forgiving of it. Policymakers could also get involved and ensure that employers do not overly restrict employees from starting businesses.

BUILD AS YOU GROW!!

Timothy Folta

Understanding the "Hybrid" theory:

Hybrid entrepreneurship refers to a type of entrepreneurship where a business owner or founder pursues both social and financial goals. Here is a business example of hybrid entrepreneurship:

Warby Parker: It was founded in 2010 with a mission to provide affordable, stylish glasses to consumers while also addressing the problem of limited access to eyewear in developing countries. For every pair of glasses sold, the company donates a pair to someone in need through its "Buy a Pair, Give a Pair" program. Warby Parker's hybrid approach has been successful, and the company has grown rapidly since its founding, with a valuation of over $1 billion in 2015.

TOMS Shoes: It was founded in 2006 with a mission to provide shoes to children in need. For every pair of shoes sold, the company donates a pair to a child in need through its "One for One" program. In addition to its social mission, TOMS also focuses on creating high-quality, stylish shoes that appeal to consumers. The company's hybrid approach has been successful, and TOMS has expanded its product line to include eyewear and coffee.

Patagonia: It was founded in 1973 with a mission to create high-quality outdoor clothing while also protecting the environment. The company has a strong commitment to sustainability and has taken several steps to reduce its environmental impact, such as using recycled materials in its products and advocating for environmental policies. Patagonia's hybrid approach has been successful, and the company has grown to become a major player in the outdoor clothing industry.

Overall, hybrid entrepreneurship is a growing trend in the business world, as more and more companies recognize the importance of social responsibility and environmental sustainability. By pursuing both financial and social goals, these companies can create value for both their shareholders and society.

Here are some Indian examples of hybrid entrepreneurship:

Goonj: It was founded in 1999 with a mission to address the issue of rural poverty and development in India. The organization collects unused and surplus materials from urban households and corporations and distributes them to rural communities. Goonj's hybrid approach combines social entrepreneurship with sustainable development, and the organization has helped to create employment opportunities for rural communities while also addressing the issue of waste management in urban areas.

Drishtee: It was founded in 2000 with a mission to provide access to essential goods and services in rural areas of India. The organization works with local entrepreneurs to set up "Drishtee centers" that provide a range of services, including access to clean water, education, and healthcare. Drishtee's hybrid approach has helped to create economic opportunities in rural areas while also addressing the issue of rural development.

Barefoot College: It was founded in 1972 with a mission to provide education and skills training to rural communities in India. The organization offers a range of programs, including solar electrification, water harvesting, and healthcare, and it works with local communities to build capacity and promote sustainable development. It is hybrid approach combines social entrepreneurship with education and capacity building, & the organization has helped to create employment opportunities for rural communities while promoting environmental sustainability.

By combining social and financial goals, these organizations have been able to create value for both their shareholders and society.

Classroom Activity: "A Creative Ideation Workshop"

Objective: To introduce readers to the concept of Hybrid Theory and encourage them to explore creative combinations of ideas and concepts to develop innovative entrepreneurial solutions.

Materials: Whiteboard or flip chart, Markers, Sticky notes & Pen/pencil for each participant.

Duration: 90 – 100 mins

Instructions:

Activity	Instructions
Intro (5 mins)	Provide an overview of Hybrid Theory, explaining its significance in entrepreneurship as the integration of diverse ideas, technologies, or business models to create novel and disruptive innovations. Highlight importance of thinking outside traditional boundaries & embracing cross-disciplinary approaches for success.
Idea Generation (10 mins)	Conduct a quick warm-up activity to stimulate creativity. Ask participants to brainstorm as many ideas as possible for solving a specific problem or addressing a market need. Encourage participants to think freely and without judgment during this ideation exercise.
Hybrid Theory Case Studies (15 mins)	Present case studies of successful entrepreneurial ventures that exemplify Hybrid Theory in action. Discuss how these ventures combined elements from different domains or industries to create unique and market-leading solutions. Encourage participants to analyze the factors that contributed to their success and what made their hybrid approaches innovative.
Hybrid Idea Generation (20 mins)	Divide participants into small groups of 4-6 people. Assign each group a specific problem or challenge related to entrepreneurship. Instruct groups to brainstorm and develop hybrid ideas by creatively combining concepts, technologies, or business models from different domains to address the given challenge.
Group Idea Pitch (15 mins)	Ask each group to present their hybrid ideas to the rest of the participants. Facilitate a collaborative discussion, allowing other groups to provide feedback and suggestions to further enhance the hybrid solutions.
Reflection (10 mins)	Individually, ask participants to reflect on the creative process of generating hybrid ideas and identify any challenges or breakthrough moments they experienced. Encourage them to refine and elaborate on their initial hybrid ideas based on the feedback received during the group presentations.
Pitching & Evaluation (15 mins)	Organize a pitching session where each participant will present their refined hybrid idea to a panel of "investors" or peers. The panel can provide feedback, ask questions, and evaluate the feasibility and innovativeness of the hybrid ideas.

Wrap-up (5 mins)	Summarize the key takeaways from the activity, emphasizing the power of Hybrid Theory in fostering innovative thinking and problem-solving in entrepreneurship. Encourage participants to apply the principles of Hybrid Theory in their entrepreneurial endeavors, exploring diverse perspectives and embracing creative combinations to drive disruptive innovations. Provide additional resources and reading materials on Hybrid Theory and creativity in entrepreneurship for those interested in further exploration.

Conclusion: This activity will ignite participants' creativity and showcase their potential in generating innovative solutions for entrepreneurial challenges. Through collaborative brainstorming & case studies, participants will discover the transformative power of combining diverse ideas, technologies, and business models to create market-leading ventures. This exploration will inspire participants to embrace cross-disciplinary approaches & think boldly, unlocking new possibilities for future entrepreneurial success through creative combination.

12.14 Individual Ambidexterity

Most new ventures are founded by former employees of organizations. Employees make discoveries while working for organizations and decide to exploit them on their own, especially when parent firms do not see the value in their discoveries or choose not to exploit them due to a lack of fit with the firm's strategy. When employees leave to start new ventures, we call their ventures employee spinouts. Ambidextrous behaviors have been observed in entrepreneurs. Entrepreneurs display ambidextrous through boundary-spanning relationships, by avoiding excess exploitation and keeping time aside for exploration, by using platforms for discussing issues related to exploration, and by shifting focus from exploration to exploitation and vice versa as the current situation requires (Volery et al., 2013). The entrepreneurial process is often conceptualized as stage based. For example, Kazanjian and Drazin (1990) suggest four stages: conception and development, commercialization, growth, and stability. The early stages are more in line with exploration activities and the later stages are more like exploration activities, again suggesting entrepreneurs need to be able to do both types of activities. Mom et al. (2015) proposes that individuals working within organizations are ambidextrous if they are involved in both exploration and exploitation activities. Exploration and exploitation involve different types of learning and thus offer different preparatory experiences for individuals involved in them. According to March (1991), exploration involves activities such as search, play, experimentation, ideation, radical innovation, and formulation, whereas exploitation involves activities like refinement, execution, selection, implementation, and incremental improvement. Yeganegi et al. (2019) propose that entrepreneurial preparation within their employing firms is important for employees turned entrepreneurs. Work experiences may be sources of entrepreneurial opportunities that employees can use to create new businesses and to potentially increase their economic and social mobility. The above argument suggests that when employees experience both exploration and exploitation (i.e., individual-level ambidexterity) in an organizational setting, they are mimicking the same stage-based processes that they will likely encounter in entrepreneurship. Seeing the whole cycle of the business activity may enable employees to better recognize opportunities, reduce their uncertainty, increase the depth and breadth of their knowledge, and increase their perceptions of self-efficacy—all of which are expected to increase the likelihood of that they will become nascent entrepreneurs. The authors distinguish between exploration and exploitation experiences, thus drawing on the individual ambidexterity literature for inspiration. Using data from the Global Entrepreneurship Monitor, their analyses suggest that employees who experience individual-level ambidexterity, that is exposure to both the exploration and exploitation phases in the corporate venturing process, are more likely to become nascent entrepreneurs. The degree of ambidexterity that an individual may experience as a member of an organization is likely to differ according to the context internal to the organization. For example, organizations that break up exploration and exploitation tasks with structural separations may use differentiated incentive schemes (i.e., different rewards for those who are engaging in exploration than those for individuals specializing in exploitation). Alternatively, they may disallow overlapping cultures to form around exploration and exploitation activities and therefore be less likely to employ individuals who will experience ambidexterity at work. By contrast, organizations that practice contextual ambidexterity (Gibson and Birkinshaw, 2004), where both exploration and exploitation occur within the same organizational units are likely to accommodate ambidexterity experiences for more individuals.

Understanding the "Ambidexterity" theory:

Individual ambidexterity refers to an individual's ability to balance exploration and exploitation activities in their work. Here is a business example of individual ambidexterity:

Google: It is known for fostering a culture of individual ambidexterity among its employees. For example, the company encourages its engineers to spend 20% of their time working on projects outside of their core responsibilities, which allows them to explore new ideas and technologies. At the same time, Google also places a strong emphasis on execution and delivering results, which requires employees to be able to effectively exploit existing knowledge and capabilities.

Apple: It encourages individual ambidexterity among its employees. The company has a strong culture of innovation and encourages employees to think creatively and explore new ideas. At the same time, Apple also places a strong emphasis on execution and delivering high-quality products, which requires employees to be able to effectively exploit existing knowledge and capabilities.

Procter & Gamble: It has implemented several programs to foster individual ambidexterity among its employees. For example, the company has a "Connect + Develop" program that encourages employees to collaborate with external partners to develop new products and technologies. The company also encourages employees to rotate through different roles and functions, which helps to develop their ability to explore new ideas while also effectively exploiting existing knowledge and capabilities.

By encouraging employees to balance exploration & exploitation activities, these companies can drive innovation and growth while also delivering high-quality products & services.

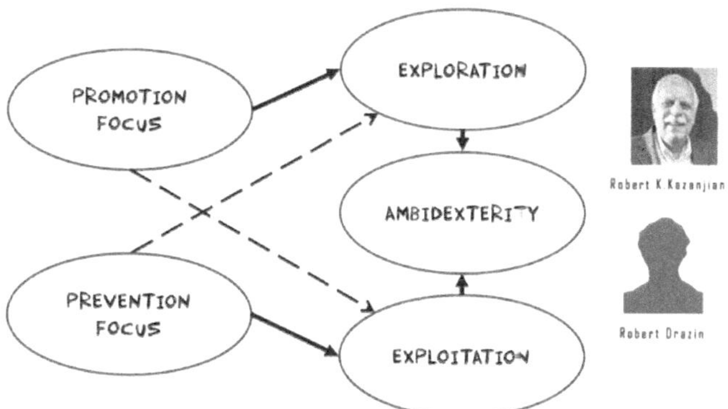

Classroom Activity: "Balancing the Paradox: Ambidexterity"

Objective: To introduce participants to the theory & help them understand how entrepreneurs can effectively balance exploration & exploitation behaviors to drive innovation & sustainable growth.

Materials: Whiteboard or flip chart, Markers, Sticky notes & Pen/pencil for each participant.

Duration: 60 minutes

Instructions:

Activity	Instructions
Intro (10 mins)	Introduce topic of "Individual Ambidexterity Theory." Explain that Individual Ambidexterity Theory focuses on how entrepreneurs can simultaneously explore new opportunities while exploiting existing resources and capabilities to achieve long-term success & innovation.
Understanding Individual Ambidexterity (15 mins)	Distribute the handout on Individual Ambidexterity Theory to participants. Take some time to go through the key concepts: a. Exploration: The ability to pursue new ideas, ventures, and opportunities for innovation. b. Exploitation: The ability to optimize and leverage existing resources, knowledge, and capabilities. c. The paradox of ambidexterity: Balancing exploration and exploitation, which often involves trade-offs and challenges.
Case Studies (20 mins)	Optionally, provide participants with case studies of successful entrepreneurs or companies that have effectively demonstrated individual ambidexterity. Instruct participants to analyze the case studies and identify: a. How the entrepreneurs or companies balanced exploration and exploitation in their strategies. b. The impact of individual ambidexterity on their innovation and sustained growth. Let everyone share their views individually & groups
Interactive Discussion (10 mins)	Facilitate a group discussion on the insights gained from the case studies and examples. Encourage participants to share their thoughts on the challenges and benefits of embracing individual ambidexterity in entrepreneurship. Discuss strategies that entrepreneurs can adopt to better manage the paradox and foster ambidextrous behaviors.

Reflection and Action (5 mins)	Ask participants to reflect on their own entrepreneurial ventures or business ideas. Have them consider how they can apply individual ambidexterity principles to enhance their decision-making and overall approach to innovation and growth.
Wrap-up (Varies)	Summarize the main takeaways from the activity, emphasizing the significance of Theory in entrepreneurship. Remind participants that embracing the paradox of exploration and exploitation can lead to more resilient and successful entrepreneurial ventures. Encourage them to continually assess their strategies and adapt to changing circumstances, striking a balance between innovation and efficiency for sustained success.

Conclusion: The exploration of the Theory has illuminated the art of balancing exploration and exploitation for entrepreneurs, leading to enhanced innovation and sustained growth. Embracing this paradox empowers entrepreneurs to thrive in dynamic markets, continually adapt, and achieve long-term success in their ventures.

12.15 Informal Entrepreneurship

Informal entrepreneurship happens outside of the formal economy. The formal economy is the part that is legal and legitimate. The legal economy is where companies and entrepreneurs pay taxes, abide by regulations, and attain licenses that are set out by governments or institutions.

Informal entrepreneurship is not about purely black-market enterprises, like illegal gambling rings, outlaw biker gangs, or illegal fireworks factories. Informal entrepreneurship can involve everything from street vendors to domestic work within the home. In many societies, informal entrepreneurship is a major part of the economy, especially in developing countries. Often informal entrepreneurship is so normalized in a society that it is considered legitimate in the minds of the majority, even if it might also be illegal (Webb et al., 2009). According to Suchman (1995), legitimacy is: *"a generalized perception or assumption that the actions of an entity are desirable, proper, or appropriate within some socially constructed system of norms, values, beliefs, and definitions"*. Thus, one way of conceiving of informal entrepreneurship is to think of it as entrepreneurship that is legitimate, but not legal. Webb et al. suggest that entrepreneurship that is both illegal and illegitimate is part of the renegade economy, not the informal economy. According to Williams and Nadin (2010): *"legitimizing this hidden enterprise culture [informal entrepreneurship] could be an important means of promoting enterprise and economic development".* All of this suggests recognizing informal entrepreneurship is a new avenue for economic development that is not just focused on innovation, high-growth business models, or technology venture, which receive the bulk of the attention.

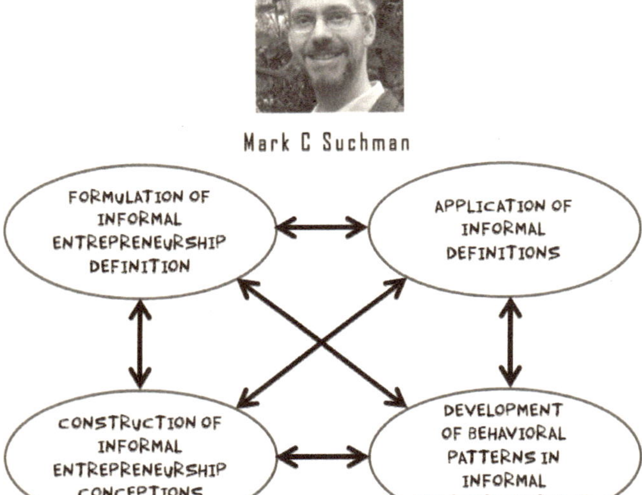

Mark C Suchman

Understanding the "Informal Entrepreneurship" theory:

Informal entrepreneurship refers to business activities that are conducted outside of formal business structures, such as traditional businesses or corporations. For example;

Street vendors: They are a common example of informal entrepreneurship. In many cities around the world, street vendors sell a variety of goods, including food, clothing, and souvenirs. These vendors often operate without a formal business license or other legal documents, and their business activities are not regulated by the government. Despite these challenges, many street vendors earn a living & support themselves and their families through their business activities.

Freelance workers: Graphic designers, writers, and consultants, are another example of informal entrepreneurship. These workers often operate on a project-by-project basis and are not formally employed by a company or organization. Instead, they rely on their skills and reputation to find new clients and generate income. Freelance work can be a flexible and rewarding career path, but it can also be challenging due to the need to constantly find new clients and manage the administrative aspects of running a business.

Family businesses: Family businesses, such as small shops or restaurants may operate without formal legal structures or business plans, and they may rely on family members to provide labor and management support. Despite these challenges, many family businesses can succeed and grow over time, due in part to the strong social and cultural ties that bind family members together.

Informal entrepreneurship plays an important role in many economies around the world. While these businesses may face significant challenges, they also offer opportunities for individuals and families to generate income, create jobs, and contribute to their communities.

Classroom Activity: Exploring Informal Entrepreneurship

Objective: To help readers understand and explore the concept of informal entrepreneurship, its characteristics, and its significance in various economies.

Materials: Whiteboard or flip chart, Markers, Sticky notes & Pen/pencil for each participant.

Duration: 90 – 100 mins

Instructions:

Activity	Instructions
Intro (10 mins)	Introduce the topic of informal entrepreneurship. Briefly explain what informal entrepreneurship means and its key features. Emphasize that informal entrepreneurs operate outside the traditional regulatory frameworks & often play a crucial role in economies worldwide.
Research (20 mins)	Ask readers to conduct research on informal entrepreneurship. They can use the internet, books, or other available resources to gather information. Provide them with a set of guiding questions, such as: • Define informal entrepreneurship? • Characteristics of the informal entrepreneurs? • Difference between in informal & formal entrepreneurship? • Examples of successful informal entrepreneurs? • Challenges faced by informal entrepreneurs? • How does informal entrepreneurship contribute to economy?

Group Discussion (15 mins)	Divide the readers into small groups (3-5 people per group) and encourage them to share their findings. Facilitate a group discussion where they can exchange ideas and insights related to the theory of informal entrepreneurship. Each group should appoint a spokesperson to summarize their findings.
Real-life Examples (15 mins)	Present real-life examples of informal entrepreneurs who have made a significant impact on their communities or industries. Include stories of street vendors, artisans, or online businesses that started informally and grew into successful ventures. Discuss how these examples illustrate principles of informal entrepreneurship.
Advantages /Disadvantages (10 mins)	Guide readers in brainstorming the advantages and disadvantages of informal entrepreneurship. Ask them to consider the benefits of flexibility, low entry barriers, and rapid adaptation, as well as the challenges related to lack of legal protections, limited access to financing, and informality's potential limitations for scalability.
Case Study Analysis (20 mins)	Provide readers with a case study focused on an informal entrepreneur or a business that operates in the informal sector. They should analyze the case study and identify the factors that contributed to the entrepreneur's success or hindered their growth.
Reflection and Wrap-up (10 mins)	Gather the readers' insights and reflections on the theory of informal entrepreneurship. Engage discussion with questions like: • How informal entrepreneurship impacts economies globally? • What can formal entrepreneurs & policymakers learn from the characteristics of informal entrepreneurship? • Can formal & informal entrepreneurship coexist & complement each other?

Conclusion: The sheds light on the vital role played by these ventures in economies worldwide. Through real-life examples, group discussions, and case study analysis, readers have gained insights into the advantages, challenges, and unique contributions of informal entrepreneurs. By understanding how formal and informal entrepreneurship can coexist and learning from each other, participants empower to embrace the potential of informality in their entrepreneurial endeavors.

12.16 Information Asymmetry

Information asymmetry refers to a condition whereby two parties in a market or organizational relationship have access to different information about the exchange. It can be seen as an alternative to the classical assumption of "perfect information" in economics. Information asymmetries have been acknowledged by regulators who have made laws forbidding insider trading. Insiders have special access to the real financial picture of a company and have an unfair advantage when buying and selling company stock (Abocdy, 2000). Company executives, like CEOs also have fiduciary responsibilities toward their investors which require them to be truthful and forthcoming. Information asymmetry is also a potential source of problems in entrepreneurship. For example, an entrepreneur knows much more about the real potential of their ventures because they have inside access to knowledge about their customers and the issues with production. The investors, on the other hand, have less information about the true probabilities, so usually demands a higher return or interest rate to compensate them (see the pecking order Theory). There is potential for abuse of investors when entrepreneurs reveal information selectively, or make statements that are difficult to verify. For instance, when Elon Musk tweeted that he had secured investment to take the company private, investors responded positively, but the Securities and Exchange Commission was not impressed. Even within the startup founding team, more technical founders may have better information about the potential of an innovation but may not disclose it if it would undermine the motivations of sales and business-oriented founders (see agency Theory). It is quite common for technical founders to lead on their business partners and boards. Lowe (2001) proposes that information asymmetry creates problems in contracting between inventors and outside companies (would-be licensing partners) causing the inventors to seek to build their own organizations to bring their inventions to market. Similarly, an inventor within a company may see more potential in their technology than their managers do leading them to spin out the new technology into a new startup (i.e., a spinout). Information asymmetries may also help to explain why entrepreneurs & firms often make poor partner selections when entering joint ventures (Balakrishnan and Koza, 1993).

Understanding the "Information Asymmetry" theory:

Information asymmetry refers to a situation where one party in a business transaction has more information than the other party, giving them an advantage in the transaction. For example.

Used car sales: When buying a used car, the seller typically has more information about the car's condition and history than the buyer. The seller may know about previous accidents or repairs or may have a better understanding of the car's overall condition. This information asymmetry can put the buyer at a disadvantage, as they may not be able to accurately assess the true value of the car and may end up paying more than it's worth.

Mitchell P Koza | Srinivasan Balakrishnan

SELLER THINKS VALUE IS 20LAC

BUYER THINKS VALUE IS 15 LAC

Insurance policies: When purchasing an insurance policy, the insurance company typically has more information about the risk being insured than the policyholder. For example, the insurance company may have access to data on the likelihood of certain events occurring (such as car accidents or house fires) that the policyholder does not have. This information asymmetry can lead to situations where the insurance company charges higher premiums than necessary or denies coverage to certain policyholders.

Investment opportunities: When considering an investment opportunity, investors may not have access to all the information they need to make an informed decision. For example, a company seeking investment may withhold information about its financial performance or prospects, giving it an advantage in negotiations. This information asymmetry can lead to situations where investors make poor investment decisions or are taken advantage of by unscrupulous companies.

Businesses can work to mitigate the impacts of information asymmetry by being transparent and providing as much information as possible to all parties involved in a transaction.

Classroom Activity: Unveiling the Information Asymmetry

Objective: To help readers understand the concept of information asymmetry in entrepreneurship, its implications, and strategies to mitigate its effects.

Materials: Whiteboard or flip chart, Markers, Sticky notes & Pen/pencil for each participant.

Duration: 90 – 100 mins

Instructions:

Activity	Instructions
Intro (10 mins)	Begin by introducing the topic of information asymmetry in entrepreneurship. Explain that information asymmetry occurs when one party in a transaction possesses more or better information than the other party. Emphasize its relevance in influencing decision-making, risk assessment, and market dynamics.
Case Studies (20 mins)	Present case studies or examples that illustrate information asymmetry in different entrepreneurial scenarios. This could include situations where startups seek funding from investors, consumers purchasing products or services, or when hiring employees or forming partnerships. Discuss the consequences of information asymmetry in each case and its impact on the outcomes.
Information Gathering (15 mins)	Divide readers into small groups and assign each group a specific entrepreneurial scenario where information asymmetry plays a significant role. Ask them to brainstorm and discuss the type of information imbalances that could occur in that situation and how it may affect the decision-making process for all parties involved.

Strategies for Mitigation (15 mins)	Gather the readers and have each group share their findings. Facilitate a collective brainstorming session to explore strategies for mitigating information asymmetry in entrepreneurship. Encourage creative & practical solutions that can help level the information playing field, such as transparency, reputation systems, third-party certifications, & data sharing initiatives.
Real-life Examples (15 mins)	Present real-life examples of entrepreneurs or businesses that have successfully navigated information asymmetry challenges. Discuss how these individuals or companies implemented strategies to address misinformation & how it positively impacted their ventures.
Reflection and Discussion (10 mins)	Engage the whole group in a reflective discussion about the significance of understanding information asymmetry for entrepreneurs. Encourage participants to share their insights, challenges, and potential applications of the strategies discussed. Discuss how being aware of information asymmetry can influence entrepreneurial decision-making & foster trust in business deals.
Wrap-up (5 mins)	Reiterate the importance of acknowledging and addressing information imbalances to foster more efficient and trustworthy entrepreneurial ecosystems.

Conclusion: By exploring real-life examples, brainstorming mitigation strategies, and engaging in reflective discussions, participants will be well-prepared to navigate information imbalances, make informed decisions, and foster trust in their entrepreneurial endeavors, contributing to more resilient and thriving ventures.

12.17 Lean launchpad

The Lean Launchpad was developed by Steve Blank (serial entrepreneurs and adjunct professor at Stanford) and colleagues as a repeatable process to create a startup. It is probably the most popular methodology today, featuring in a great number of entrepreneurship programs for students and mature students. It is also the method used at Lean Campus Startups and other top incubator programs. Despite its popularity, there is little empirical research examining the method.

Assumptions behind the Lean Launchpad: The Theory behind the Lean Launchpad can be described as a discovery Theory. The entrepreneurship literature is divided about the nature of entrepreneurial opportunities. At one end of the spectrum is the creationist school that views entrepreneurship as a process of opportunity creation led by teams and individuals (McMullen and Dimov, 2013). At the opposite end of the spectrum, the discovery school defends an objective view of entrepreneurship where opportunities exist independently from the entrepreneurs who race to discover and exploit them (Baron, 2006). Creationist theories tend to dismiss incumbents because they believe entrepreneurs' visions already consider what incumbents will do. The discovery perspective tends to view incumbents as competitors in sensing and seizing opportunities. The Lean Launchpad can be described as a discovery Theory because potential entrepreneurs start with a customer segment and then search to identify problems worth solving by talking to (interviewing) early adopters in the customer segment. Potential entrepreneurs develop product and service ideas with respect to validated problems only. Both of these tenets of the Lean Launchpad method are grounded in a belief about reality where problems are real and can be objectively (or inter-subjectively) identified and verified, and solutions to validated problems can be iterated through to come to a profitable product/service via an elimination.

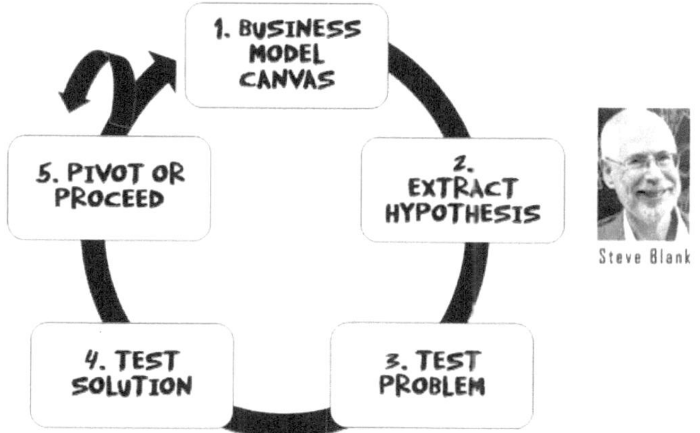

Understanding the "Lean Launchpad" theory:

Lean Launchpad is a method for launching a new business idea that involves conducting customer discovery and validation before investing significant resources into building a product or service. For example.

Dropbox: The company's founders, Drew Houston and Arash Ferdowsi, initially created a video demonstration of the product and posted it online to gauge interest. They then conducted interviews with potential customers to better understand their needs and pain points related to file sharing. Based on this feedback, the founders were able to refine their product and secure early adopters before investing significant resources into building the full product.

Airbnb: The company's founders, Brian Chesky and Joe Gebbia initially rented out air mattresses in their San Francisco apartment during a conference to earn some extra cash. They then conducted interviews with their customers to better understand their needs and preferences related to travel accommodations. Based on this feedback, the founders were able to refine their product and secure early adopters before investing significant resources into building the full platform.

Uber: The company's founders, Travis Kalanick & Garrett Camp initially launched a beta version of the app in San Francisco to test the concept and gain feedback from early adopters. They then expanded to other cities, using customer feedback to refine their product & improve UX.

Lean Launchpad is a powerful tool for launching new business ideas that can help entrepreneurs avoid costly mistakes and better understand their customers' needs and preferences. By focusing on customer discovery and validation before investing significant resources into building a product, entrepreneurs can increase their chances of success and build businesses that truly meet the needs of their target market.

Classroom Activity for Educators: Lean Launchpad Simulation

Objective: To provide readers with a hands-on experience of the theory, emphasizing customer validation, iterative development, & rapid experimentation to build successful & customer-focused startups.

Materials: Whiteboard or flip chart, Markers, Sticky notes & Pen/pencil for each participant.

Duration: 110 – 120 mins

Instructions:

Activity	Instructions
Intro (10 mins)	Introduce the theory, explaining its core principles, such as customer development, business model canvas, and the build-measure-learn feedback loop. Emphasize the importance of focusing on customer needs and constant experimentation to drive startup success.

Startup Teams (5 mins)	Divide readers into small groups (3-5 participants per group) and assign each group as a startup team. Encourage diversity within the teams to bring different perspectives and skills to the simulation.
Identify Ideas (10 mins)	Have each team brainstorm potential startup ideas that address real-world problems or needs. They should write each idea on a sticky note and present it to the rest of the group briefly.
Customer Discovery (15 mins)	Instruct each startup team to select idea from their list and conduct customer discovery interviews within the group. They should take turns playing the roles of potential customers and entrepreneurs, seeking to validate the problem, target market, & potential solution.
Pivot or Persevere (10 mins)	After the customer discovery interviews, each team should analyze the feedback received and decide whether to pivot their startup idea (make a significant change) or persevere (keep the idea as is). They must present their decision & reasoning to other participants.
Build Measure (15 mins)	In the build-measure-learn phase, each startup team should create a basic prototype or MVP (Minimum Viable Product) of their startup idea. They can use paper prototypes, mockups, or simple digital versions. After building, they should present their MVP to other teams for feedback and measure the responses.
Iterative (15 mins)	Following the feedback received each startup team should discuss and implement improvements to their MVP. Encourage iterative development quick iterations to enhance the product based on real-time insights.
Pitch (10 mins each team)	Conclude the activity with each startup team delivering a pitch presentation to the rest of the participants. They should showcase their final MVP highlight customer validation results, and explain their business model. After each pitch, allow time for Q&A and feedback from the audience.
Reflection (10 mins)	Engage the whole group in a reflective discussion on the Lean Launchpad simulation experience. Encourage participants to share their key takeaways, challenges, and the value of customer-centric approaches in entrepreneurship.

Wrap-up (5 mins)	Conclude the activity by summarizing the key principles of the Lean Launchpad theory and how it fosters innovation and customer-focused startups. Encourage participants to apply these learnings in their future entrepreneurial endeavors and utilize the build-measure-learn feedback loop for continuous improvement.

Conclusion: The activity empowers participants with practical insights into customer validation, iterative development, and the build-measure-learn approach in entrepreneurship. Through teamwork, real-world problem-solving, and pitch presentations, readers gain valuable experiences to foster innovation, adaptability, and customer-centricity in their future startup endeavors, laying the foundation for successful and impactful ventures.

12.18 Mental disorders

Mental disorders are usually studied as problems in need of remedies like medication, interventions, or counseling. However, some entrepreneurship researchers have suggested that mental disorders can be positively associated with entrepreneurship. The idea is that a disorder may be due to a mismatch between person and context. Perhaps people who may have mental disorders preventing them from, for example, taking a cubical job, may thrive in a more entrepreneurial environment. Maybe entrepreneurship is an outlet allowing people that might be dysfunctional employees to succeed (See Wiklund et al., 2018). Bogan et al. (2013) suggest that mood disorders cause difficulties for people in the job market and therefore leads them to pursue self-employment. Their data corroborate this. Some mental disorders may also confer advantages upon their hosts, at least for some entrepreneurial tasks. For instance, Wiklund et al. (2016) find that individual with ADHD may be more likely thrive doing fast-paced multitasking in environments that require creativity. Wiklund et al. (2018) argue that mental disorders require individuals to develop coping mechanisms and resilience that can be transferred into entrepreneurship. Logan (2009) suggests that individuals with dyslexia may be more likely to thrive as entrepreneurs because it encourages them to delegate of tasks (even simple reading and writing tasks). This new literature provides a positive spin on some mental disorders. It remains unclear though if mental disorders help with business startup but hinder subsequent business growth. It is also not clear if having a little or a lot of a particular disorder is helpful. For instance, being a little bit dyslexic might boost entrepreneurship, while being very dyslexic might be disabling. More research is needed!

Understanding the "Mental Disorder" theory:
Mental disorder theories are used by mental health professionals to better understand and treat mental health conditions, but they should not be used to label or discriminate against individuals in a business setting. It is important for businesses to prioritize mental health and well-being in the workplace, and to provide resources and support to employees who may be struggling with mental health conditions.

This can include offering mental health benefits, providing flexible work arrangements, promoting work-life balance, and creating a culture of openness and understanding around mental health. By creating a supportive and inclusive work environment, businesses can help to reduce the stigma around mental health conditions and support the overall well-being of their employees.

Johan Wiklund | Isabella Hatak | Holger Patzelt | Dean A. Shepherd

STAY HUNGRY?
STAY FOOLISH?
STAY CRAZY?

Classroom Activity: Understanding Mental Disorders

Objective: To help readers gain a deeper understanding of mental disorders theory, its impact on individuals and society, and the importance of mental health awareness in entrepreneurship.
Materials: Whiteboard or flip chart, Markers, Sticky notes & Pen/pencil for each participant.
Duration: 90 – 100 mins

Instructions:

Activity	Instructions
Intro (10 mins)	Introduce the theory & explain that mental disorders are medical conditions affecting a person's thinking, feeling, mood, and behavior, and that understanding mental health is crucial for promoting well-being and productivity in entrepreneurial ventures.
Research and Group Discussion (20 mins)	Divide readers into small groups (3-5 participants per group) and assign each group a specific mental disorder (e.g., depression, anxiety, bipolar disorder). Instruct them to research and discuss the causes, symptoms, and potential impact of the assigned disorder on an entrepreneur's personal & professional life. Encourage open communication and empathy during the discussion.
Case Studies (15 mins)	Present case studies or real-life examples of entrepreneurs who have openly shared their struggles with mental health issues and how it affected their journey. Discuss the challenges they faced, coping mechanisms, & support they sought to understand the complexities & stigma surrounding mental health in entrepreneurship.
Mental Health Strategies (15 mins)	Facilitate a brainstorming session where each group shares strategies to support mental health in entrepreneurial settings. Encourage the exploration of ways to foster a supportive and inclusive environment, such as implementing wellness programs, promoting work-life balance, and normalizing conversations around mental health.
Mindfulness & Self-Care (10 mins)	Introduce mindfulness and self-care techniques that entrepreneurs can incorporate into their daily routines to reduce stress and maintain mental well-being. Guided breathing exercises or brief meditation sessions can be practiced during this segment to give participants firsthand experience with these practices.
Reflective Writing (10 mins)	Take a few mins to reflect writing on the importance of mental health awareness in entrepreneurship. They should write about how this understanding can positively impact their own ventures & contribute to building a supportive & resilient entrepreneurial community.

Group Sharing (10 mins)	Invite participants to share their reflections with the group. Encourage an open & supportive atmosphere where individuals feel comfortable discussing their thoughts & experiences related to mental health in entrepreneurship.
Wrap-up & Takeaways (5 mins)	Summarize the key in the context of entrepreneurship. Emphasize the significance of destigmatizing mental health issues, promoting self-care, & fostering a culture of empathy & support within entrepreneurial ecosystem.

Conclusion: This activity empowers participants with a deeper understanding of the theory. By exploring case studies, brainstorming mental health strategies, and practicing mindfulness, readers gain valuable insights to foster a supportive and resilient entrepreneurial community, promoting well-being and empathy in their ventures and interactions. The significance of destigmatizing mental health issues & prioritizing self-care is emphasized, creating a positive impact on both individual entrepreneurs and the broader entrepreneurial ecosystem.

12.19 Physiological Theory

Could your physiology make you more entrepreneurial? Research examining the physiology of entrepreneurs is rather new and underdeveloped. Very little is known about how our physiology can affect our propensity for entrepreneurship. One study examined how testosterone level experienced in the womb can affect us. Testosterone exposure in utero is linked to competitiveness, aggressiveness, and other traits that have been linked to some extend with entrepreneurs.[1] The researchers used a technique of measuring finger length ratios that are markers of testosterone exposure. Survey respondents were supplied with rulers and instructions and self-reported the lengths of their index and ring fingers. To calculate the ratio (2D:4D), one divides the length of the index finger by the length of the ring finger on the same hand. A higher ratio (i.e., relatively long index finger) is associated with many different traits including sexuality, aggressiveness, assertiveness, unprovoked violence, etc. Studies in management have gone much further than those in entrepreneurship.[2] They investigated the role of hormones like dopamine, testosterone, oxytocin, serotonin, and cortisol. They have looked at physical characteristics like height, weight, physique, athleticism, energy & attractiveness. They have looked at conditions like cardio, diabetes, musculoskeletal, & blood pressure.

TESTOSTERONE LEVELS

BIOLOGICAL FACTORS

WERNER BÖNTE

RISK ABILITY

PSYCHOLOGICAL FACTORS

VIVIEN PROCHER

STARTUP EXPERIENCE

BEHAVIORAL FACTORS

DIEMO URBIG

Understanding the "Physiological" theory:
Physiological theories are often related to how the body responds to different stimuli and how these responses can impact behavior in a business setting. For example.

Fight or Flight Response: It is a physiological reaction that occurs when an individual perceives a threat or danger. In a business setting, this response can be triggered by a high-pressure situation, such as an important presentation or a crisis. Understanding the fight or flight response can help businesses to manage stress and anxiety in the workplace & provide resources to help employees cope with these feelings.

Maslow's Hierarchy of Needs: It describes how human needs are organized in a hierarchy, with basic physiological needs such as food, water, and shelter at the bottom and higher-level needs such as self-actualization at the top. In a business setting, this theory can help organizations to design programs & policies that meet employees' basic needs and promote their overall well-being.

Sleep Deprivation: It is a physiological state that can impact an individual's cognitive and emotional functioning, including memory, attention, and mood. In a business setting, sleep deprivation can impact productivity, decision-making, and interpersonal relationships. Understanding the impact of sleep on employee performance and well-being can help businesses to create policies and practices that prioritize adequate rest and work-life balance.

Herzberg's Two-Factor Theory: It is based on the idea that certain factors in the workplace (such as hygiene factors like salary and working conditions) are necessary for employee satisfaction, but do not necessarily lead to motivation or higher job performance. Instead, it is the presence of motivational factors like recognition, achievement, and growth opportunities that can lead to increased motivation and job satisfaction. This theory can be applied to businesses by recognizing the importance of providing a supportive work environment that fosters employee growth and development, encourages autonomy and creativity, and recognizes and rewards high performance.

Cognitive Load Theory: It is based on the idea that the working memory of an individual has a limited capacity for processing information. This theory suggests that businesses should design tasks and activities in a way that minimizes the cognitive load on employees, allowing them to focus on important tasks and make decisions more effectively. This can be achieved using clear and concise communication, simple and intuitive software interfaces, and well-organized work processes that minimize distractions and cognitive overload.

Classroom Activity: Exploring Physiology in Entrepreneurship

Objective: To help readers understand the role of physiological factors in entrepreneurship and how they can impact an entrepreneur's performance, decision-making, and overall well-being.

Materials: Speakers, Whiteboard, Markers, Sticky notes & Pen/pencil for each participant.

Duration: 90 – 100 mins

Instructions:

Activity	Instructions
Intro (10 mins)	Explain that physiological factors, such as stress, sleep, nutrition, and exercise, play a crucial role in an entrepreneur's cognitive abilities, emotional regulation, and physical health Emphasize the importance of understanding these factors to enhance entrepreneurial performance & well-being.
Teams (5 mins)	Divide readers into small groups (3-5 participants per group) and assign each group a specific physiological factor (e.g., stress, sleep, nutrition, exercise).

Discuss (20 mins)	Instruct them to research and discuss how their assigned factor can impact an entrepreneur's daily life and decision-making. Encourage open discussions about personal experiences and strategies for managing these factors effectively.
Case Studies (15 mins)	Present case studies or real-life examples of entrepreneurs who have experienced significant physiological challenges during their entrepreneurial journey. Discuss how these challenges affected their performance, creativity, & ability to cope with stress. Analyze outcomes & lessons learned from each case.
Strategies (15 mins)	Facilitate a brainstorming session to shares strategies & promote positive physiological habits in an entrepreneurial setting. Encourage discussions on stress management techniques, sleep hygiene, healthy eating habits, & integrating exercise in routine.
Relax (10 mins)	Introduce mindfulness & relaxation exercises that entrepreneurs can practice reducing stress and enhance overall well-being. Guided mindfulness sessions or relaxation techniques can be practiced during this segment for first-hand experience.
Reflect (10 mins)	Ask participants to reflect writing on how they can implement the physiological strategies discussed in their own entrepreneurial lives. Encourage them to set personal goals and action plans for better well-being.
Group Sharing (10 mins)	Invite participants to share their reflections and action plans with the group. Encourage a supportive atmosphere where individuals can offer feedback and support to each other in their pursuit of positive physiological habits.
Wrap (5 mins)	Summarize key takeaways & emphasize about self-care, stress management, & adopting healthy habits to thrive as entrepreneurs. Encourage participants to prioritize their well-being, in their journey.

Conclusion: This activity equips participants with a comprehensive understanding of the impact of physiological factors on entrepreneurship. By exploring case studies, brainstorming strategies, and reflecting on personal well-being, readers are empowered to prioritize self-care, stress management, and healthy habits, fostering a resilient and successful entrepreneurial journey with improved performance and overall satisfaction. The significance of integrating physiological awareness into entrepreneurship is highlighted, fostering a culture of well-being to promote long-term entrepreneurial success.

12.20 Real options

EDWARD H. BOWMAN | DILEEP HURRY

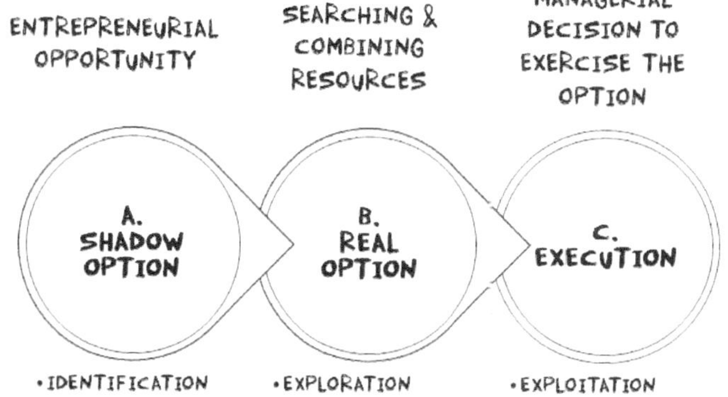

Real options Theory is concerned with investments in real assets that are similar in structure to financial options like put and call options that allow investors to bet on the upside or downside of stocks without tying up too much capital (Bowman and Hurry, 1993). According to McGrath (1999), real options Theory is supposed to be superior to net present value analysis and other time value calculations, especially under conditions of uncertainty. The fundamental idea behind real options Theory is that an opportunity that has a way out is worth more than one that does not have a way out. For example, startups can be merged, one startup can be stripped of resources to help another, a team can be moved from one opportunity to another etc. Thus, entrepreneurs and investors in entrepreneurial ventures are apt to view failure as a learning opportunity that contributes to the assessment of future projects. Real options thinking reduces the social cost of failure and thus increases the risk that potential entrepreneurs and investors will be willing to take in the future. Lee et al. (2007) uses real options logic to argue that bankruptcy laws should not punish entrepreneurs too severely because it could have the unintended consequence of reducing the number of individuals pursuing opportunities that are both very high risk and very high in potential reward. O'Brian et al. (2003) find that individuals considering entrepreneurial entry decisions seem to use a real options logic. They find the entrepreneurs are less likely to enter an industry where uncertainty is higher and where investments are irreversible.

Understanding the "Real Options" theory:

Real options theory is a financial theory that focuses on the value of flexibility and the ability to make decisions in the future based on new information. For example.

Investing in R&D: One example of applying real options theory in a business context is investing in research and development (R&D). By investing in R&D, a company is essentially creating an option to pursue a future project or product that may have significant value if successful. The decision to invest in R&D is based on the belief that the potential value of the project or product will exceed the costs of development, and that the company will have the flexibility to decide whether to pursue the project based on the outcomes of the research.

Flexible manufacturing capacity: Another example of applying real options theory in a business context is having flexible manufacturing capacity. By investing in flexible manufacturing technology or processes, a company creates an option to adjust production levels or shift production to different products or markets as needed. This allows the company to take advantage of new opportunities or respond to changing market conditions while minimizing costs and risks.

Delaying investment decisions: Real options theory can also be applied to investment decisions by considering the option value of delaying the decision to invest. By delaying investment decisions, a company can wait to gather additional information or to see how market conditions develop before committing resources to a project or investment. This allows the company to reduce the risk of investing in projects that may not have as much value as initially anticipated. Real options theory can be a valuable tool for businesses to better understand the value of flexibility and the option to make decisions based on new information. By applying this theory, businesses can make more informed investment decisions and take advantage of new opportunities while minimizing risks and costs.

Classroom Activity: Exploring Real Options Theory for Startups

Objective: This activity is to help readers understand the concept of real options theory and its application in entrepreneurial decision-making. Participants will explore how real options theory allows entrepreneurs to make more informed and flexible choices in uncertain and dynamic business environments.

Materials: Whiteboard, Markers, Sticky notes & Pen/pencil for each participant.

Duration: 95 – 110 mins

Instructions:

Activity	Instructions
Intro (10 mins)	Introduce the theory & explain that real options theory is an approach that allows entrepreneurs to treat business decisions as options, like financial options. Emphasize that it helps in evaluating the potential benefits of delaying, expanding, or abandoning projects in uncertainty.
Concepts & Principles (15 mins)	Explain the fundamental concepts & principles of real options theory, such as identifying investment opportunities as real options, recognizing the value of flexibility in decision-making, & considering various stages of project development as options.
Case Studies (20 mins)	Present case studies of real-life entrepreneurial ventures that effectively used real options theory to make strategic decisions. Discuss how these entrepreneurs benefited from the flexibility provided by the approach & how it impacted their business success.
Real Options Analysis (20 mins)	Divide readers into small groups (3-5 participants per group) and assign each group a hypothetical entrepreneurial scenario. Instruct them to conduct a real options analysis for their scenario, considering factors like market uncertainty, competitive landscape, and potential payoffs from various decisions. Encourage participants to think critically and creatively during the analysis.
Group Pitch (15 mins)	Have each group present their real options analysis to the rest of the participants. Allow time for questions and discussions after each presentation. This segment encourages participants to learn from one another's insights and interpretations of real options theory in different entrepreneurial contexts.
Application (10 mins)	Engage participants in a guided discussion on how they can apply real options theory to their own entrepreneurial ventures or business ideas. Encourage them to identify specific aspects of their ventures where real options thinking could lead to more informed and adaptive decision-making.

Benefits & Limitations (10 mins)	Discuss the potential benefits and limitations of real options theory in entrepreneurship. Encourage participants to share their perspectives on how this approach can be effectively implemented and any challenges they foresee.
Wrap-up (5 mins)	Summarize the key takeaways from exploring real options theory in entrepreneurship. Emphasize how real options thinking can enhance decision-making in uncertain markets and dynamic business environments, enabling entrepreneurs to be more agile and resilient in pursuing opportunities & managing risks.

Conclusion: This activity equips participants with a deeper understanding of real options theory and its application in entrepreneurial decision-making. By exploring case studies, conducting real options analysis, and discussing benefits and limitations, readers gain valuable insights to make informed and flexible choices, enabling them to navigate uncertainties and enhance their entrepreneurial ventures' success.

12.21 Risk

Peltzman's (1975) pioneering study of automobile accidents revealed that expected positive effects of safety regulations rarely materialized upon implementation. He argued that when drivers feel safer, they take more risks, which compensate for the safety interventions. Support for what is now dubbed the 'Pelzman effect' (or risk compensation Theory) is far reaching and extends to varying contexts including new rules in NASCAR racing, mandated visor use in hockey, consumer vigilance in response to food safety messages, and bike helmet laws. But does this phenomenon also explain greater entrepreneurial risk-taking in the presence of social safety nets? There is emerging evidence that social safety nets can have positive benefits for entrepreneurs by reducing the risk associated with entry. Olds (2016a) finds that states that provided more food stamps have more limited liability company registrations among members of newly covered households. The author argues that these individuals felt entrepreneurship to be a less risky option because of the availability of food stamps, should they be needed. Similarly, Olds (2016b) finds that when children received government health insurance, their parents were 12% more likely to start a business, and that business quality improved (i.e., they noted a 36% increase in incorporated ventures).

Hombert, Schoar, Sraer and Thesmar (2014) studied a unique reform in France that provided employment insurance benefits to entrepreneurs for up to three years while they developed their ventures. They found an immediate increase in monthly firm creation of 25% and conclude that the program increased productivity by spurring the creation of new firms that are more productive to replace older less productive ones.

Caliendo and Künn (2011) review the literature on start-up subsidy programs targeting the unemployed and conclude that positive results are most common, followed by null effects, whereas negative results are very rare. In their own study of German unemployed receiving startup subsidies, 80% were found to be productive after five years, earning a relatively high income, and feeling notably happier with their lives.

Fairlie, Kapur and Gates (2011) find that government provided health care boosts entrepreneurship and that employer-sponsored medical insurance strengthens the ties of employees to their jobs, increasing the risks associated with venturing. Basic income programs may also allow individuals to fund their own health care programs while they develop their startups, thus reducing employment lock.

In short, while more research is needed, we do seem to have good preliminary evidence that social safety nets encourage entrepreneurial risk-taking. This is especially relevant today as the concept of a "universal basic income" is being vigorously debated. By extending a safety net beneath all, a universal basic income may alleviate the need for entrepreneurship out of desperation from insufficient employment options. However, it also is likely to encourage risk-taking by those who already have employment. As more and more regions and nations experiment with universal basic income programs, we will likely get access to the data we need to test impacts on entrepreneurial risk-taking.

Understanding the "Risk" theory:

Risk theory is a concept in business that deals with the identification, assessment, and management of potential risks that may impact an organization's operations or goals. For example.

Enterprise Risk Management (ERM): An insurance company can use ERM to assess the risks associated with insuring a new type of policy, such as cyber insurance, and implement strategies to mitigate those risks.

Investment Risk Management: A venture capital firm may use risk theory to evaluate potential investments in start-up companies. The firm would assess the risks associated with each investment, such as market risks or operational risks, and develop strategies to manage those risks.

Operational Risk Management: A manufacturing company may use risk theory to identify potential risks associated with its production processes, such as equipment failure or supply chain disruptions, and develop strategies to mitigate those risks.

Financial Risk Management: A bank may use risk theory to identify potential risks associated with lending money to a new customer and develop strategies to manage those risks.

By using risk theory, businesses can make more informed decisions, minimize risks, and ultimately achieve their goals more effectively.

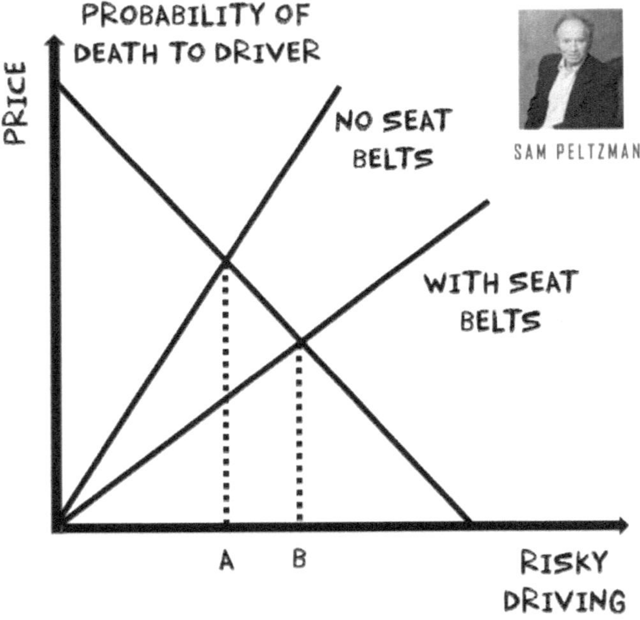

Classroom Activity: Understanding Risk in Entrepreneurship

Objective: This activity is to help readers comprehend the concept of risk theory in entrepreneurship and how it impacts decision-making, risk assessment, and business strategies. Participants will explore various types of risks and develop strategies to mitigate them.

Materials: Whiteboard, Markers, Sticky notes & Pen/pencil.

Duration: 105 – 110 mins

Instructions:

Activity	Instructions
Introduction (10 mins)	Begin by introducing the topic of risk theory in entrepreneurship. Explain that risk is an inherent part of entrepreneurial endeavors, and understanding the types of risks and how to manage them is crucial for success. Emphasize the significance of risk assessment and the role of risk-taking in innovation and business growth.
Types of Risks (15 mins)	Discuss various types of risks entrepreneurs face, such as market risk, financial risk, operational risk, competitive risk, and technological risk. Explain each type and provide real-world examples of companies that encountered and navigated these risks effectively or faced challenges due to them.
Risk Mitigation (20 mins)	Divide readers into small groups (3-5 participants per group) and assign each group a specific type of risk. Instruct them to brainstorm and discuss strategies to mitigate the assigned risk in an entrepreneurial setting. Encourage creativity and critical thinking to develop practical and innovative risk management approaches.
Case Studies (20 mins)	Present case studies of successful entrepreneurs who made strategic decisions based on risk analysis. Discuss how they identified potential risks, developed risk management strategies, and turned risks into opportunities. Analyze the outcomes and lessons learned from each case study.
Risk Assessment (15 mins)	Provide participants with a hypothetical entrepreneurial scenario or business idea. Instruct them to conduct a risk assessment for the given situation, identifying potential risks and evaluating their potential impact on the venture. Participants should propose risk mitigation strategies based on the principles discussed earlier.
Group Pitch (10 mins)	Have each group present their risk assessment exercise and the strategies they developed to mitigate the identified risks. Allow time for questions and discussions after each presentation. Encourage participants to learn from each other's risk management approaches.
Reflection/ Discussion (10 mins)	Engage the whole group in a reflective discussion on the significance of risk theory in entrepreneurship. Encourage participants to share their insights on managing risks effectively and how it influences their entrepreneurial decision-making process.

Wrap-up (5 mins)	Conclude the activity by summarizing the key takeaways from exploring risk theory in entrepreneurship. Emphasize the importance of understanding and managing risks to seize opportunities and drive business success. Encourage participants to apply the insights gained in their entrepreneurial ventures to make informed and strategic decisions.

Conclusion: This activity empowers participants to grasp the intricacies of risk theory in entrepreneurship. By delving into various risk types, real-world case studies, and hands-on risk assessment exercises, readers gain valuable insights into managing risks effectively, enabling them to make informed decisions and seize opportunities for business success. Emphasizing the significance of risk awareness and mitigation, this activity equips aspiring entrepreneurs to navigate uncertainties with confidence and resilience in their entrepreneurial journey.

12.22 Self-competition

Elias Khalil (1997) at Monash University asks why is it that some entrepreneurs that have prior accomplishments continue to risk their capital again and again? Why don't they retire? One possibility is that these entrepreneurs are trying to be the best in the world or in each territory or space. Another possibility is that they are striving just to be better than their former selves. Self-competition Actor's main assumption is that individuals develop the desire to improve themselves, or rather, upon their former selves. Entrepreneurship can be viewed as behaviors that individuals use to better themselves. The Theory also assumes that individuals keep track of their personal best and can compare themselves to their former bests. For example, one might try to obtain a return on investment that is double what a previous venture was able to provide. Or one might try to expand the scale of the venture to be larger than previous ventures, or to span more territories. The Theory suggests that individuals that actively compare themselves to their former selves may develop a motivation to improve. The Theory seems to have links with the self-actualization Theory that Maslow described in his need's hierarchy. One may also be motivated by past failures to improve. For example, rather than feeling a sense of loss, and entrepreneur may try to learn from the experience and try again. The Theory is like prospect Theory and regulatory focus Theory. It is also related to self-efficacy Theory and hubris Theory.

INNOVATE WITHIN YOUR INDUSTRY

"DISRUPT YOURSELF"

BEFORE YOUR COMPETITION DOES

ELIAS KHALIL

Understanding the "Self-Competition" theory:

Self-competition, also known as intra-industry competition, is a situation where a company competes against its own products or services, rather than against other companies in the same industry. For example.

Product line extension: A fast-food chain may introduce new menu items that compete with its existing menu items, such as adding new burger options that compete with its existing burgers.

Cannibalization: A smartphone manufacturer may introduce a new model that has more features than its existing models, causing some customers to switch to new model & reducing sales of its older models.

Brand extension: A clothing retailer may introduce a new line of clothing under a different brand name that competes with its existing clothing lines.

Franchising: A company may open new franchises in locations that compete with its existing franchises. For e.g., a coffee shop chain may open new locations that compete with existing locations in same area.

Self-competition can be both a challenge and an opportunity for businesses forcing them to continuously improve their products and services to stay ahead of the competition, even if that competition is with their own products or services.

Classroom Activity: Exploring Self-Competition in Startups

Objective: To introduce readers to the concept of self-competition theory in entrepreneurship and its implications for business growth and innovation. Participants will explore how self-competition can drive continuous improvement & enhance competitive advantage.

Duration: 95 – 110 mins

Instructions:

Activity	Instructions
Intro (10 mins)	Introduce & explain what drive's entrepreneurs to continuously challenge & surpass their previous achievements rather than focusing solely on external competitors. Emphasize how it fosters innovation, adaptability, & sustainability.

Concepts and Principles (15 mins)	Discuss the fundamental concepts and principles of self-competition theory, such as: - The importance of setting ambitious yet achievable goals for personal and business growth. - Encouraging a culture of experimentation and risk-taking to push boundaries. - Emphasize value of learning from failures & successes to sustainability.
Case Studies (20 mins)	Present case studies of entrepreneurs or companies that have exemplified self-competition in their journey. Analyze how their pursuit of self-improvement and innovation has contributed to their success and sustained competitive advantage. Encourage participants to draw lessons from these examples.
Self-Competition Exercise (20 mins)	Divide readers into small groups (3-5 participants per group) and assign each group a hypothetical entrepreneurial scenario. Instruct them to brainstorm and discuss how the concept of self-competition can be applied in their given scenario to foster growth and innovation. Encourage creative thinking and practical strategies.
Group Pitch (15 mins)	Have each group present their self-competition exercise to the rest of the participants. Allow time for questions and discussions after each presentation. This segment encourages participants to learn from one another's insights and interpretations of self-competition theory in different entrepreneurial contexts.
Reflection (10 mins)	Engage the whole group in a reflective discussion on the significance of self-competition theory in entrepreneurship. Encourage participants to share their insights on how embracing self-competition can positively impact their entrepreneurial mindset and business strategies.
Wrap-up (5 mins)	Conclude the activity by summarizing the key takeaways from exploring self-competition theory in entrepreneurship. Emphasize how adopting a self-competition mindset can drive continuous growth, innovation, and sustainable competitive advantage within entrepreneurial ventures. Encourage participants to integrate this approach into their entrepreneurial journey to achieve lasting success.

Conclusion: This activity exposes participants to the concept of self-competition theory and its significance in the entrepreneurial context.

By exploring fundamental principles, real-world case studies, and engaging in self-competition exercises, readers gain valuable insights into fostering innovation, continuous improvement, and sustainable growth within their entrepreneurial ventures. Emphasizing the adoption of a self-competition mindset, this activity equips aspiring entrepreneurs with essential tools to thrive in a competitive landscape and achieve long-term success.

12.23 Serial

Serial entrepreneurship refers to the repeated behaviors of entrepreneur— "There are two types of entrepreneurs: novice entrepreneurs, who launch a business for the first time, and habitual entrepreneurs, which include serial entrepreneurs, who launch businesses sequentially, and portfolio entrepreneurs, who run multiple businesses concurrently." Plehn-Dujowich suggests that serial entrepreneurs differ substantially from first time entrepreneurs. They argue that the serial entrepreneurs develop new capabilities over time that makes them more effective entrepreneurs. For instance, they may develop heuristics that guide their decision processes that reduce the analysis task needed to assess risks. These types of advantage lead to equal or higher success rates for serial entrepreneurs and a higher likelihood of sticking to entrepreneurship as a career choice.

Serial entrepreneurship Theory starts with the idea that entrepreneurs need to decide whether to stay in business, leave the business to start a new business, or leave the business to enter employment. The process of starting businesses then exiting them to start new ones that seem even more promising is the serial entrepreneur's way. Each business is a steppingstone to the next, a means to an end, not an end. A policy implication that stems from the study is that reducing the cost of shutting down a business is just as important as reducing the cost of stating a new business. Some scholars have argued that serial entrepreneurship is temporal portfolio entrepreneurship since most entrepreneurs would like to launch more than one business but may feel unable to deal with more than one at a time. Perhaps entrepreneurs may prefer to learn from each experience sequentially rather than deal with too many variables all at once.

Understanding the "Serial" theory:

Serial entrepreneurship is a term used to describe individuals who start and run multiple businesses over their careers. These entrepreneurs tend to have a passion for creating new businesses and are often driven

by a desire to solve problems or create new opportunities. Here are some examples of serial entrepreneurship in business:
Elon Musk: A well-known serial entrepreneur who has founded several successful businesses, including SpaceX, Tesla, Neuralink, and The Boring Company. Each of these companies operates in a different industry and focuses on solving different problems, but they all share Musk's vision of creating a better future for humanity.
Richard Branson: He is another famous serial entrepreneur who has founded numerous businesses, including Virgin Group, Virgin Atlantic, and Virgin Galactic. Branson is known for his ability to spot new opportunities and create innovative businesses that disrupt traditional industries.

Steve Jobs: The co-founder of Apple was a serial entrepreneur who also founded Pixar Animation Studios and NeXT. Jobs was known for his ability to create products that were not only innovative but also highly desirable to consumers.
Jeff Bezos: The founder of Amazon, is also a serial entrepreneur who has founded several other businesses, including Blue Origin and The Washington Post. Bezos is known for his ability to spot new opportunities and create businesses that disrupt traditional industries, as he did with Amazon.

The serial theory in entrepreneurship is a critical driver of innovation and economic growth, as it creates new businesses and new jobs that can drive progress in various industries.

Classroom Activity: Serial Theory - Unleashing Innovativeness

Objective: The workshop is to empower participants with the mindset and tools of "Serial Theory" entrepreneurs. Through interactive exercises and discussions, participants will explore the process of ideation, experimentation, and adaptation to create groundbreaking innovations.

Duration: 3-4 hours

Materials: Whiteboard or flipchart with markers, Sticky notes and pens/pencils, Handout with brief descriptions of real-life successful entrepreneurs and their serial theory approach (e.g., Elon Musk, Richard Branson, Steve Jobs) & a Projector or screen for multimedia presentations

Instruction:

Activity	Instructions
Intro (30 mins)	Introduce "Serial Theory" & its significance in entrepreneurship. Share success stories of renowned entrepreneurs as examples of serial theorists. Present the agenda.
Ideation Session (60 mins)	Divide participants into small groups or pairs. Brainstorm and generate innovative business ideas related to a theme/industry. Encourage expansive thinking & challenging conventional ideas.
Pitch & Selection (30 mins)	Each group presents their top three business ideas to the workshop. Facilitate Q&A sessions for feedback and insights from participants. Groups vote on the most promising idea.
Proto-type (60 mins)	Each group creates a plan for experimentation or prototyping. Emphasize setting clear goals, metrics, and adaptable timelines. Encourage participants to be agile and open to feedback.
Execute & Test (60 mins)	Participants work on implementing experiments or creating prototypes. Provide necessary resources and support.
Refine (45 mins)	Analyze results and gather insights from experimentation. Facilitate discussions on adapting initial hypotheses based on findings.

Close (15 mins)	Gather participants ^ discuss key takeaways, emphasizing the importance of a serial theory mindset. Provide resources & recommendations.
Optional Extension (Varies)	Invite successful entrepreneurs as guest speakers to share insights. Conduct a "Pitch Competition" for refined ideas with judges/investors. Offer follow-up support or mentorship for pursuing experimental ideas beyond the workshop.

Conclusion: The workshop equipped participants with the mindset and tools of innovative entrepreneurs who continually explore new possibilities. Through ideation, experimentation, and adaptation, attendees embraced a relentless pursuit of groundbreaking ideas. Armed with the serial theory approach, they are now better prepared to drive entrepreneurial success by daring to challenge the status quo and evolve their ventures dynamically.

12.24 Slacker

It is passed around more as rumor than formal theoretical framework. The Theory starts with a premise about how entrepreneurial ventures come about. Entrepreneurial opportunities are viewed as difficult to discover or create, requiring a lot of time and trial and error. Perhaps slackers have nothing more important to do, allowing them the resilience to keep trying, even after repeated failures. The slacker Theory suggests that people with slack time and slack resources have an advantage in entrepreneurship. They are able to pursue ideas that may not be profitable and are still able to survive. This means they can take risks and experiment. Perhaps this elicits the image of a young adult from a well-to-do family that engages in social activities and gambles (engages in risky behaviors) rather than pursuing a real job or taking education seriously. The slacker Theory would suggest that if one is born or thrust into a situation that affords them considerable slack, then the chance that they will be afforded the option and resources to try out entrepreneurship increases dramatically. The family safety net (privilege), which is manifest in name recognition, reputation and even credit worthiness, confers untold advantages. Thus, slackers from well-funded parents and relatives have an advantage and can slack off more often and more fully. This is like the concept of organizational slack which largely points to a positive relationship between organizational slack defined as availability of resources and innovation outcomes for firms (Marlin and Geiger, 2015). Another interpretation is that any subculture that is composed of individuals with survival needs covered can mature into something more. Leisure time is key, when individuals can spend time playing, experimenting, and spending time and trading thoughts with others. Entrepreneurship is time consuming and unrewarding at the beginning, so one needs to be sustained in the short run by some other flow of resources. This is consistent with recent advances in the study of social safety nets and entrepreneurship. The slacker Theory is related to the Great Man Theory of entrepreneurship in the sense that both theories try to explain the 'garage entrepreneurs': usually young people with time to tinker with new ideas along with their friends. Slacker-friendly college campuses can often become incubators of excellent startup ideas as students avoid their studies in favor of the glamor of entrepreneurship. It seems there is little academic literature testing the slacker Theory of entrepreneurship. It would be interesting to see if entrepreneurs are more likely to be among people that could have been categorized as slackers at the time, they founded their ventures.

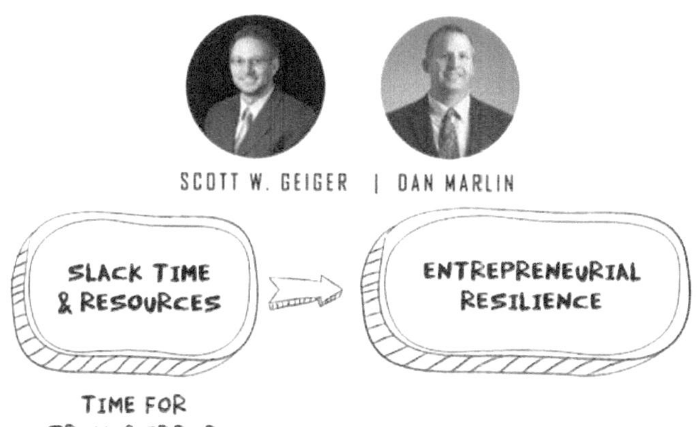

Understanding the "Slacker" theory:

A slacker is a person who avoids work or responsibilities and puts in minimal effort to get by. In a business context, a slacker can have a negative impact on productivity and morale, leading to decreased performance and outcomes. For example.

John works as a software developer for a tech company. Although he is highly skilled and capable, he frequently misses deadlines and takes longer than necessary to complete tasks. He often shows up late to meetings and is unresponsive to emails and messages. His colleagues frequently must pick up the slack and cover for him, which leads to frustration and resentment. As a result of John's slacking, the company's projects are delayed, and clients are unhappy with the service. The team's productivity suffers, and they struggle to meet their targets. The manager eventually confronts John about his behavior, but he shows little interest in improving and continues to put in minimal effort. Slackers can have a negative impact on a business's performance and morale. It is essential for managers to identify and address these behaviors to ensure that the team is functioning at its best and meeting its goals.

Classroom Activity: "Overcoming Slacker Startup Drive"

Objective: To help readers understand and overcome the slacker theory mindset that hinders entrepreneurial success. By identifying and addressing these limiting beliefs, participants will be encouraged to develop a growth-oriented entrepreneurial mindset and take proactive steps towards achieving their business goals.

Duration: 60 – 90 mins

Materials: Whiteboard, Markers, Sticky notes, Handouts, Case studies & Awards for participation

Instruction:

Activity	Instructions
Intro (10 mins)	Introduce the "Slacker Theory" & its relevance to entrepreneurship with its negative impact on Startup success.
Identifying Beliefs (15 mins)	Break participants into small groups. Provide sticky notes and markers. Instruct them to brainstorm beliefs associated with the slacker theory hindering entrepreneurial progress. Share findings with the entire audience.
Debunking the Theory (20 mins)	Facilitate a discussion on each identified belief. Encourage participants to challenge these beliefs with evidence and counterarguments. Present examples of successful entrepreneurs who overcame challenges through dedication and hard work.
Mindset (15 mins)	Introduce characteristics of an entrepreneurial mindset (resilience, adaptability, creativity, growth-oriented attitude). Explain how adopting these qualities helps overcome slacker theory tendencies. Share strategies for developing the mindset.

Case Studies (15 mins)	Present case studies of successful entrepreneurs who faced and conquered obstacles. Analyze their mindset and actions in achieving success. Encourage participants to derive insights and apply them to their own entrepreneurial ventures.
Goal Setting & Action Plan (15 mins)	Have participants set specific and achievable short-term and long-term entrepreneurial goals. Stress the importance of breaking goals into actionable steps with deadlines. Encourage sharing goals for accountability.
Close (5 mins)	Recap key points and importance of challenging the slacker theory mindset. Offer additional resources for self-improvement in entrepreneurship. Thank participants for their engagement.

Conclusion: This activity sheds light on the detrimental impact of the theory on entrepreneurial aspirations and success. By challenging these limiting beliefs and cultivating an entrepreneurial mindset grounded in dedication and perseverance, participants are now equipped to take proactive steps towards achieving their business goals. Let us embrace the journey of entrepreneurship with a growth-oriented attitude, knowing that hard work and resilience pave the way to realizing our entrepreneurial dreams.

12.25 Social Entrepreneurship

The concept of social entrepreneurship is relatively new and may not be thought of as a Theory. It is more like a domain or niche phenomenon that may deserve attention. According to Dees (2017), social entrepreneurship has largely emerged out of discontent with the performance of government and charitable organizations in tackling social problems. Governments are often underfunded, ineffective, and too political to do what is right for all. Charities are busy fighting for funds and justifying their existence and many successful such organizations use many of their donors' funds for internal development purposes. If governments and charities would be more effective at tackling poverty, health issues, and inequality, then there would not be a need for social entrepreneurs to try to pick up the slack. This is also a core idea in the stakeholder Theory of entrepreneurship. Social entrepreneurs bring market logic and business acumen to bear in combating social problems. They are change agents in the social sector. They aim to make a profit (even a slim one) to be able to maintain and expand business operations and to do better for their mission groups. Each social venture typically has a mission to aid a specific underprivileged sub-population or group. Social ventures mix for-profit and not-for-profit elements. Examples include food banks that providing job training, and development banks. Social entrepreneurs have a strong sense of accountability toward their mission populations. Many of the social goods produced by social entrepreneurs are difficult to measure or quantify. This makes it difficult to ensure that social ventures are succeeding in their missions. Nonetheless, social ventures must try to demonstrate positive outcomes when they compete for support, donations, and volunteers. Dacin et al. (2010) argue that social entrepreneurship may not need new Theory at all and encourage researchers to look to existing entrepreneurship theories to support the concept.

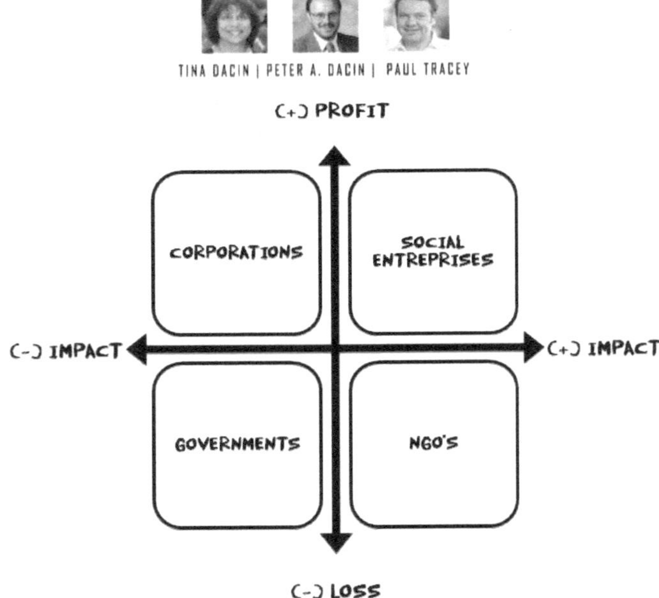

Understanding the "Social Entrepreneurship" theory:

Social entrepreneurship is the practice of using business principles and techniques to create positive social or environmental outcomes. Some examples of Indian businesses that exemplify social entrepreneurship:

Fabindia: It sells a range of handmade & eco-friendly products, including clothing, home furnishings, & personal care items while working closely with rural artisans and craftspeople, helping to promote their traditional skills & provide them with sustainable livelihoods.

D.light Design: It's a social enterprise that produces solar-powered lighting solutions for off-grid communities in developing countries. The company's products are affordable and durable, providing a reliable source of clean energy to people who lack access to electricity.

Goonj: It collects and distributes clothing and other essential items to people in need across India. The organization also runs a range of initiatives focused on community development, such as providing clean water and promoting education.

Sarvajal: It operates a network of water purification and distribution kiosks in rural areas of India. The company provides clean and affordable drinking water to communities that lack access to safe water sources, improving public health and reducing water-borne diseases.

Jaipur Rugs: It produces handmade rugs and carpets using traditional techniques. The company works with over 40,000 rural artisans across India, providing them with a reliable source of income and preserving their traditional skills.

These businesses demonstrate how social entrepreneurship can have a positive impact on society and the environment, while also generating sustainable profits. They have created innovative solutions to address some of India's most pressing social and environmental challenges, helping to create a more equitable and sustainable future for all.

Here are some global examples of social entrepreneurship theory in practice:

TOMS Shoes: It is a company that has built its business around a "one-for-one" model. For every pair of shoes sold, the company donates a pair to a child in need. The company's mission is to improve the lives of people in need, while also running a profitable business.

Grameen Bank: It is a microfinance institution founded by Nobel laureate Muhammad Yunus. The bank provides small loans to poor people, particularly women, to help them start businesses and improve their economic situation. The bank has helped millions of people escape poverty and become financially self-sufficient.

Warby Parker: It is a company that sells eyeglasses and sunglasses online. The company has built its business around a social mission to provide affordable eyewear to people in need. For every pair of glasses sold, the company donates a pair to a person in need.

BRAC: It is a development organization founded in Bangladesh that has since expanded to other countries. The organization operates a range of programs focused on improving education, healthcare, and economic opportunities for people living in poverty. BRAC has helped millions of people improve their lives and escape poverty.
These examples demonstrate how social entrepreneurship theory can be applied in practice to create positive social change and address pressing social and environmental challenges.

Classroom Activity: "Empowering Change: Sociopreneurship"

Objective: To introduce the theory and engage readers in exploring how innovative business models can address social and environmental challenges. Participants will gain a deeper understanding of Social Entrepreneurship theory and be encouraged to think creatively about leveraging entrepreneurial skills for positive impact.
Duration: 90 – 120 mins
Materials:
Instructions:

Activity	Instructions
Intro (15 mins)	Begin by defining Social Entrepreneurship and its significance in addressing social and environmental issues. Explain that Social Entrepreneurs aim to create sustainable ventures with a focus on positive societal impact while maintaining financial viability. Provide examples of successful social enterprises and their contributions to their communities or causes.
Identifying Social Issues (20 mins)	Divide participants into small groups and provide them with sticky notes and markers. Instruct each group to identify one or more pressing social or environmental issues that resonate with them. Encourage creative thinking & consider local, national, or global challenges. After 20 mins, let each group present their chosen issues & briefly explain why they find them important.
Social Solutions (25 mins)	In their groups, have participants brainstorm innovative business ideas or solutions that could address the identified social or environmental challenges. Encourage them to consider unique approaches, partnerships, and potential impact. Each group should write their ideas & present them to the entire audience.

Social Impact (15 mins)	Facilitate a discussion on measuring and evaluating social impact in the context of Social Entrepreneurship. Explain different metrics and methods used by social enterprises to assess their effectiveness. Discuss how quantifiable and qualitative indicators can help gauge success in creating positive change.
Case Studies (15 mins)	If available, share case studies or examples of successful social entrepreneurs and their ventures. Analyze their business models, strategies, and impact on the communities they serve. Discuss the challenges they faced and the lessons that can be learned from their experiences.
Developing Mindset (20 mins)	Guide participants in reflecting on the key traits and skills required to be a successful Social Entrepreneur. Discuss qualities such as empathy, resilience, creativity, and the ability to adapt to change. Encourage participants to recognize their own strengths and areas for development in fostering a social entrepreneurial mindset.
Action Planning (15 mins)	Have each participant individually or within their groups develop a preliminary action plan for a social entrepreneurial venture. Encourage them to outline their objectives, target audience, impact metrics, and potential partners or resources needed. Share insights and feedback with each other.
Conclusion (5 mins)	Summarize the key takeaways from the activity, emphasizing the power of Social Entrepreneurship to drive positive change. Encourage participants to continue exploring social issues, developing innovative solutions, and making a difference in their communities through entrepreneurial initiatives.
Optional Follow-up (Varies)	Provide articles, books, or websites, to further deepen their understanding of the topic. Offer support and guidance for those interested in pursuing their social entrepreneurial ventures & create a platform for ongoing discussion & collaboration on such initiatives.

Conclusion: This activity introduces participants to the transformative potential of Social Entrepreneurship in addressing pressing social and environmental issues. By fostering an entrepreneurial mindset focused on positive impact, participants are empowered to develop innovative solutions that create meaningful change in their communities.

12.26 Social Exchange

Social exchange Theory regards trading relations as built on norms of reciprocity and mutual attraction (Emerson, 1981; De Clercq et al., 2010). Reciprocity is the exchange of privileges between parties based on mutual trust. For instance, a lunch or round of drinks may be purchased by one individual, with the understanding that other will pay back the debt at some unspecified time. In extended reciprocity, the assumption is that the environment will pay it forward to ensure repayment, even if indirectly over time. Mutual attraction implies that one party is not predating on the other, that both parties that have something to gain. There is therefore an assumption of trust between the parties. For example, it has been observed that in traditional subsistence cultures, tribes will often donate their surpluses to neighboring tribes with no time bound expectations of repayment. Social exchange and entrepreneurship: There seem to be some budding evidence that the mechanisms that allow social exchanges to occur matter considerably. Overall, the advice coming from this stream of research is that we should probably give each other the benefit of the doubt. In contrast to other theories about entrepreneurship, such as psychological theories that suggest that individuals are the key units of measure in entrepreneurship, the social exchange perspective is focused on the entrepreneur's relationships. Successful entrepreneurs nurture the processes of social exchange with their stakeholders. They are careful to build a reputation for fairness over time, which engenders trust from stakeholders. Individual characteristics may matter most as antecedents of social exchange processes. For instance, some individuals may be more predisposed to nurture trusting relationships, while others may prefer arms-length relationships. Social exchange processes need continual care to keep them flowing efficiently. A reputation for reciprocity may be path dependent, making it difficult to recover from a tarnished reputation.

Understanding the "Social Exchange" theory:

Social exchange theory suggests that individuals engage in social interactions based on the expectation of receiving rewards and minimizing costs. This theory can be applied to various situations in business, such as employee-employer relationships, customer-merchant relationships, and business partnerships. One business example of social exchange theory is the relationship between a company and its customers. In this scenario, the company provides a product or service to the customer in exchange for payment. The customer evaluates the product or service and decides whether it is worth the price. If the product or service meets customer's expectations & provides a positive experience, customer may be more likely to return & make future purchases.

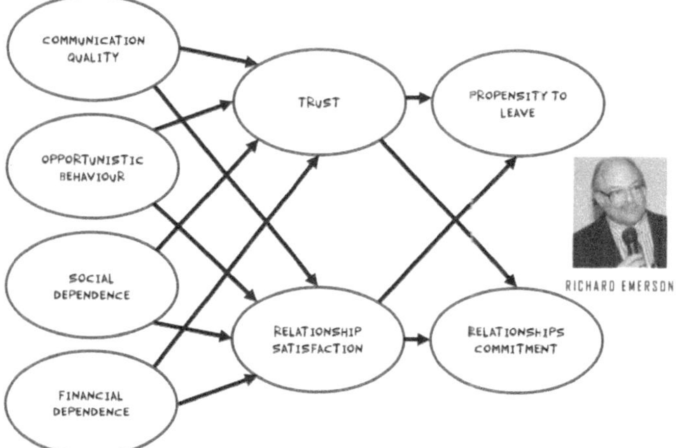

In this case, both the company and the customer benefit from the exchange, as the company earns revenue and the customer obtains a product or service that satisfies their needs or wants. Another example is the relationship between an employer and employee. The employer provides a salary, benefits, and a work environment to the employee in exchange for their labor and contributions to the company. The employee evaluates the benefits and opportunities provided by the company and decides whether it is worth their effort and time. If the employer offers fair compensation and opportunities for growth and development, the employee may be more likely to be committed and engaged in their work. In this case, both the employer & employee benefit from the exchange, as the employer obtains the skills and contributions of the employee, & the employee earns income and gains experience and skills. In both examples, theory suggests that individuals engage in social interactions based on the expectation of receiving rewards and minimizing costs. By understanding this theory, businesses can develop strategies to enhance the benefits of their products or services, improve their relationships with customers and employees, and ultimately achieve success.

Classroom Activity: "Building Bridges: Social Startups"

Objective: To help readers understand the concept of Social Exchange Theory and its application in entrepreneurship. Participants will engage in a practical exercise that encourages them to analyze and apply the principles of social exchange to entrepreneurial scenarios.

Duration: 100 – 120 mins

Materials: Whiteboard or flipchart, Markers, Sticky notes, Handouts about the theory.

Instructions:

Activity	Instructions
Intro (10 mins)	Introduce the Theory and its relevance to entrepreneurship. Provide a brief overview of the theory, explaining how it relates to the interactions and relationships that entrepreneurs have with stakeholders, customers, employees, and partners.
Real-life Examples (15 mins)	Divide the participants into small groups or pairs. Distribute sticky notes and ask each group to come up with real-life examples of social exchange in entrepreneurship. Encourage them to think about situations where entrepreneurs provide value to stakeholders and receive something in return, either tangible (e.g., money) or intangible (e.g., trust, loyalty). Each group can write down their examples on separate sticky notes.
Sharing (20 mins)	Ask each group to share their examples on the whiteboard or flipchart, sticking their sticky notes in a visible area. Facilitate a discussion about the examples, encouraging participants to identify common themes and patterns related to social exchange in entrepreneurship. Discuss the importance of creating mutually beneficial relationships with stakeholders and how this can contribute to long-term business success.
Analyzing Entrepreneurial Relationships (20 mins)	Present a few entrepreneurial scenarios to the participants, where social exchange principles may come into play. Examples: a. A startup founder seeking investment from venture capitalists. b. An online retailer building a loyal customer base. c. An entrepreneur negotiating a partnership with a supplier. In their groups, participants should analyze these scenarios through the lens of Social Exchange Theory, identifying the potential motivations, costs, rewards, and risks involved.

Role-playing Exercise (30 mins)	Assign different roles to participants within each group, such as entrepreneur, customer, investor, supplier, etc. Using the scenarios from above step, have participants engage in role-playing exercises where they act out the interactions between the stakeholders. Encourage them to embody the principles of social exchange in their roles, understanding the give-and-take dynamics and how these interactions can influence the success of the entrepreneurial endeavor.
Wrap-up (5 mins)	Bring the activity to a close with a brief recap of the key insights gained from exploring Social Exchange Theory in the context of entrepreneurship. Emphasize the significance of fostering positive and mutually beneficial relationships in the entrepreneurial journey.
Extended Activity (Vary)	Encourage participants to conduct interviews with entrepreneurs or business owners they know to gain real-world insights into how social exchange principles have played a role in their ventures. Participants can then share their findings in the next session or through a written report.

Conclusion: This activity theory provides participants with valuable insights into the significance of cultivating mutually beneficial relationships with stakeholders. Through real-life examples, role-playing exercises, and thoughtful analysis, participants gain a deeper understanding of how social exchange principles shape entrepreneurial success. Emphasizing the role of trust, reciprocity, and value creation, this activity reinforces the importance of leveraging social exchange dynamics to build thriving and sustainable ventures.

12.27 Social Judgement

The central concept in social judgement Theory is legitimacy (Suchman, 1995), as the buyers and suppliers of any new venture must believe that the startup is legitimate in order to commit their scarce resources or risk capital. A startup must meet the regulatory, normative and cognitive institutional requirements of the markets where it competes. A social judgment Theory of entrepreneurship looks to the entrepreneurs' stakeholders' social judgement about their ventures. These judgments are important because of the way that stakeholders make decisions to support a burgeoning venture or not to. Impression management? Perhaps and interesting critique of the social judgement theory as stated above is that it may be descriptive rather than prescriptive. For example, if the Theory is considered prescriptive (i.e., normative), then an entrepreneur might thus manage the impressions that stakeholders build about them to bring about favorable outcomes. More than just impressions: Legitimacy has been variously described as the right to exist, social fitness, desirability, properness, appropriateness, endorsement, and acceptance (Bitektine, 2011). Jones et al. (2008) present an interesting extension of this idea when they explain how firms get competitive advantage from engaging in just behaviors. Gaining a reputation for fair play may allow stakeholders to open and give access to their tacit knowledge, which gives insight into true wants, needs and abilities. Entrepreneurs are therefore at a disadvantage because they do not have a reputation for fair play already established, and in environments with many benevolent incumbencies, new entry may be difficult. This also helps to explain why employee spinouts perform better than other types of startups. The spinout founders have special access to their parent firm networks because of their prior work experiences. Some similarities with Google's ranking algorithm: Google's page rank algorithm work a bit like social judgement Theory. It rewards pages that are linked to by authoritative pages. Authoritative pages are those that have many links from other pages with many links. Thus, any new webpage starts with the problem of needing to attract back-links from existing websites. Probably the reason that you found this page today is because someone with access to an authority page linked to me and gave me "link juice". Otherwise, this page would be on Google's page 5 somewhere. It is interesting to see how users use Google. The first result gets about forty percent of the traffic, the second gets twenty percent, the third gets ten percent, and so on nearly halving all the way down, though with a relatively long tail. Why? Because Google is usually, right? Because we are lazy? No. Because authoritative websites said (in html) that the result is the best and we seem to trust that.

Understanding the "Social Judgement" theory:

Social judgment theory suggests that people make judgments about others based on their preexisting attitudes and beliefs, and that these judgments can affect their behavior towards those individuals. In a business context, the theory can be observed in the way that people make decisions about which products to buy, which companies to do business with & which employees to hire or work with. One example of social judgment theory in a business context is the way that consumers evaluate different brands of products or services. Consumers often have preexisting attitudes and beliefs about different brands, based on factors such as advertising, word-of-mouth recommendations, and their own past experiences with those brands.

When making purchasing decisions, consumers will judge different brands based on how well they align with their preexisting attitudes and beliefs. For example, a consumer who values environmentally friendly products may choose to purchase a brand that advertises their commitment to sustainability. Another example of social judgment theory in a business context is the way that employers evaluate job candidates during the hiring process. Employers often have preexisting attitudes and beliefs about what makes a good employee, based on factors such as their own past experiences, the requirements of the job, and the culture of the company. When evaluating job candidates, employers will judge them based on how well they align with these preexisting attitudes and beliefs. For example, an employer who values teamwork may be more likely to hire a candidate who has a track record of working well with others.

An example of social judgment theory in business is the use of celebrity endorsements in advertising. Companies often use celebrities to promote their products or services because they believe that the celebrity's positive image and popularity will influence consumer attitudes and behaviors. However, the effectiveness of celebrity endorsements depends on the consumer's existing attitudes and beliefs about the celebrity. If the consumer has a positive opinion of the celebrity, they are more likely to be influenced by the endorsement. On the other hand, if the consumer has a negative opinion of the celebrity, the endorsement may have the opposite effect and reduce their willingness to purchase the product.

Another example is the use of social proof in marketing. Social proof refers to the phenomenon where individuals conform to the actions and opinions of others in their social group. In business, this can be applied to customer reviews and testimonials. By showcasing positive reviews and testimonials from satisfied customers, companies can influence the opinions and attitudes of potential customers and increase their likelihood of purchasing the product. However, social proof may be less effective if the individual has pre-existing negative attitudes or beliefs about the product or brand.

This theory can have a significant impact on business decisions and outcomes. By understanding how people make judgments based on their preexisting attitudes and beliefs, businesses can develop strategies to appeal to those attitudes and beliefs and improve their chances of success.

MARK C. SUCHMAN

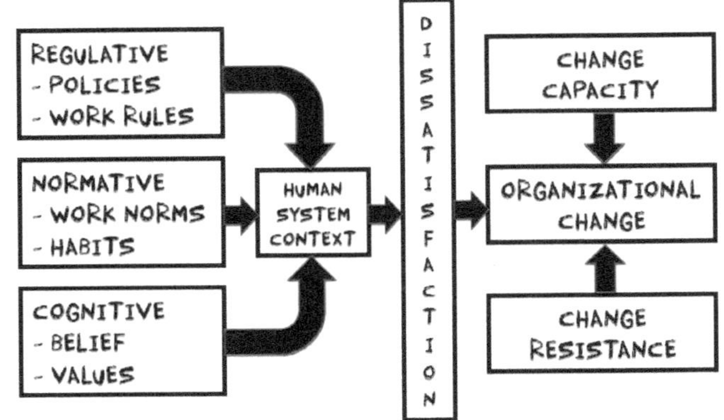

Classroom Activity: "Social Judgment in Startups"

Objective: To introduce readers to the Theory and demonstrate its relevance and application in the context of entrepreneurship. Participants will gain insights into how social judgments influence entrepreneurial decision-making, behavior, and success.

Materials: Handouts, Whiteboard, markers, Sticky notes, Pen/pencil.

Duration: 60 mins

Instructions:

Activity	Instructions
Intro (10 mins)	Begin by introducing the topic of Social Judgment Theory and its relevance in the entrepreneurial context. Explain that Social Judgment Theory explores how people form judgments and make decisions based on the information they receive & their prior beliefs.
Theory Pitch (15 mins)	Provide a brief presentation on the theory, including the points: Explanation of the three judgment categories: Acceptance, Rejection, and Non-commitment. The concept of the "Latitude of Acceptance" and "Latitude of Rejection." The role of "Ego Involvement" in influencing judgment. Discussion on the "Assimilation Contrast Effect" & its impact on perceptions.

Real-life Examples (15 mins)	Divide participants into small groups or pairs and distribute sticky notes or index cards to each group. Instruct them to brainstorm and write down real-life examples of situations where Social Judgment Theory might come into play for entrepreneurs. Encourage them to think about scenarios such as product launches, pitching to investors, or dealing with customers.
Discuss (15 mins)	Bring the groups back together and facilitate a group discussion. Each group should share at least one of their real-life examples and explain how Social Judgment Theory could influence the decisions and actions of entrepreneurs in that situation.
Application Exercise (5 mins)	Now, ask the participants to imagine they are entrepreneurs facing a specific business challenge. Distribute a case study or describe a hypothetical situation. They should individually write down their responses to the following questions: How would their own social judgments impact their decision-making in this scenario? How might they leverage the theory to improve their decision-making process and outcomes?
Group Pitch (5 mins)	Invite volunteers to share their individual responses and insights with the whole group. Encourage open discussions and provide feedback on their application of the theory in the given scenario.
Takeaways (5 mins)	Summarize the key points covered during the activity and emphasize the importance of understanding Social Judgment Theory for entrepreneurs. Highlight how awareness of this theory can lead to better decision-making, effective communication, and enhanced interpersonal skills.
Closing Remarks (Vary)	Encourage the participants to continue exploring the theory and its implications for entrepreneurship. Suggest further reading and resources to deepen their understanding. Remind them that being aware of how social judgments influence their own and others' actions can be a valuable skill in their entrepreneurial journey.

Conclusion: The activity introduces participants to the concept and its significance. Through real-life examples and application exercises, participants gain insights into how social judgments impact decision-making and learn to leverage this knowledge for better outcomes. By understanding the role of Social Judgment Theory, entrepreneurs can enhance their decision-making, communication, and interpersonal skills, leading to greater success in their entrepreneurial endeavors.

12.28 Spinout versus spinoff

When I talk to entrepreneurs and managers, there is much confusion about the difference between spinouts and spinoffs. This confusion is due to the ambiguous use of these terms both in practice and academia. Although there exist many opinions about the differences between spinouts and spinoffs, I will focus here on the authority behind a spinout or spinoff. **Spinoffs** (often called "corporate spinoffs") are the outcome of a corporate decision-making process (Agarwal, Audretsch, and Sarkar, 2007). A parent company's managers decide to make a division or subsidiary of the corporation into a separate legal entity with different (albeit often overlapping) owners. Spinoffs are often used to increase corporate coherence and to give new ventures the independence they need to flourish. Spinoffs are a form of corporate restructuring decision that involves divestment. Owners of shares in the parent receive shares in the spinoff, which is a new legal entity with its own equity. The actual implementation of a spinoff may vary, for example, a pure-play, split-off, or carve-out. The term "starburst" is also used in practice to describe a series of simultaneous or sequential spinoffs.

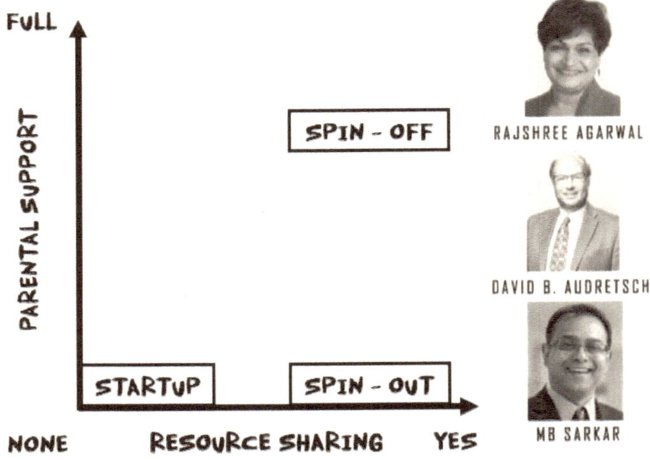

Spinouts (often called "employee spinouts") are the outcome of the independent decisions of employees that leave the parent firm to start new ventures. Neither the parent firms, nor their investors receive any ownership shares in a spinout as spinouts are typically owned and controlled by former employees and their own investors (e.g., venture capitalists). Because they are not authorized, spinouts are often met with hostility from parent firm managers and owners (Walter, Heinrichs, and Walter, 2014). Parent firms often try to litigate against spinouts for violating non-compete, non-solicitation, and non-disclosure agreements, all of which may increase the cost of venturing for the spinout. Spinouts may be considered by primary parent firm stakeholders to be disloyal or treacherous, as in the case of the Traitorous Eight. Nonetheless, spinouts led by employees have been among the most successful types of startups owning to the knowledge they transfer from their parents. Among the most success spinouts involve those with large founding teams, thus taking with them large swaths of talent and their established stakeholder relationships. In the education and research industries, academic spinoff usually involves university professors or researchers, but also typically also provide equity to universities. For the sake of clarity, it might be better to use the term "academic spinoff" where the university retain equity, and "academic spinout" where the university gets nothing. Spinouts are related but distinct from hybrid entrepreneurship.

Understanding the Spinout versus Spinoff theory:

In the context of business, a spinout refers to the creation of a new company or business unit from an existing company's assets or operations. This can occur for various reasons, such as to focus on a specific product or service, to capitalize on a new market opportunity, or to raise additional funding. An example of a spinout is the creation of Waymo, which is a self-driving car company that was spun out of Google's parent company, Alphabet, in 2016. Waymo was created to focus specifically on the development and commercialization of self-driving car technology, which was a new and rapidly growing market at the time. By spinning out Waymo, Google was able to raise additional funding and attract strategic partners to support the development of the technology, while also creating a separate entity that could focus solely on this area of business. Another example of a spinout is the creation of PayPal, which was originally part of eBay. In 2015, PayPal was spun out into a separate publicly traded company, with the goal of allowing both companies to focus on their core businesses and pursue independent growth strategies. The spinout allowed PayPal to operate independently and raise additional capital, while also allowing eBay to focus on its e-commerce business. In both scenarios, spinout allowed the new company to focus specifically on a particular area of business and pursue growth opportunities independently of the parent company. By doing so, the parent company was able to unlock additional value from its assets & operations, while also creating a new company with the potential for significant growth & success.

Classroom Activity: "Understanding Spinout versus Spinoff"

Objective: To introduce readers to the concepts of "Spinout" and "Spinoff" in entrepreneurship and help them understand the differences, benefits, and challenges associated with each approach.

Materials: Handouts, Whiteboard with markers, Sticky notes, Pen/pencil for each participant.

Duration: 60 mins

Instructions:

Activity	Instructions
Intro (10 mins)	Begin by introducing the topic of "Spinout versus Spinoff Theory" in entrepreneurship. Explain that these are two different strategies that established companies use to commercialize their innovations & create new ventures. Participants will understand the importance of this topic in the entrepreneurial context.
Theory Presentation (15 mins)	Provide a brief presentation on the key concepts of Spinout and Spinoff theories. Define Spinout as a scenario where a new venture is formed by employees or researchers who leave an existing company to commercialize technology or intellectual property developed within that company. Define Spinoff as a situation where a parent company establishes a new venture as a separate entity to commercialize its non-core assets or divisions. Discuss the motivations, benefits, and challenges associated with each approach. Present examples of successful spinouts and spinoffs to illustrate real-world applications, to grasp the practical relevance.
Spinout and Spinoff (10 mins)	Divide participants into small groups or pairs and provide each group with sticky notes or index cards. Instruct them to brainstorm & write down the key differences between Spinout & Spinoff theories, including advantages & potential risks for each strategy. Foster interaction & discussion to encourage critical thinking about the distinctions between the two entrepreneurial approaches.

Group Discussions (15 mins)	Bring the groups back together and facilitate a group discussion. Each group should share their findings, and the facilitator can write the key points on the flipchart or whiteboard. Encourage participants to ask questions, challenge assumptions, & engage in a lively discussion about the merits & drawbacks of each approach.
Application Exercise (10 mins)	Ask participants to imagine they are either part of an established company or a group of entrepreneurs with innovative ideas. In this exercise, they must decide whether to pursue a spinout or spinoff strategy for commercializing their technology or intellectual property. Participants should individually write down their decision and the reasons behind it, encouraging them to consider the strategic fit of each option for their specific context.
Group Pitch (10 mins)	Invite volunteers to share their individual decisions & reasoning with the whole group. Encourage open discussions & provide feedback on their chosen approach & its alignment with their goals which promotes knowledge sharing & peer learning.
Conclusion and Takeaways (5 mins)	Summarize the key points covered during the activity, emphasizing the importance of understanding Spinout and Spinoff theories as viable entrepreneurial strategies. Highlight that each approach has its unique advantages and challenges, and the choice should align with the specific context and objectives of the venture. Participants will have clearer understanding of these strategies & their potential application in real-world business scenarios.
Closing Remarks (Vary)	Encourage participants to continue explore the concepts of Spinout & Spinoff theories in entrepreneurship, suggesting further reading and resources to deepen their understanding. Remind them to apply this knowledge to impact their entrepreneurial endeavors positively & decision-making processes. Participants will be motivated to explore more innovative business strategies & make informed choices when considering spinouts or spinoffs.

References

Achievement Motivation

Collins, C. J., Hanges, P. J., and Locke, E. A. (2004). The relationship of achievement motivation to entrepreneurial behavior: A meta-analysis. Human performance, 17(1), 95-117.

McClelland, D. C. (1967). Achieving society. Simon and Schuster.

Stewart, W. H., and Roth, P. L. (2007). A meta-analysis of achievement motivation differences between entrepreneurs and managers. Journal of Small Business Management, 45(4), 401-421.

-Network

Latour, B. (1999). On recalling ANT. The Sociological Review,47(1_suppl), 15-25.

Korsgaard, S. (2011). Entrepreneurship as translation: Understanding entrepreneurial opportunities through actor-network. Entrepreneurship & Regional Development, 23(7-8), 661-680.

Actualization

Ramoglou, S., and Tsang, E. W. (2016). A realist perspective of entrepreneurship: Opportunities as propensities. Academy of Management Review, 41(3), 410-434.

Agency

Eisenhardt, K. M. (1989). Agency: An assessment and review. Academy of management review, 14(1), 57-74.

Jensen, M. C., and Meckling, W. H. (1976). of the firm: Managerial behavior, agency costs and ownership structure. Journal of financial economics, 3(4), 305-360.

Agglomeration

Delgado, M., Porter, M. E., and Stern, S. (2010). Clusters and entrepreneurship. Journal of economic geography, 10(4), 495-518.

Cordes, C., Richerson, P. J., and Schwesinger, G. (2014). A corporation's culture as an impetus for spinoffs and a driving force of industry evolution. Journal of Evolutionary Economics, 24(3), 689–712.

Cusmano, L., Morrison, A., and Pandolfo, E. (2015). Spin-off and clustering: a return to the Marshallian district. Cambridge Journal of Economics, 39(1), 49–66.

Berchicci, L., King, A., and Tucci, C. L. (2011). Does the apple always fall close to the tree? The geographical proximity choice of spin-outs. Strategic Entrepreneurship Journal, 5(2), 120–136.

Alertness (-)

Ambiguity Tolerance

Schere, J. L. (1982, August). Tolerance of Ambiguity as a Discriminating Variable Between Entrepreneurs and Managers. In Academy of management proceedings (Vol. 1982, No. 1, pp. 404-408).
Academy of Management.

Mac Donald Jr, A. P. (1970). Revised scale for ambiguity tolerance: Reliability and validity. Psychological reports, 26(3), 791-798.

Architectural of Entrepreneurship

Henderson, R. M., & Clark, K. B. (1990). Architectural innovation: The reconfiguration of existing product technologies and the failure of established firms. *Administrative science quarterly*, 9-30.

Tushman, M. L., & Anderson, P. (1986). Technological discontinuities and organizational environments. *Administrative science quarterly*, 439-465.

Ulrich, K. (1995). The role of product architecture in the manufacturing firm. *Research policy*, *24*(3), 419-440.

Attribution

Shaver, K. G., Gartner, W. B., Crosby, E., Bakalarova, K., and Gatewood, E. J. (2001). Attributions about entrepreneurship: A framework and process for analyzing reasons for starting a business. Entrepreneurship and Practice, 26(2), 5-28.

Baumol's

Baumol, W. J. (1996). Entrepreneurship: Productive, unproductive, and destructive. Journal of business venturing, 11(1), 3-22.921.

Bicultural

Al-Shammari, M., and Al Shammari, H. (2018). Biculturalism and entrepreneurship: An introductory research note (A). International Journal of Entrepreneurship, 22(1), 1-11.

Al-Shammari, M., and Al Shammari, H. (2018). The impact of bicultural knowledge, skills, abilities and other experiences (ksaos) on individual entrepreneurial behavior: the context of entrepreneurial discovery, evaluation and implementation. International Journal of Entrepreneurship, 22(2).

Birth Order

Robinson, P. B., and Keith Hunt, H. (1992). Entrepreneurship and birth order: Fact or folklore. Entrepreneurship and Regional Development, 4(3), 287-298.

Hisrich, R. D., and Brush, C. G. (1983). The woman entrepreneur: Implications of family, educational, and occupational experience. Frontiers of entrepreneurship research, 255-270.

Watkins, J. M., and Watkins, D. S. (1983). The female entrepreneur: Her background and determinants of business choice-some British data. Frontiers of entrepreneurship research, 271-288.

Rychlak, J. F. 1981, Introduction to Personality and Psychotherapy: A - Construction Approach, 2nd edition (Boston, MA: Houghton Mifflin Company).

Born Global Startups

Knight, G. A., and Cavusgil, S. T. (2004). Innovation, organizational capabilities, and the born-global firm. *Journal of international business studies*, *35*(2), 124-141.

Leung, A, & Chiu, C. Y. (2008). Interactive effects of multicultural experiences and openness to experience on creative potential. *Creativity Research Journal*, 20(4), 376–382. https://doi.org/10.1080/10400410802391371

McCormick, M., & Somaya, D. (2020). Born globals from emerging economies: Reconciling early exporting with theories of internationalization. Global Strategy Journal, 10(2), 251-281. https://doi.org/10.1002/gsj.1368

Pidduck, R. J. (2019). *Three essays unpacking the role of cross-cultural experience on entrepreneurship*. shareok.org. https://hdl.handle.net/11244/321093

Brain Parasite

Houdek, P. (2017). Puppet master: possible influence of the parasite Toxoplasma gondii on managers and employees. Academy of Management Perspectives, 31(1), 63-81.

Johnson Stefanie K., Fitza Markus A., Lerner Daniel A., Calhoun Dana M., Beldon Marissa A., Chan Elsa T. and Johnson Pieter T. J. (2018.) Risky business: linking Toxoplasma gondii infection and entrepreneurship behaviours across individuals and countries. Proc. R. Soc. B.28520180822 http://doi.org/10.1098/rspb.2018.0822

Lerner, D. A., Alkærsig, L., Fitza, M. A., Lomberg, C., & Johnson, S. K. (2021). Nothing Ventured, Nothing Gained: Parasite Infection is Associated with Entrepreneurial Initiation, Engagement, and Performance. Entrepreneurship and Practice, 45(1), 118–144. https://doi.org/10.1177/1042258719890992

Bricolage

Lévi-Strauss, C. (1962). La pensée sauvage (Vol. 289). Paris: Plon.

Baker, T., and Nelson, R. E. (2005). Creating something from nothing: Resource construction through entrepreneurial bricolage. Administrative science quarterly, 50(3), 329-366.

Cantillon

Rothbard, M. N. (1995). An Austrian Perspective on the History of Economic Thought: Classical Economics (Vol. 2). Ludwig von Mises Institute.

Cantillon, R. The cradle of political economy.

Cognitive Evaluation

Keh, H. T., Der Foo, M., and Lim, B. C. (2002). Opportunity evaluation under risky conditions: The cognitive processes of entrepreneurs. Entrepreneurship and practice, 27(2), 125-148.

Competence Destruction

Christensen, C. M., & Bower, J. L. (1996). Customer power, strategic investment, and the failure of leading firms. *Strategic management journal*, *17*(3), 197-218.

Tushman, M. L., & Anderson, P. (1986). Technological discontinuities and organizational environments. *Administrative science quarterly*, 439-465.

Contingency

Lawrence, P. R., and Lorsch, J. W. (1967). Differentiation and integration in complex organizations. Administrative science quarterly, 1-47.

Wiklund, J., and Shepherd, D. (2005). Entrepreneurial orientation and small business performance: a configurational approach. Journal of business venturing, 20(1), 71-91.

Miller, D., and Toulouse, J. M. (1986). Chief executive personality and corporate strategy and structure in small firms. Management science, 32(11), 1389-1409.

Chowdhury, Sanjib. "The moderating effects of customer driven complexity on the structure and growth relationship in young firms." Journal of Business Venturing 26, no. 3 (2011): 306-320.

Creative Destruction

Schumpeter, J. A. (1947) The Creative Response in Economic History. Journal of Economic History, Vol. 7 149–59.

Schumpeter, Joseph (1942). Capitalism, Socialism and Democracy. New York: Harper and Roe Publishers. p. 82.

Stam, F.C. (2018) Enabling Creative Destruction: An Entrepreneurial Ecosystem Approach to Industrial Policy. Working Paper series, volume 18, issue 05. U.S.E. Research Institute

Critical

Alvesson, M., and Willmott, H. (1992). On the idea of emancipation in management and organization studies. Academy of management review, 17(3), 432-464.

Jennings, P. L., Perren, L., and Carter, S. (2005). Guest editors' introduction: Alternative perspectives on entrepreneurship research. Entrepreneurship and Practice, 29(2), 145-152.

Ogbor, J. O. (2000). Mythicizing and reification in entrepreneurial discourse: Ideology-critique of entrepreneurial studies. Journal of management studies, 37(5), 605-635.

Perren, L., and Jennings, P. L. (2005). Government discourses on entrepreneurship: issues of legitimization, subjugation, and power. Entrepreneurship and Practice, 29(2), 173-184.

Cultural

Cochran, T. C. (1965). The entrepreneur in economic change. Explorations in Economic History, 3(1), 25-38.

Hofstede, G. (1980). Culture and organizations. International Studies of Management and Organization, 10(4), 15-41.

Davidsson, P., and Wiklund, J. (1997). Values, beliefs and regional variations in new firm formation rates. Journal of Economic psychology, 18(2), 179-199.

Shane, S. A. (1992). Why do some societies invent more than others? Journal of Business Venturing, 7(1), 29-46.

Diffusion of Innovations

Mintrom, M. (1997). Policy entrepreneurs and the diffusion of innovation. *American journal of political science*, 738-770.

Moore, G. A., & McKenna, R. (1999). Crossing the chasm. PerfectBound.

Ramani, S. V., SadreGhazi, S., & Duysters, G. (2012). On the diffusion of toilets as bottom of the pyramid innovation: Lessons from sanitation entrepreneurs. Technological Forecasting and Social Change, 79(4), 676-687.

Rogers, E. M. (2010). *Diffusion of innovations*. Simon and Schuster.

Disagreeableness

Gladwell, M. (2013). David and Goliath: Underdogs, misfits, and the art of battling giants. Hachette UK.

Disruptive Innovation

Christensen, C. M. (2003). The innovator's dilemma: The revolutionary book that will change the way you do business. New York, NY: HarperBusiness Essentials.

Markides, C. (2006). Disruptive innovation: In need of better. Journal of product innovation management, 23(1), 19-25.

Dynamic Capabilities

Eisenhardt, K. M., & Martin, J. A. (2000). Dynamic capabilities: what are they? *Strategic management journal*, *21*(10-11), 1105-1121.

Teece, D. J. (2007). Explicating dynamic capabilities: the nature and microfoundations of (sustainable) enterprise performance. *Strategic management journal*, *28*(13), 1319-1350.

Zahra, S. A., Sapienza, H. J., & Davidsson, P. (2006). Entrepreneurship and dynamic capabilities: A review, model and research agenda. Journal of Management studies, 43(4), 917-955.

Effectuation

Sarasvathy, S. D. (2001). Causation and effectuation: Toward a theoretical shift from economic inevitability to entrepreneurial contingency. Academy of management Review, 26(2), 243-263.

Chandler, G. N., DeTienne, D. R., McKelvie, A., and Mumford, T. V. (2011). Causation and effectuation processes: A validation study. Journal of business venturing, 26(3), 375-390.

Read, S., Song, M., and Smit, W. (2009). A meta-analytic review of effectuation and venture performance. Journal of Business Venturing, 24(6), 573-587.

Emancipation

Rindova, V., Barry, D., and Ketchen, D. J. (2009). Entrepreneuring as emancipation. Academy of Management Review, 34(3), 477-491

Embeddedness

Hite, J. M., and Hesterly, W. S. (2001). The evolution of firm networks: From emergence to early growth of the firm. Strategic management journal, 22(3), 275-286.

Jack, S. L. and Anderson, A. R. (2002). The effects of embeddedness on the entrepreneurial process. Journal of business Venturing, 17(5), 467-487.

Uzzi, B. (1997). Social structure and competition in interfirm networks: The paradox of embeddedness. Administrative science quarterly, 35-67.

Expectancy

Kanfer, R. (1990). Motivation and industrial and organizational psychology. Handbook of industrial and organizational psychology, 1(2), 75-130.

Renko, M., Kroeck, K. G., and Bullough, A. (2012). Expectancy and nascent entrepreneurship. Small Business Economics, 39(3), 667-684.

Vroom, V. 1963. Work and Motivation. New York, NY: Wiley.

Experiential Learning

Corbett, A. C. (2005). Experiential learning within the process of opportunity identification and exploitation. Entrepreneurship and Practice, 29(4),473–491.

Kolb, D. A. (1984). Experiential learning: Experienceas the source of learning and development (Vol.1). Englewood Cliffs, NJ: Prentice-Hall.

Sørensen, J. B. and Fassiotto, M. A. (2011). Organizations as fonts of entrepreneurship. Organization Science, 22(5), 1322-1331.

Feminist

Greer, M. J., & Greene, P. G. (2003). Feminist and the study of entrepreneurship. *New perspectives on women entrepreneurs*, 1-24.

Hurley, A. E. (1999). Incorporating feminist theories into sociological theories of entrepreneurship. Women in Management Review, 14(2), 54-62.

First Mover

Kerin, R.A., Varadarajan, P.R. and Peterson, R.A., 1992. First-mover advantage: A synthesis, conceptual framework, and research propositions. The Journal of Marketing, pp.33-52.

Teece, D. J. 1986. Profiting from technological innovation: Implications for integration, collaboration, licensing and public policy. Research policy, 15(6), 285-305.

Tushman, M.L. and Anderson, P., 1986. Technological discontinuities and organizational environments. Administrative science quarterly, pp.439-465.

Genetic

Shane, S., Nicolaou, N., Cherkas, L., and Spector, T. D. (2010). Genetics, the Big Five, and the tendency to be self-employed. Journal of Applied Psychology, 95(6), 1154.

Nicolaou, N., Shane, S., Cherkas, L., Hunkin, J., and Spector, T. D. (2008). Is the tendency to engage in entrepreneurship genetic? Management Science, 54(1), 167-179.

Great Man

Thomas Carlyle, 1840. On Heroes, Hero-worship and the Heroic in History. London: Chapman and Hall, 193 Piccadilly

Drakopoulou Dodd, S., and Anderson, A. R. (2007). Mumpsimus and the mything of the individualistic entrepreneur. International Small Business Journal, 25(4), 341-360.

Harvard School

Pradhan, Rabindra & Nath, Papri. (2011). Rethinking entrepreneurship: Developing a psychosocial framework. Journal of Indian Academy of Applied Psychology.

Mohanty, S. K. (2005). Fundamentals of entrepreneurship. PHI Learning Pvt. Ltd.

Hoselitz

Gambe, A. R. (2000). Overseas Chinese entrepreneurship and capitalist development in Southeast Asia (Vol. 9). LIT Verlag Münster.

Hoselitz, B. F. (1963). Entrepreneurship and traditional elites. Explorations in Economic History, 1(1), 36.

Hubris

Cassar, G. (2010). Are individuals entering self-employment overly optimistic? An empirical test of plans and projections on nascent entrepreneur expectations. Strategic Management Journal, 31(8), 822-840.

Hayward, M. L., Shepherd, D. A., and Griffin, D. (2006). A hubris of entrepreneurship. Management Science, 52(2), 160-172.

Hogarth, R. M., and Karelaia, N. (2012). Entrepreneurial success and failure: Confidence and fallible judgment. Organization Science, 23(6), 1733-1747.

Sundermeier, J. (2017). Start-Up (s) with Hubris-The Effects of Hubris on the Performance of Core Entrepreneurial Functions (Doctoral dissertation).

Human Capital

Becker, G. S. (1994). Human capital revisited. In Human Capital: A Theoretical and Empirical Analysis with Special Reference to Education (3rd Edition) (pp. 15-28). The University of Chicago Press.

Stuart, R. W., and Abetti, P. A. (1990). Impact of entrepreneurial and management experience on early performance. Journal of business venturing, 5(3), 151-162.

Zacharakis, A. L., and Meyer, G. D. (2000). The potential of actuarial decision models: can they improve the venture capital investment decision? Journal of Business Venturing, 15(4), 323-346.

Hybrid Entrepreneurship

Folta, T. B., Delmar, F., and Wennberg, K. (2010). Hybrid entrepreneurship. Management Science, 56(2), 253-269.

Raffiee, J., and Feng, J. (2014). Should I quit my day job? A hybrid path to entrepreneurship. *Academy of Management Journal*, *57*(4), 936-963.

Impulsivity

Wiklund, J., Patzelt, H., and Dimov, D. (2016). Entrepreneurship and psychological disorders: How ADHD can be productively harnessed. Journal of Business Venturing Insights, 6, 14-20.

Verheul, I., Block, J., Burmeister-Lamp, K., Thurik, R., Tiemeier, H., and Turturea, R. (2015). ADHD-like behavior and entrepreneurial intentions. Small Business Economics, 45(1), 85-101

Fast Company Story

Individual Ambidexterity

Gibson,C.B., and Birkinshaw, J. (2004). The Antecedents, Consequences, and Mediating Role of Organizational Ambidexterity, Academy of Management Journal, 47(2),209–226.

Kazanjian,R. K., and Drazin, R. (1990). A Stage-Contingent Model of Design and Growth forTechnology Based New Ventures, Journal of Business Venturing, 5(3),137–150.

March, J.G. (1991). Exploration and Exploitation in Organizational Learning,Organization Science, 2(1), 71–87.

Mom, T. J,Fourné, S. P., and Jansen, J. J. (2015). 'Managers' work experience,ambidexterity, & performance: The contingency role of the work context' Human Resource Management, 54(S1), 133-153.

Volery, T., Mueller, S., and von Siemens, B. (2015). Entrepreneur ambidexterity: A study of entrepreneur behaviours and competencies in growth-oriented small and medium-sized enterprises. International Small Business Journal, 33(2), 109-129.

Yeganegi, S., Laplume, A. O., Dass, P., and Greidanus, N. S. (2019) Individual-Level Ambidexterity and Entrepreneurial Entry. Journal of Small Business Management.

Individual-Opportunity Nexus

: Casson, M. (2005). The individual–opportunity nexus: a review of Scott Shane: a general of entrepreneurship. Small Business Economics, 24(5), 423-430.

Eckhardt, J. T., and Shane, S. (2010). An update to the individual-opportunity nexus. In Handbook of entrepreneurship research (pp. 47-76). Springer New York.

Shane, S. and Eckhardt, J. (2003). The individual-opportunity nexus. In Handbook of entrepreneurship research (pp. 161-191). Springer US.

Informal

Suchman, M. (1995). Managing Legitimacy: Strategic and Institutional Approaches. *The Academy of Management Review, 20*(3), 571-610. doi:10.2307/258788

Webb, J. W., Tihanyi, L., Ireland, R. D., and Sirmon, D. G. (2009). You say illegal, I say legitimate: Entrepreneurship in the informal economy. Academy of Management Review, 34(3), 492-510.

Williams, C. C., and Nadin, S. (2010). Entrepreneurship and the informal economy: An overview. Journal of Developmental Entrepreneurship, 15(04), 361-378.

Information Asymmetry

Aboody, D., Lev, B. (2000). Information asymmetry, R and D, and insider gains. The journal of Finance, 55(6), 2747-2766.

Balakrishnan, S., Koza, M. P. (1993). Information asymmetry, adverse selection and joint-ventures: and evidence. Journal of economic behavior and organization, 20(1), 99-117.

Lowe, R. A. (2001). Entrepreneurship and information asymmetry: and evidence from the University of California. Unpublished working paper, Haas School of Business.

Information Processing

Hansen, E. L., and Allen, K. R. (1992). The creation corridor: Environmental load and pre-organization information-processing ability. Entrepreneurship: and Practice, 17(1), 57-66.

Newell, A., and Simon, H. A. (1972). Human problem solving (Vol. 104, No. 9). Englewood Cliffs, NJ: Prentice-Hall.

Institutional

Bruton, G. D., Ahlstrom, D., and Li, H. L. (2010). Institutional and entrepreneurship: where are we now and where do we need to move in the future? Entrepreneurship and practice, 34(3), 421-440.

North, D. C. (1991). Institutions. Journal of economic perspectives, 5(1), 97-112.

Scott, W. R. (2001). Instituitions and organizations. Thousande Oakes: Sage.

Scott, W. R. (2005). Institutional: Contributing to a theoretical research program. Great minds in management: The process of development, 37, 460-484.

Jack of All Trades

Åstebro, T., and Thompson, P. (2011). Entrepreneurs, Jacks of all trades or Hobos? Research policy, 40(5), 637-649.

Lazear, E. P. (2004). Balanced skills and entrepreneurship. The American Economic Review, 94(2), 208-211.

Silva, O. (2007). The Jack-of-All-Trades entrepreneur: Innate talent or acquired skill? Economics letters, 97(2), 118-123.

Wagner, J. (2003). Testing Lazear's jack-of-all-trades view of entrepreneurship with German micro data. Applied Economics Letters, 10(11), 687-689.

Knowledge Spillover

Acs, Z. J., Braunerhjelm, P., Audretsch, D. B., and Carlsson, B. (2009). The knowledge spillover of entrepreneurship. Small business economics, 32(1), 15-30.

Agarwal, Rajshree, David Audretsch, and M. B. Sarkar. "Knowledge spillovers and strategic entrepreneurship." Strategic Entrepreneurship Journal 4, no. 4 (2010): 271-283

Audretsch, D. B. and Lehmann, E. E. (2005). Does the knowledge spillover of entrepreneurship hold for regions? Research Policy, 34(8), 1191-1202

Lean Launchpad

Baron, R. A. 2006. Opportunity recognition as pattern recognition: How entrepreneurs "connect the dots" to identify new business opportunities. Academy of Management Perspectives, 20(1): 104-119

Blank, S. (2012). The startup owner's manual: The step-by-step guide for building a great company.

McMullen, J. S., and Dimov, D. 2013. Time and the entrepreneurial journey: The problems and promise of studying entrepreneurship as a process. Journal of Management Studies, 50(8): 1481-1512.

Liquidity

Davidsson, P., and Honig, B. (2003). The role of social and human capital among nascent entrepreneurs. Journal of business venturing, 18(3), 301-331.

Evans, D. S., and Jovanovic, B. (1989). An estimated model of entrepreneurial choice under liquidity constraints. Journal of political economy, 97(4), 808-827.

Stuart, T., and Sorenson, O. (2003). Liquidity Events and the Geographic Distribution of Entrepreneurial Activity. Administrative Science Quarterly, 48(2), 175.

Davila, A., Foster, G., and Gupta, M. (2003). Venture capital financing and the growth of startup firms. Journal of business venturing, 18(6), 689-708.

Hurst, E., and Lusardi, A. (2004). Liquidity constraints, household wealth, and entrepreneurship. Journal of political Economy, 112(2), 319-347.

Locus of Control

Rotter, J. B. (1990). Internal versus external control of reinforcement: A case history of a variable. American psychologist, 45(4), 489

Mueller, S. L., and Thomas, A. S. (2001). Culture and entrepreneurial potential: A nine country study of locus of control and innovativeness. Journal of business venturing, 16(1), 51-75.

Schultz, D.P. and Schultz, S.E. (2005). Theories of Personality (8th ed.). Wadsworth: Thomson. ISBN 0-534-62402-2

Machiavellian

Machiavelli, N. (1940). The Prince and Discourses on the First Decade of Titus Livius. New York: The Modern Library.

Baumol, W. J. (1996). Entrepreneurship: Productive, unproductive, and destructive. Journal of business venturing, 11(1), 3-22.921

McLuhan

McLuhan, M. (1964). Understandig media. *The Extensions of Man. New York.*

McLuhan, M., McLuhan, M. A., and Lapham, L. H. (1994). Understanding media: The extensions of man. MIT press.

Tushman, M. L. and Anderson, P. (1986). Technological discontinuities and organizational environments. Administrative Science Quarterly, 439-465.

Mental Disorders

Wiklund, J., Hatak, I., Patzelt, H., and Shepherd, D. A. (2018). Mental Disorders in the Entrepreneurship Context: When being different can be an advantage. Academy of Management Perspectives, 32(2), 182-206.

Wiklund, J., Patzelt, H., and Dimov, D. (2016). Entrepreneurship and psychological disorders: How ADHD can be productively harnessed. Journal of Business Venturing Insights, 6, 14-20.

Logan, J. (2009). Dyslexic entrepreneurs: the incidence; their coping strategies and their business skills. Dyslexia, 15(4), 328-346.

Bogan, V. L., Fertig, A. R., and Just, D. R. (2014). Self-Employment and Mental Health.

Misfit

Kahn, S., La Mattina, G., and MacGarvie, M. J. (2017). "Misfits,""stars," and immigrant entrepreneurship. Small Business Economics, 1-25.

Clay, A., and Phillips, K. M. (2016). The Misfit Economy: Lessons in Creativity from Pirates, Hackers, Gangsters and Other Informal Entrepreneurs. Simon and Schuster.

Hofstede, G., N. Noorderhaven, A.R. Thurik, L. M. Uhlaner, A.R.M. Wennekers, and R.E. Wildeman. 2004. Culture's role in entrepreneurship: self-employment out of dissatisfaction. In Innovation, entrepreneurship and culture, eds. T. E. Brown and J. M. Ulijn, 162-203. Cheltenham: Edward Elgar.

Necessity Versus Opportunity

Wong, P. K., Ho, Y. P., and Autio, E. (2005). Entrepreneurship, innovation and economic growth: Evidence from GEM data. Small business economics, 24(3), 335-350.

Harding, R., Hart, M., Jones-Evans, D., and Levie, J. (2002). Global entrepreneurship monitor. London: London Business School.

Shane, S. (2009). Why encouraging more people to become entrepreneurs is bad public policy? Small business economics, 33(2), 141-149.

Lippmann, S., Davis, A., and Aldrich, H. E. (2005). Entrepreneurship and inequality. In Entrepreneurship (pp. 3-31). Emerald Group Publishing Limited.

Welter, F., Baker, T., Audretsch, D. B., and Gartner, W. B. (2017). Everyday entrepreneurship—a call for entrepreneurship research to embrace entrepreneurial diversity. Entrepreneurship and Practice, 41(3), 311-321

Niche

Hutchinson, G. E. (1978). An introduction to population ecology.

Hannan, M. T., and; Freeman, J. (1977). The population ecology of organizations. *American journal of sociology*, *82*(5), 929-964

Hardesty DL, 1972. The human ecological niche. American Anthropologist, 74: 458- 466

Passion

Thorgren, S., and Wincent, J. (2015). Passion and habitual entrepreneurship. International Small Business Journal, 33(2), 216-227

Cardon, M. S., Zietsma, C., Saparito, P., Matherne, B. P., and Davis, C. (2005). A tale of passion: new insights into entrepreneurship from a parenthood metaphor. Journal of business venturing, 20(1), 23-45

Chang, 2002. The Passion Plan at Work: Building a Passion-Driven Organization. Jossey-Bass, San Francisco, CA.

Vallerand, R. J., Blanchard, C., Mageau, G. A., Koestner, R., Ratelle, C., Léonard, M., and

Marsolais, J. (2003). Les passions de l'ame: on obsessive and harmonious passion. Journal of personality and social psychology, 85(4), 756

Gielnik, M. M., Spitzmuller, M., Schmitt, A., Klemann, D. K., and Frese, M. (2015). "I put in effort, therefore I am passionate": Investigating the path from effort to passion in entrepreneurship. Academy of Management Journal, 58(4), 1012-1031

Pecking Order

Paul, S., Whittam, G., and Wyper, J. (2007). The pecking order: does it apply to start-up firms? Journal of small business and enterprise development, 14(1), 8-21.

Physiological

Bönte, W., Procher, V. D., and Urbig, D. (2016). Biology and selection into entrepreneurship—The relevance of prenatal testosterone exposure. Entrepreneurship and Practice, 40(5), 1121-1148.

Nofal, A. M., Nicolaou, N., Symeonidou, N., and Shane, S. (2018). Biology and management: A review, critique, and research agenda. Journal of Management, 44(1), 7-31.

Planned Behavior

Ajzen, I. (1991). The theory of planned behavior. Organizational behavior and human decision processes, 50(2), 179-211.

Population Ecology

Hannan, M. T., and Freeman, J. (1977). The population ecology of organizations. American journal of sociology, 82(5), 929-964

Freeman, J., Carroll, G. R., and Hannan, M. T. (1983). The liability of newness: Age dependence in organizational death rates. American sociological review, 692-710

Procedural Justice

Kim, W. C., and Mauborgne, R. A. (1991). Implementing global strategies: The role of procedural justice. *Strategic Management Journal*, *12*(S1), 125-143.

Sapienza, H. J., and Korsgaard, M. A. (1996). Procedural justice in entrepreneur-investor relations. *Academy of management Journal*, *39*(3), 544-574.

Procedural justice: A psychological perspective JW Thibaut, L Walker - 1975 - Hillsdale, NJ: Erlbaum

Prospect

Busenitz, L. W., West III, G. P., Shepherd, D., Nelson, T., Chandler, G. N., and Zacharakis, A. (2003). Entrepreneurship research in emergence: Past trends and future directions. Journal of management, 29(3), 285-308

Hsu, D. K., Wiklund, J., and Cotton, R. D. (2017). Success, failure, and entrepreneurial reentry: An experimental assessment of the veracity of self-efficacy and prospect. Entrepreneurship and Practice, 41(1), 19-47

Tversky, A., and Kahneman, D. (1986). Rational choice and the framing of decisions. Journal of business, S251-S278

Radical Subjectivism

Chiles, T. H., Bluedorn, A. C., and Gupta, V. K. (2007). Beyond creative destruction and entrepreneurial discovery: A radical Austrian approach to entrepreneurship. Organization Studies, 28(4), 467-493.

Lachmann, L. M. (1977). Capital, expectations, and the market process. Kansas City.

Real Options

Bowman, E. H. and Hurry, D. (1993). Strategy through the option lens: An integrated view of resource investments and the incremental-choice process. Academy of management review, 18(4), 760-782.

Lee, S. H., Peng, M. W., and Barney, J. B. (2007). Bankruptcy law and entrepreneurship development: A real options perspective. Academy of Management Review, 32(1), 257-272.

McGrath, R. G. (1999). Falling forward: Real options reasoning and entrepreneurial failure. Academy of Management review, 24(1), 13-30.

O'Brien, J. P., Folta, T. B., and Johnson, D. R. (2003). A real options perspective on entrepreneurial entry in the face of uncertainty. Managerial and Decision Economics, 24(8), 515-533.

Regulatory Focus

Baas, M., De Dreu, C. K., and Nijstad, B. A. (2008). A meta-analysis of 25 years of mood-creativity research: Hedonic tone, activation, or regulatory focus? Psychological bulletin, 134(6), 779.

Brockner, J., Higgins, E. T., and Low, M. B. (2004) Regulatory focus theory and the entrepreneurial process. Journal of Business Venturing, 19(2), 203-220.

Higgins, E. T. (1998). Promotion and prevention: Regulatory focus as a motivational principle. In Advances in experimental social psychology (Vol. 30, pp. 1-46). Academic Press.

Hmieleski, K. M., and Baron, R. A. (2008). Regulatory focus and new venture performance: A study of entrepreneurial opportunity exploitation under conditions of risk versus uncertainty. Strategic Entrepreneurship Journal, 2(4), 285-299.

Religious

Weber, M. (1904). Die protestantische Ethik und der Geist des Kapitalismus.

Resilience

Ayala, J. C., and Manzano, G. (2014). The resilience of the entrepreneur. Influence on the success of the business. A longitudinal analysis. *Journal of Economic Psychology*, *42*, 126-135.

Bullough, A., Renko, M., and Myatt, T. (2014). Danger zone entrepreneurs: The importance of resilience and self-efficacy for entrepreneurial intentions. *Entrepreneurship and Practice*, *38*(3), 473-499.

Luthar, S. S., Cicchetti, D., and Becker, B. (2000). The construct of resilience: A critical evaluation and guidelines for future work. *Child development*, *71*(3), 543-562.

Resource Based

Barney, J. (1991). Firm resources and sustained competitive advantage. Journal of management, 17(1), 99-120.

Barney, J. B. (2018). Why resource-based Actor's model of profit appropriation must incorporate a stakeholder perspective. *Strategic Management Journal*, *39*(13), 3305-3325.

Alvarez, S. A., and Barney, J. B. (2007). Discovery and creation: Alternative theories of entrepreneurial action. Strategic entrepreneurship journal, 1(1-2), 11-26.

Resource Dependency

Pfeffer, J., and Salancik, G. R. (2003). The external control of organizations: A resource dependence perspective. Stanford University Press.

Katila, R., Rosenberger, J. D., and Eisenhardt, K. M (2008). Swimming with sharks: Technology ventures, defense mechanisms and corporate relationships. Administrative Science Quarterly, 53(2), 295-332.

Yli-Renko, H., Sapienza, H. J., and Hay, M. (2001). The role of contractual governance flexibility in realizing the outcomes of key customer relationships. Journal of Business Venturing, 16(6), 529-555.

Resource Scarcity

Oxenfeld, A.R. and Kelly, A.O. (1969). Will successful franchise systems become wholly-owned chains? Journal of Retailing 44, 69–83.

Audretsch, D. B. (1995). Innovation, growth and survival. International journal of industrial organization, 13(4), 441-457.

Combs, J. G., and Ketchen, D. J. (1999). Can capital scarcity help agency explain franchising? Revisiting the capital scarcity. Academy of Management Journal, 42(2), 196-207.

Stanworth, J., and Curran, J. (1999). Colas, burgers, shakes, and shirkers: Towards a sociological model of franchising in the market economy. Journal of Business Venturing, 14(4), 323-344.

Shane, S. A. (1996). Hybrid organizational arrangements and their implications for firm growth and survival: A study of new franchisors. Academy of management journal, 39(1), 216-234.

Risk

Caliendo,M., and Künn, S. (2011). Start-up subsidies for the unemployed: Long-termevidence and effect heterogeneity. Journal of Public Economics, 95(3-4),311-331.

Fairlie, R.W., Kapur, K., and Gates, S. (2011). Is employer-based health insurance abarrier to entrepreneurship? Journal of Health Economics, 30(1), 146-162.

Hombert,J., Schoar, A., Sraer, D., and Thesmar, D. (2014). Can unemployment insurance spur entrepreneurial activity? (No. w20717). National Bureau of Economic Research

Olds, G(2016a). Food Stamp Entrepreneurs. Harvard Business School Working Paper, No.16-143, June.

Olds, G.(2016b) Entrepreneurship and Public Health Insurance. Harvard Business School Working Paper, No. 16-144, June.

Peltzman,S. (1975). The effects of automobile safety regulation. Journal of politicalEconomy, 83(4), 677-725.

Self-Competition

Khalil, E. L. (1997). Buridan's Ass, Risk, Uncertainty, and Self-Competition: A theory of Entrepreneurship. Kyklos, 50(2), 147-163

Self-Efficacy

Bandura, A. (1977). Self-efficacy: toward a unifying of behavioral change. Psychological review, 84(2), 191

Scherer, R. F., Adams, J. S., and Wiebe, F. A. (1989). Developing entrepreneurial behaviours: A social learning perspective. Journal of Organizational Change Management, 2(3), 16-27

Serial Entrepreneurship

Plehn-Dujowich, J. (2010). A theory of serial entrepreneurship. Small Business Economics, 35(4), 377-398.

Sarasvathy, S. D., Menon, A. R., & Kuechle, G. (2013). Failing firms and successful entrepreneurs: Serial entrepreneurship as a temporal portfolio. Small business economics, 40(2), 417-434

Signaling

Bhattacharya, S. (1979). Imperfect information, dividend policy, and" the bird in the hand" fallacy. The Bell Journal of Economics, 259-270

Connelly, B. L., Certo, S. T., Ireland, R. D., and; Reutzel, C. R. (2011). Signaling: A review and assessment. Journal of Management, 37(1), 39-67

Slacker

Marlin, D. and Geiger, S. W. (2015). A reexamination of the organizational slack and innovation relationship. Journal of Business Research, 68(12), 2683-2690

Social Capital

Burt, R. S. (2002). The social capital of structural holes. The new economic sociology: Developments in an emerging field, 148-190.

Granovetter, M. S. (1973). The strength of weak ties. American journal of sociology, 78(6), 1360-1380.

Greve, A. and Salaff, J. W. (2003). Social networks and entrepreneurship. Entrepreneurship and practice, 28(1), 1-22.

Walker, G., Kogut, B. and Shan, W. (1997). Social capital, structural holes and the formation of an industry network. Organization science, 8(2), 109-125.

Social Entrepreneurship

Dees, J. G. (2017). 1 The Meaning of Social Entrepreneurship. In Case Studies in Social Entrepreneurship and Sustainability (pp. 34-42). Routledge.

Dacin, P. A., Dacin, M. T., and Matear, M. (2010). Social entrepreneurship: Why we don't need a new and how we move forward from here. Academy of management pesrspectives, 24(3), 37-57.

Social Exchange

De Clercq, D., Dimov, D., and Thongpapanl, N. T. (2010). The moderating impact of internal social exchange processes on the entrepreneurial orientation–performance relationship. Journal of business venturing, 25(1), 87-103.

Emerson, R. M. (1981). Social exchange. Social psychology: Sociological perspectives. New York: Basic Books

Social Identity

Huddy, L. (2001). From social to political identity: A critical examination of social identity. Political psychology, 22(1), 127-156.

Obschonka, M., Goethner, M., Silbereisen, R. K., and Cantner, U. (2012). Social identity and the transition to entrepreneurship: The role of group identification with workplace peers. Journal of Vocational Behavior,80(1), 137-147.

Tajfel, H. and Turner, J. C. (1979). An integrative of intergroup conflict. The social psychology of intergroup relations,33(47), 74

Social Judgement

Bitektine, A. (2011). Toward a theory of social judgments of organizations: The case of legitimacy, reputation, and status. Academy of Management Review, 36(1), 151-179.

Jones, T. M., Harrison, J. S., and; Felps, W. (2018). How applying instrumental stakeholder can provide sustainable competitive advantage. Academy of Management Review, (ja).

Suchman, M. C. (1995). Managing legitimacy: Strategic and institutional approaches. *Academy of management review*, *20*(3), 571-610.

Spinout

Agarwal, R., Audretsch, D., and Sarkar, M. B. (2007). The process of creative construction: knowledge spillovers, entrepreneurship, & economic growth. Strategic Entrepreneurship Journal, 1(3–4), 263–286.

Walter, S. G., Heinrichs, S., and Walter, A. (2014). Parent hostility and spin-out performance. *Strategic Management Journal*, *35*(13), 2031-2042.

Stages
Bhave, M. P. (1994). A process model of entrepreneurial venture creation. Journal of business venturing, 9(3), 223-242.
Kazanjian, R. K., and Drazin, R. (1990). A stage-contingent model of design and growth for technology based new ventures. Journal of business venturing, 5(3), 137-150.
Stakeholder
Barney, J. B. (2018). Why resource-based Actor's model of profit appropriation must incorporate a stakeholder perspective. *Strategic Management Journal*, *39*(13), 3305-3325.
Laplume, A., Walker, K., Zhang, Z., & Yu, X. (2020). Incumbent Stakeholder Management Performance and New Entry. *Journal of Business Ethics*, 1-16.
Mitchell, R. K. (2002). Entrepreneurship and Stakeholder: Comment on Ruffin Lecture# 2—Delivered by Professor S. Venkataraman. The Ruffin Series of the Society for Business Ethics, 3, 175-195.
Venkataraman, S., 2002. Stakeholder value equilibration and the entrepreneurial process. The Ruffin Series of the Society for Business Ethics, 3, pp.45-57.
Stewardship
Argryis, C. 1964. Integrating the individual and the organization. New York: Wiley.
Donaldson, L., and Davis, J. H. (1991). Stewardship or agency: CEO governance and shareholder returns. Australian Journal of management, 16(1), 49-64.
Davis, J. H., Schoorman, F. D., and Donaldson, L. (1997). Toward a stewardship of management. Academy of Management Review, 22(1), 20-47.
Rechner, P. L., and Dalton, D. R. (1991). CEO duality and organizational performance: A longitudinal analysis. Strategic Management Journal, 12(2), 155-160.
Strategic Disagreements
Bhide, A. (1994). How entrepreneurs craft strategies that work. HBR, 72(2), 150-161
Klepper, S. (2007). Disagreements, spinoffs, and the evolution of Detroit as the capital of the US automobile industry. Management Science, 53(4), 616-631
Klepper, S., and Thompson, P. (2010). Disagreements and intra-industry spinoffs. International Journal of Industrial Organization, 28(5), 526-538
Stieglitz, N., and Heine, K. (2007). Innovations and the role of complementarities in a strategic of the firm. Strategic Management Journal, 28(1), 1-15
Thompson, P., and Chen, J. (2011). Disagreements, employee spinoffs and the choice of technology. Review of Economic Dynamics, 14(3), 455-474
Transaction Cost
Coase, Ronald H. 1937. The nature of the firm. Economica, 4: 386.
Dahlman, C. 1979. The problem of externality. Journal of Law and Economics 22 (1): 141-162
Oliver, W. 1975. Markets and hierarchies: Analysis & antitrust implications. New York, NY: Free Press.

Uncertainty-Bearing

Emmett, R. B. (2011). Frank H. knight on the 'entrepreneur function" in modern enterprise. Seattle University Law Review, 34(4), 1139.

Knight, F. H. (1921). Risk, Uncertainty and Profit. The Riverside Press Cambridge.

Upper Echelons

Hambrick, D. C., and Mason, P. A. (1984). Upper echelons: The organization as a reflection of its top managers. Academy of management review, 9(2), 193-206

Vanaelst, I., Clarysse, B., Wright, M., Lockett, A., Moray, N., and S'Jegers, R. (2006) Entrepreneurial team development in academic spinouts: An examination of team heterogeneity. Entrepreneurship and Practice, 30(2), 249-271

Patzelt, H., Zu Knyphausen-Aufseß, D., and Nikol, P. (2008). Top management teams, business models, and performance of biotechnology ventures: An upper echelon perspective. British Journal of Management, 19(3), 205-221

Utility

Douglas, E. J. and Shepherd, D. A. (2002). Self-employment as a career choice: Attitudes, entrepreneurial intentions, & utility maximization. Entrepreneurship and practice, 26(3), 81-90.

Mill, John Stuart (1998). Crisp, Roger, ed. Utilitarianism. Oxford University Press.

Weak Ties

Granovetter, M. S. (1977). The strength of weak ties. In Social networks (pp. 347-367).

Withdrawal of Status Respect

Hagen, E. E. (1963). How economic growth begins: a theory of social change. Journal of Social Issues, 19(1), 20-34

Dana, L. P. (1995). Entrepreneurship in a remote sub-Arctic community. Entrepreneurship and Practice, 20, 57-72

X-Efficiency

Leibenstein, H. (1966). Allocative efficiency vs." X-efficiency". The American Economic Review, 392-415

Leibenstein, H. (1978). On the basic proposition of X-efficiency. The American Economic Review, 328-332

Acknowledgement

As I stand here, on the threshold of another book, "Startup Theories, Examples & Activities", I am overwhelmed with gratitude for the incredible journey that has brought me to this point. This book represents the culmination of my passion for startups, entrepreneurship education, and the unwavering support of countless individuals who have played an instrumental role in shaping my career.

First and foremost, I would like to express my heartfelt appreciation to my readers. Your unyielding encouragement and enthusiasm for my previous works, "The Fun of Being in a Startup" and "Startup Chanakya," have been the driving force behind my continued dedication to writing and sharing knowledge in the entrepreneurial realm. To my family, thank you for being my pillar of strength throughout my career. Your unwavering support, understanding, and love have been the bedrock of my success, providing me with the confidence to chase my dreams relentlessly. My heartfelt gratitude goes out to my friends and colleagues in the startup community, both old and new, who have shared their experiences, insights, and challenges with me. Your willingness to open and share your stories has been invaluable in shaping the content of this book and making it relatable to aspiring entrepreneurs.

Over the past 13 years, I have had the privilege of working with numerous students and aspiring entrepreneurs in various educational institutions and workshops. To all my students and mentees, thank you for constantly challenging me to refine and expand my understanding of entrepreneurship. Your thirst for knowledge has been the driving force behind my continuous exploration of new theories, examples, and activities that I could incorporate into this book.

Finally, I want to acknowledge the incredible impact that the startup ecosystem has had on me personally and professionally. The tenacity, innovation, and passion exhibited by startups and entrepreneurs worldwide have been a constant source of inspiration. I am truly humbled and privileged to be a part of this vibrant community.

"Startup Theories, Examples & Activities" would not have been possible without the unwavering support, love, and guidance of all the individuals mentioned above. This book is a tribute to the startup world, the entrepreneurs who dare to dream, and the educators who strive to empower them with knowledge. Thank you all for being an indispensable part of this journey.

With sincere gratitude,

Umesh Santoshkumar Yashoda Rathod
www.umeshrathod.in

www.ingramcontent.com/pod-product-compliance
Lightning Source LLC
LaVergne TN
LVHW091139150826
845672LV00005B/985

9798891864641